EDENS ZERO

4 NEW FRIENDS

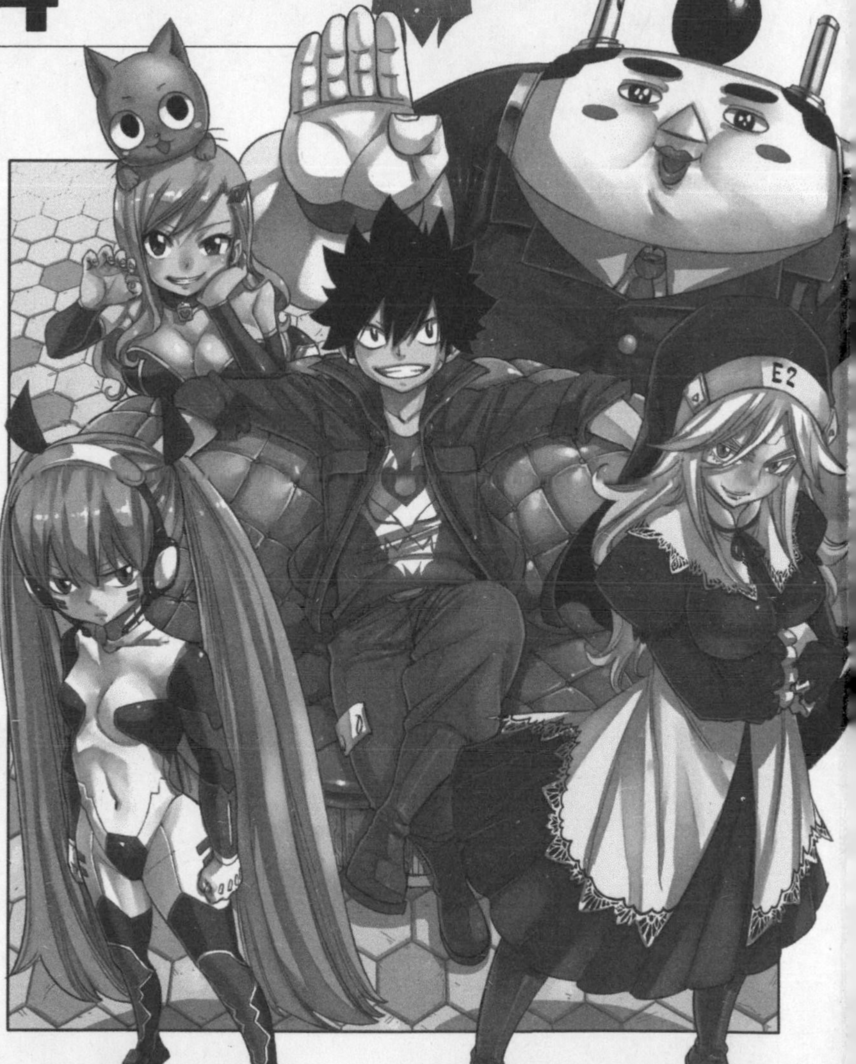

HIRO MASHIMA

EDENS ZERO 4 contents

EDENS ZERO

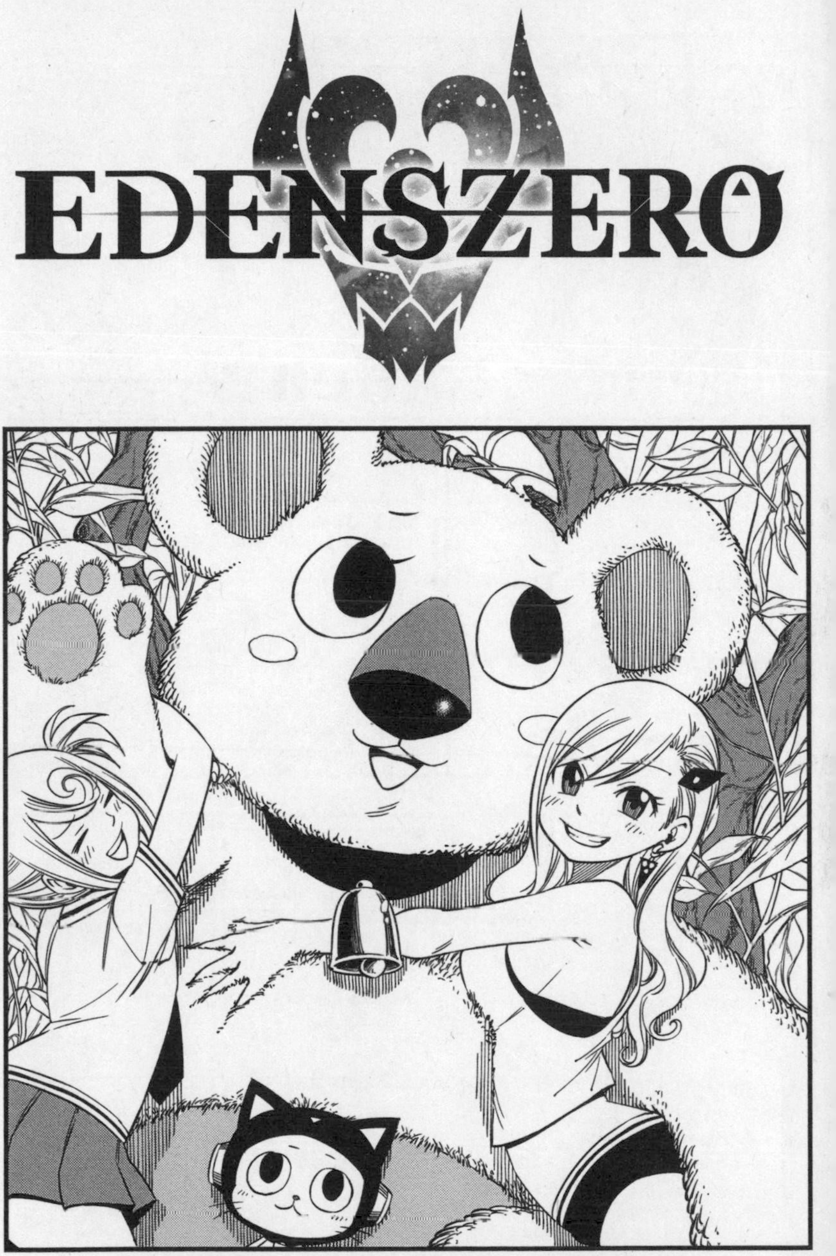

CHAPTER 24: SISTER IVRY

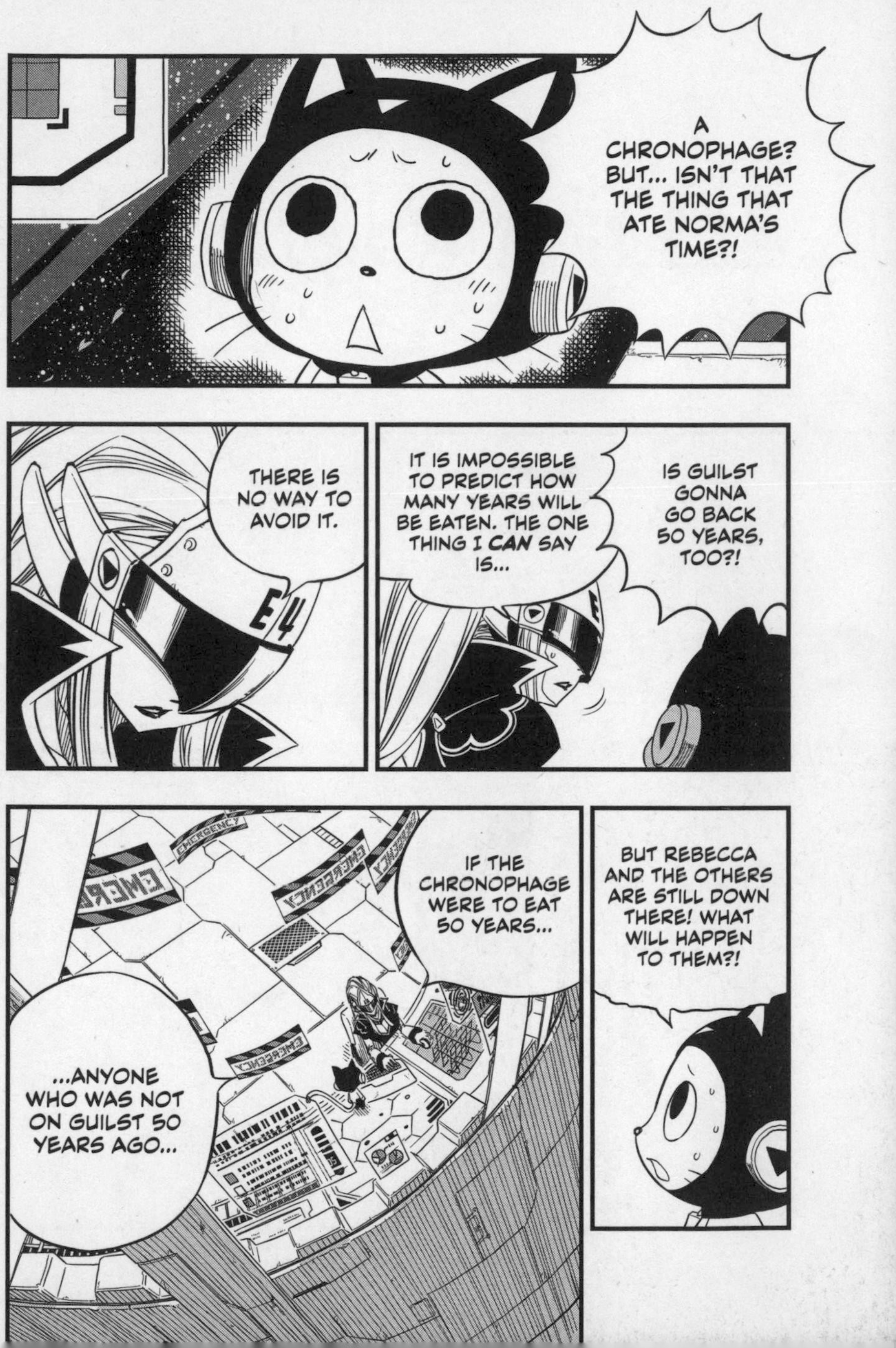
A CHRONOPHAGE? BUT... ISN'T THAT THE THING THAT ATE NORMA'S TIME?!
THERE IS NO WAY TO AVOID IT.
IS GUILST GONNA GO BACK 50 YEARS, TOO?!
IT IS IMPOSSIBLE TO PREDICT HOW MANY YEARS WILL BE EATEN. THE ONE THING I CAN SAY IS...
IF THE CHRONOPHAGE WERE TO EAT 50 YEARS...
...ANYONE WHO WAS NOT ON GUILST 50 YEARS AGO...
BUT REBECCA AND THE OTHERS ARE STILL DOWN THERE! WHAT WILL HAPPEN TO THEM?!

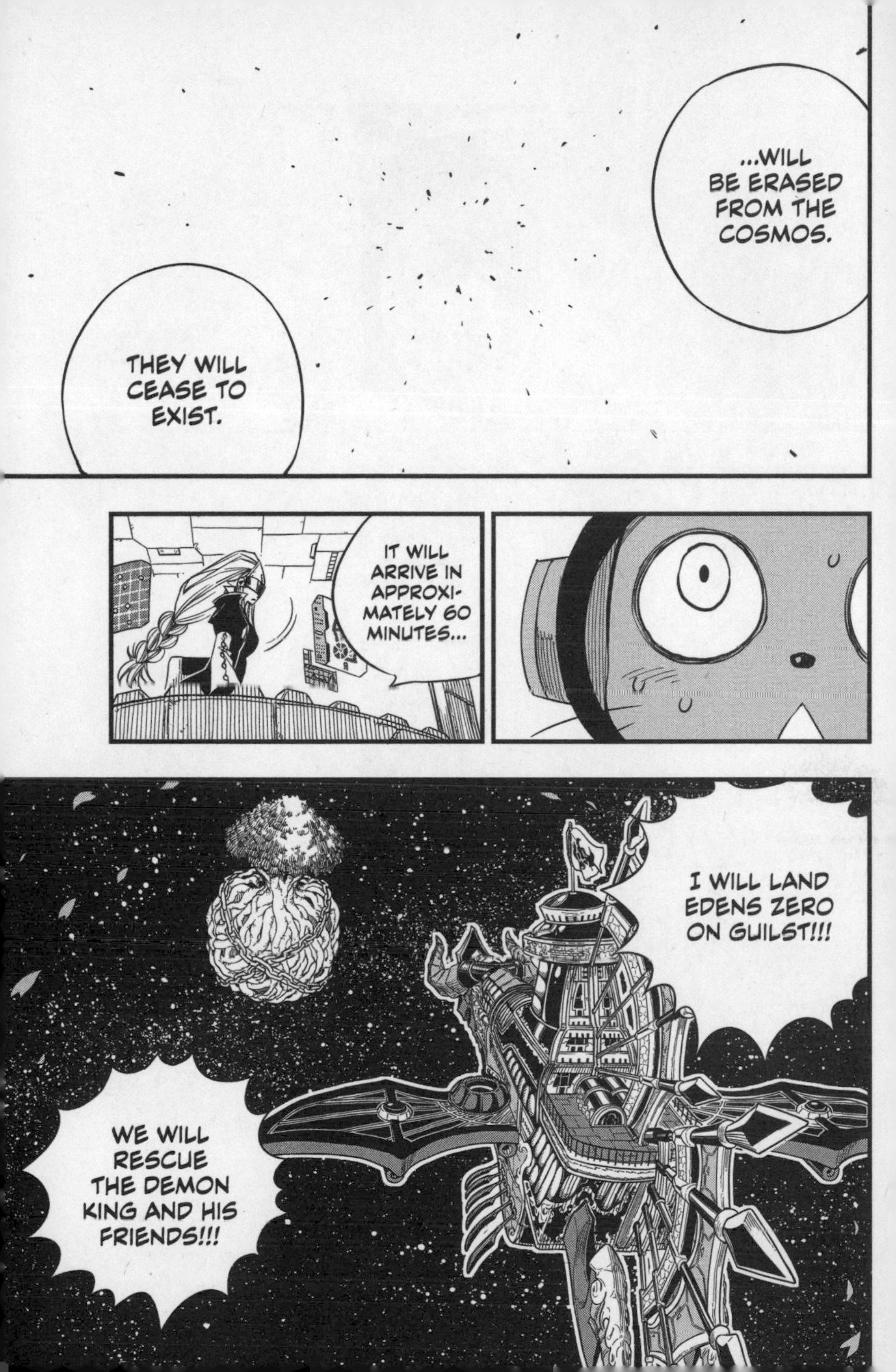
THEY WILL CEASE TO EXIST.
...WILL BE ERASED FROM THE COSMOS.
IT WILL ARRIVE IN APPROXI-MATELY 60 MINUTES...
I WILL LAND EDENS ZERO ON GUILST!!!
WE WILL RESCUE THE DEMON KING AND HIS FRIENDS!!!

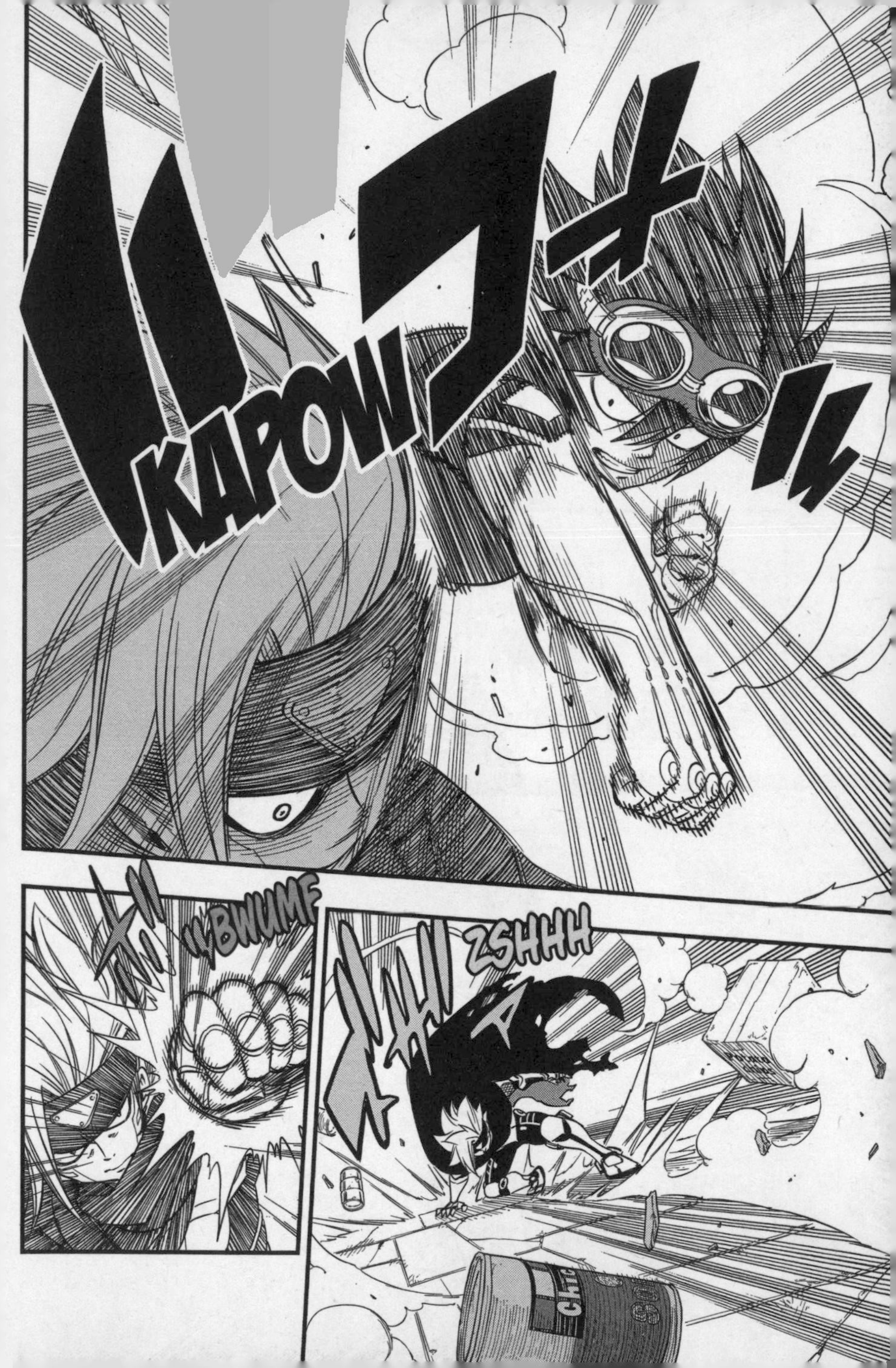
KAPOW
ZSHHH
BWUMF

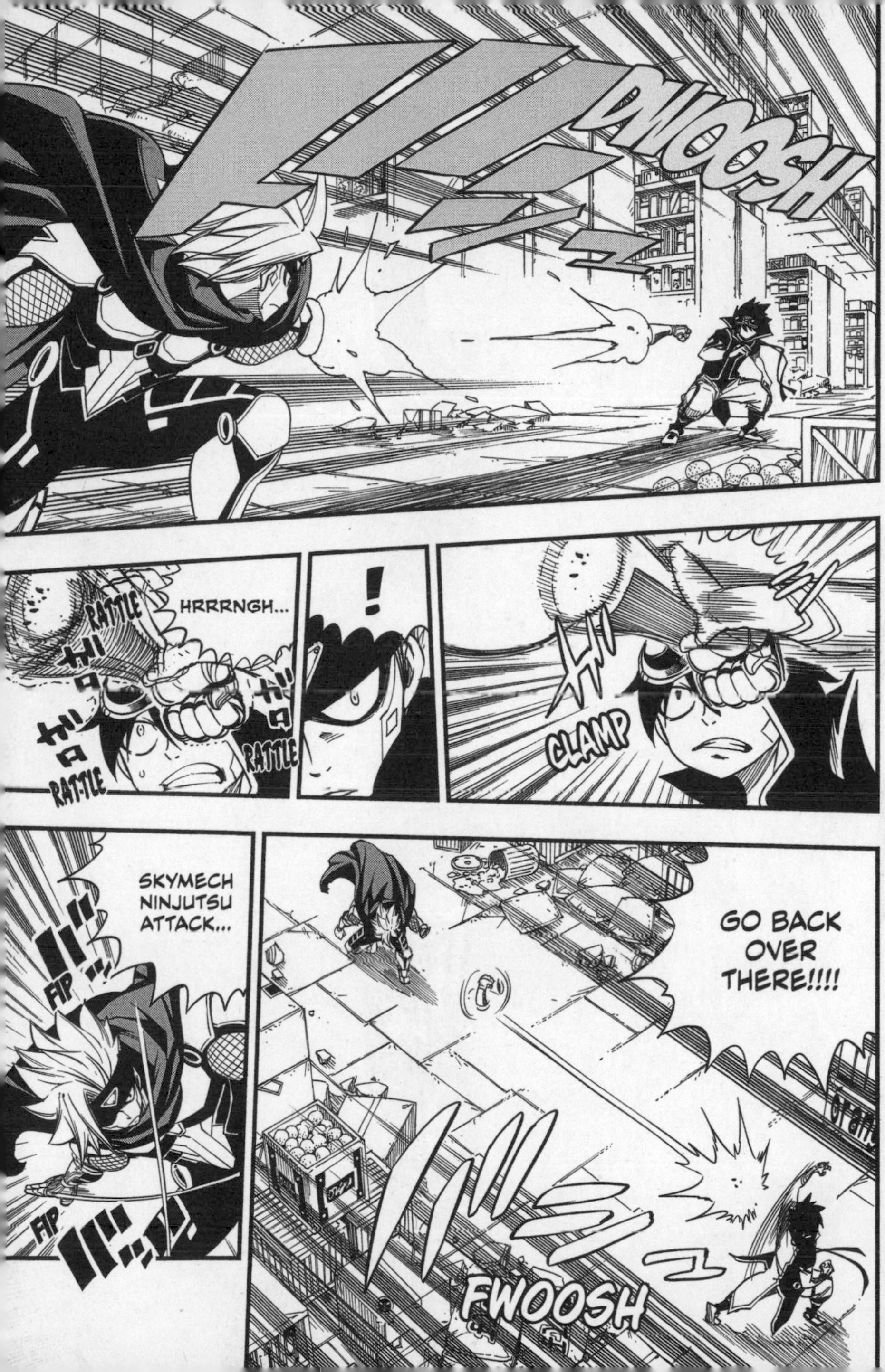
DWOOSH
CLAMP
!
HRRRNGH...
RATTLE
RATTLE
RATTLE
GO BACK OVER THERE!!!!
FWOOSH
SKYMECH NINJUTSU ATTACK...
FIP
FIP

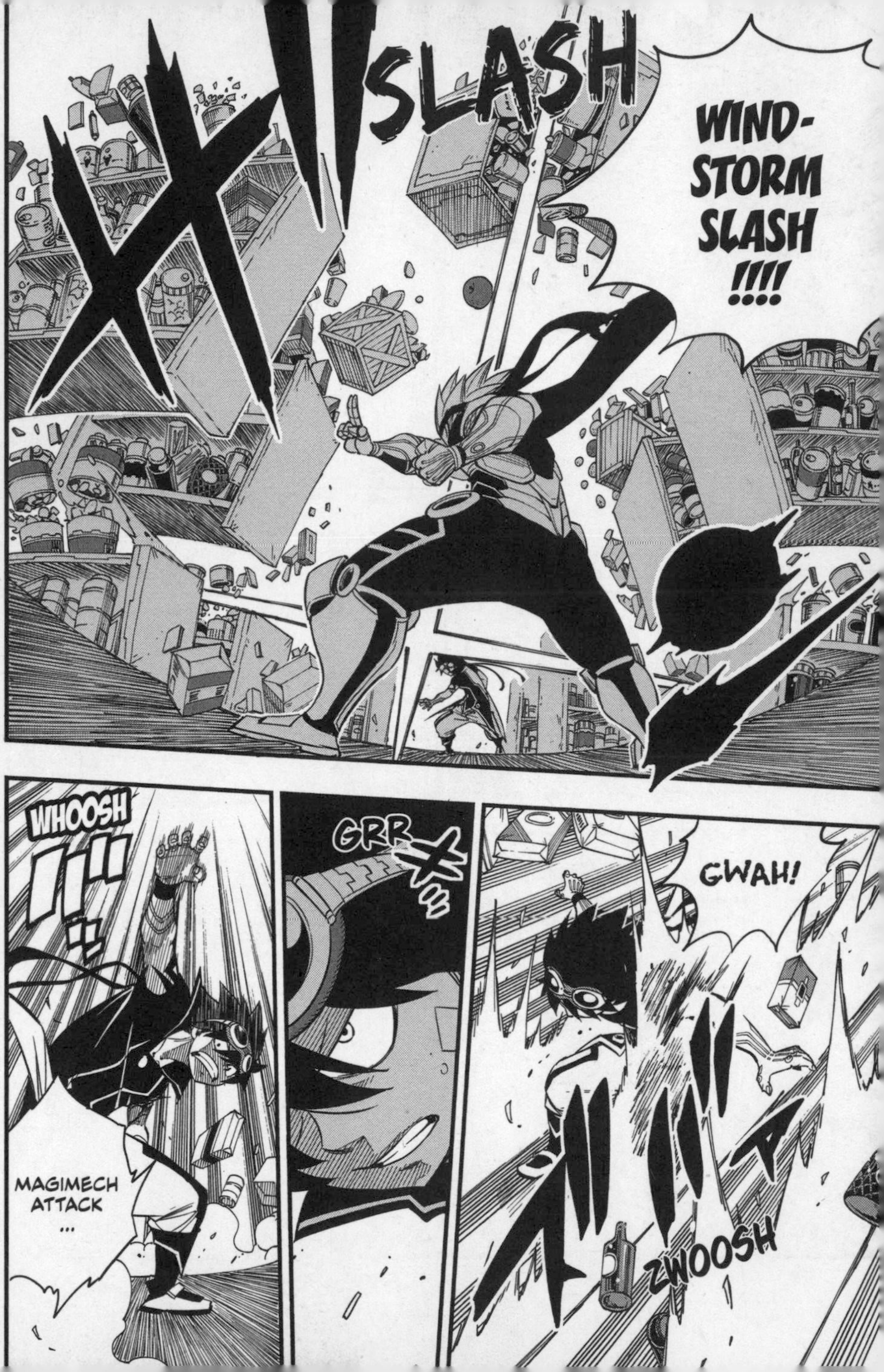
WIND-STORM SLASH !!!!
SLASH
GWAH!
ZWOOSH
GRR
WHOOSH
MAGIMECH ATTACK ...

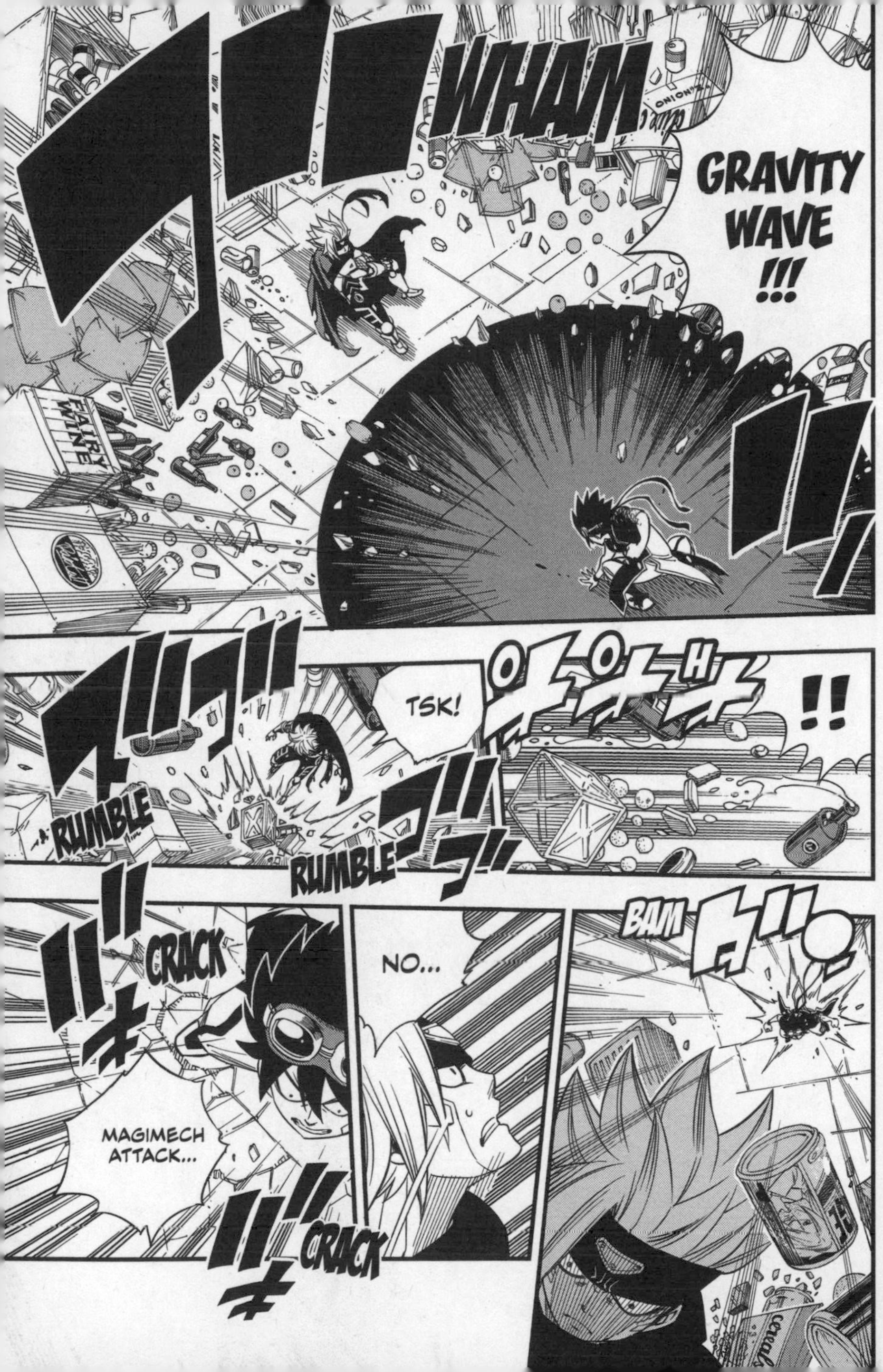
GRAVITY WAVE !!!
WHAM
FAIRY WINE
OOH!!
TSK!
RUMBLE
RUMBLE
BAM
NO...
CRACK
MAGIMECH ATTACK...
CRACK

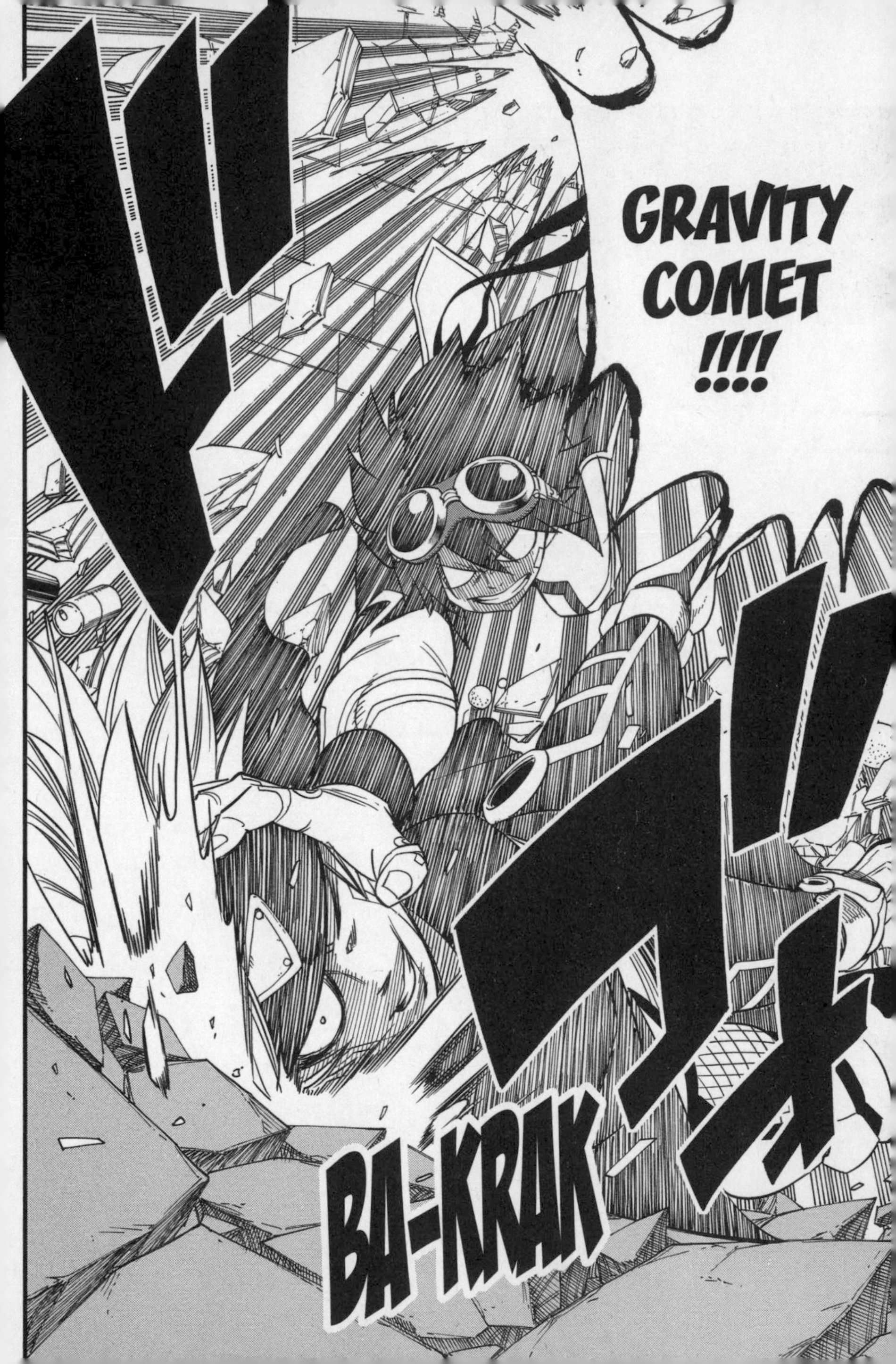
GRAVITY
COMET
!!!!
BA-KRAK

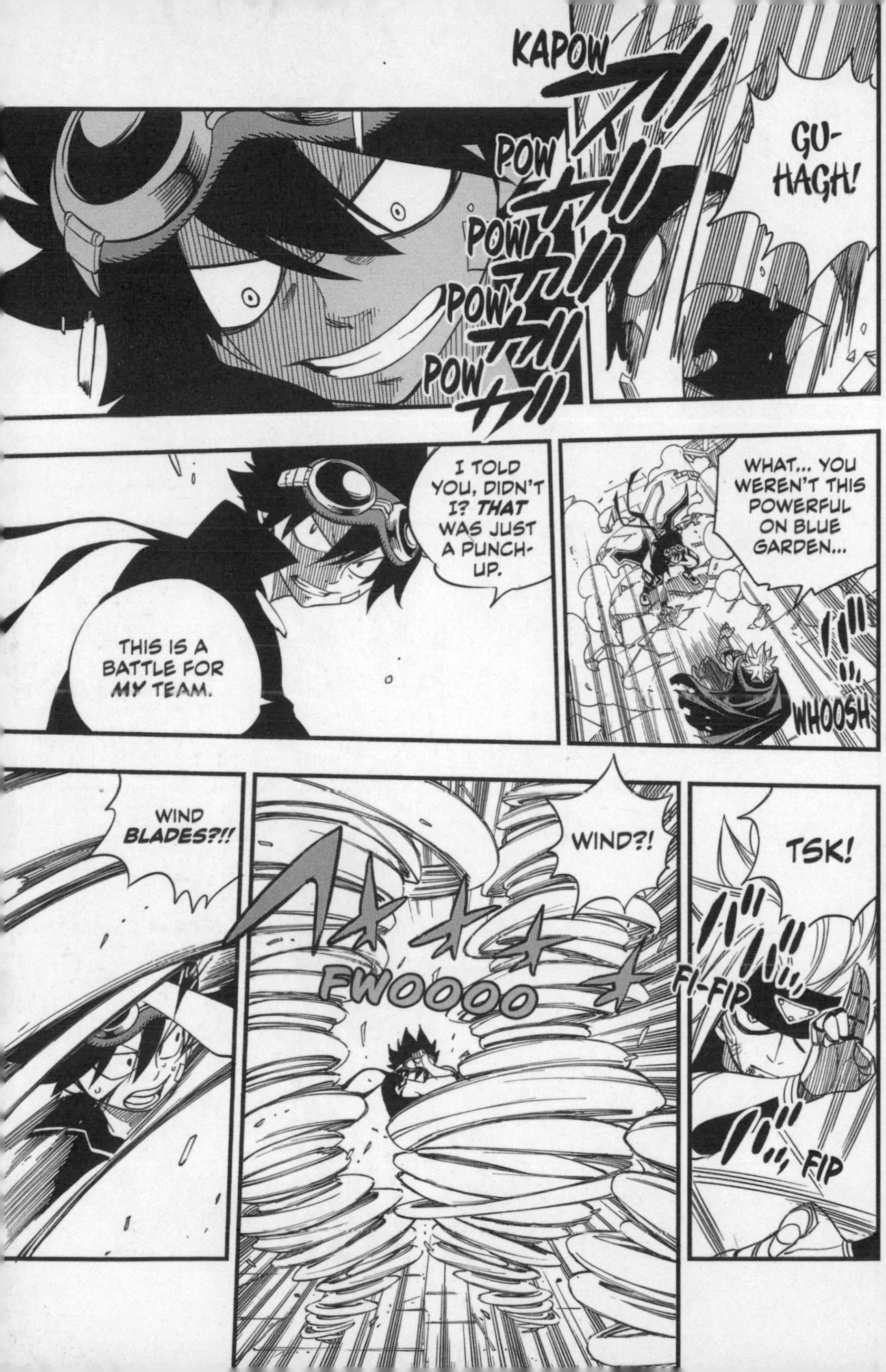
KAPOW
GU-HAGH!
POW
POW
POW
POW
WHAT... YOU WEREN'T THIS POWERFUL ON BLUE GARDEN...
WHOOSH
I TOLD YOU, DIDN'T I? *THAT* WAS JUST A PUNCH-UP.
THIS IS A BATTLE FOR *MY* TEAM.
TSK!
FI-FIP
FIP
WIND?!
FWOOOO
WIND *BLADES?!!*

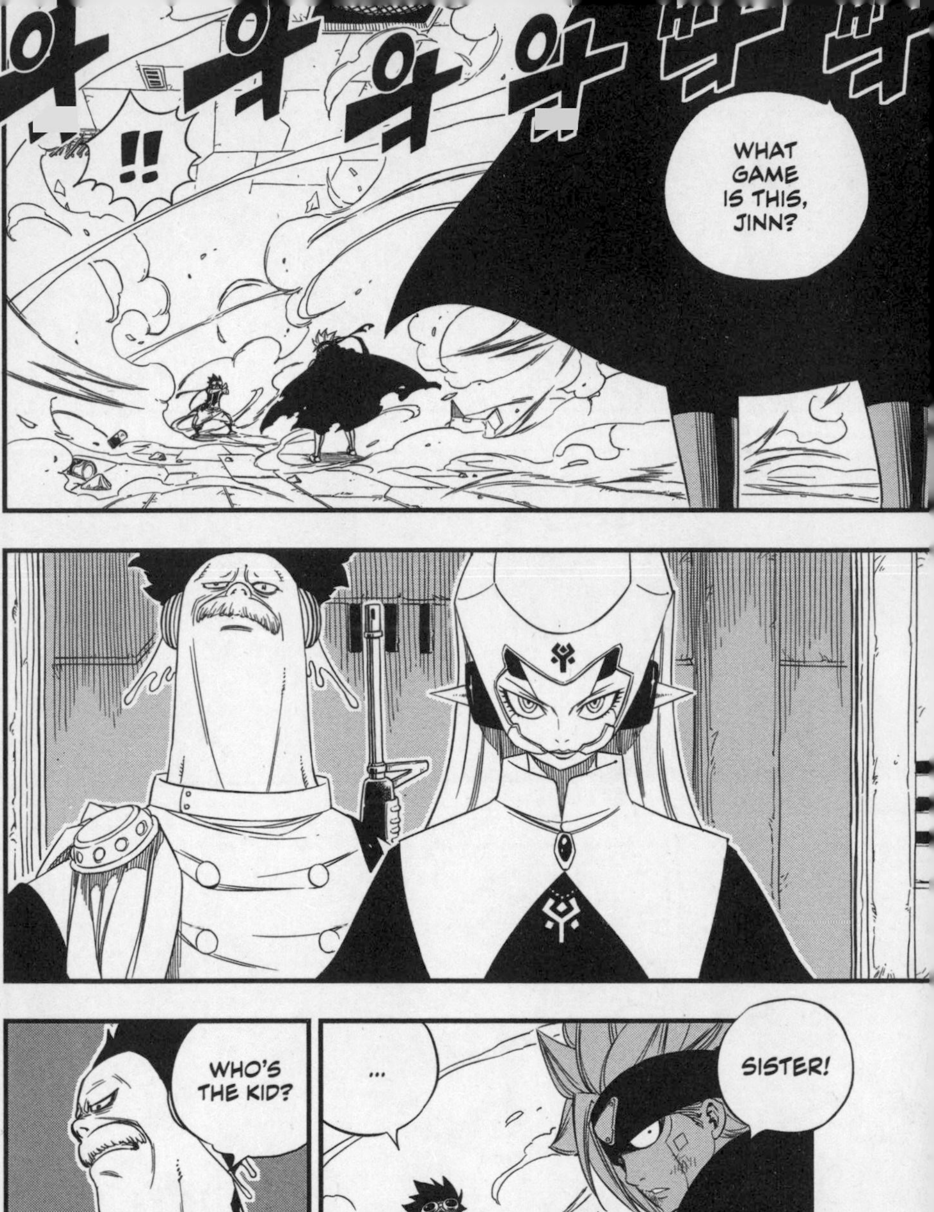
!!
WHAT GAME IS THIS, JINN?
SISTER!
...
WHO'S THE KID?

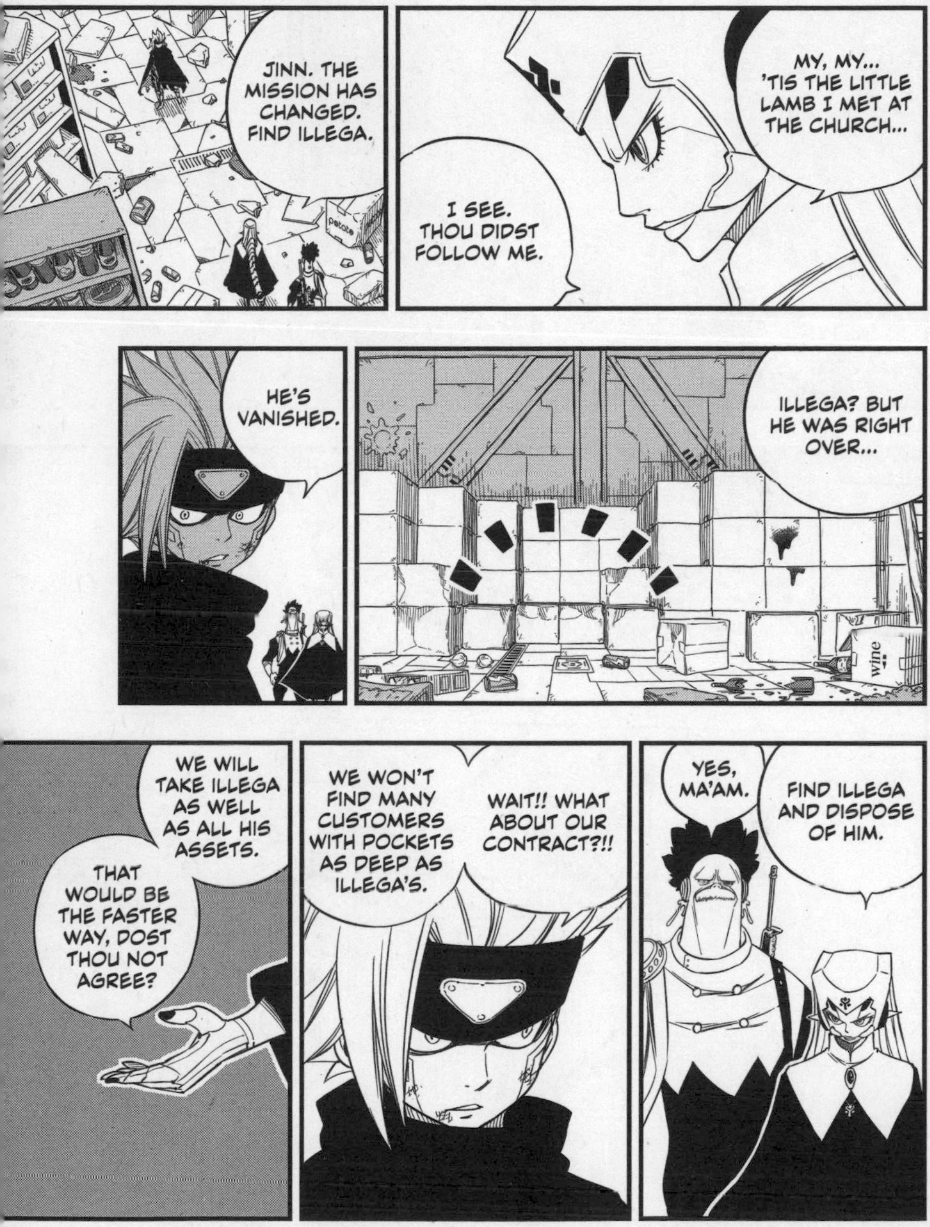
MY, MY... 'TIS THE LITTLE LAMB I MET AT THE CHURCH...
I SEE. THOU DIDST FOLLOW ME.
JINN. THE MISSION HAS CHANGED. FIND ILLEGA.
ILLEGA? BUT HE WAS RIGHT OVER...
HE'S VANISHED.
FIND ILLEGA AND DISPOSE OF HIM.
YES, MA'AM.
WAIT!! WHAT ABOUT OUR CONTRACT?!!
WE WON'T FIND MANY CUSTOMERS WITH POCKETS AS DEEP AS ILLEGA'S.
WE WILL TAKE ILLEGA AS WELL AS ALL HIS ASSETS.
THAT WOULD BE THE FASTER WAY, DOST THOU NOT AGREE?

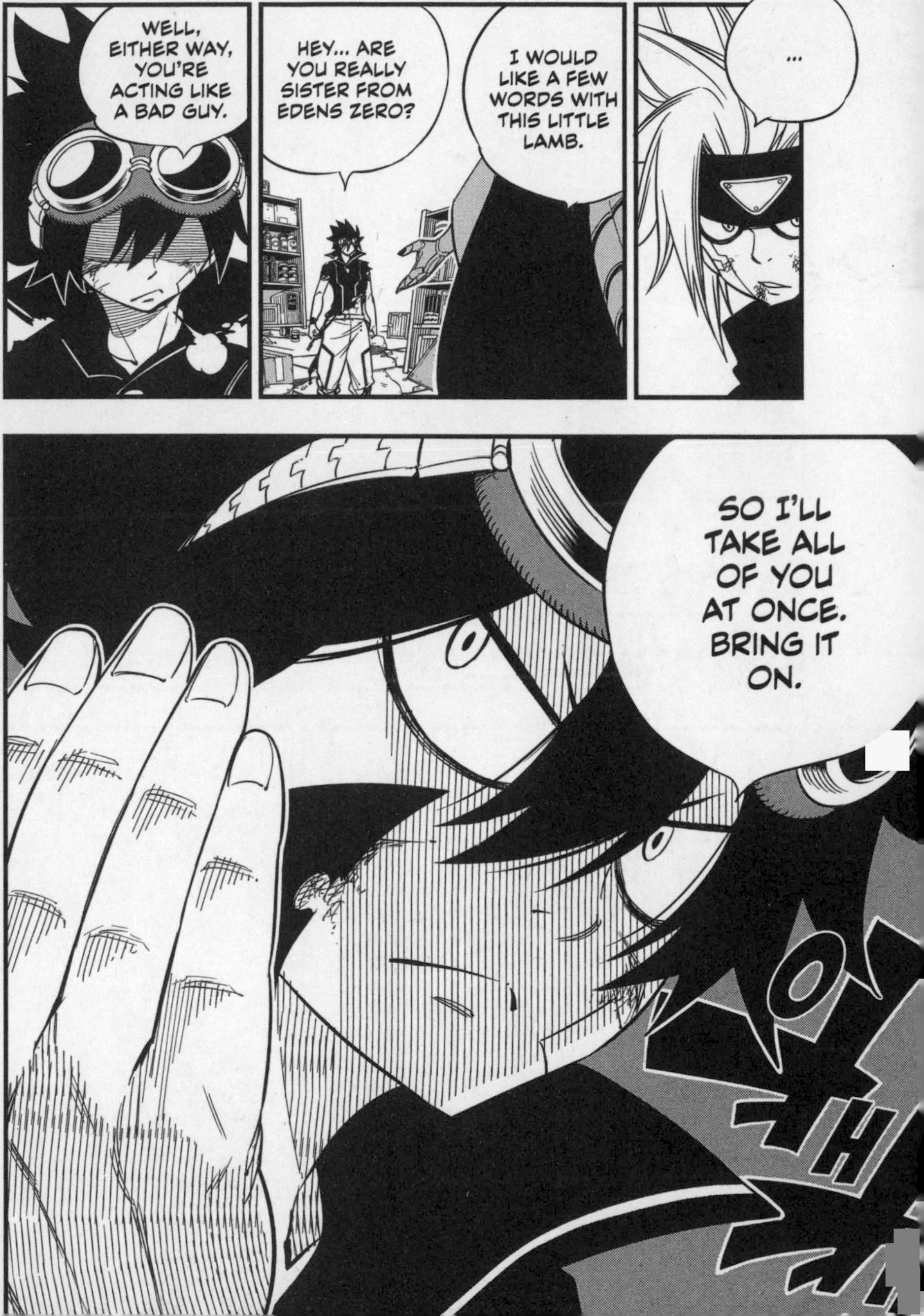
...
I WOULD LIKE A FEW WORDS WITH THIS LITTLE LAMB.
HEY... ARE YOU REALLY SISTER FROM EDENS ZERO?
WELL, EITHER WAY, YOU'RE ACTING LIKE A BAD GUY.
SO I'LL TAKE ALL OF YOU AT ONCE. BRING IT ON.

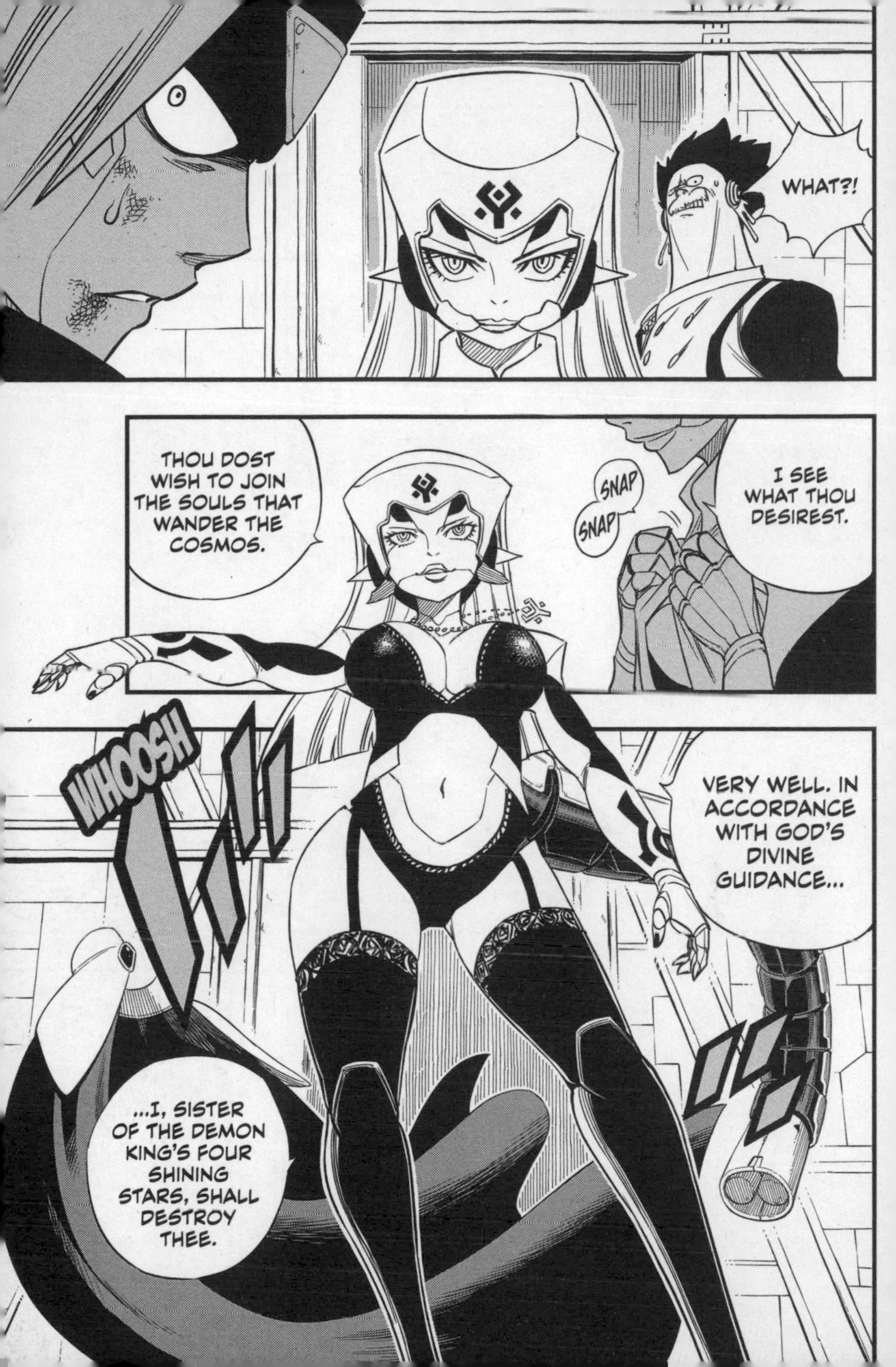
WHAT?!
I SEE WHAT THOU DESIREST.
SNAP
SNAP
THOU DOST WISH TO JOIN THE SOULS THAT WANDER THE COSMOS.
VERY WELL. IN ACCORDANCE WITH GOD'S DIVINE GUIDANCE...
WHOOSH
...I, SISTER OF THE DEMON KING'S FOUR SHINING STARS, SHALL DESTROY THEE.

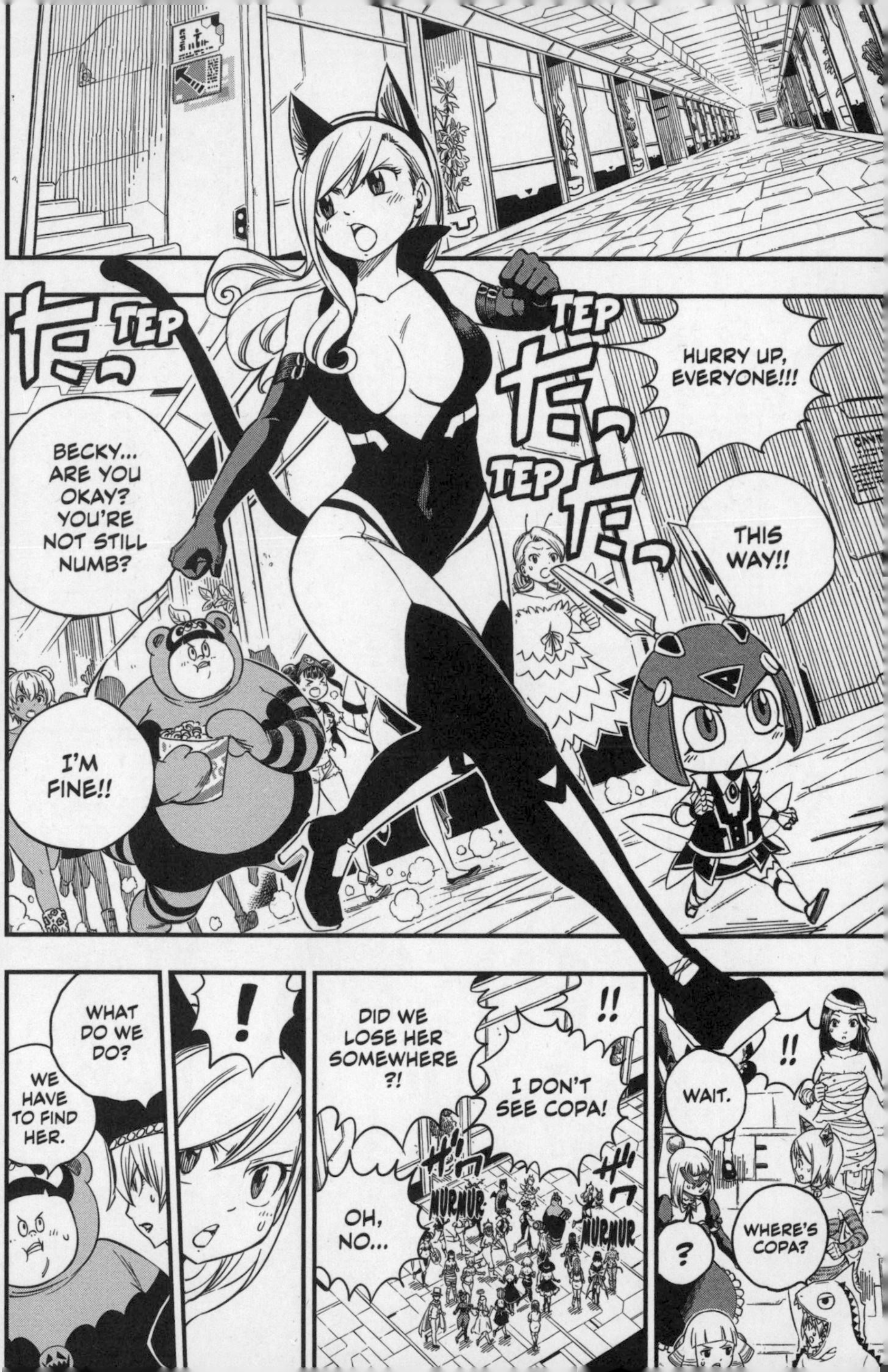

HURRY UP, EVERYONE!!!
TEP
だっ
TEP
だっ
THIS WAY!!
TEP
だっ
BECKY... ARE YOU OKAY? YOU'RE NOT STILL NUMB?
I'M FINE!!
!!
WAIT.
WHERE'S COPA?
?
!!
DID WE LOSE HER SOMEWHERE?!
I DON'T SEE COPA!
ザワ
MURMUR
ザワ
MURMUR
OH, NO...
!
WHAT DO WE DO?
WE HAVE TO FIND HER.

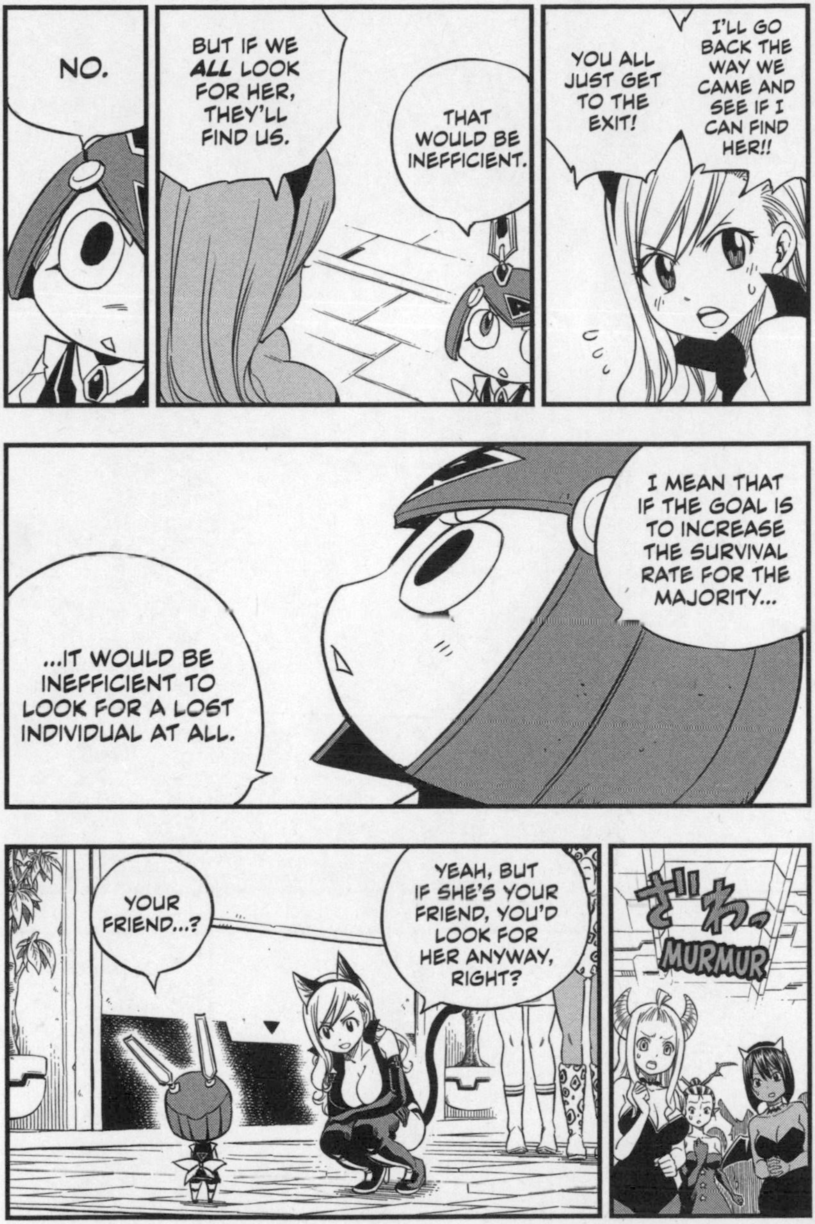
I'LL GO BACK THE WAY WE CAME AND SEE IF I CAN FIND HER!!
YOU ALL JUST GET TO THE EXIT!
THAT WOULD BE INEFFICIENT.
BUT IF WE ***ALL*** LOOK FOR HER, THEY'LL FIND US.
NO.
I MEAN THAT IF THE GOAL IS TO INCREASE THE SURVIVAL RATE FOR THE MAJORITY...
...IT WOULD BE INEFFICIENT TO LOOK FOR A LOST INDIVIDUAL AT ALL.
ざわっ
MURMUR
YEAH, BUT IF SHE'S YOUR FRIEND, YOU'D LOOK FOR HER ANYWAY, RIGHT?
YOUR FRIEND...?

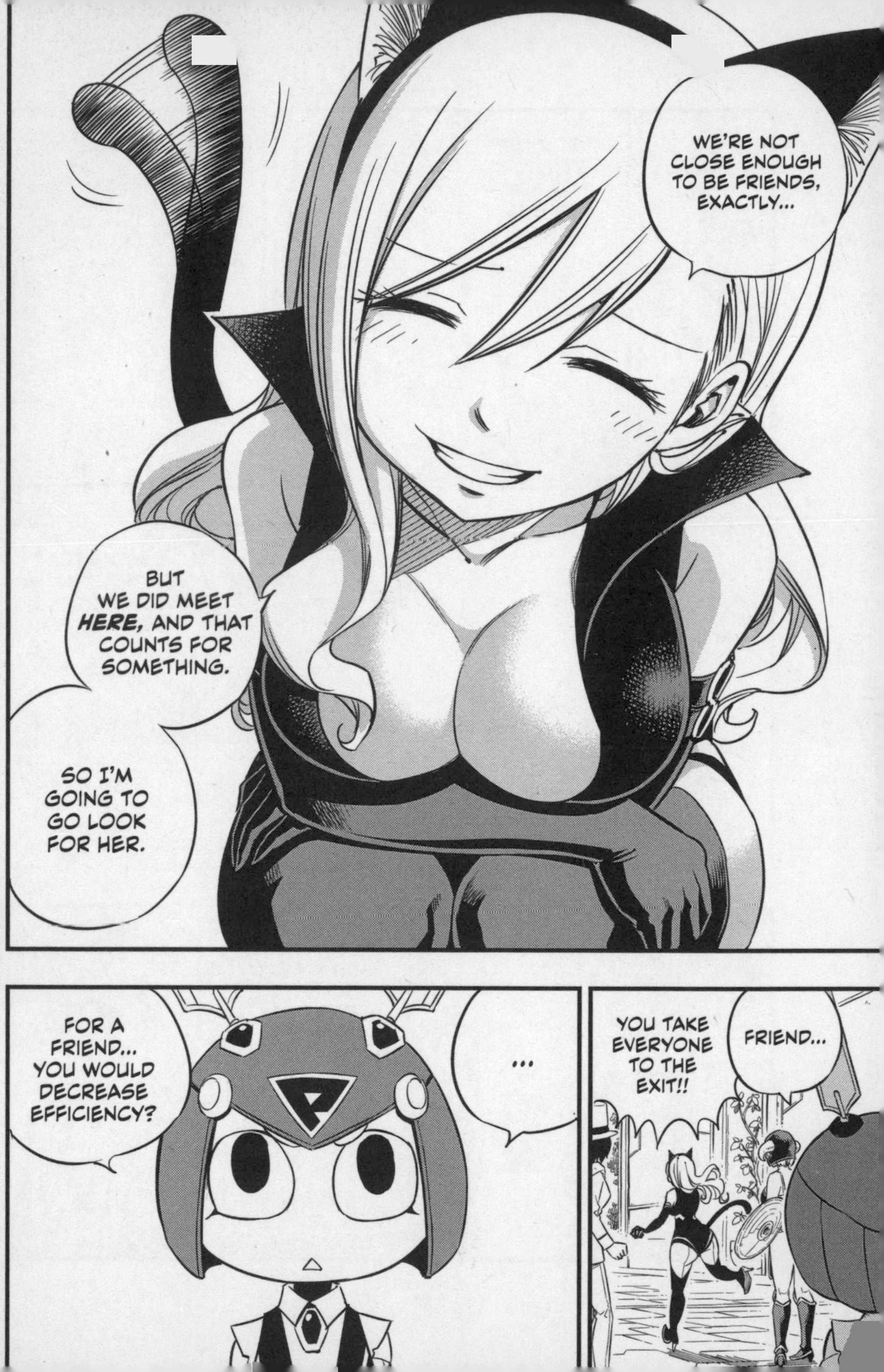
WE'RE NOT CLOSE ENOUGH TO BE FRIENDS, EXACTLY...
BUT WE DID MEET ***HERE,*** AND THAT COUNTS FOR SOMETHING.
SO I'M GOING TO GO LOOK FOR HER.
FRIEND...
YOU TAKE EVERYONE TO THE EXIT!!
...
FOR A FRIEND... YOU WOULD DECREASE EFFICIENCY?

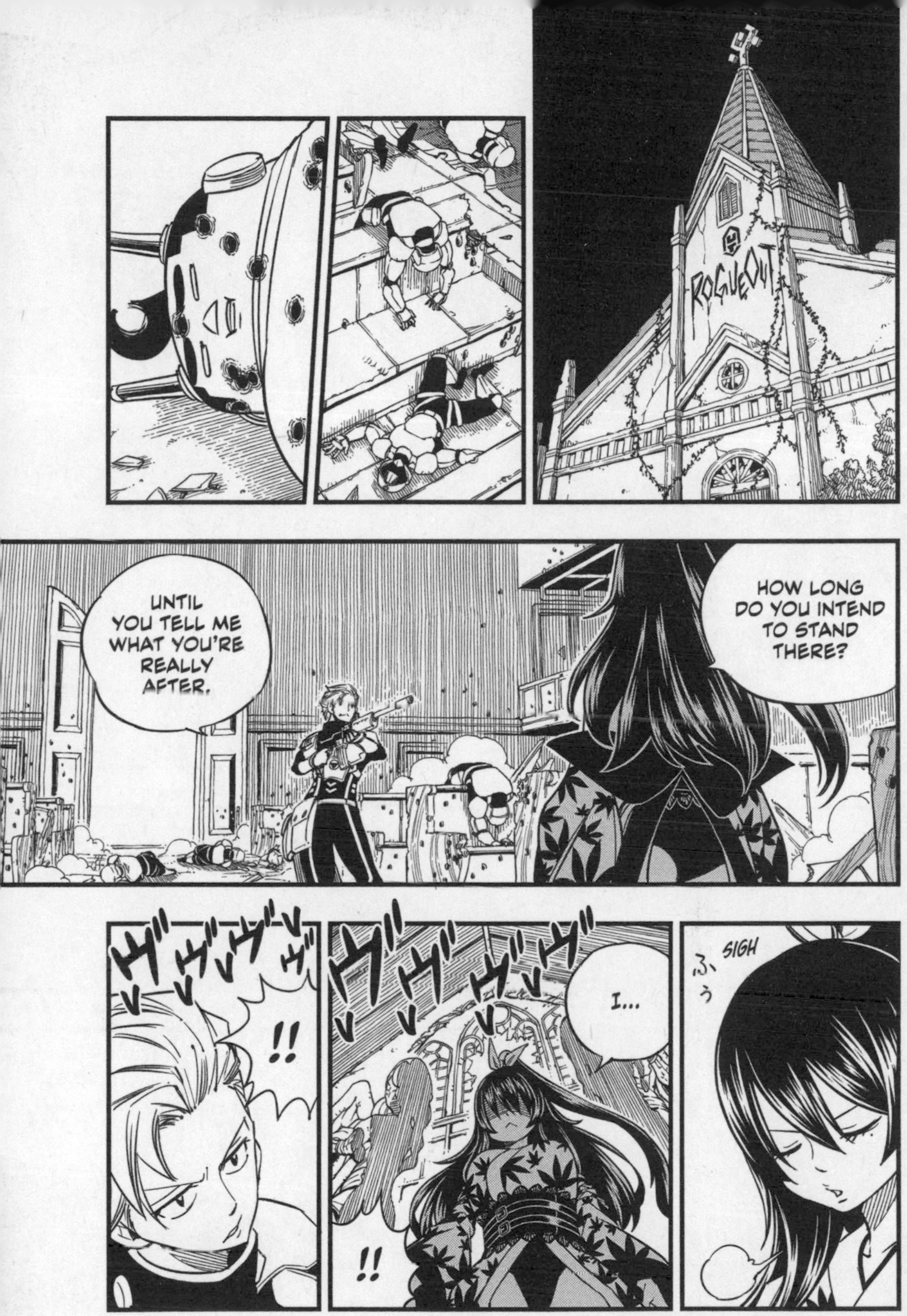
ROGUEOUT
HOW LONG DO YOU INTEND TO STAND THERE?
UNTIL YOU TELL ME WHAT YOU'RE REALLY AFTER.
ふぅ
SIGH
I...
!!
!!

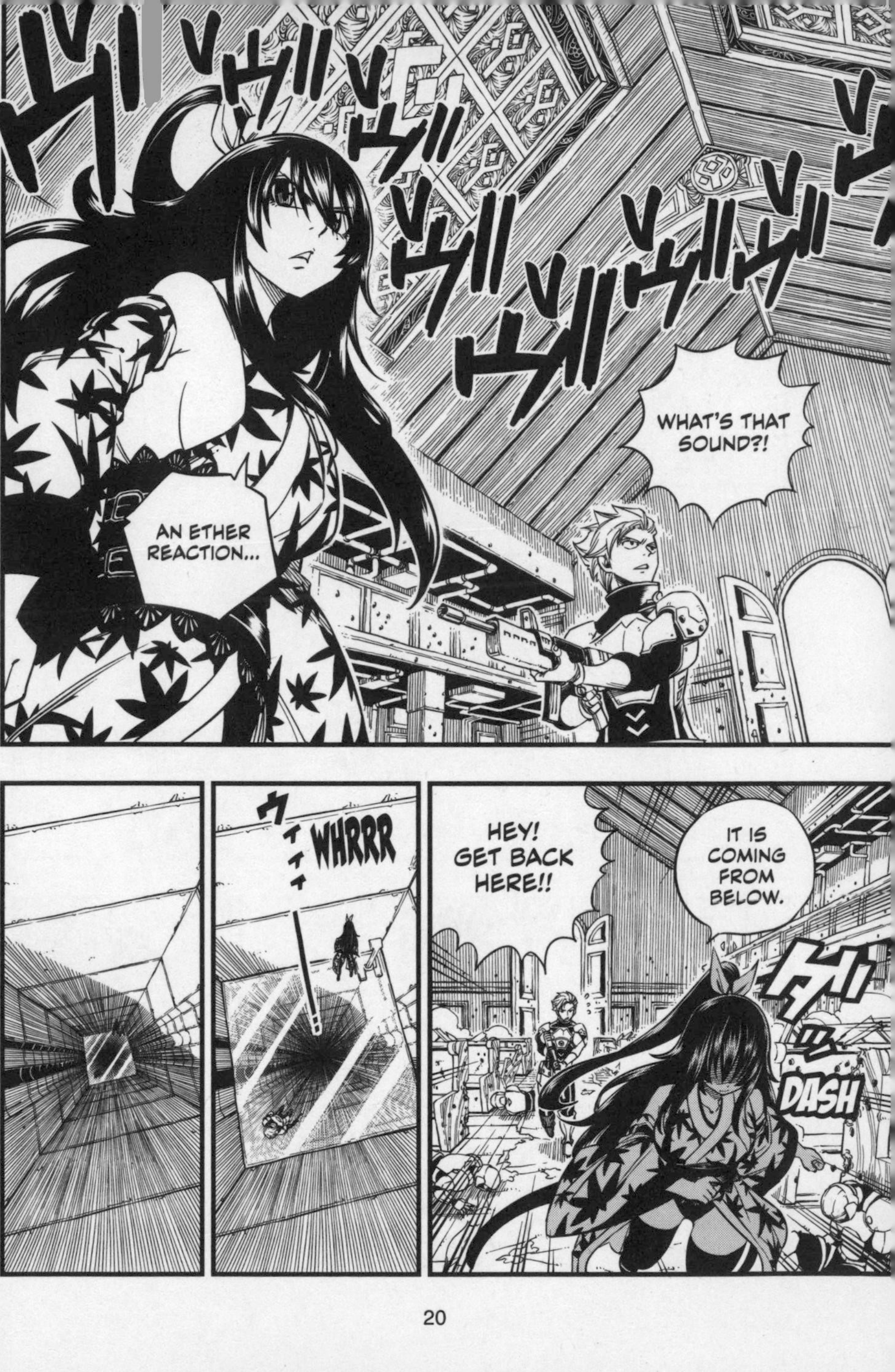
WHAT'S THAT SOUND?!
AN ETHER REACTION...
IT IS COMING FROM BELOW.
HEY! GET BACK HERE!!
DASH
WHRRR

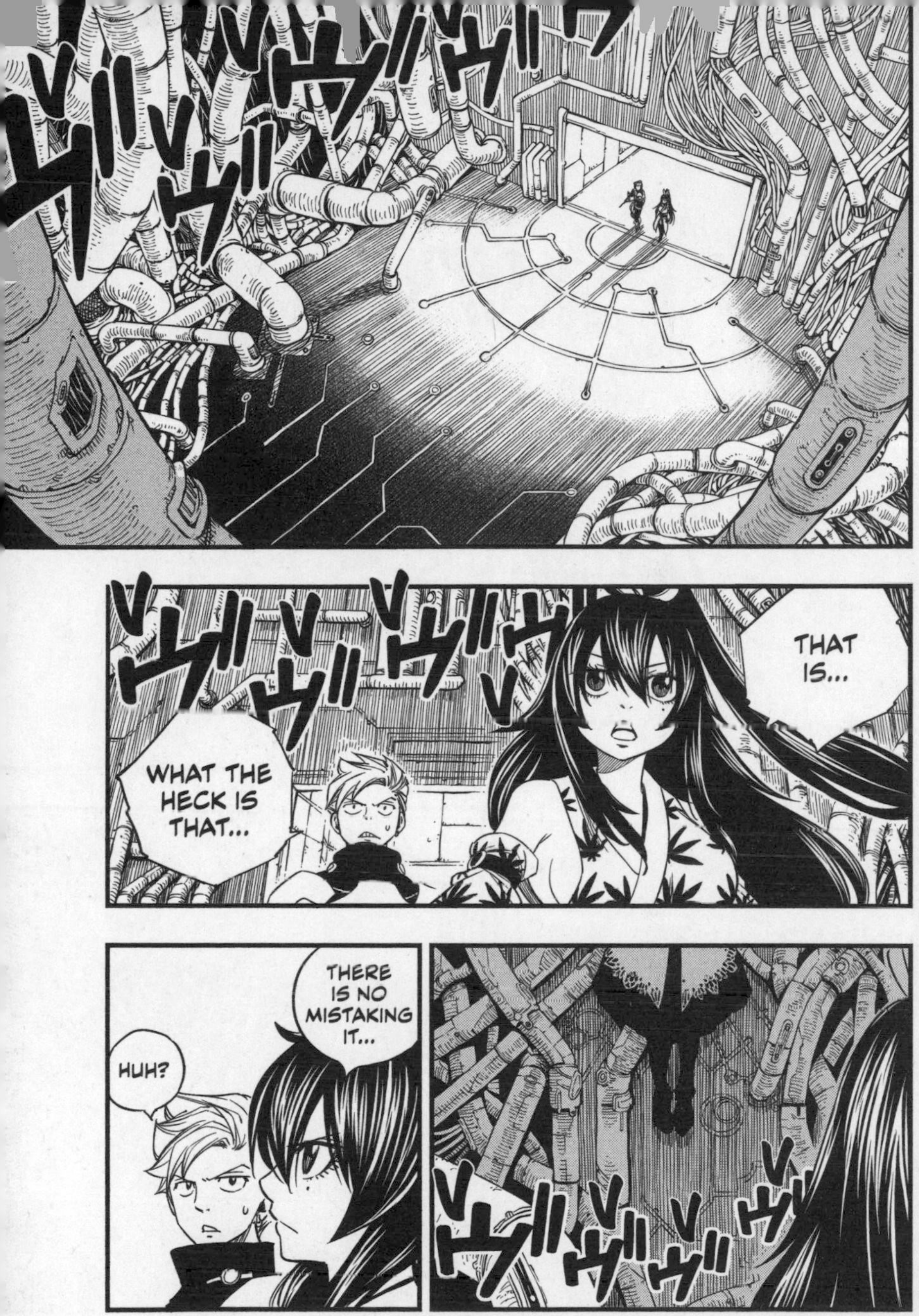
THAT IS...
WHAT THE HECK IS THAT...
THERE IS NO MISTAKING IT...
HUH?

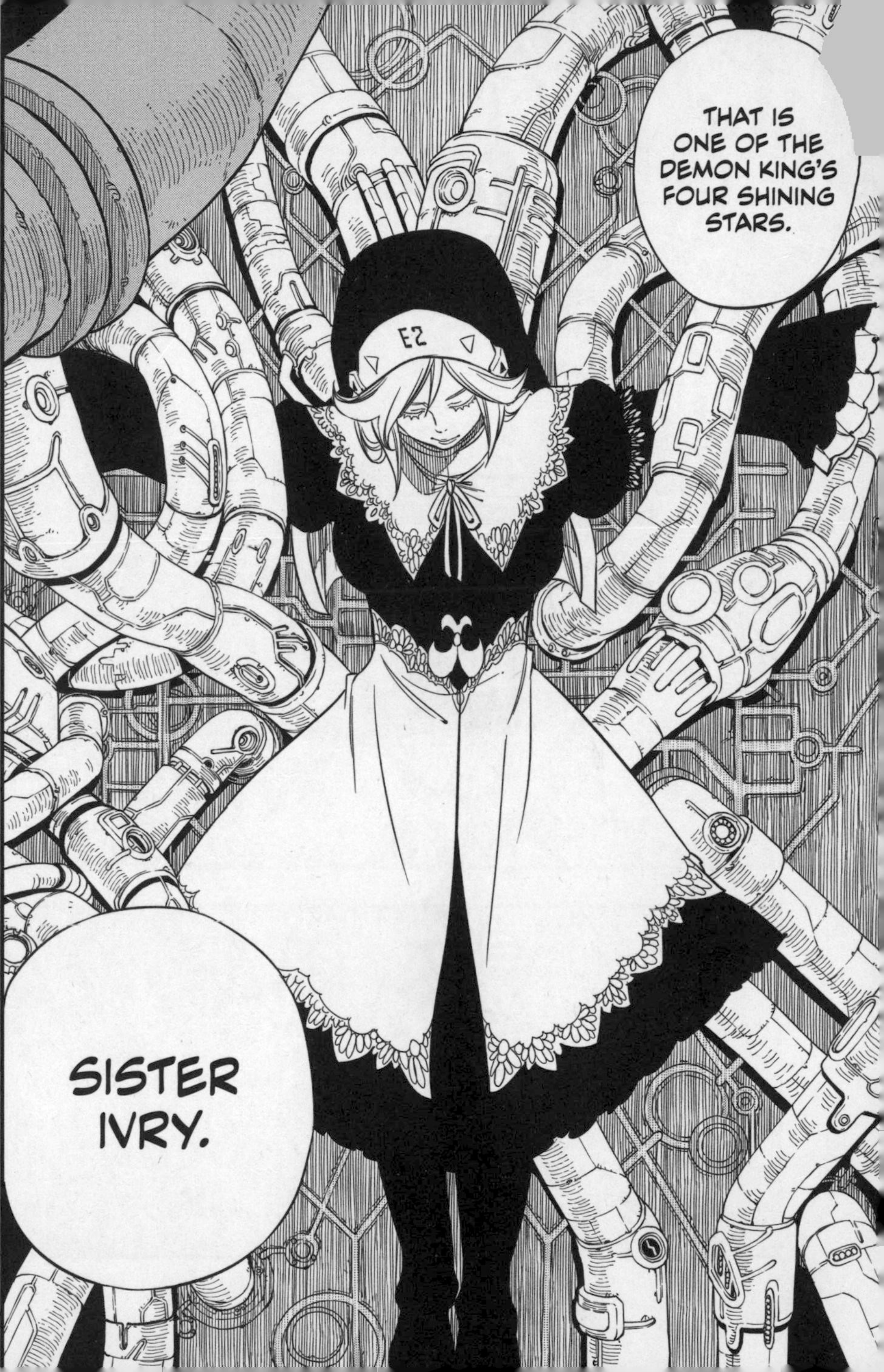
THAT IS ONE OF THE DEMON KING'S FOUR SHINING STARS.
SISTER IVRY.

EDENS ZERO

BIF

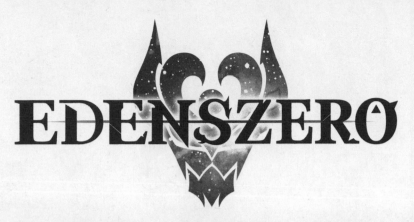

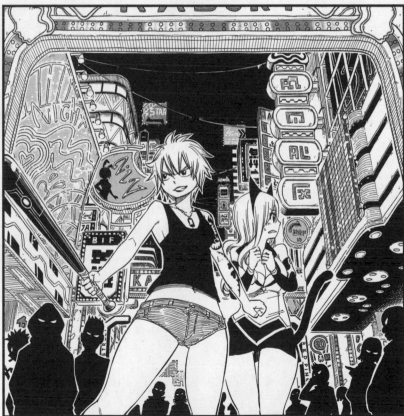

CHAPTER 25: TAKE AIM

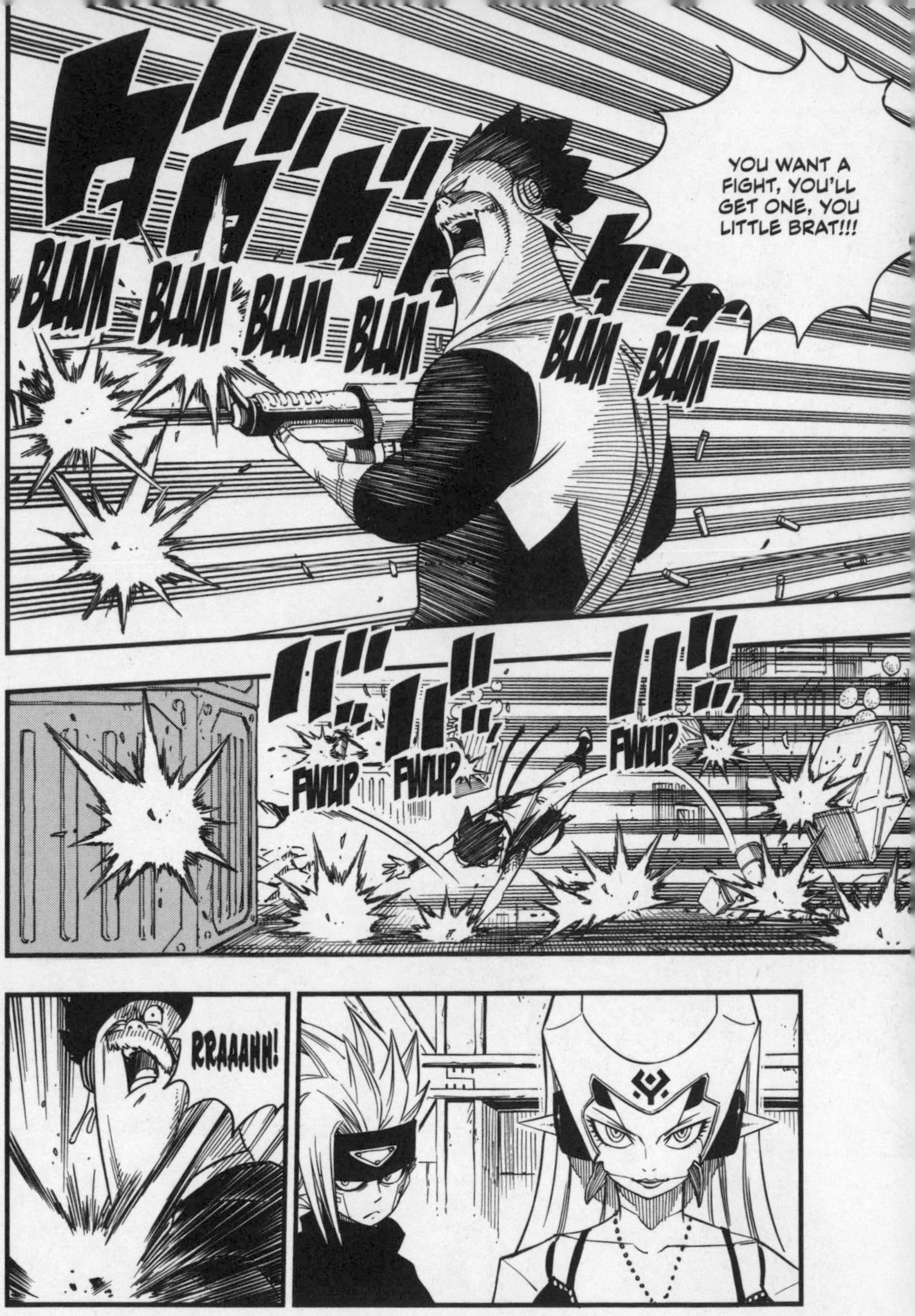
YOU WANT A FIGHT, YOU'LL GET ONE, YOU LITTLE BRAT!!!
BLAM BLAM
BLAM BLAM BLAM BLAM
FWUP
FWUP FWUP
RRAAAHH!

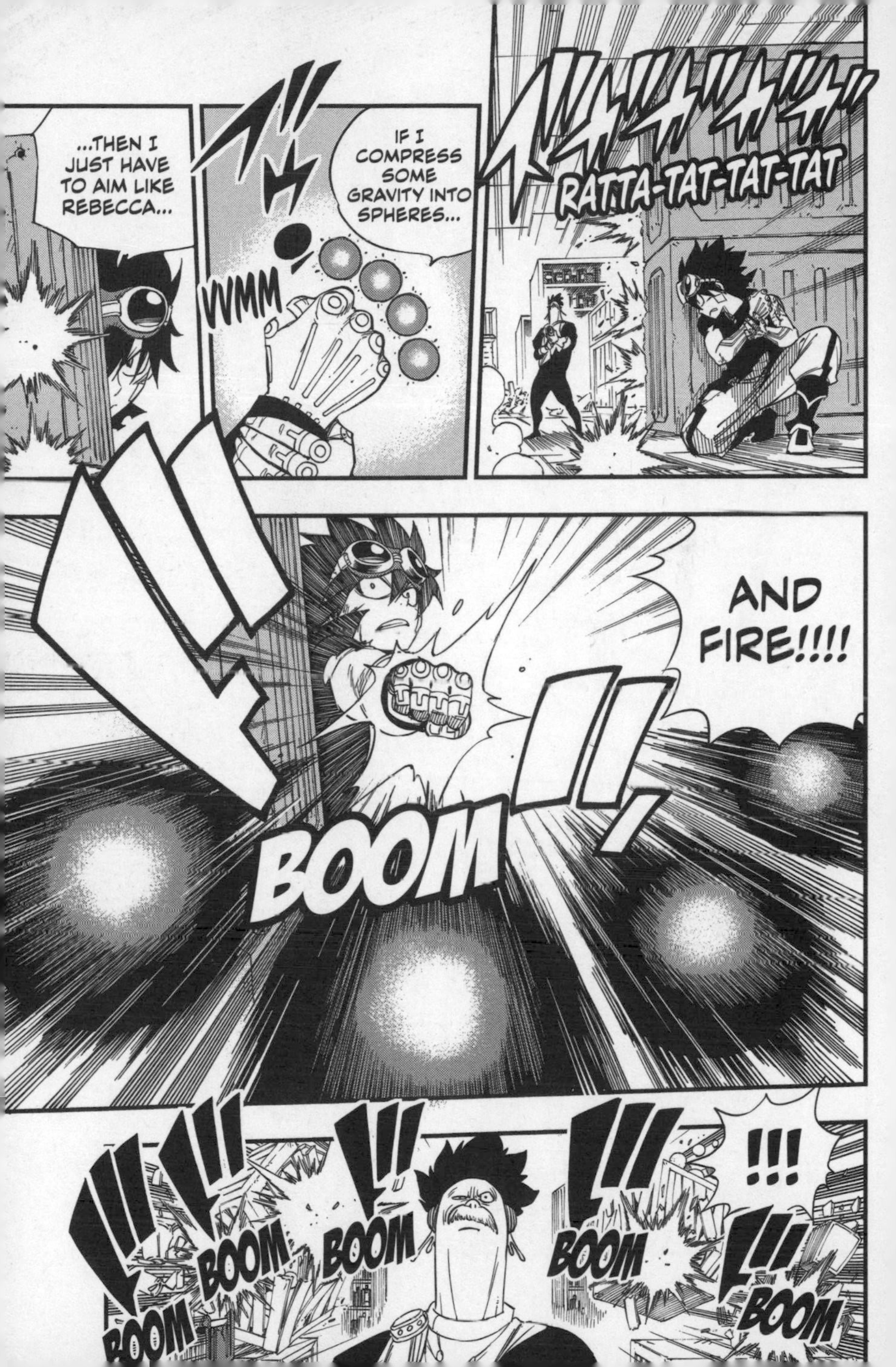
RATTA-TAT-TAT-TAT
IF I COMPRESS SOME GRAVITY INTO SPHERES...
VVMM
...THEN I JUST HAVE TO AIM LIKE REBECCA...
AND FIRE!!!!
BOOM
!!!
BOOM
BOOM
BOOM
BOOM
BOOM

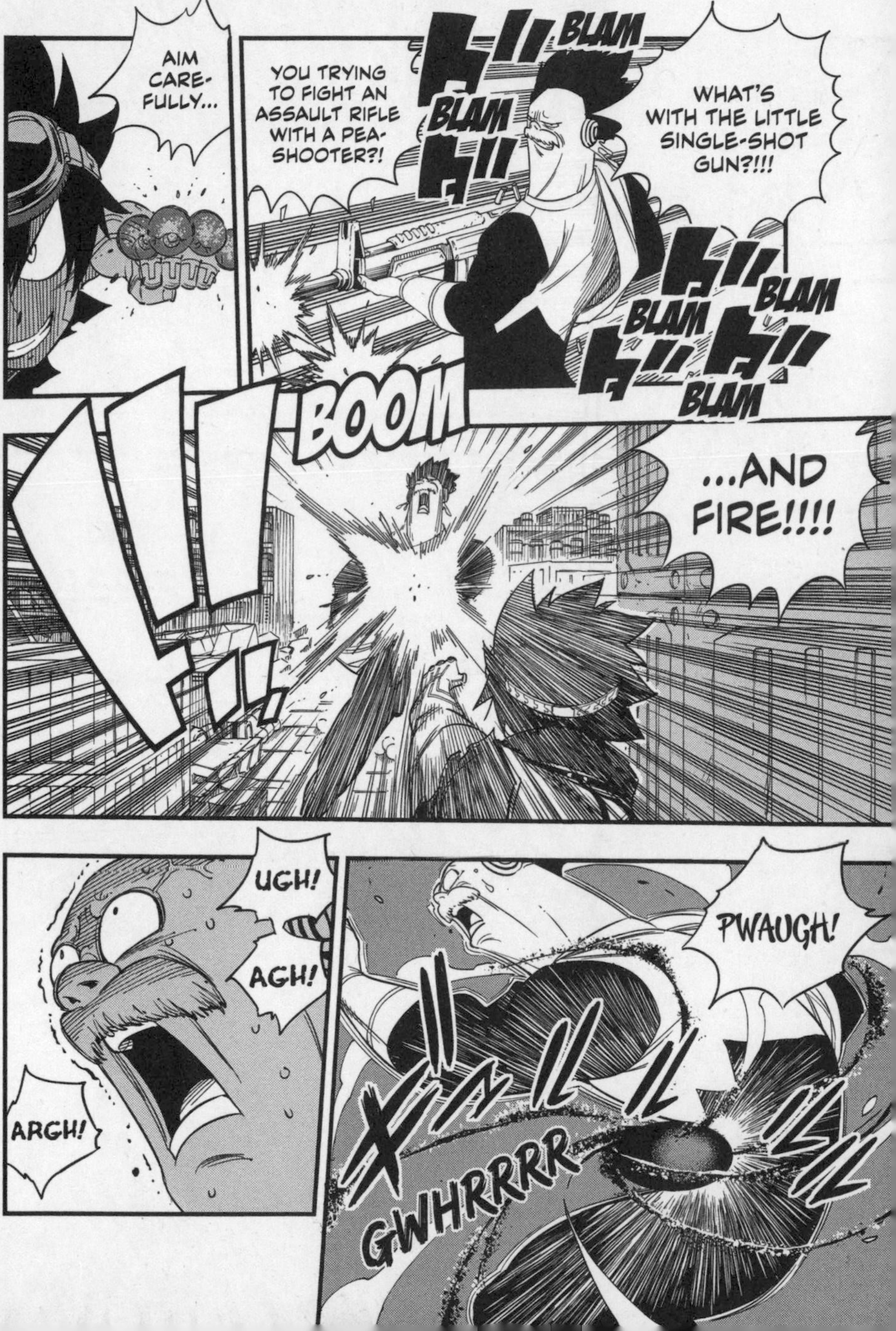
BLAM
WHAT'S WITH THE LITTLE SINGLE-SHOT GUN?!!!
BLAM
YOU TRYING TO FIGHT AN ASSAULT RIFLE WITH A PEA-SHOOTER?!
BLAM
BLAM
BLAM
BLAM
AIM CARE-FULLY...
...AND FIRE!!!!
BOOM
PWAUGH!
GWHRRRR
UGH!
AGH!
ARGH!

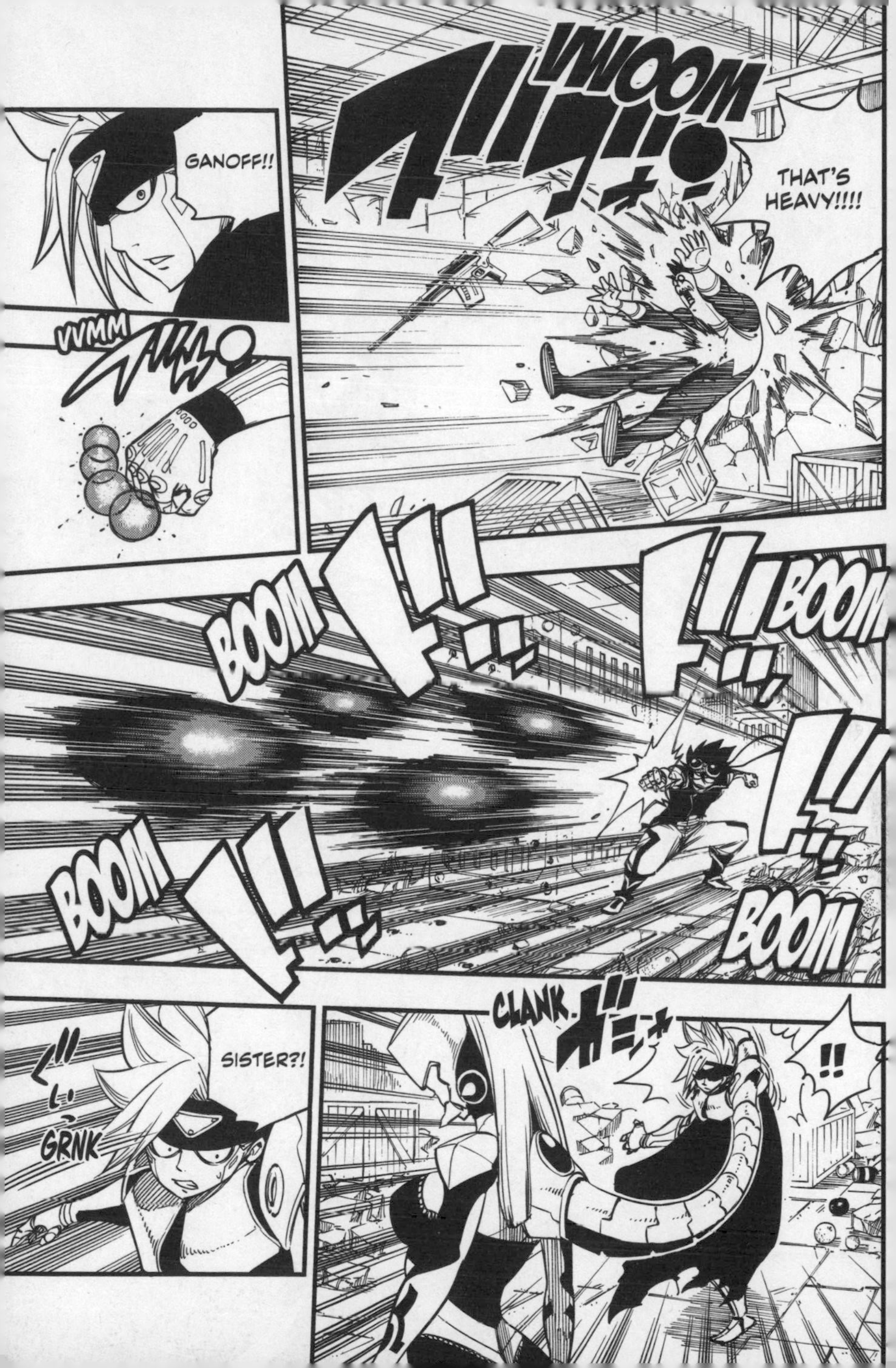

VWOOM
THAT'S HEAVY!!!!
GANOFF!!
VVMM
BOOM
BOOM
BOOM
BOOM
!!
CLANK
SISTER?!
GRNK

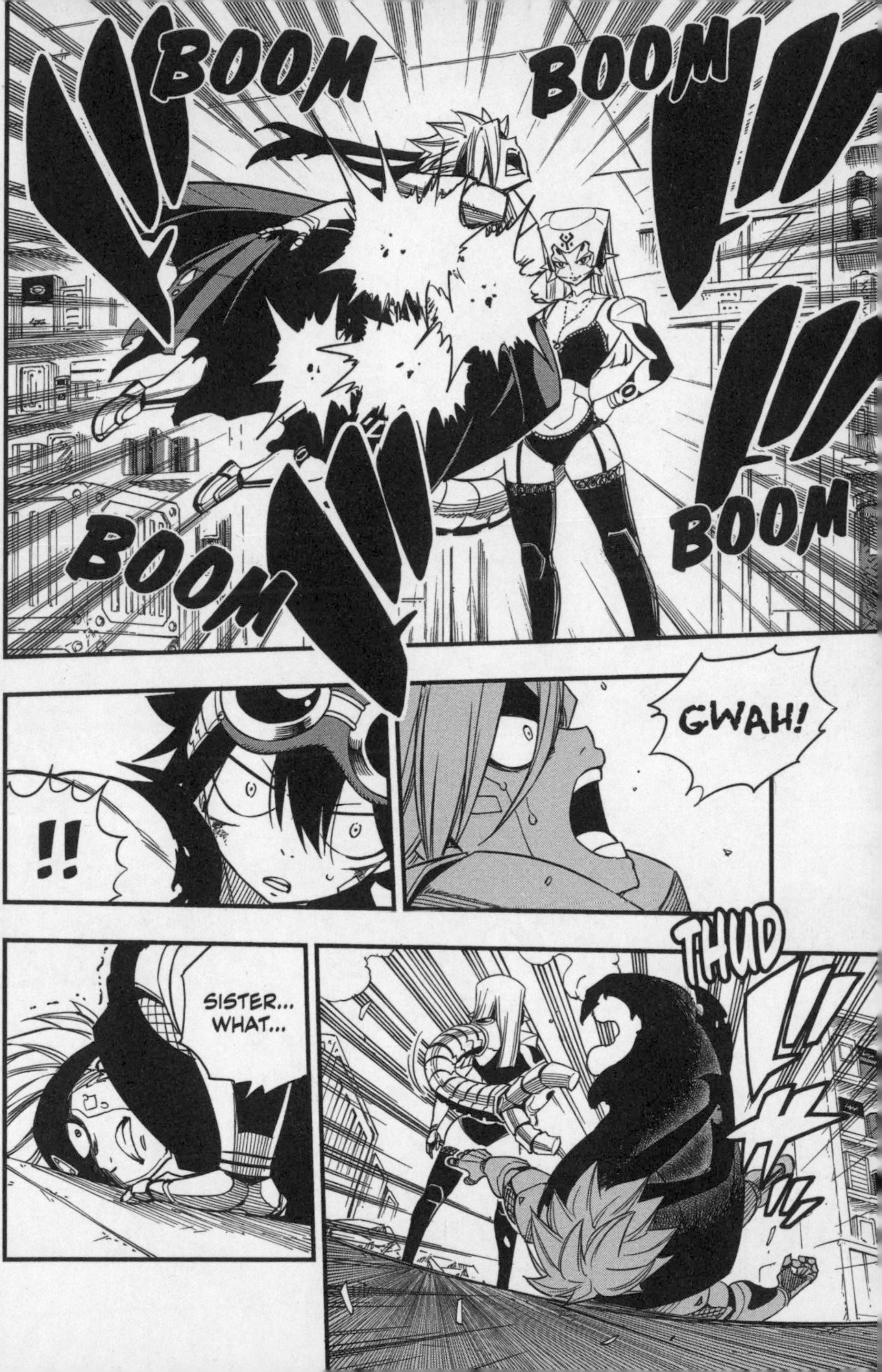
BOOM
BOOM
BOOM
BOOM
GWAH!
!!
THUD
SISTER... WHAT...

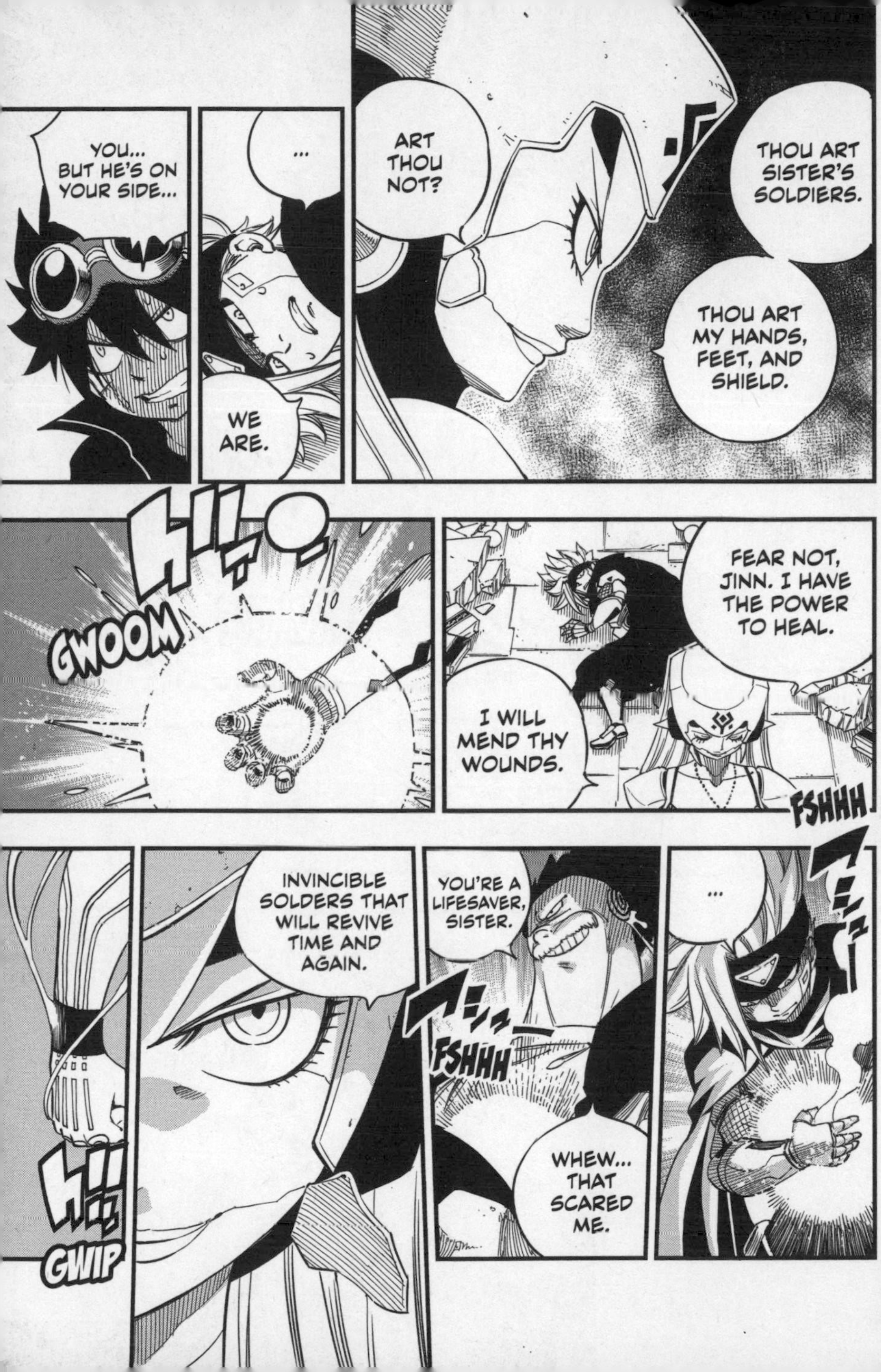
THOU ART SISTER'S SOLDIERS.
THOU ART MY HANDS, FEET, AND SHIELD.
ART THOU NOT?
...
WE ARE.
YOU... BUT HE'S ON YOUR SIDE...
FEAR NOT, JINN. I HAVE THE POWER TO HEAL.
I WILL MEND THY WOUNDS.
FSHHH
GWOOM
...
YOU'RE A LIFESAVER, SISTER.
FSHHH
WHEW... THAT SCARED ME.
INVINCIBLE SOLDERS THAT WILL REVIVE TIME AND AGAIN.
GWIP

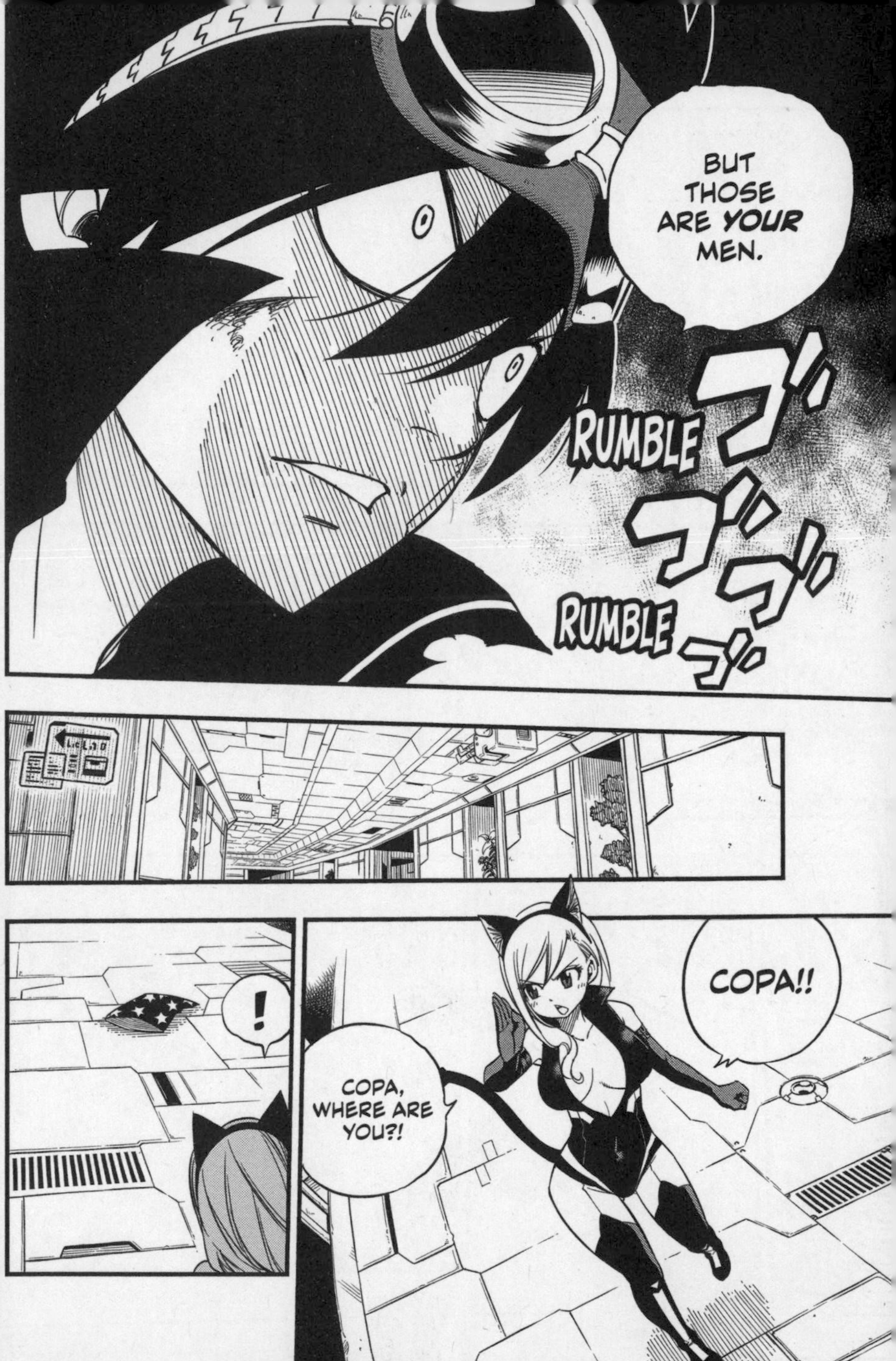

BUT THOSE ARE YOUR MEN.
RUMBLE
RUMBLE
COPA!!
COPA, WHERE ARE YOU?!
!

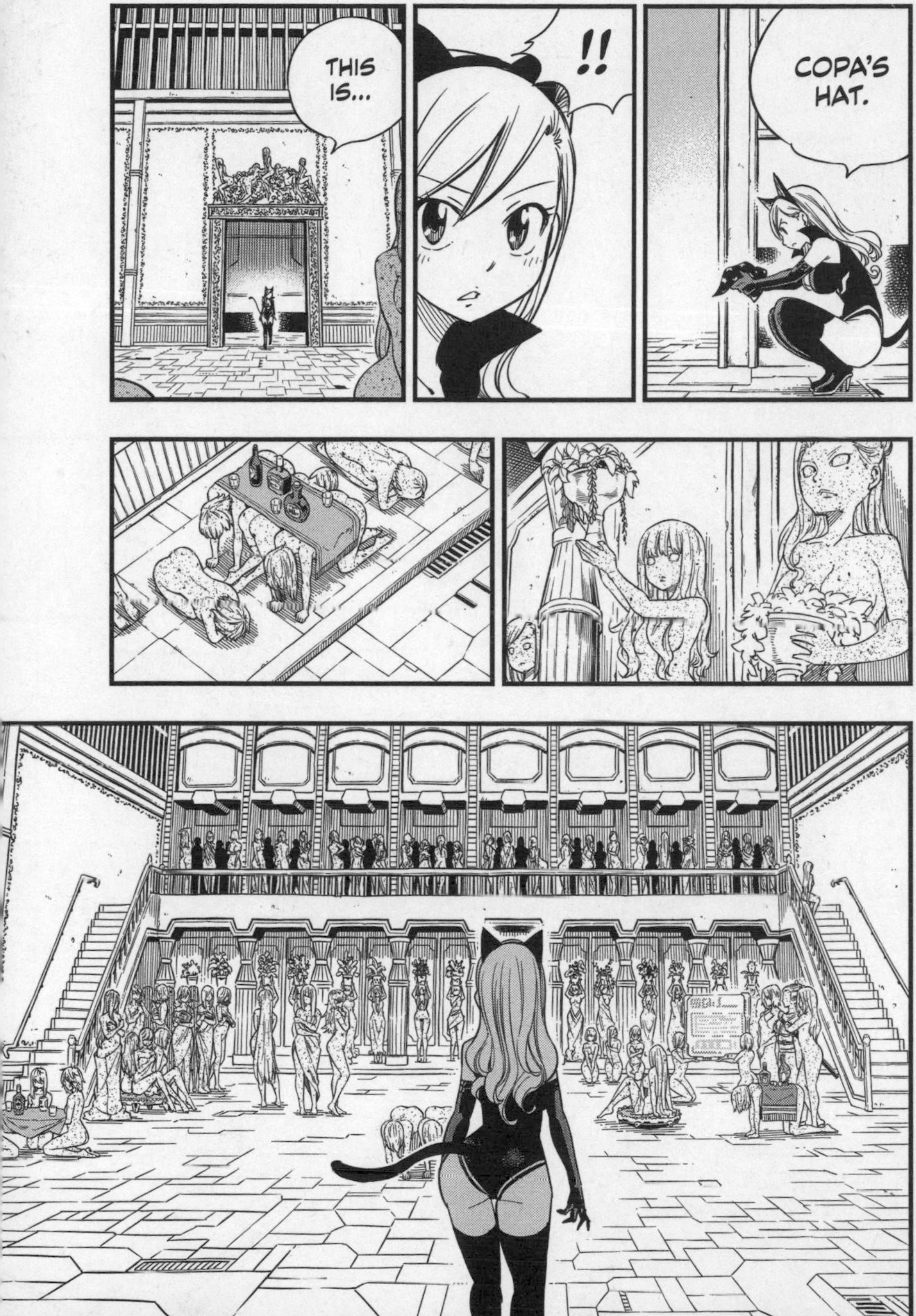
COPA'S HAT.
!!
THIS IS...

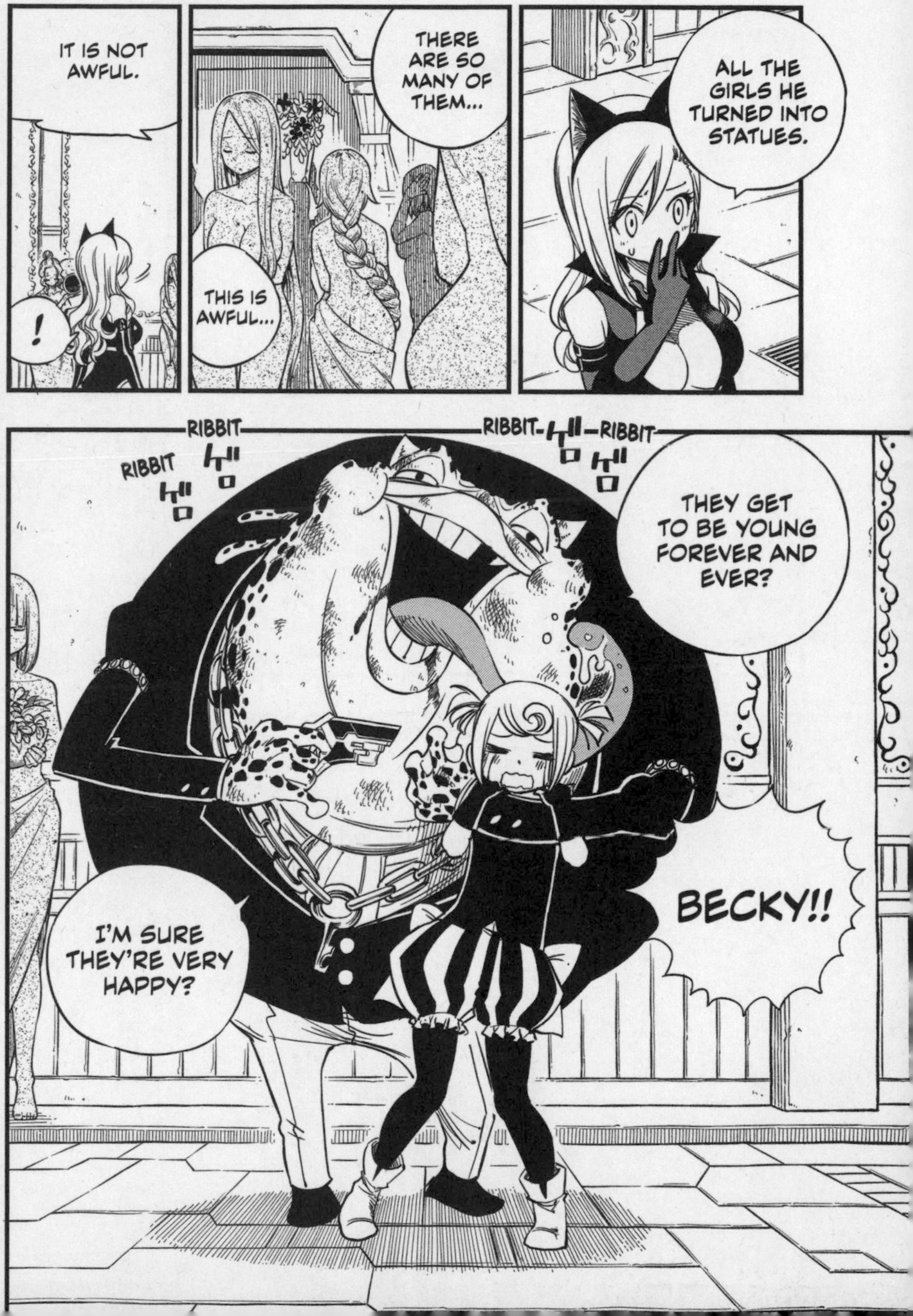
ALL THE GIRLS HE TURNED INTO STATUES.
THERE ARE SO MANY OF THEM...
THIS IS AWFUL...
IT IS NOT AWFUL.
!
RIBBIT ゲロ RIBBIT ゲロ
THEY GET TO BE YOUNG FOREVER AND EVER?
BECKY!!
RIBBIT ゲロ RIBBIT ゲロ
I'M SURE THEY'RE VERY HAPPY?

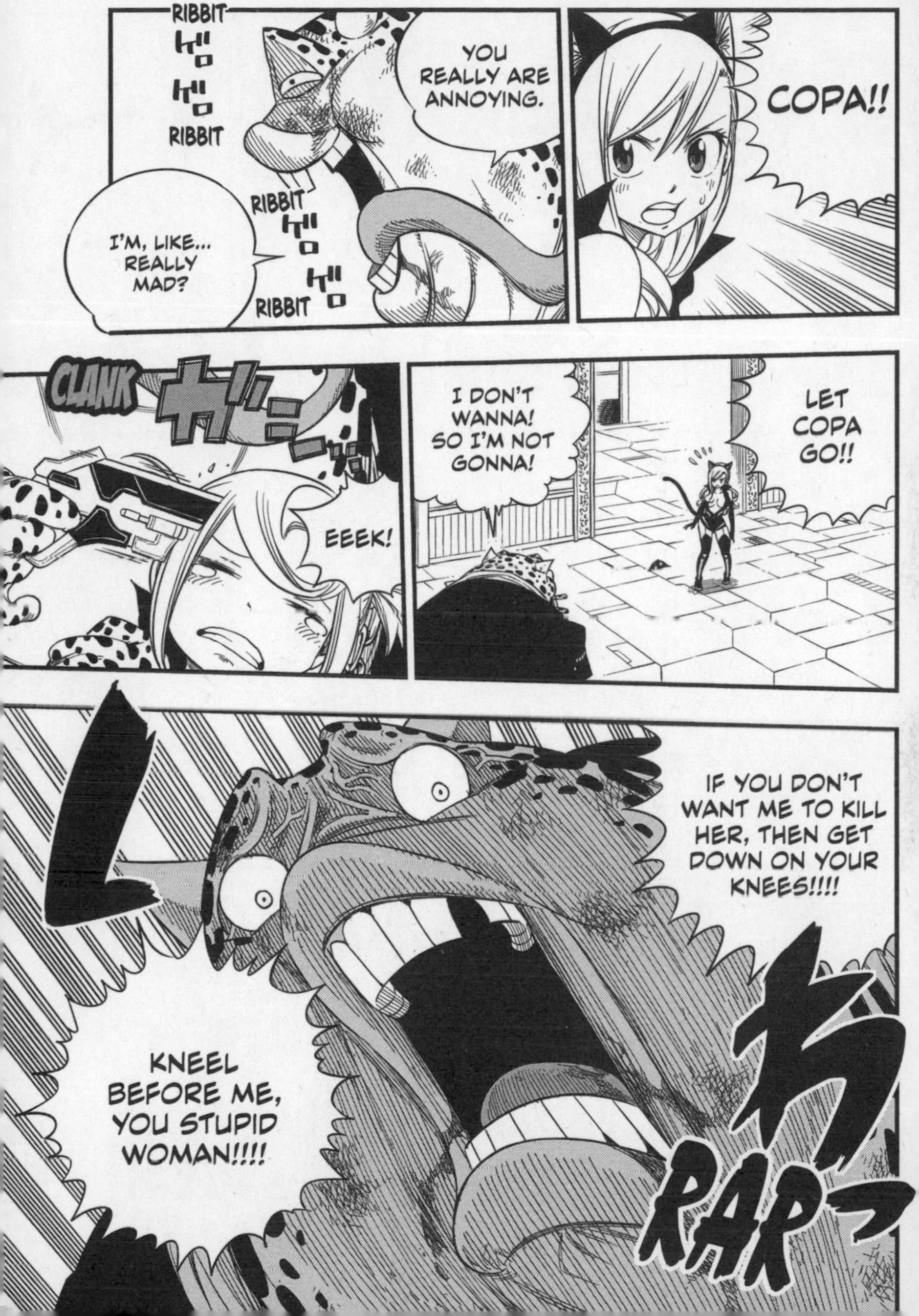

COPA!!
YOU REALLY ARE ANNOYING.
RIBBIT ゲロ ゲロ RIBBIT
RIBBIT ゲロ ゲロ RIBBIT
I'M, LIKE... REALLY MAD?
LET COPA GO!!
I DON'T WANNA! SO I'M NOT GONNA!
CLANK
EEEK!
IF YOU DON'T WANT ME TO KILL HER, THEN GET DOWN ON YOUR KNEES!!!!
KNEEL BEFORE ME, YOU STUPID WOMAN!!!!
RAP

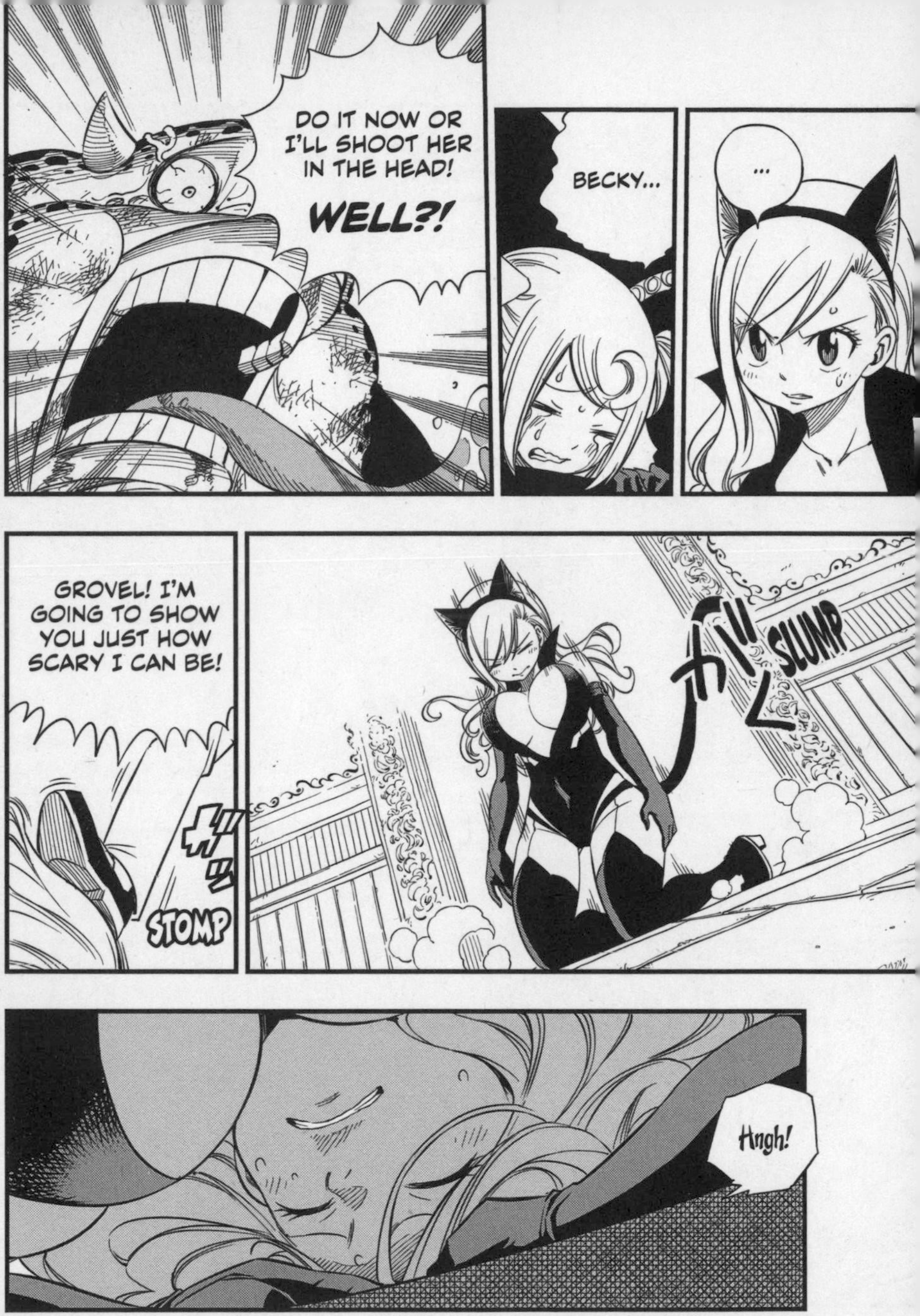
...
BECKY...
DO IT NOW OR I'LL SHOOT HER IN THE HEAD!
WELL?!
SLUMP
GROVEL! I'M GOING TO SHOW YOU JUST HOW SCARY I CAN BE!
STOMP
Hngh!

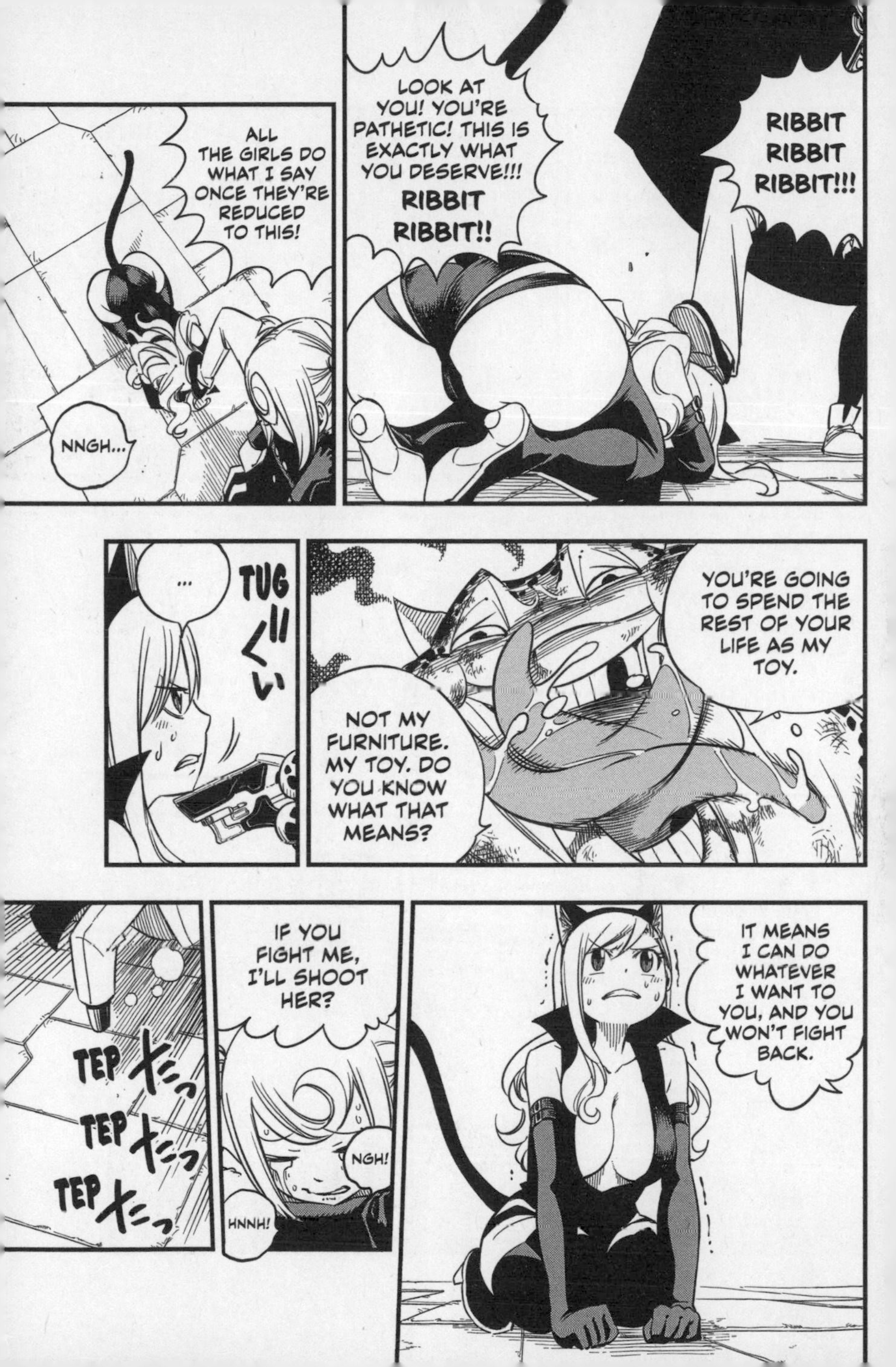
RIBBIT RIBBIT RIBBIT!!!
LOOK AT YOU! YOU'RE PATHETIC! THIS IS EXACTLY WHAT YOU DESERVE!!! RIBBIT RIBBIT!!
ALL THE GIRLS DO WHAT I SAY ONCE THEY'RE REDUCED TO THIS!
NNGH...
YOU'RE GOING TO SPEND THE REST OF YOUR LIFE AS MY TOY.
NOT MY FURNITURE. MY TOY. DO YOU KNOW WHAT THAT MEANS?
...
TUG くい
IT MEANS I CAN DO WHATEVER I WANT TO YOU, AND YOU WON'T FIGHT BACK.
IF YOU FIGHT ME, I'LL SHOOT HER?
NGH!
HNNH!
TEP たっ
TEP たっ
TEP たっ

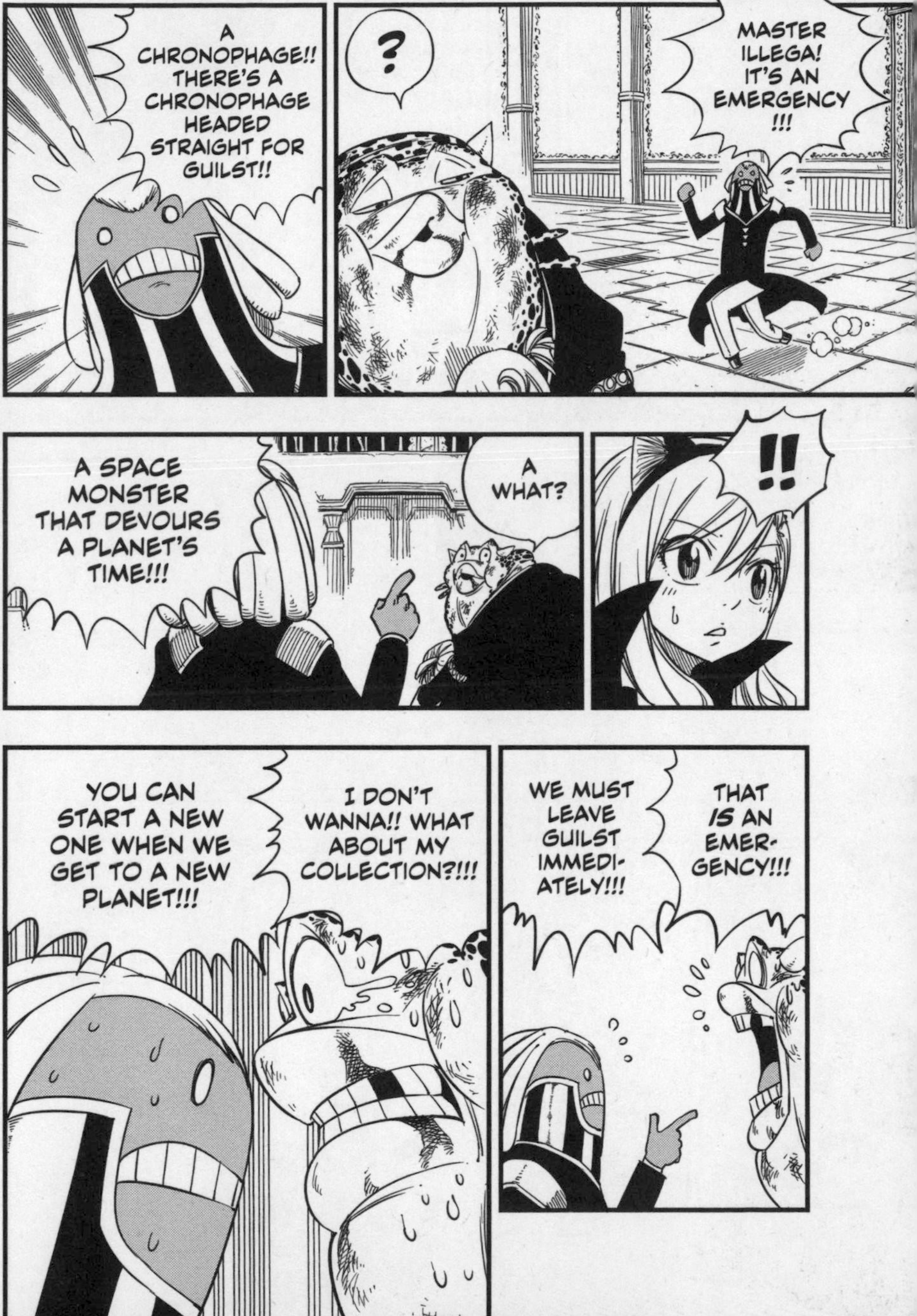
MASTER ILLEGA! IT'S AN EMERGENCY!!!
?
A CHRONOPHAGE!! THERE'S A CHRONOPHAGE HEADED STRAIGHT FOR GUILST!!
!!
A WHAT?
A SPACE MONSTER THAT DEVOURS A PLANET'S TIME!!!
THAT *IS* AN EMERGENCY!!!
WE MUST LEAVE GUILST IMMEDIATELY!!!
I DON'T WANNA!! WHAT ABOUT MY COLLECTION?!!!
YOU CAN START A NEW ONE WHEN WE GET TO A NEW PLANET!!!

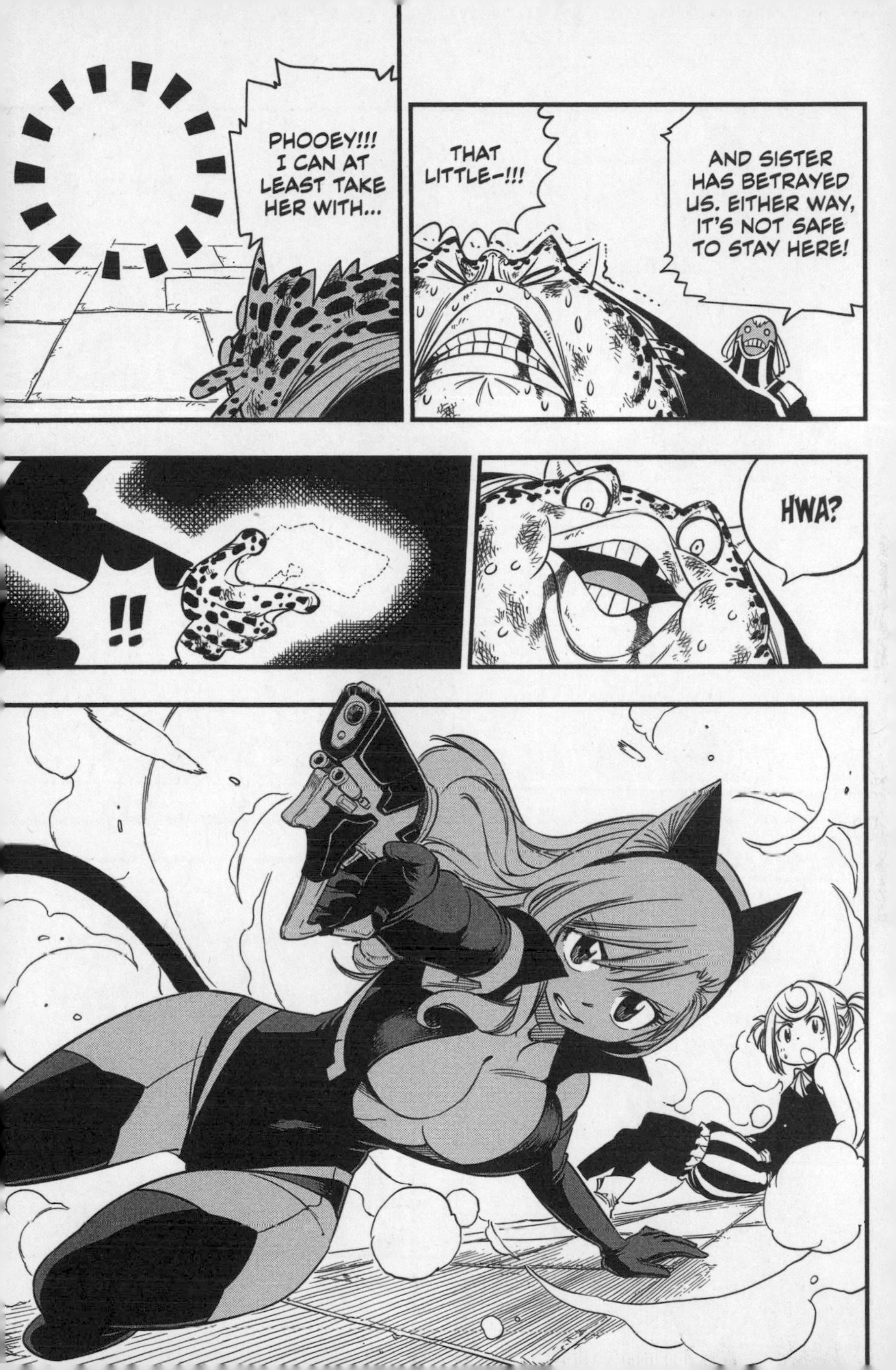
AND SISTER HAS BETRAYED US. EITHER WAY, IT'S NOT SAFE TO STAY HERE!
THAT LITTLE-!!!
PHOOEY!!! I CAN AT LEAST TAKE HER WITH...
HWA?
!!

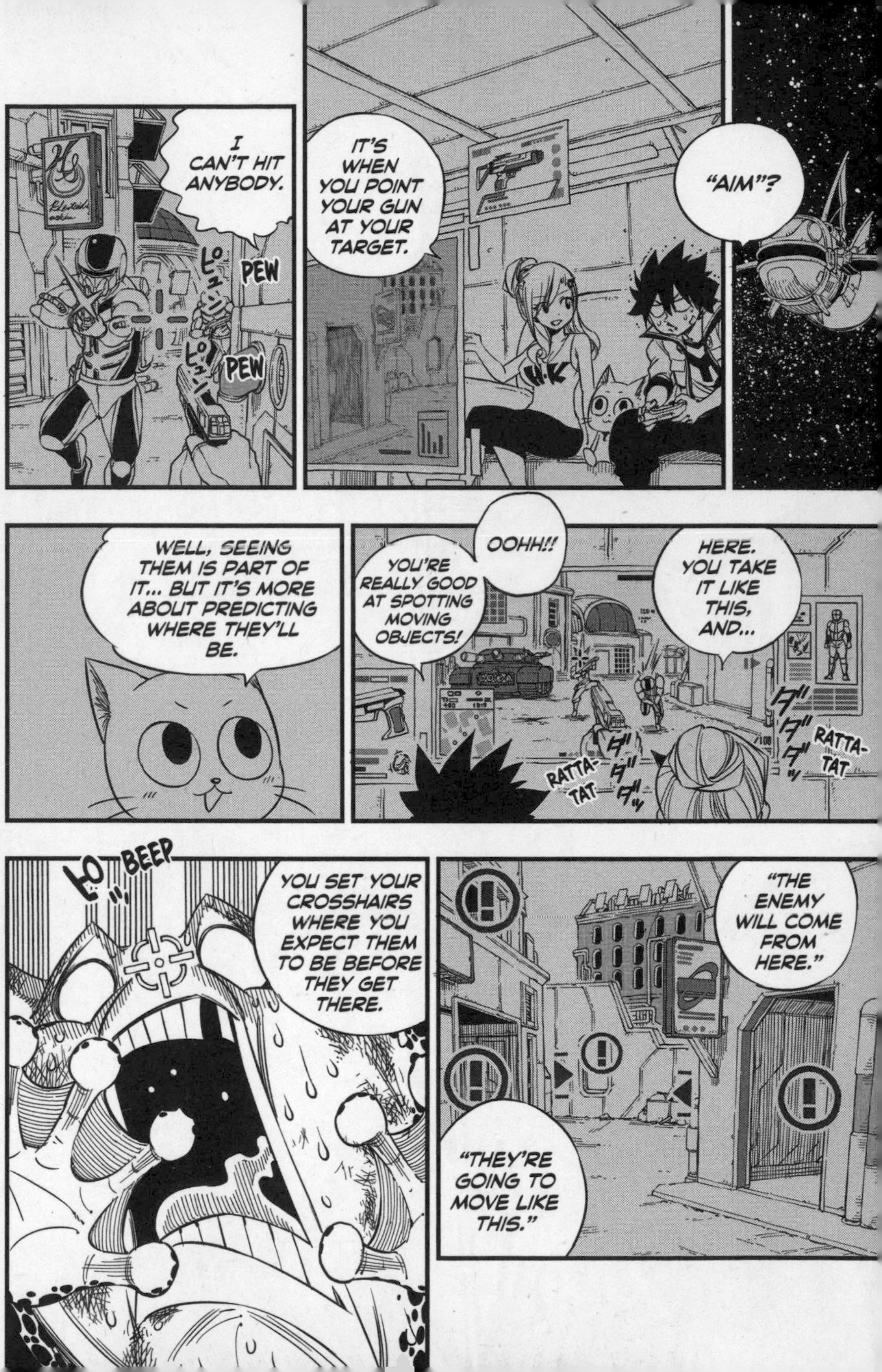
"AIM"?
IT'S WHEN YOU POINT YOUR GUN AT YOUR TARGET.
I CAN'T HIT ANYBODY.
PEW
PEW
HERE. YOU TAKE IT LIKE THIS, AND...
OOHH!!
YOU'RE REALLY GOOD AT SPOTTING MOVING OBJECTS!
RATTA-TAT
RATTA-TAT
WELL, SEEING THEM IS PART OF IT... BUT IT'S MORE ABOUT PREDICTING WHERE THEY'LL BE.
"THE ENEMY WILL COME FROM HERE."
"THEY'RE GOING TO MOVE LIKE THIS."
BEEP
YOU SET YOUR CROSSHAIRS WHERE YOU EXPECT THEM TO BE BEFORE THEY GET THERE.

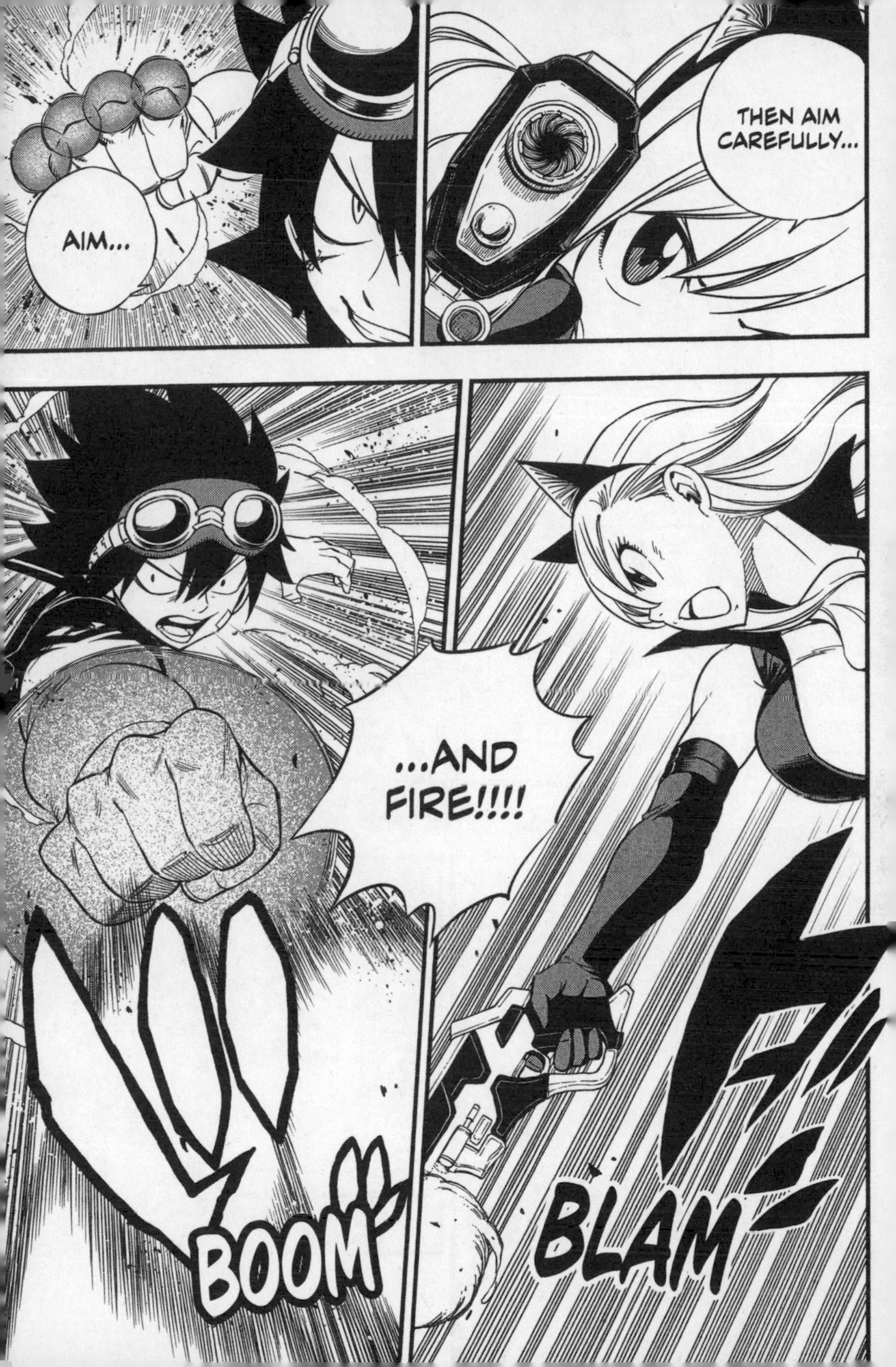
THEN AIM CAREFULLY...
AIM...
...AND FIRE!!!!
BLAM
BOOM

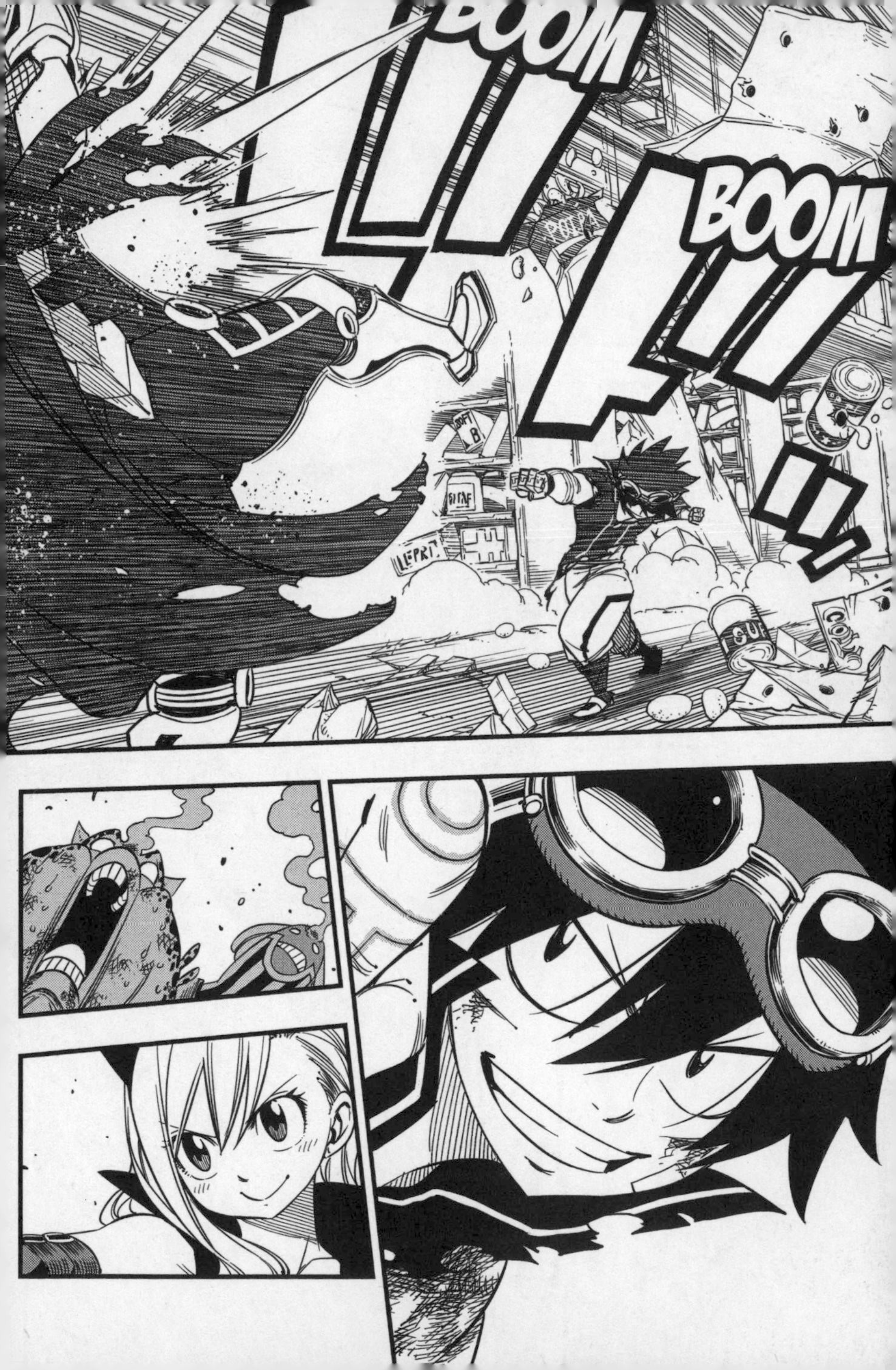
BOOM!!
BOOM!!

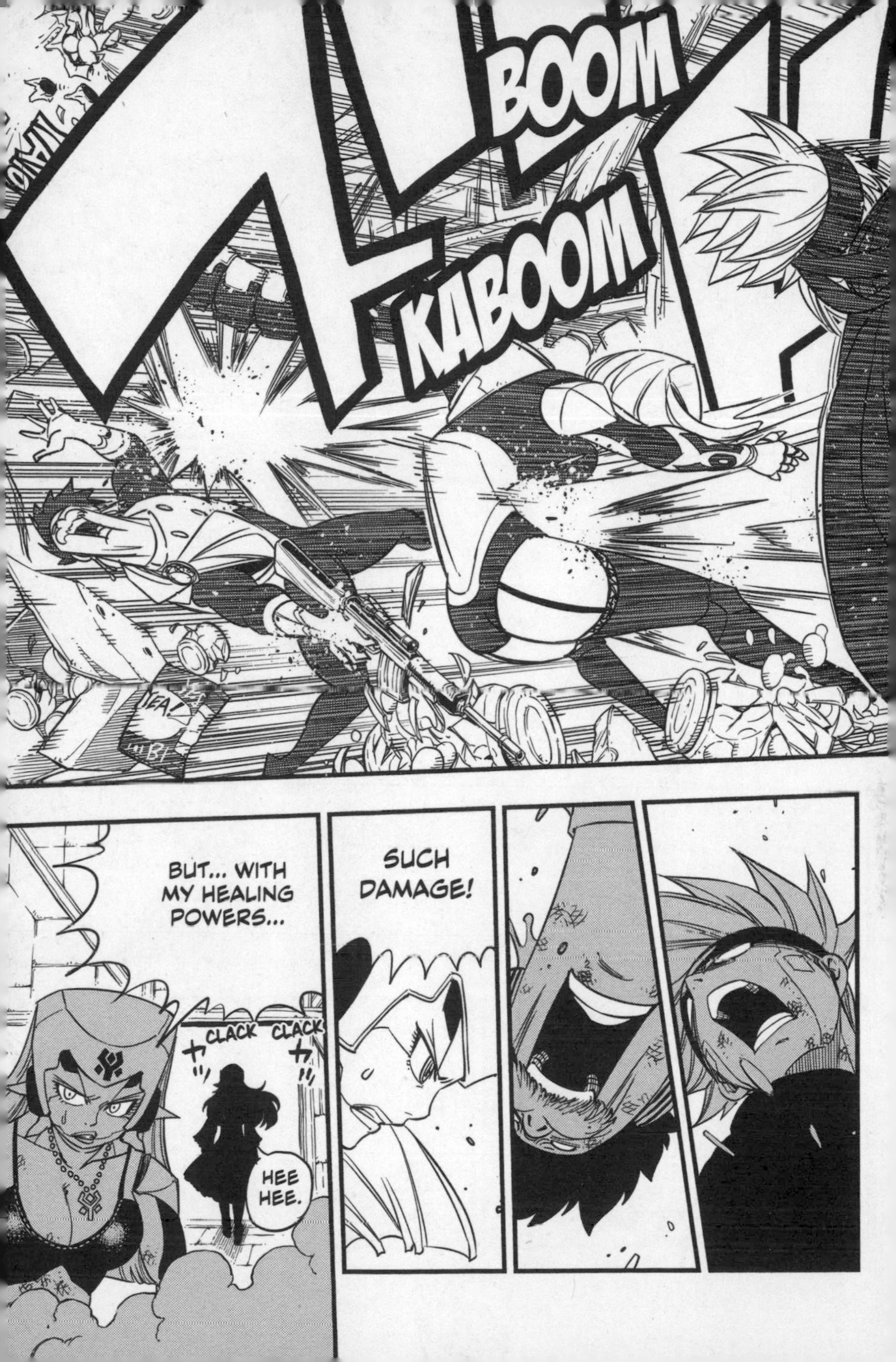
BOOM
KABOOM
SUCH DAMAGE!
BUT... WITH MY HEALING POWERS...
CLACK CLACK
HEE HEE.

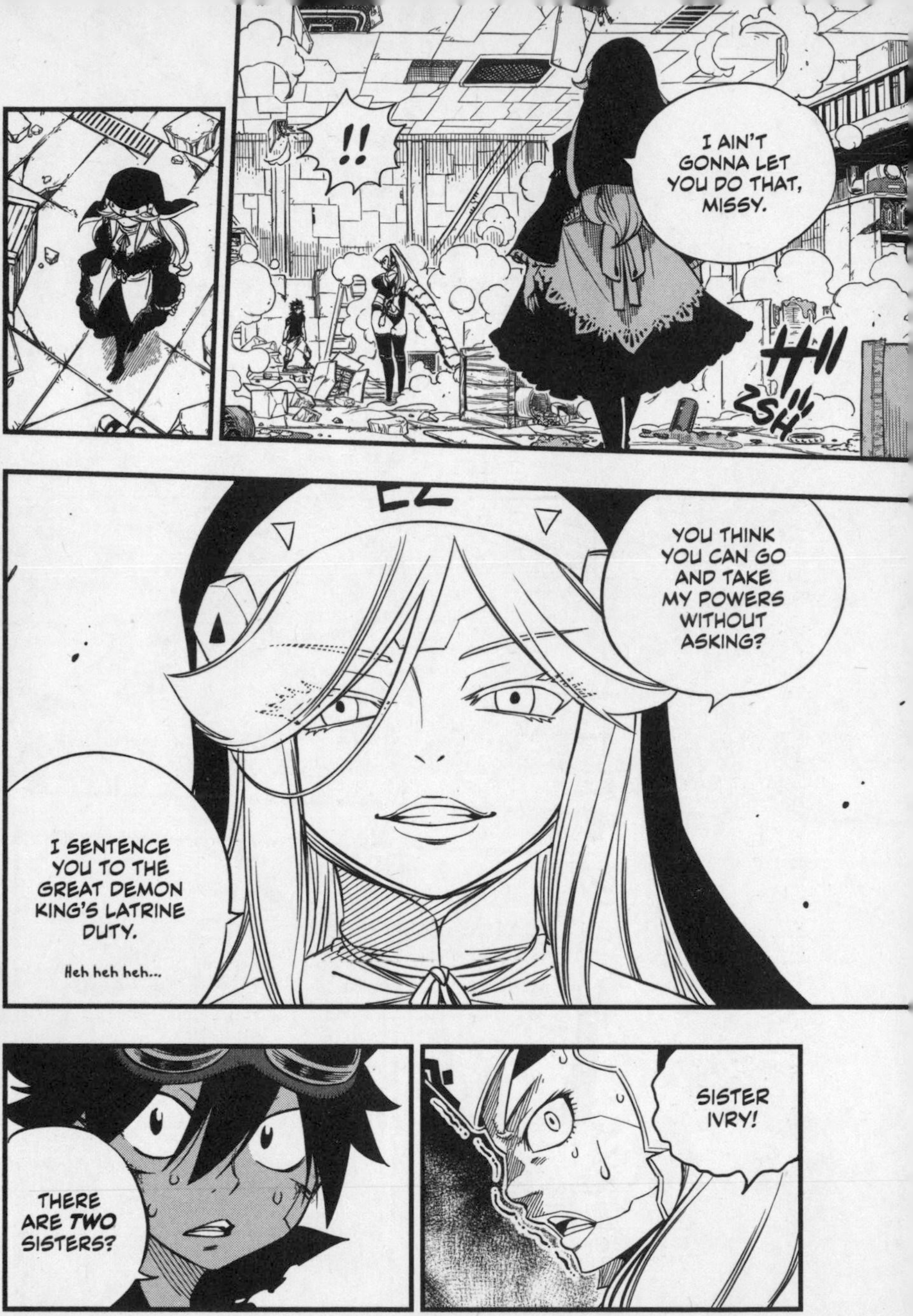
I AIN'T GONNA LET YOU DO THAT, MISSY.
!!
ZSH
YOU THINK YOU CAN GO AND TAKE MY POWERS WITHOUT ASKING?
I SENTENCE YOU TO THE GREAT DEMON KING'S LATRINE DUTY.
Heh heh heh...
SISTER IVRY!
THERE ARE *TWO* SISTERS?

EDENS ZERO

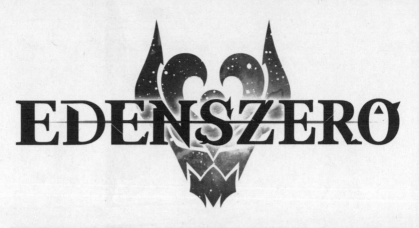

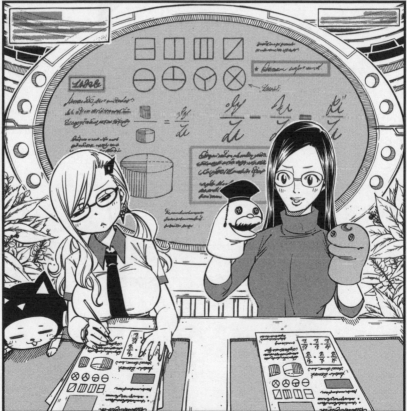

CHAPTER 26: TWO SISTERS

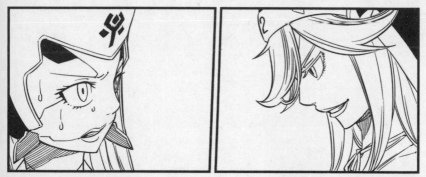

ROGUE OUT

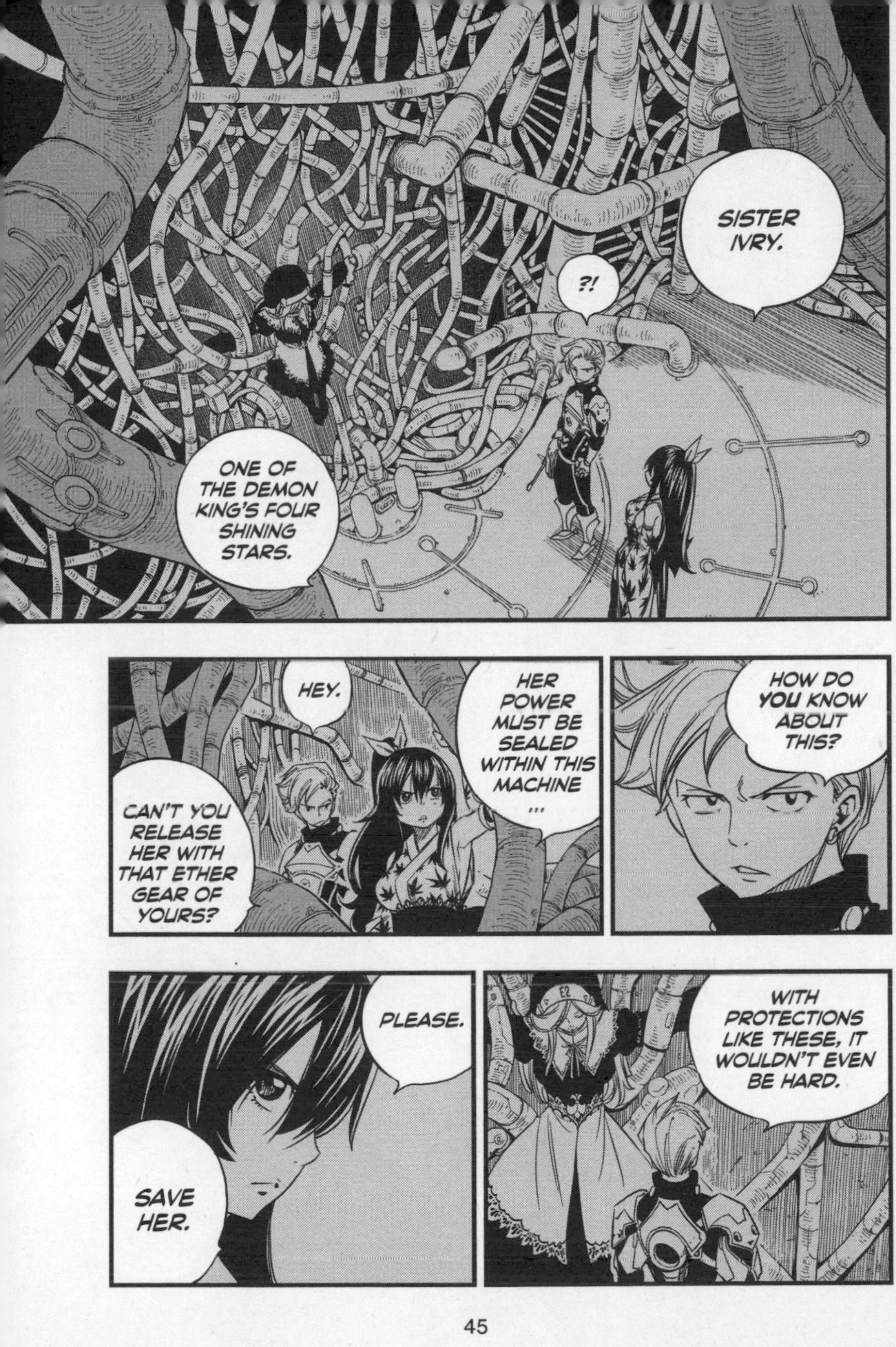
SISTER IVRY.
?!
ONE OF THE DEMON KING'S FOUR SHINING STARS.
HOW DO YOU KNOW ABOUT THIS?
HER POWER MUST BE SEALED WITHIN THIS MACHINE ...
HEY.
CAN'T YOU RELEASE HER WITH THAT ETHER GEAR OF YOURS?
WITH PROTECTIONS LIKE THESE, IT WOULDN'T EVEN BE HARD.
PLEASE.
SAVE HER.

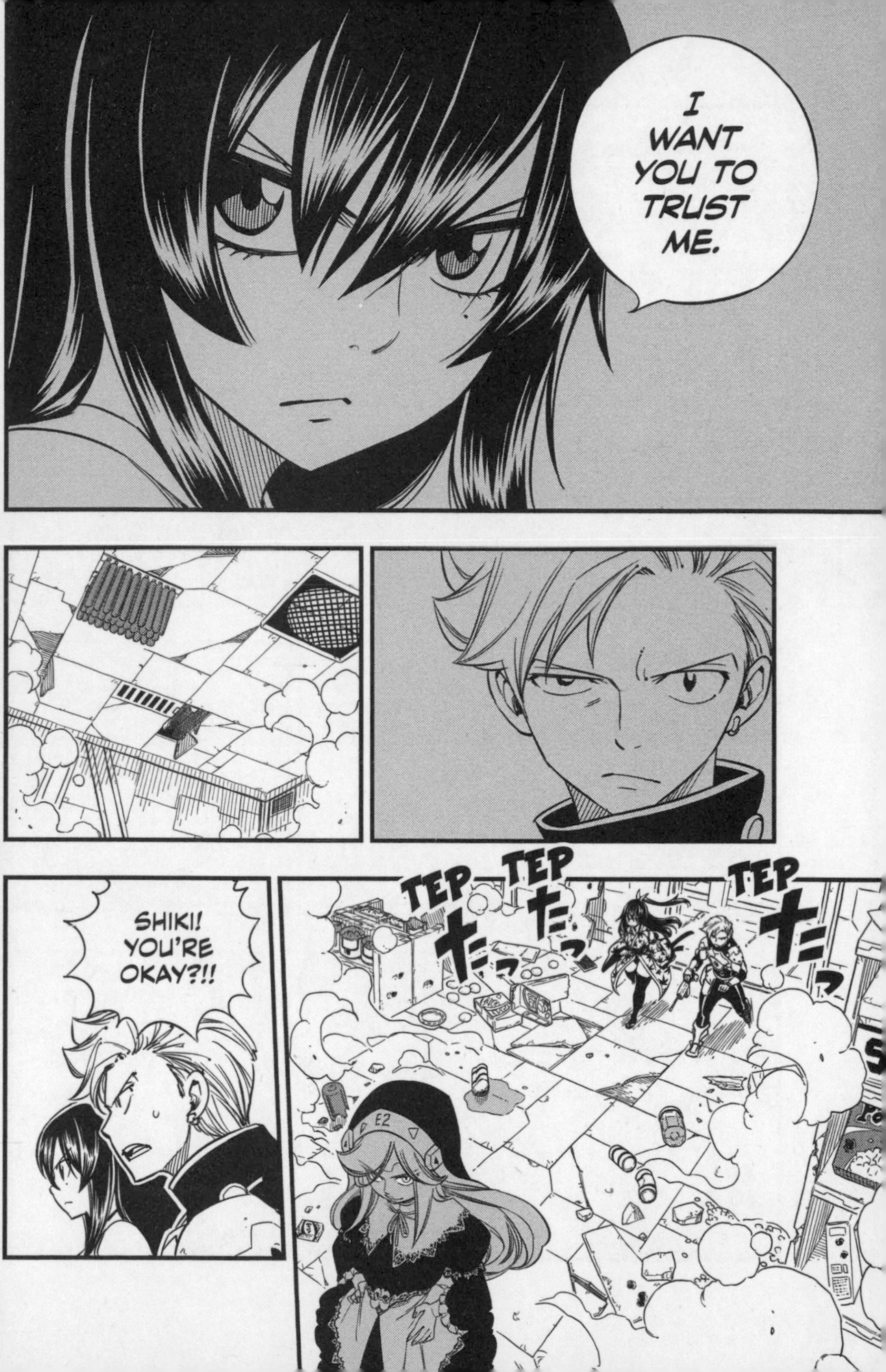
I WANT YOU TO TRUST ME.
TEP
TEP
TEP
SHIKI! YOU'RE OKAY?!!

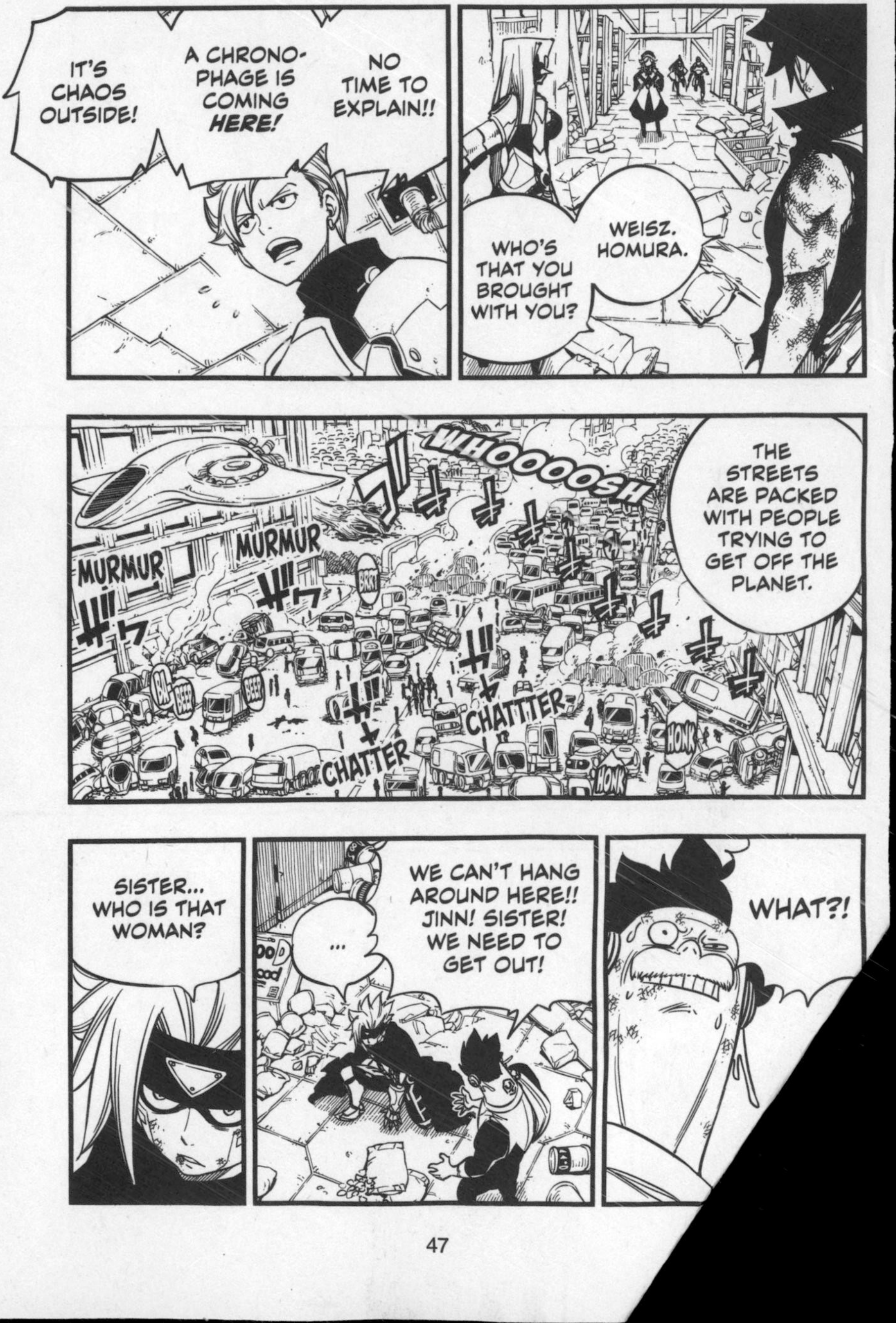
WEISZ. HOMURA.
WHO'S THAT YOU BROUGHT WITH YOU?
IT'S CHAOS OUTSIDE!
A CHRONOPHAGE IS COMING HERE!
NO TIME TO EXPLAIN!!
THE STREETS ARE PACKED WITH PEOPLE TRYING TO GET OFF THE PLANET.
WHOOOOOSH
MURMUR
MURMUR
BRRT
BEEP
BEEP
CHATTER
CHATTER
HONK
HONK
WHAT?!
WE CAN'T HANG AROUND HERE!! JINN! SISTER! WE NEED TO GET OUT!
...
SISTER... WHO IS THAT WOMAN?

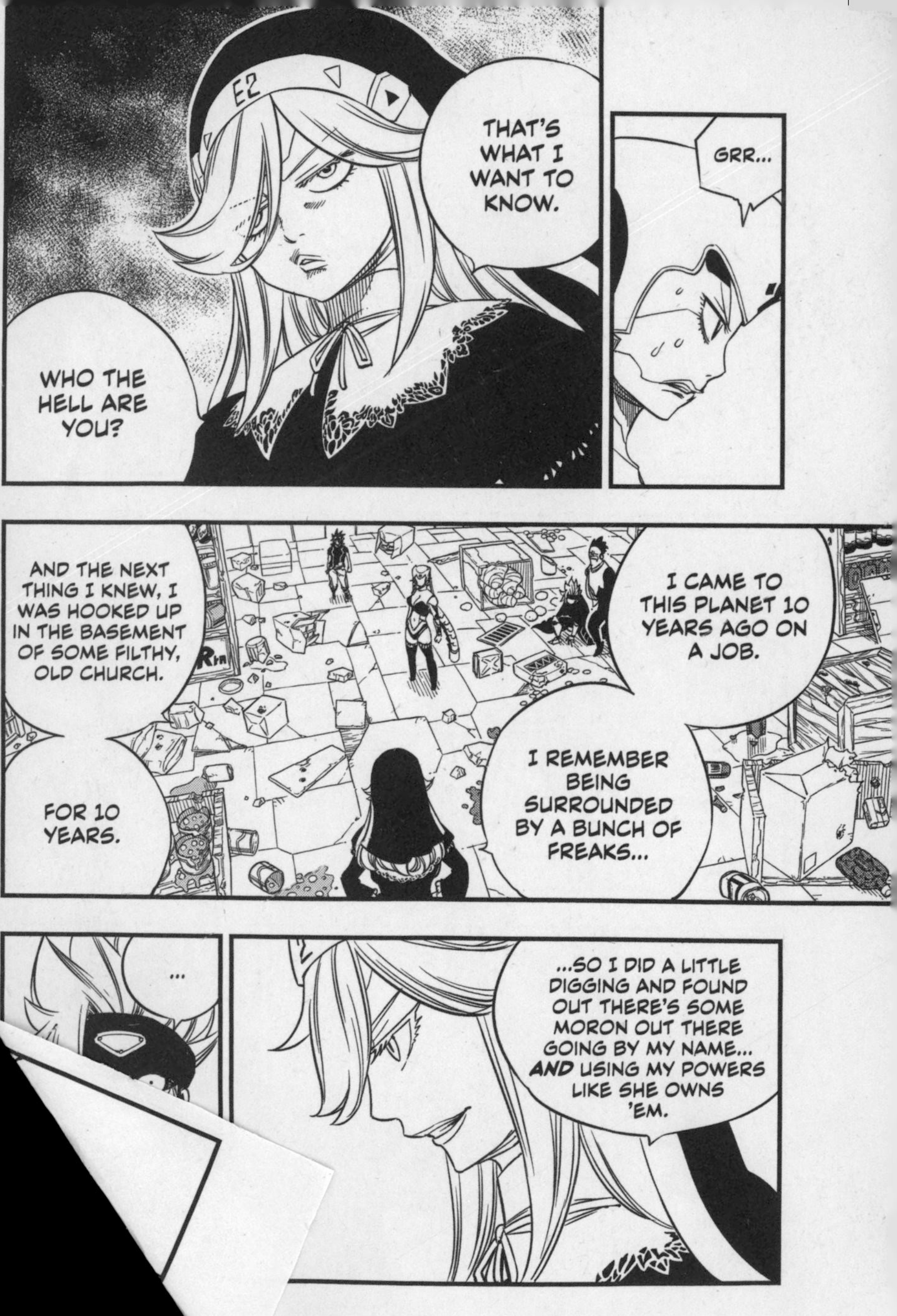
GRR...
THAT'S WHAT I WANT TO KNOW.
WHO THE HELL ARE YOU?
I CAME TO THIS PLANET 10 YEARS AGO ON A JOB.
I REMEMBER BEING SURROUNDED BY A BUNCH OF FREAKS...
AND THE NEXT THING I KNEW, I WAS HOOKED UP IN THE BASEMENT OF SOME FILTHY, OLD CHURCH.
FOR 10 YEARS.
...SO I DID A LITTLE DIGGING AND FOUND OUT THERE'S SOME MORON OUT THERE GOING BY MY NAME... **AND** USING MY POWERS LIKE SHE OWNS 'EM.
...

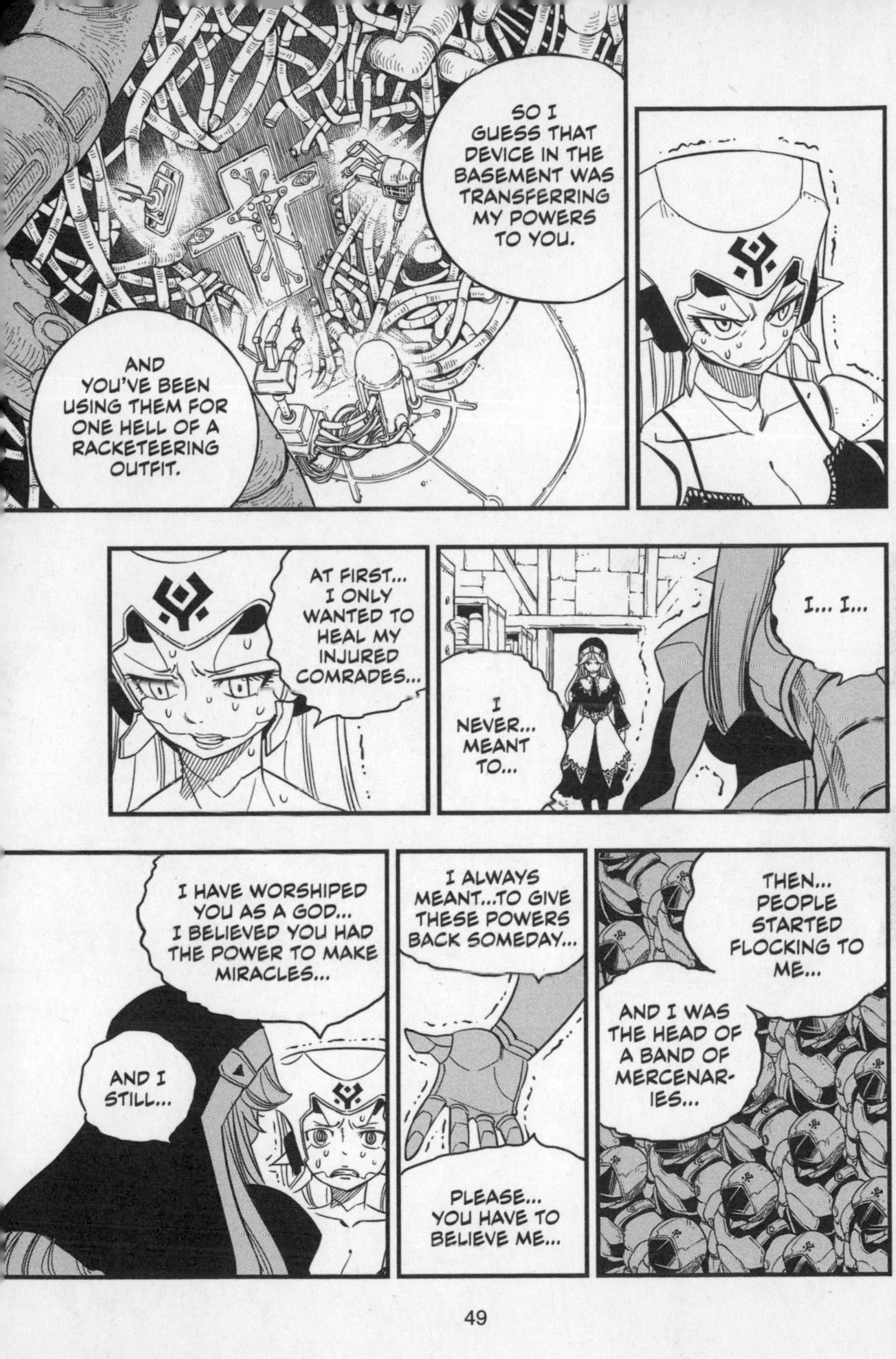
SO I GUESS THAT DEVICE IN THE BASEMENT WAS TRANSFERRING MY POWERS TO YOU.
AND YOU'VE BEEN USING THEM FOR ONE HELL OF A RACKETEERING OUTFIT.
I... I...
I NEVER... MEANT TO...
AT FIRST... I ONLY WANTED TO HEAL MY INJURED COMRADES...
THEN... PEOPLE STARTED FLOCKING TO ME...
AND I WAS THE HEAD OF A BAND OF MERCENAR-IES...
I ALWAYS MEANT...TO GIVE THESE POWERS BACK SOMEDAY...
PLEASE... YOU HAVE TO BELIEVE ME...
I HAVE WORSHIPED YOU AS A GOD... I BELIEVED YOU HAD THE POWER TO MAKE MIRACLES...
AND I STILL...

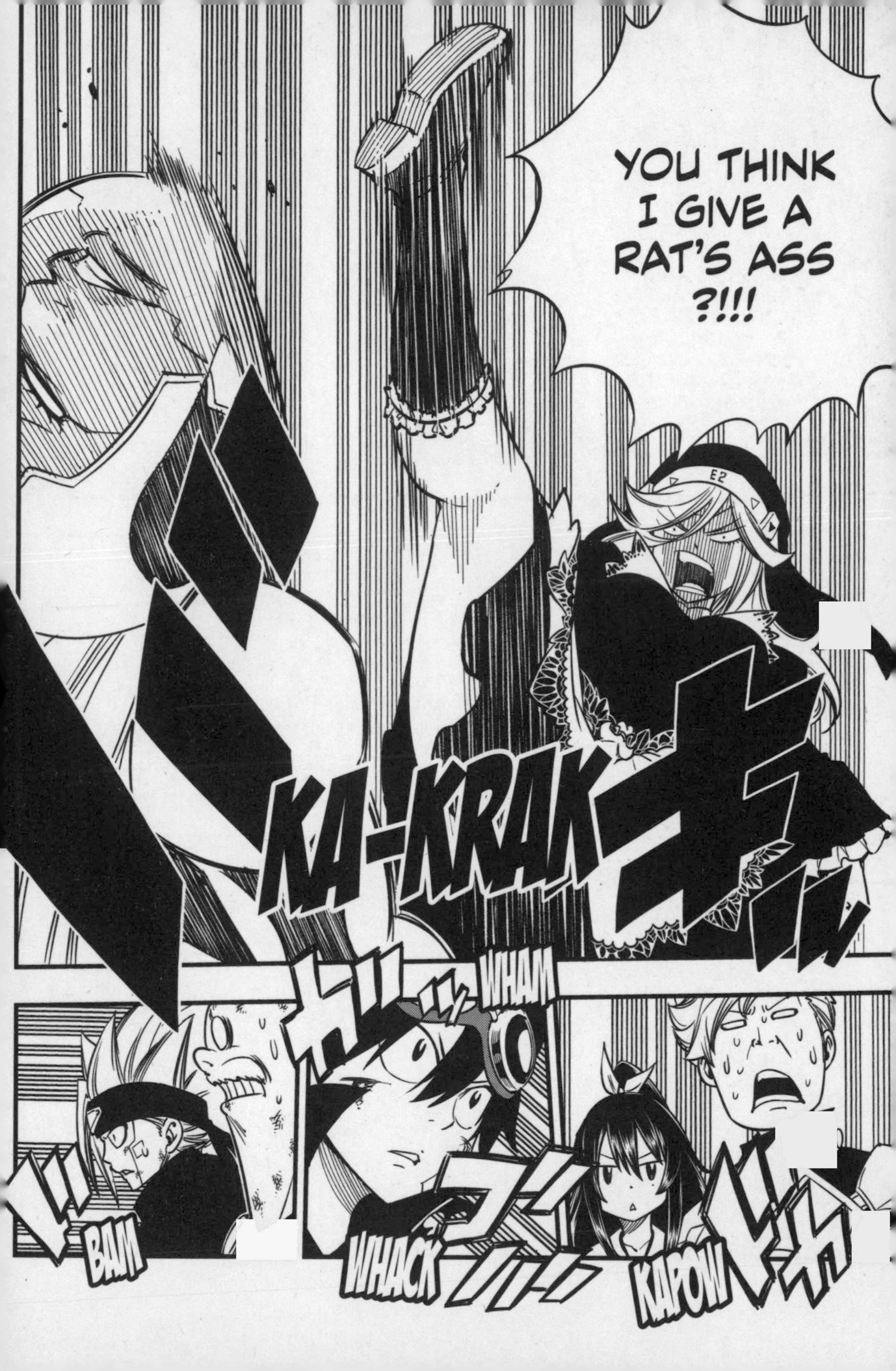

YOU THINK I GIVE A RAT'S ASS ?!!!
KA-KRAK
KAPOW
WHAM
WHACK
BAM

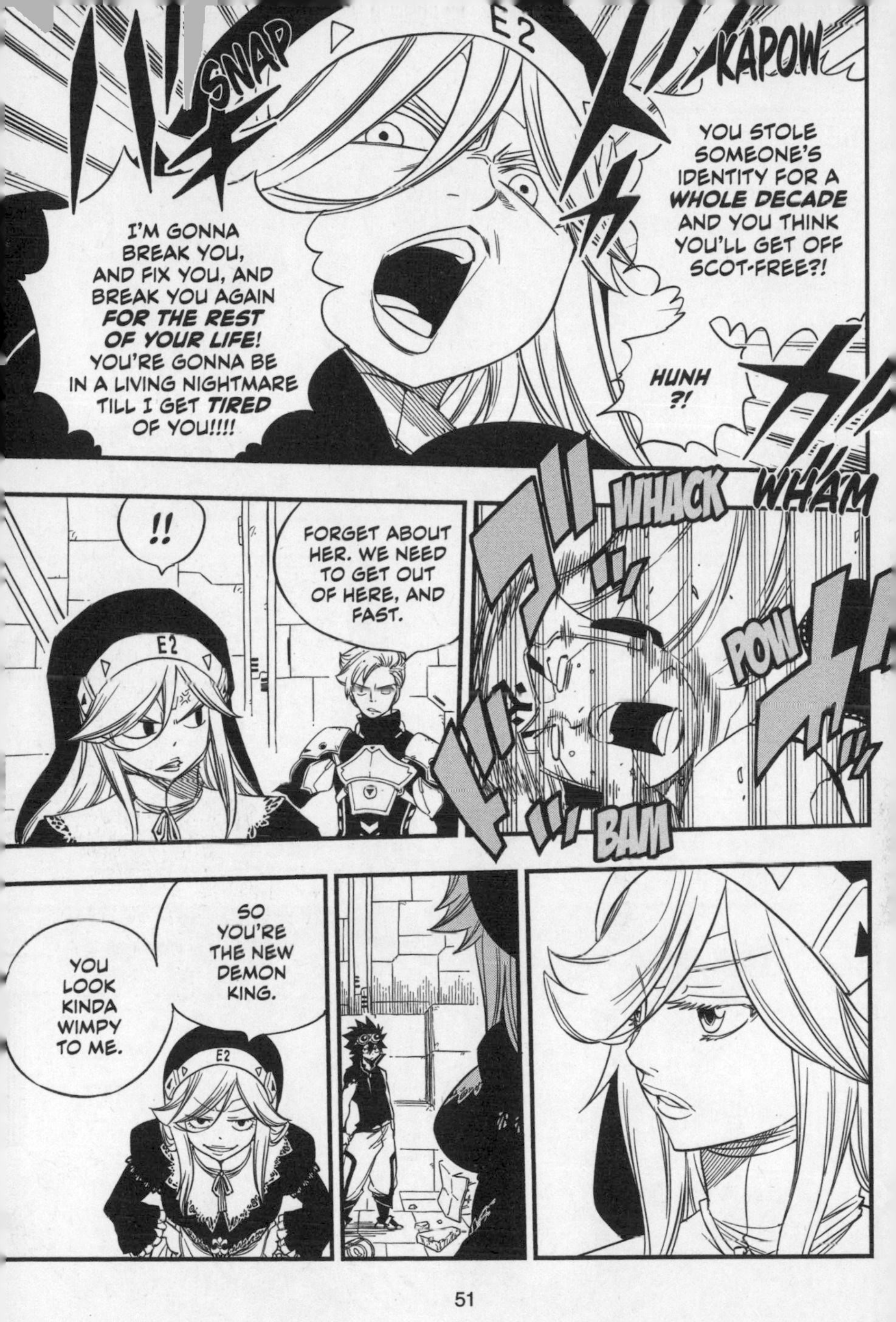
KAPOW
YOU STOLE SOMEONE'S IDENTITY FOR A ***WHOLE DECADE*** AND YOU THINK YOU'LL GET OFF SCOT-FREE?!
SNAP
I'M GONNA BREAK YOU, AND FIX YOU, AND BREAK YOU AGAIN ***FOR THE REST OF YOUR LIFE!*** YOU'RE GONNA BE IN A LIVING NIGHTMARE TILL I GET ***TIRED*** OF YOU!!!!
HUNH ?!
WHAM
WHACK
POW
BAM
FORGET ABOUT HER. WE NEED TO GET OUT OF HERE, AND FAST.
!!
SO YOU'RE THE NEW DEMON KING.
YOU LOOK KINDA WIMPY TO ME.

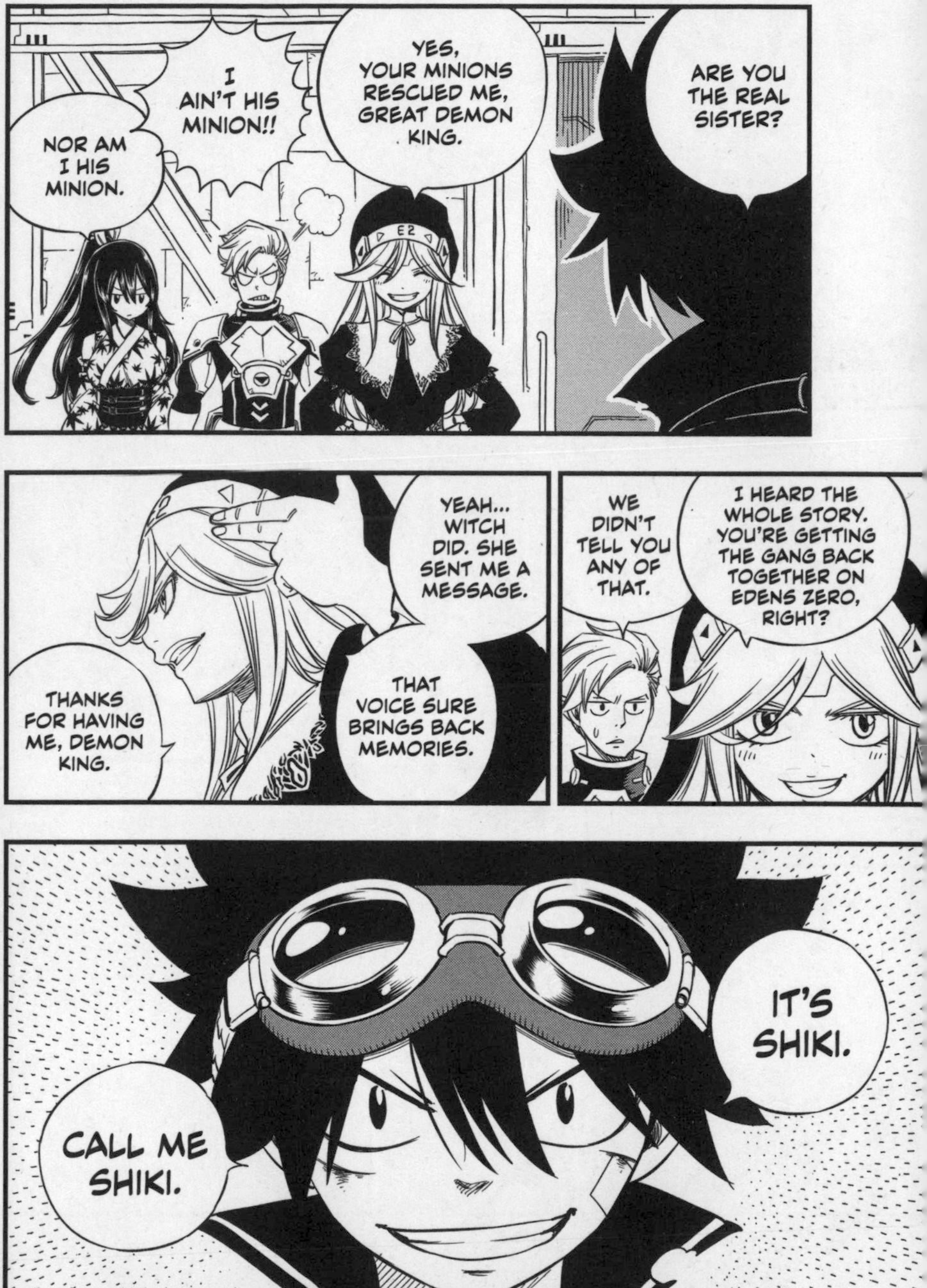
ARE YOU THE REAL SISTER?
YES, YOUR MINIONS RESCUED ME, GREAT DEMON KING.
I AIN'T HIS MINION!!
NOR AM I HIS MINION.
I HEARD THE WHOLE STORY. YOU'RE GETTING THE GANG BACK TOGETHER ON EDENS ZERO, RIGHT?
WE DIDN'T TELL YOU ANY OF THAT.
YEAH... WITCH DID. SHE SENT ME A MESSAGE.
THAT VOICE SURE BRINGS BACK MEMORIES.
THANKS FOR HAVING ME, DEMON KING.
IT'S SHIKI.
CALL ME SHIKI.

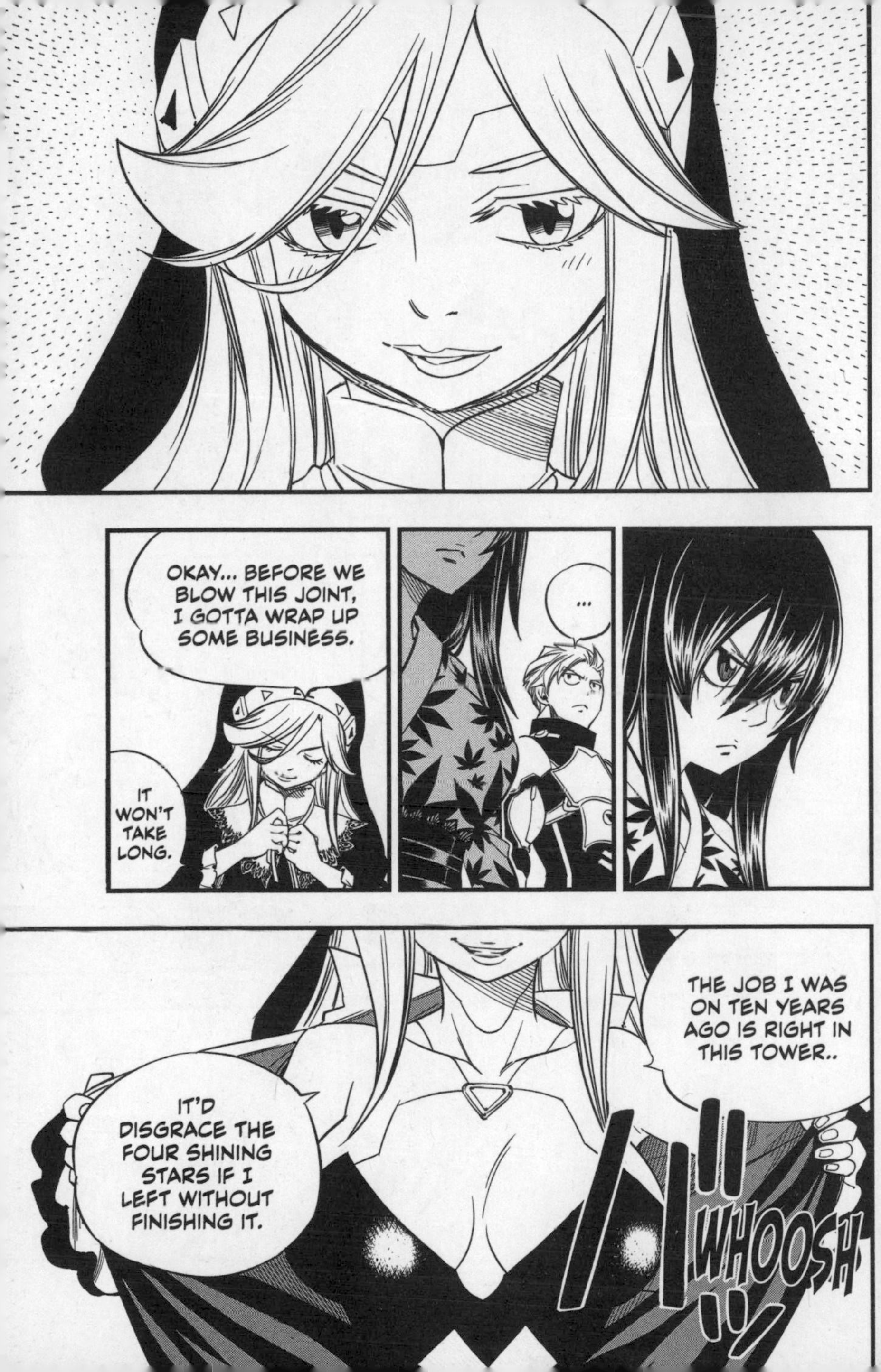
...
OKAY... BEFORE WE BLOW THIS JOINT, I GOTTA WRAP UP SOME BUSINESS.
IT WON'T TAKE LONG.
THE JOB I WAS ON TEN YEARS AGO IS RIGHT IN THIS TOWER..
IT'D DISGRACE THE FOUR SHINING STARS IF I LEFT WITHOUT FINISHING IT.
WHOOSH

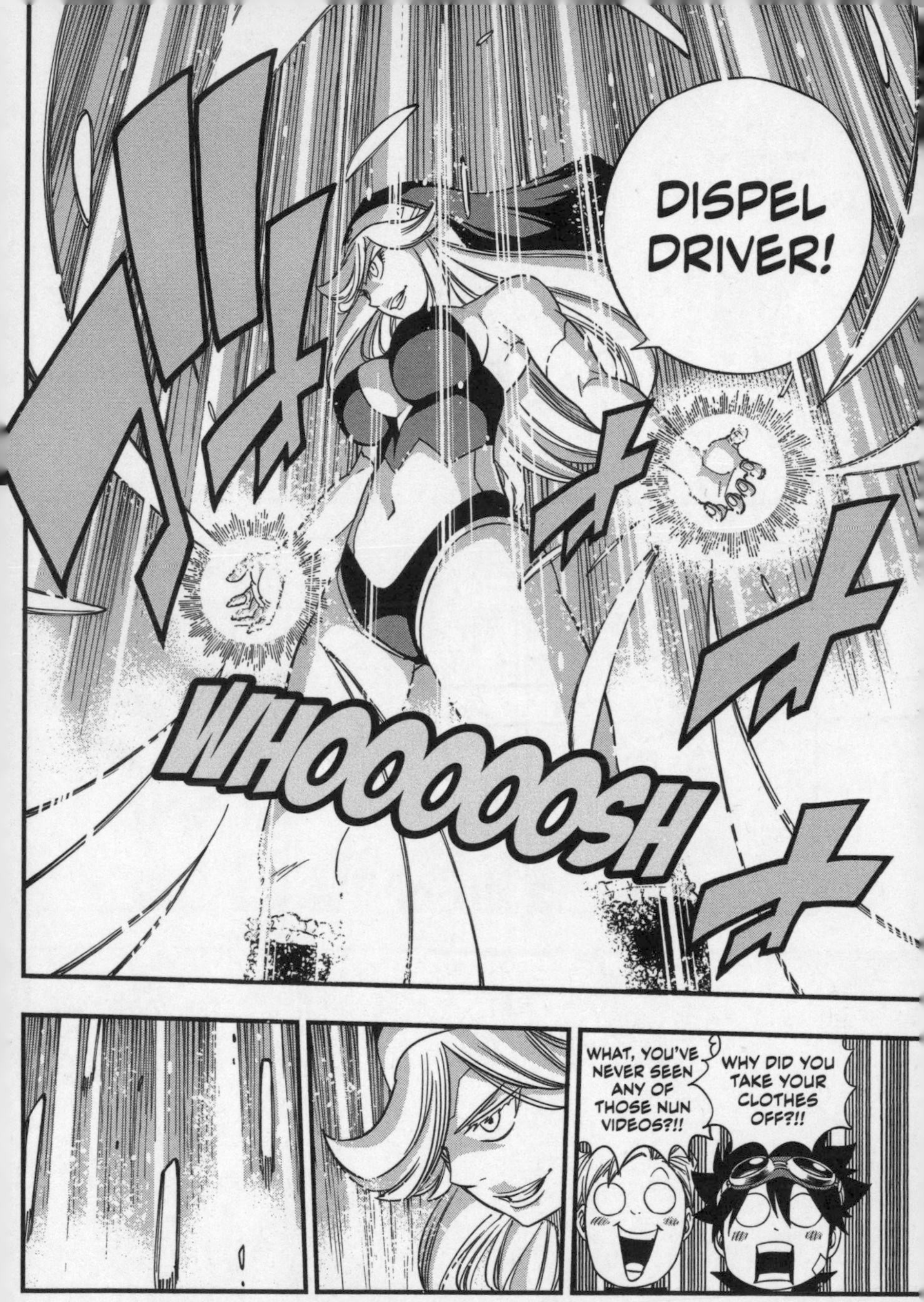
DISPEL DRIVER!
WHOOOOOSH
WHY DID YOU TAKE YOUR CLOTHES OFF?!!
WHAT, YOU'VE NEVER SEEN ANY OF THOSE NUN VIDEOS?!!

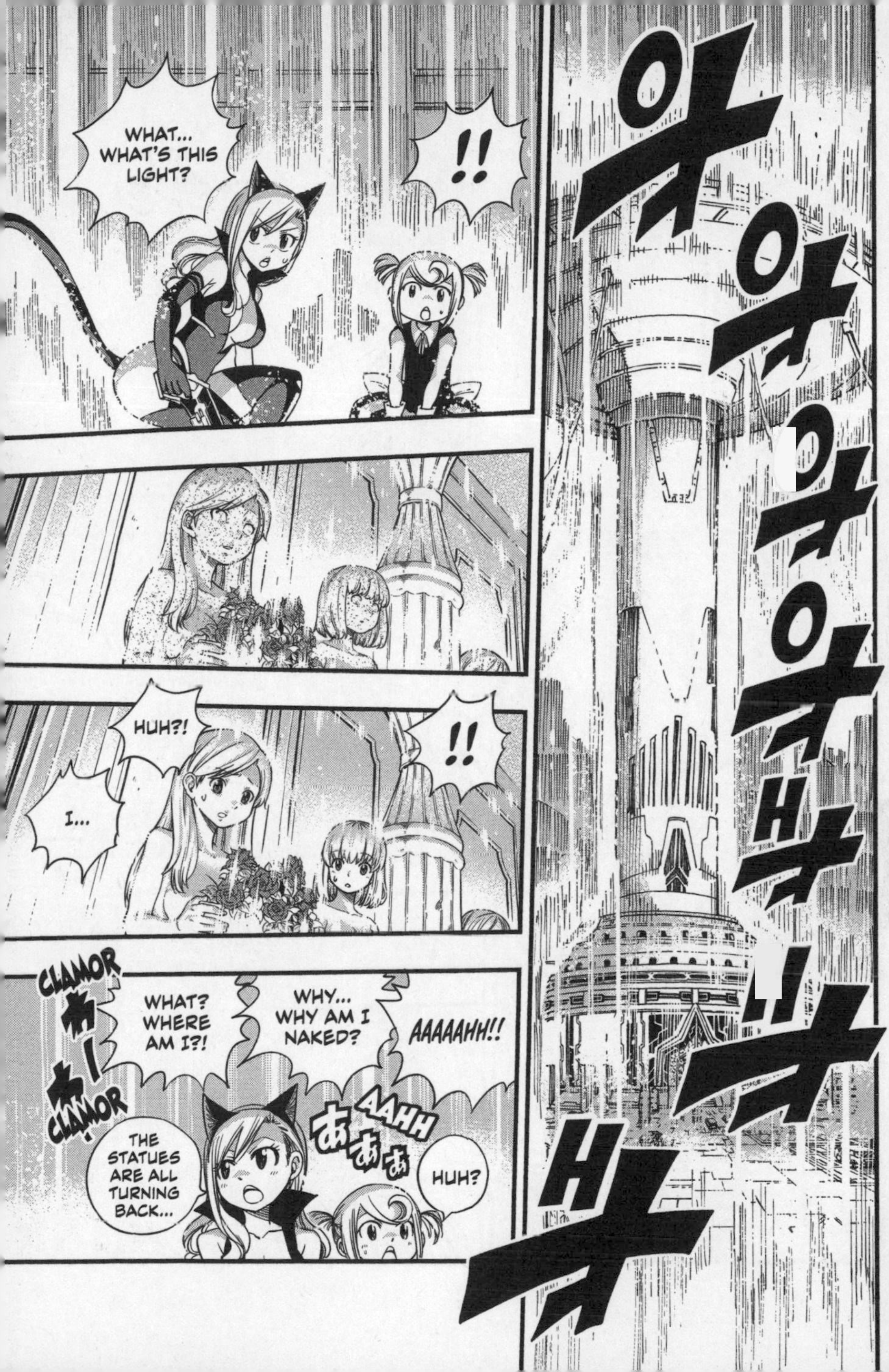
!!
WHAT... WHAT'S THIS LIGHT?
!!
HUH?!
I...
AAAAAHH!!
WHY... WHY AM I NAKED?
WHAT? WHERE AM I?!
CLAMOR CLAMOR
HUH?
AAHH
THE STATUES ARE ALL TURNING BACK...

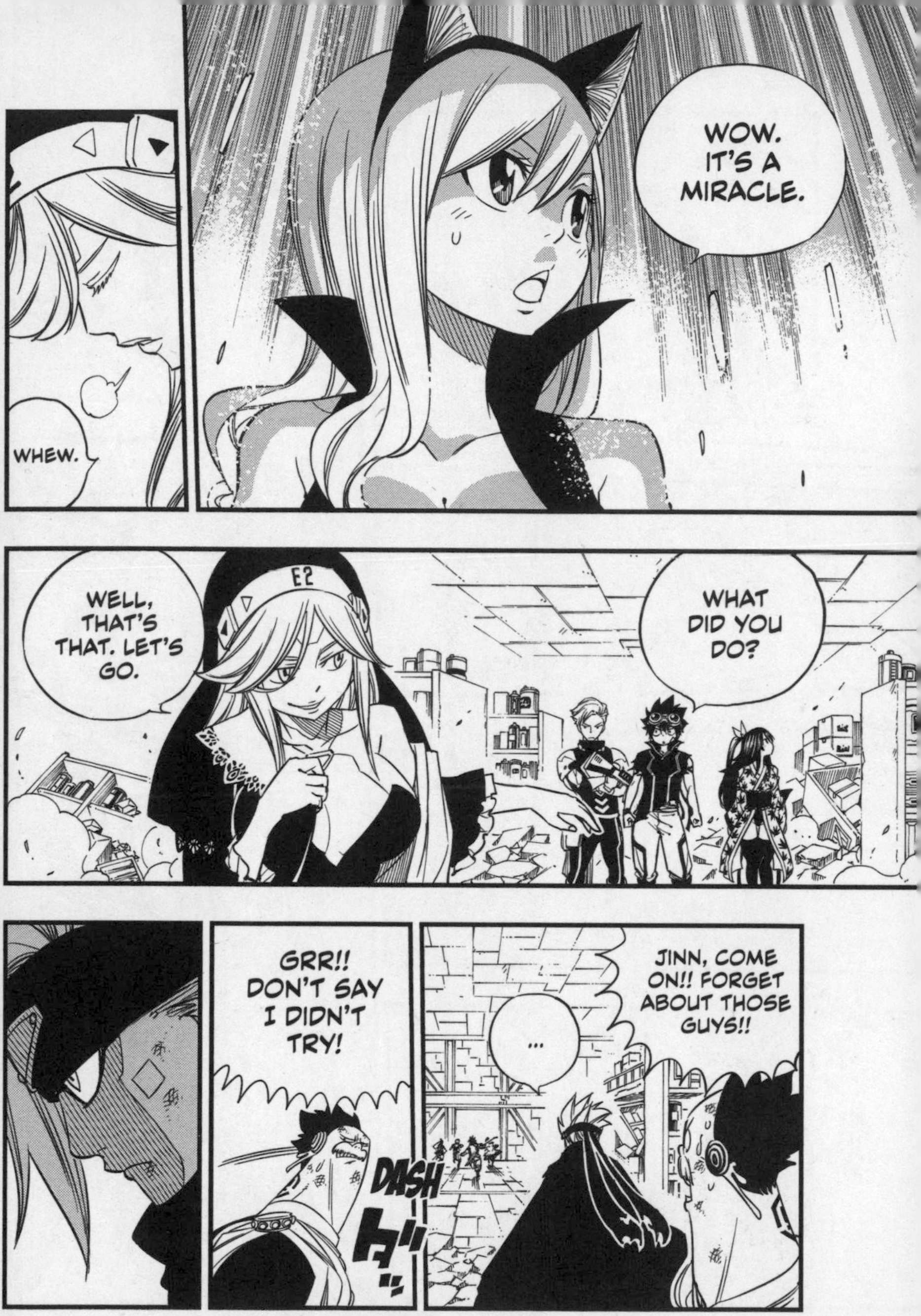
WOW. IT'S A MIRACLE.
WHEW.
WHAT DID YOU DO?
WELL, THAT'S THAT. LET'S GO.
JINN, COME ON!! FORGET ABOUT THOSE GUYS!!
...
GRR!! DON'T SAY I DIDN'T TRY!
DASH

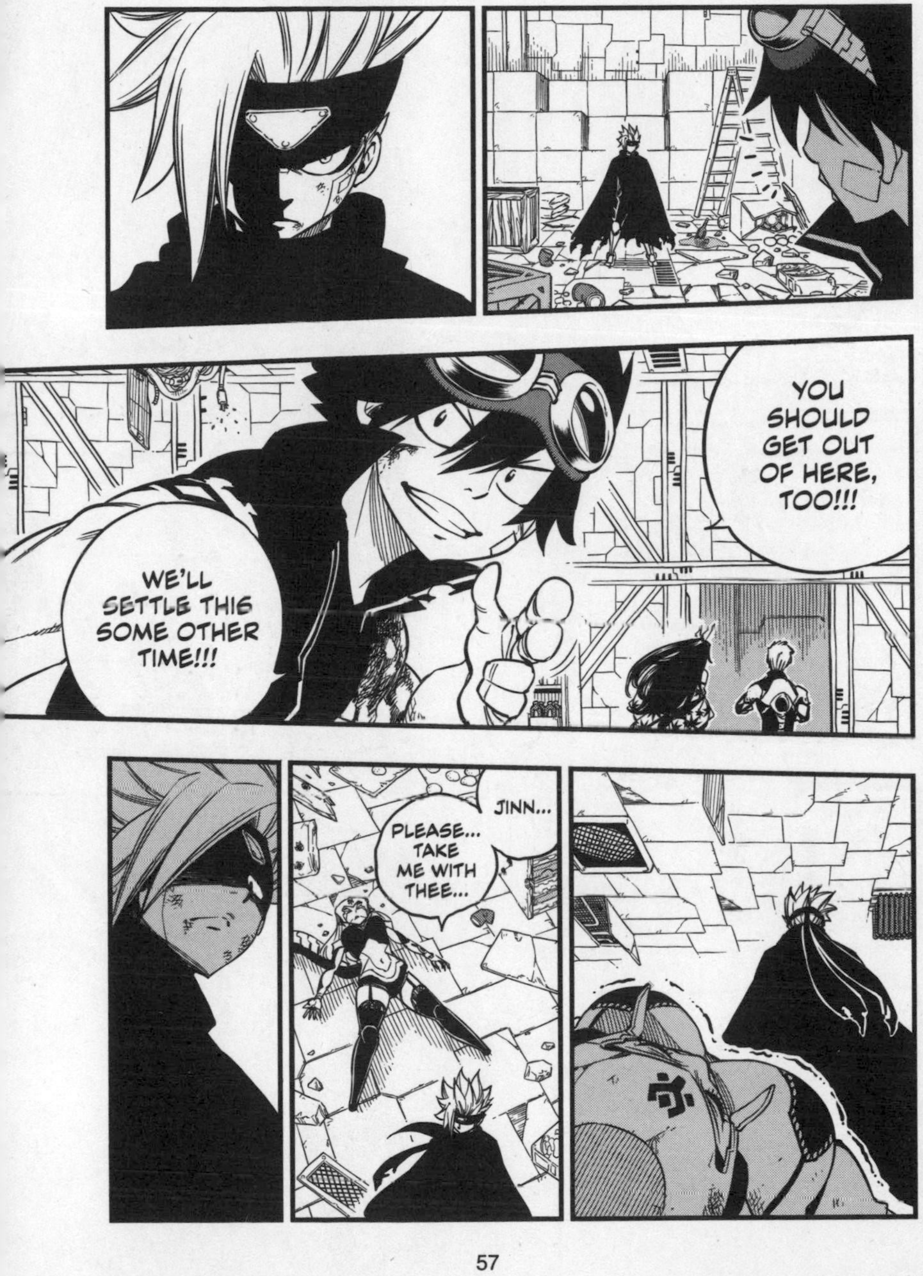
YOU SHOULD GET OUT OF HERE, TOO!!!
WE'LL SETTLE THIS SOME OTHER TIME!!!
JINN...
PLEASE... TAKE ME WITH THEE...

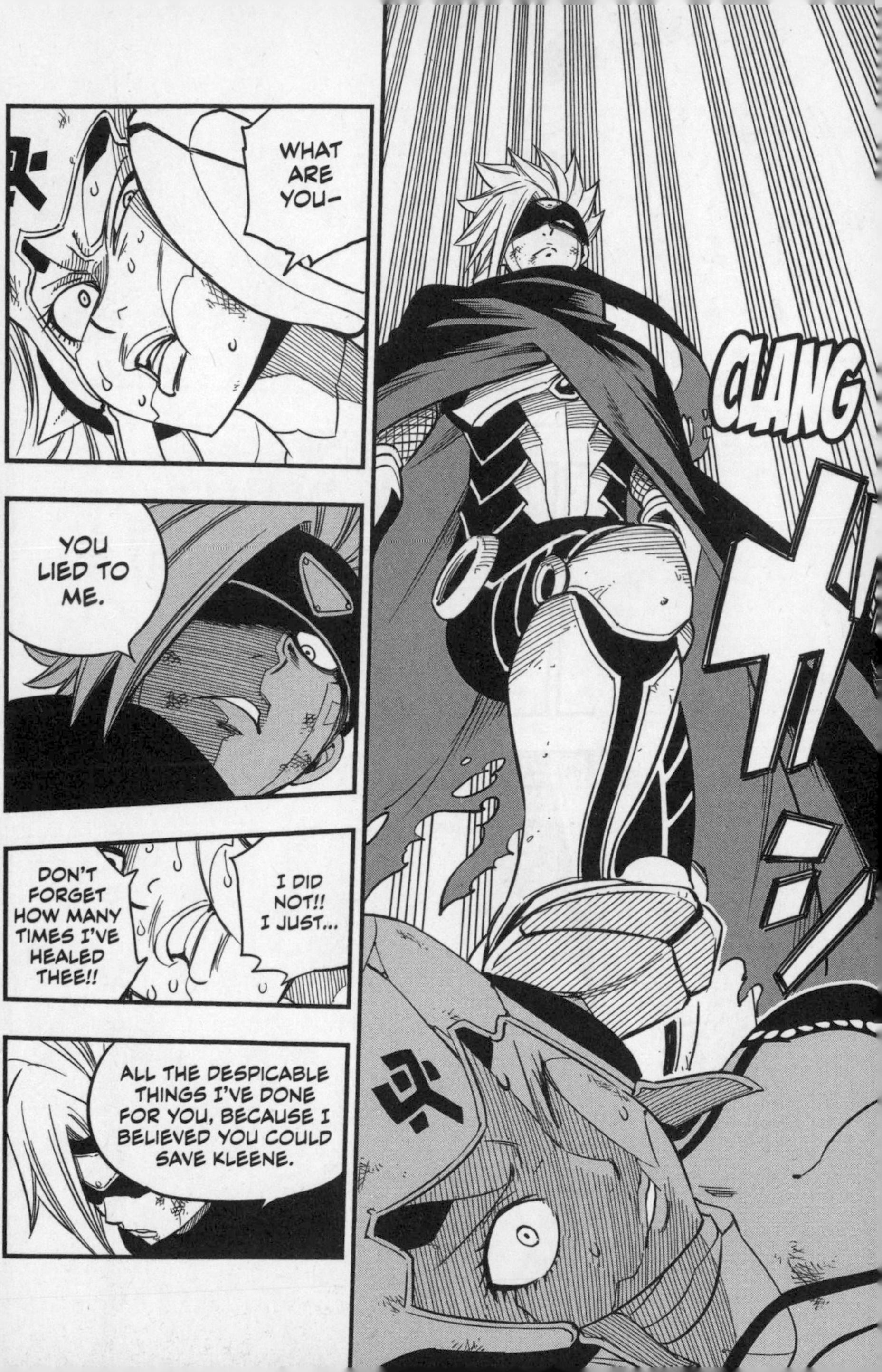
CLANG
WHAT ARE YOU-
YOU LIED TO ME.
I DID NOT!! I JUST...
DON'T FORGET HOW MANY TIMES I'VE HEALED THEE!!
ALL THE DESPICABLE THINGS I'VE DONE FOR YOU, BECAUSE I BELIEVED YOU COULD SAVE KLEENE.

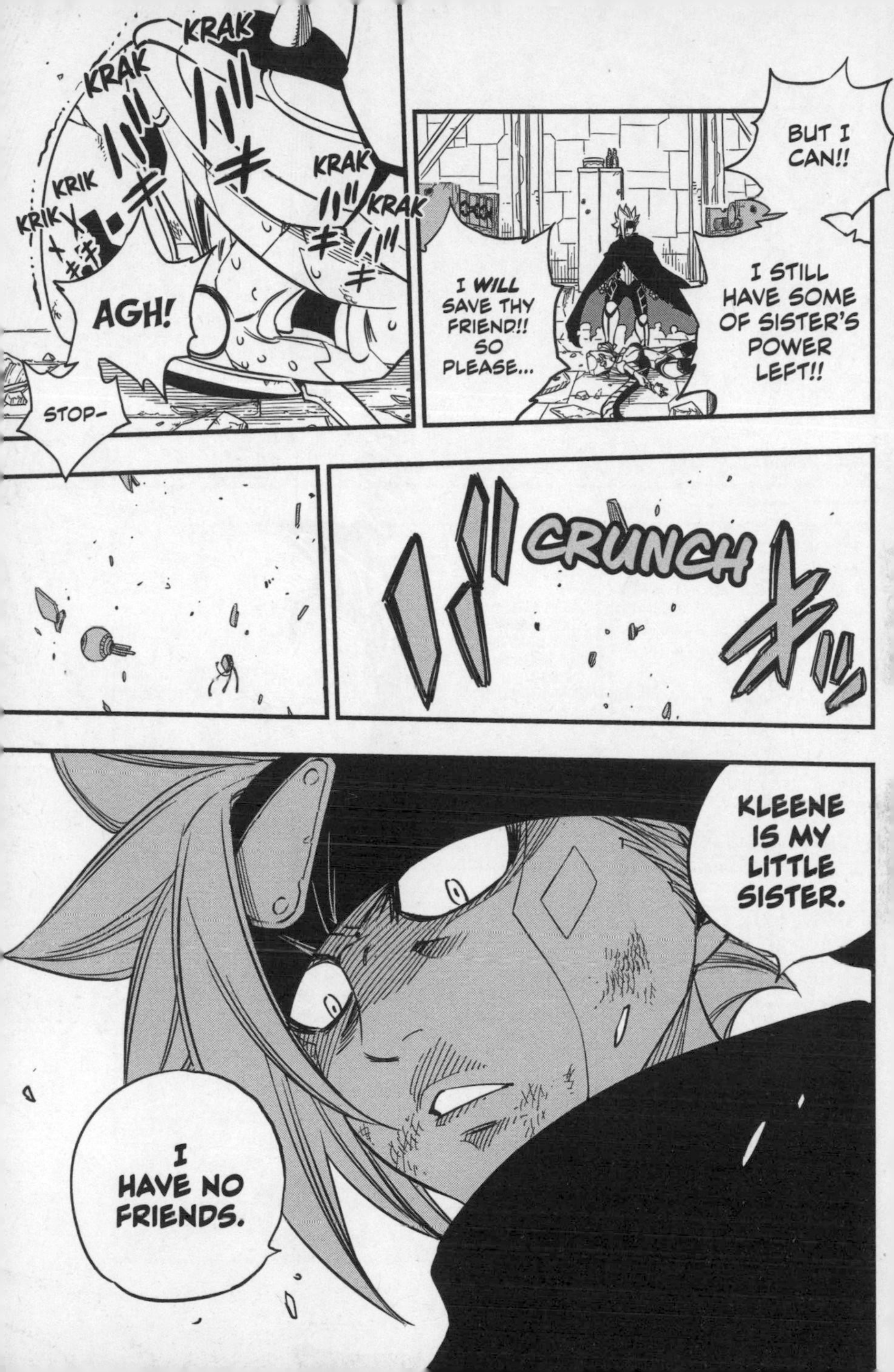
BUT I CAN!!
I STILL HAVE SOME OF SISTER'S POWER LEFT!!
I WILL SAVE THY FRIEND!! SO PLEASE...
KRAK
KRAK
KRAK
KRAK
KRIK
KRIK
AGH!
STOP-
CRUNCH
KLEENE IS MY LITTLE SISTER.
I HAVE NO FRIENDS.

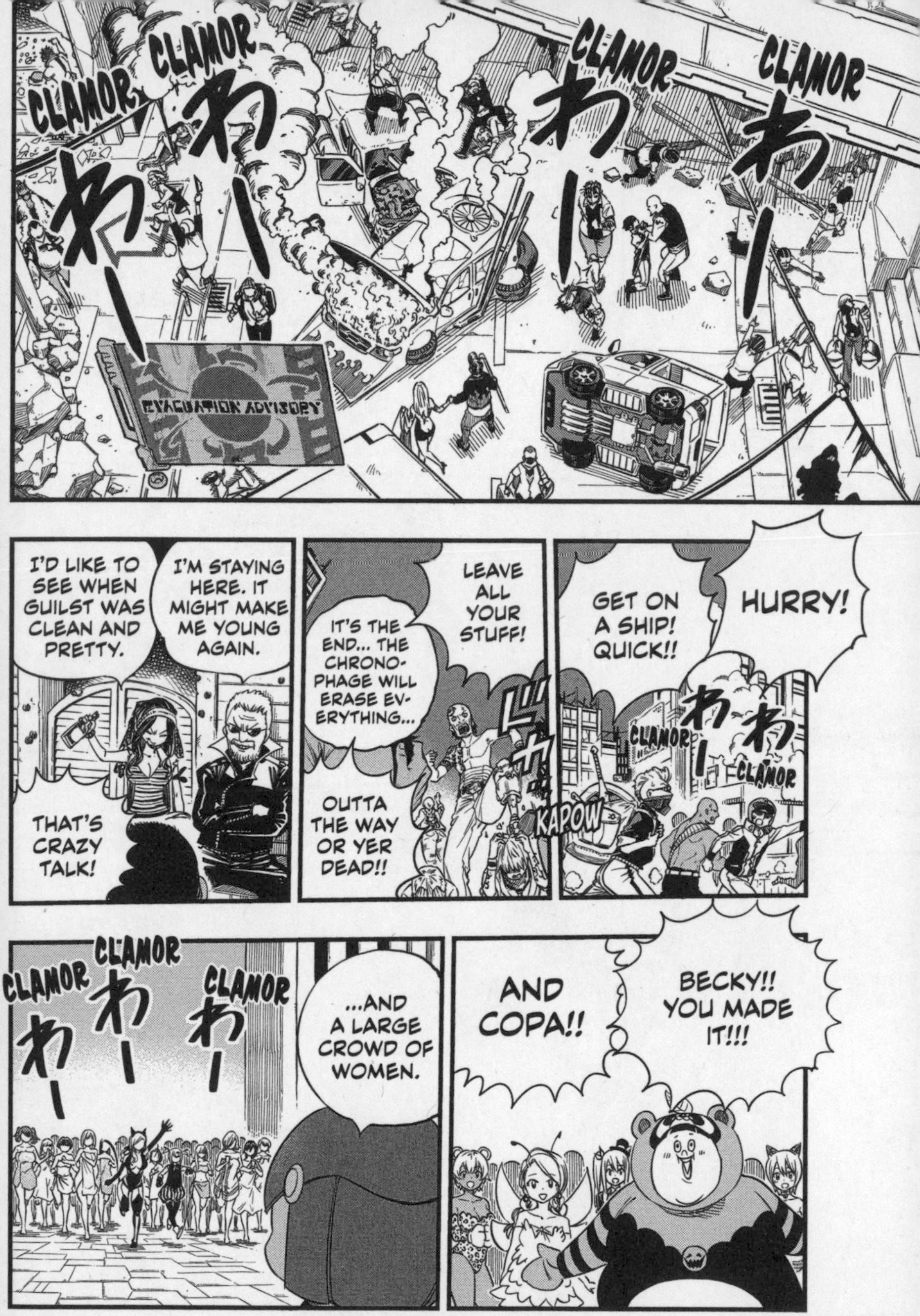
CLAMOR
CLAMOR
CLAMOR
CLAMOR
EVACUATION ADVISORY
HURRY!
GET ON A SHIP! QUICK!!
CLAMOR
CLAMOR
LEAVE ALL YOUR STUFF!
IT'S THE END... THE CHRONO-PHAGE WILL ERASE EV-ERYTHING...
OUTTA THE WAY OR YER DEAD!!
KAPOW
I'M STAYING HERE. IT MIGHT MAKE ME YOUNG AGAIN.
I'D LIKE TO SEE WHEN GUILST WAS CLEAN AND PRETTY.
THAT'S CRAZY TALK!
BECKY!! YOU MADE IT!!!
AND COPA!!
...AND A LARGE CROWD OF WOMEN.
CLAMOR
CLAMOR
CLAMOR

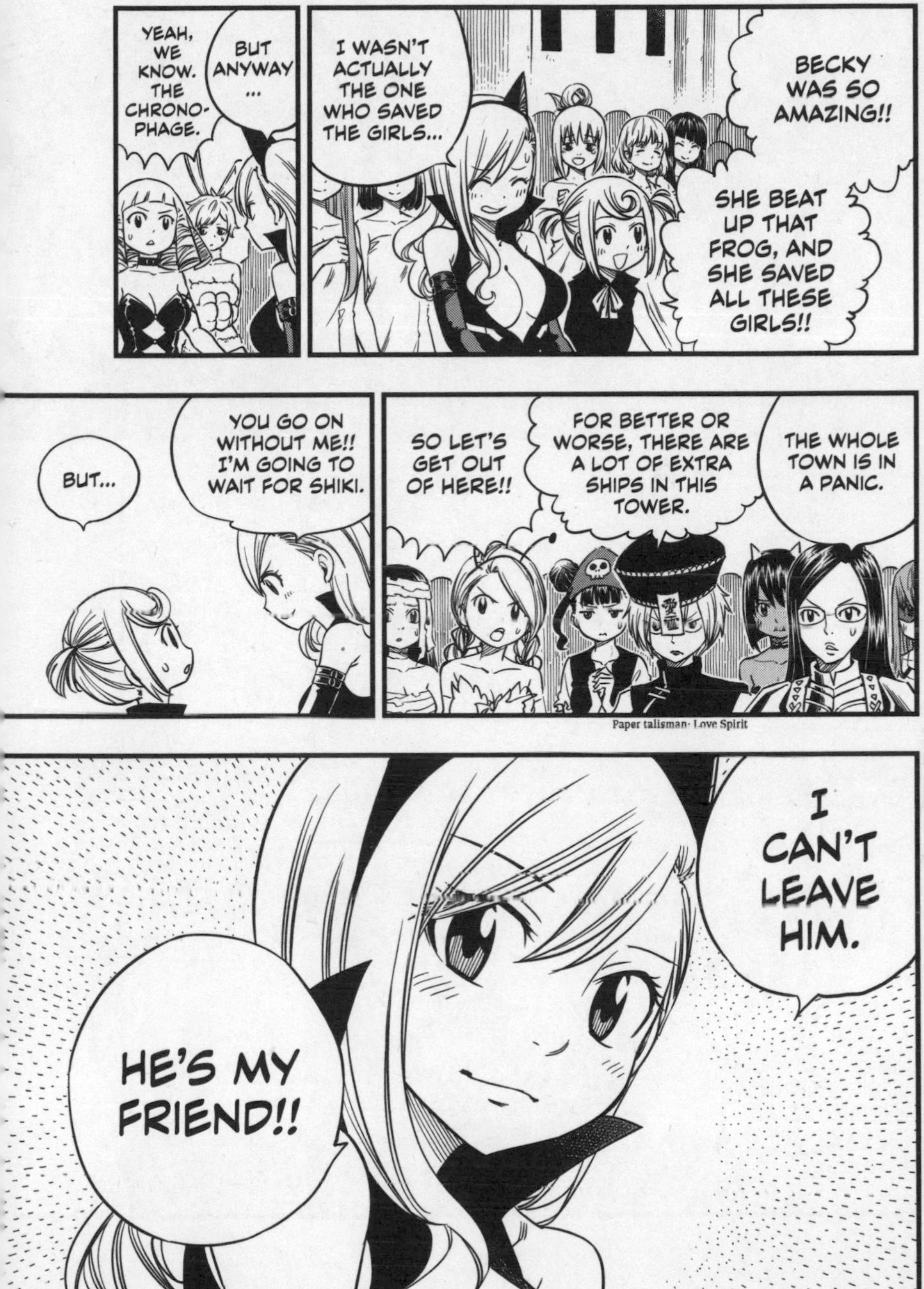
BECKY WAS SO AMAZING!!
SHE BEAT UP THAT FROG, AND SHE SAVED ALL THESE GIRLS!!
I WASN'T ACTUALLY THE ONE WHO SAVED THE GIRLS...
BUT ANYWAY ...
YEAH, WE KNOW. THE CHRONO-PHAGE.
THE WHOLE TOWN IS IN A PANIC.
FOR BETTER OR WORSE, THERE ARE A LOT OF EXTRA SHIPS IN THIS TOWER.
SO LET'S GET OUT OF HERE!!
YOU GO ON WITHOUT ME!! I'M GOING TO WAIT FOR SHIKI.
BUT...
I CAN'T LEAVE HIM.
HE'S MY FRIEND!!

Paper talisman: Love Spirit

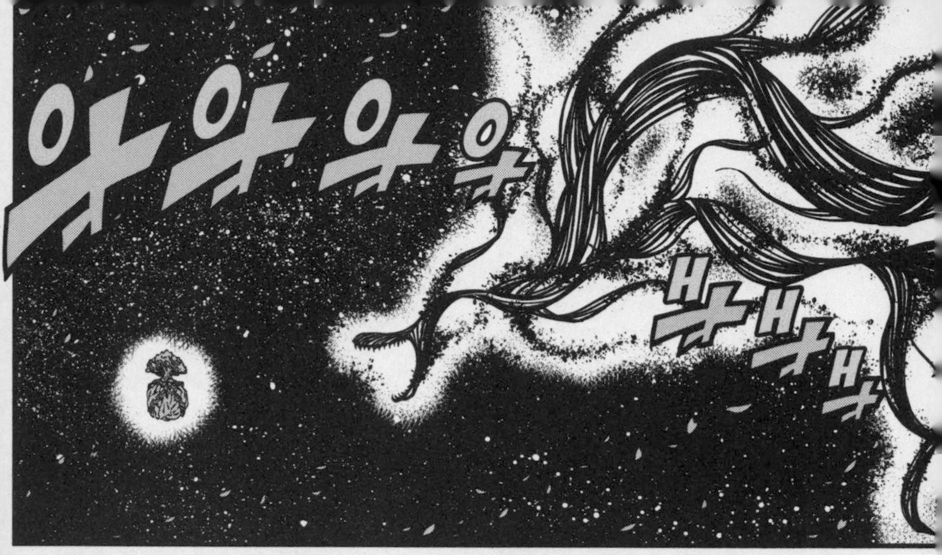

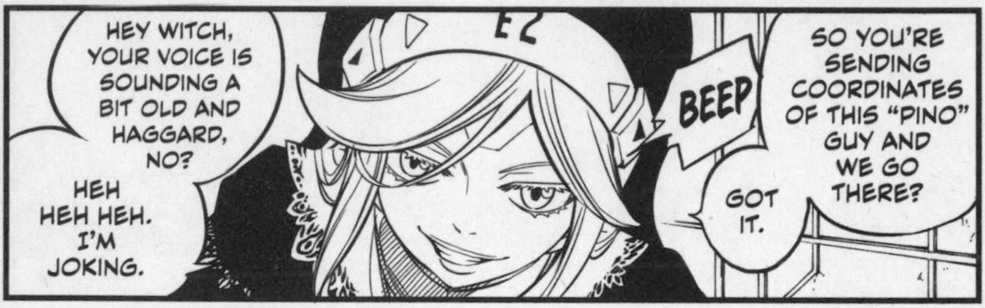
SO YOU'RE SENDING COORDINATES OF THIS "PINO" GUY AND WE GO THERE?
BEEP
GOT IT.
HEY WITCH, YOUR VOICE IS SOUNDING A BIT OLD AND HAGGARD, NO?
HEH HEH HEH. I'M JOKING.

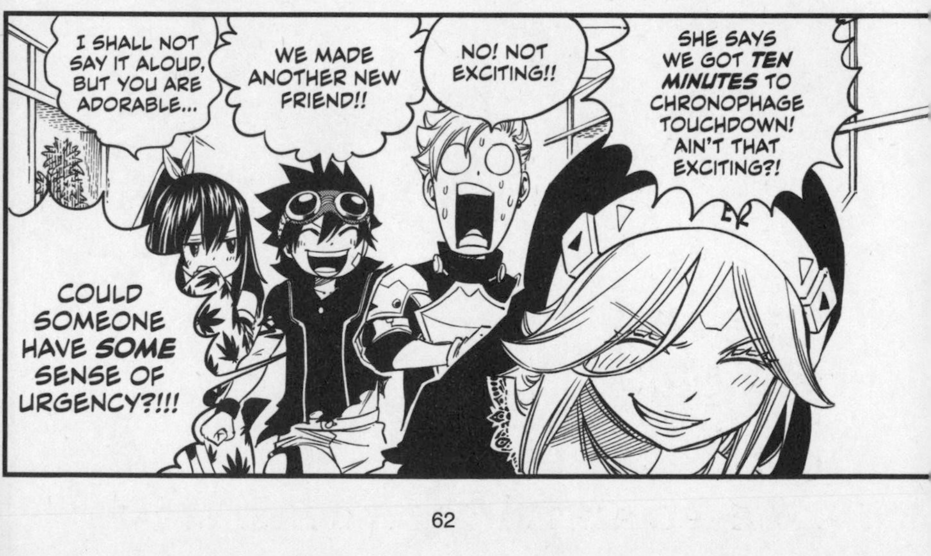
SHE SAYS WE GOT **TEN MINUTES** TO CHRONOPHAGE TOUCHDOWN! AIN'T THAT EXCITING?!
NO! NOT EXCITING!!
WE MADE ANOTHER NEW FRIEND!!
I SHALL NOT SAY IT ALOUD, BUT YOU ARE ADORABLE...
COULD SOMEONE HAVE **SOME** SENSE OF URGENCY?!!!

EDENSZERO

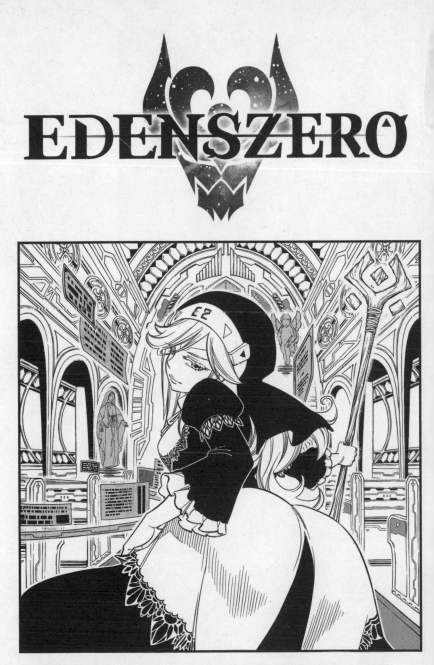

CHAPTER 27: THE GREAT GUILST ESCAPE

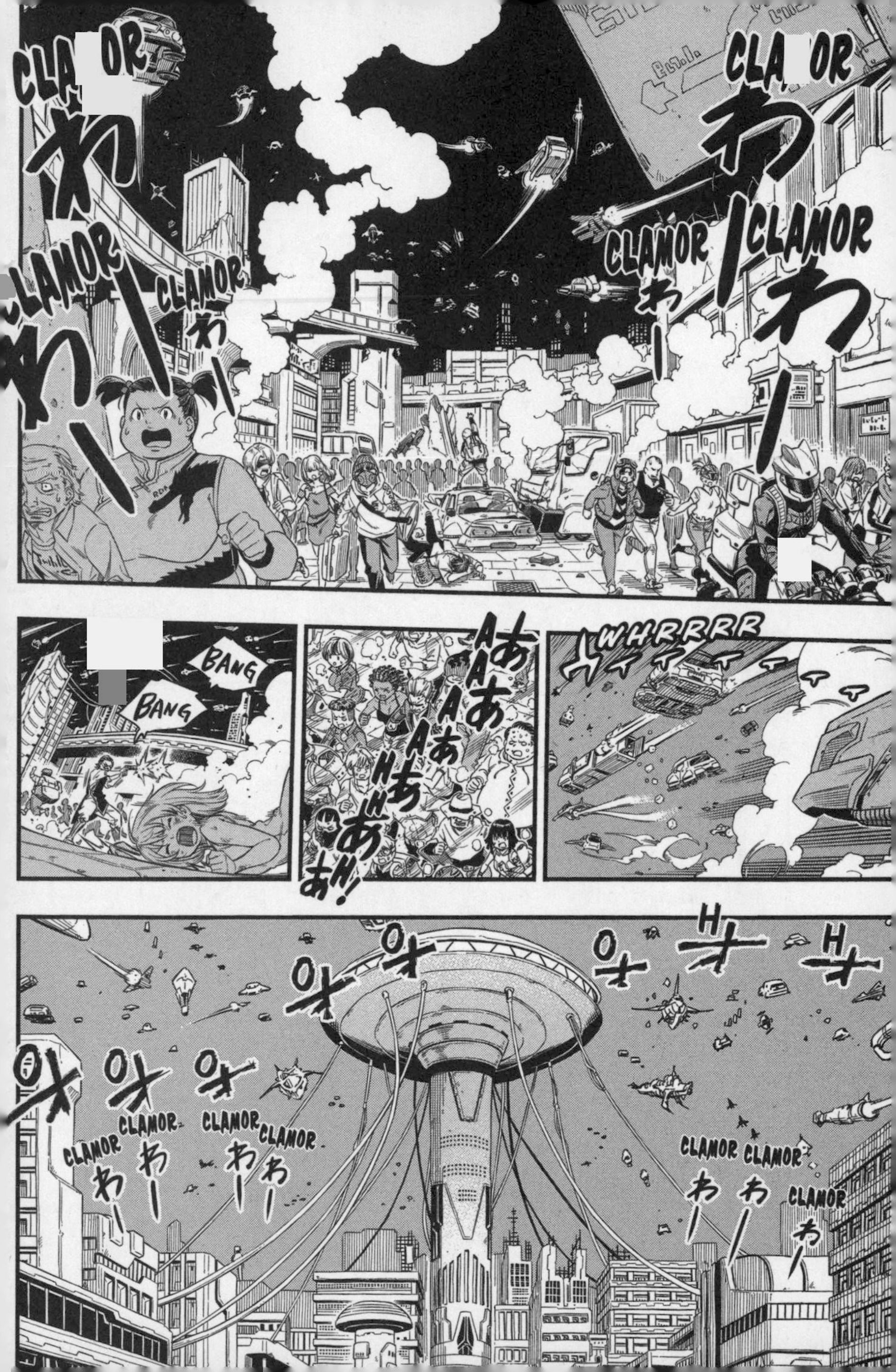

CLA OR
わっ
CLAMOR
わー
CLAMOR
わっ
CLAMOR
わー
CLAMOR
わっ
CLA OR
わっ
WHRRRR
AAAAHH!
BANG
BANG
H
H
O
O
O
O
O
O
CLAMOR
CLAMOR
CLAMOR
CLAMOR
CLAMOR
CLAMOR
CLAMOR

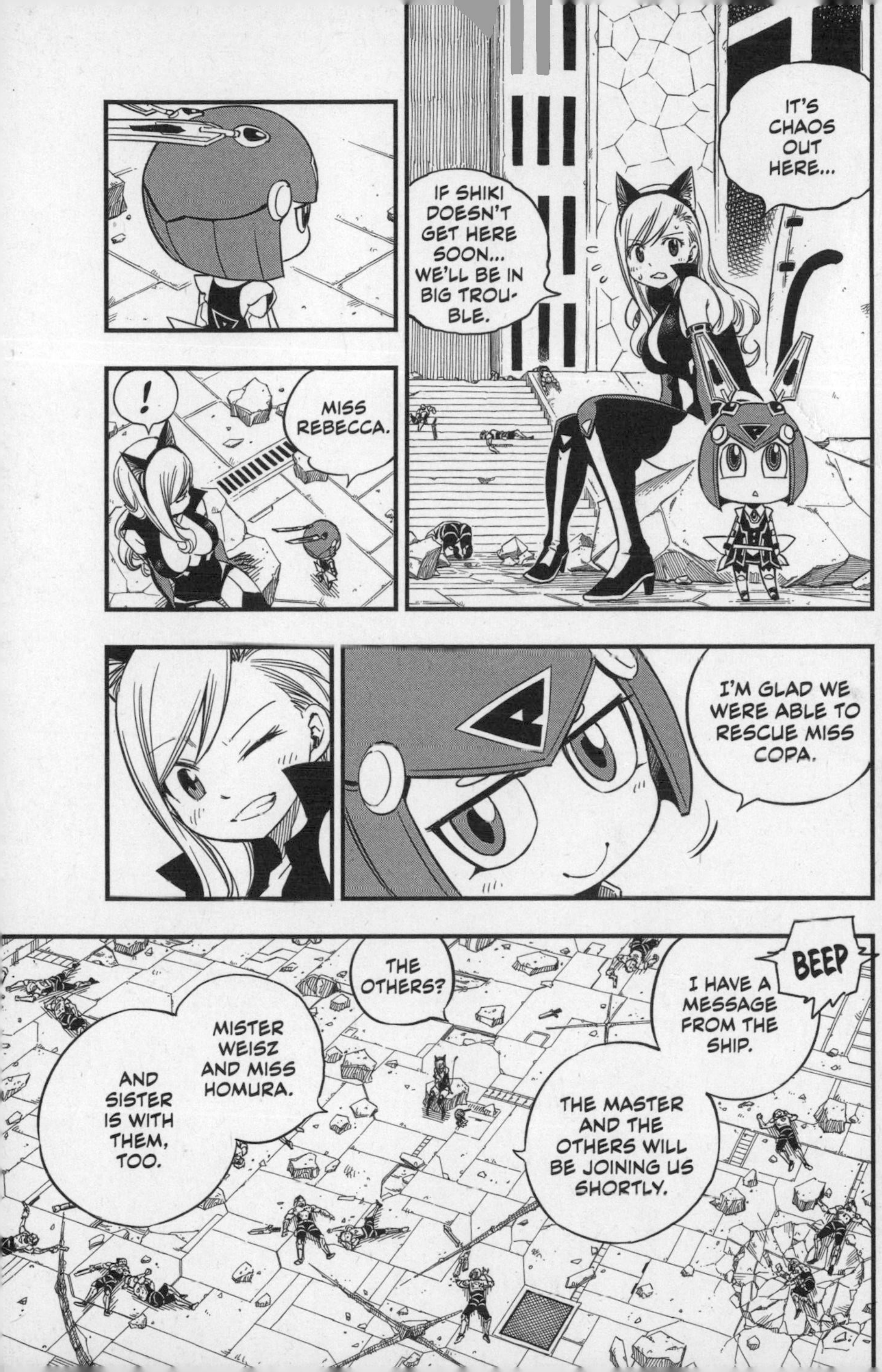
IT'S CHAOS OUT HERE...
IF SHIKI DOESN'T GET HERE SOON... WE'LL BE IN BIG TROUBLE.
!
MISS REBECCA.
I'M GLAD WE WERE ABLE TO RESCUE MISS COPA.
BEEP
I HAVE A MESSAGE FROM THE SHIP.
THE MASTER AND THE OTHERS WILL BE JOINING US SHORTLY.
THE OTHERS?
MISTER WEISZ AND MISS HOMURA.
AND SISTER IS WITH THEM, TOO.

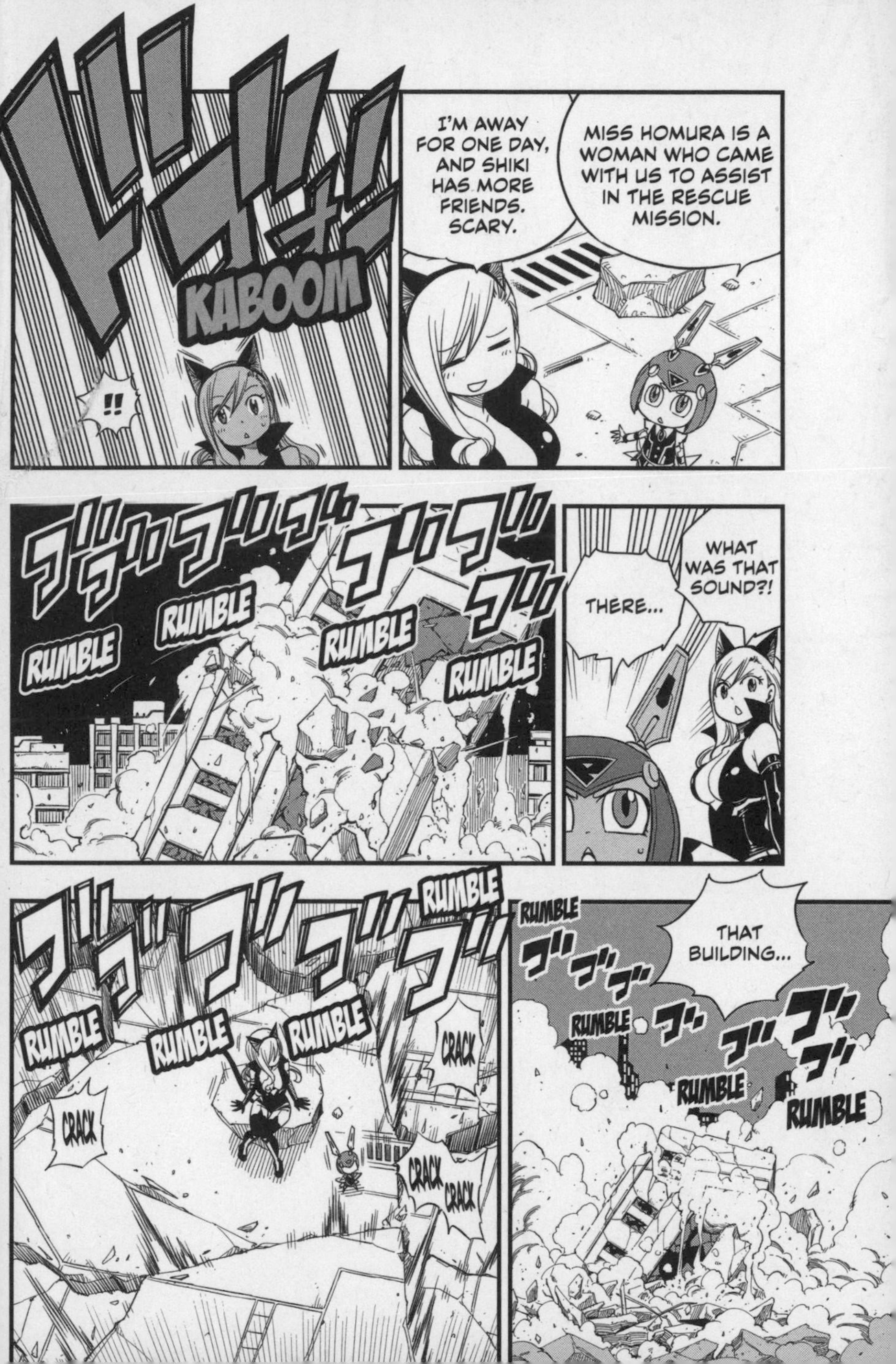
MISS HOMURA IS A WOMAN WHO CAME WITH US TO ASSIST IN THE RESCUE MISSION.
I'M AWAY FOR ONE DAY, AND SHIKI HAS MORE FRIENDS. SCARY.
KABOOM
!!
WHAT WAS THAT SOUND?!
THERE...
RUMBLE
RUMBLE
RUMBLE
RUMBLE
THAT BUILDING...
RUMBLE
RUMBLE
RUMBLE
RUMBLE
RUMBLE
RUMBLE
RUMBLE
RUMBLE
CRACK
CRACK
CRACK
CRACK

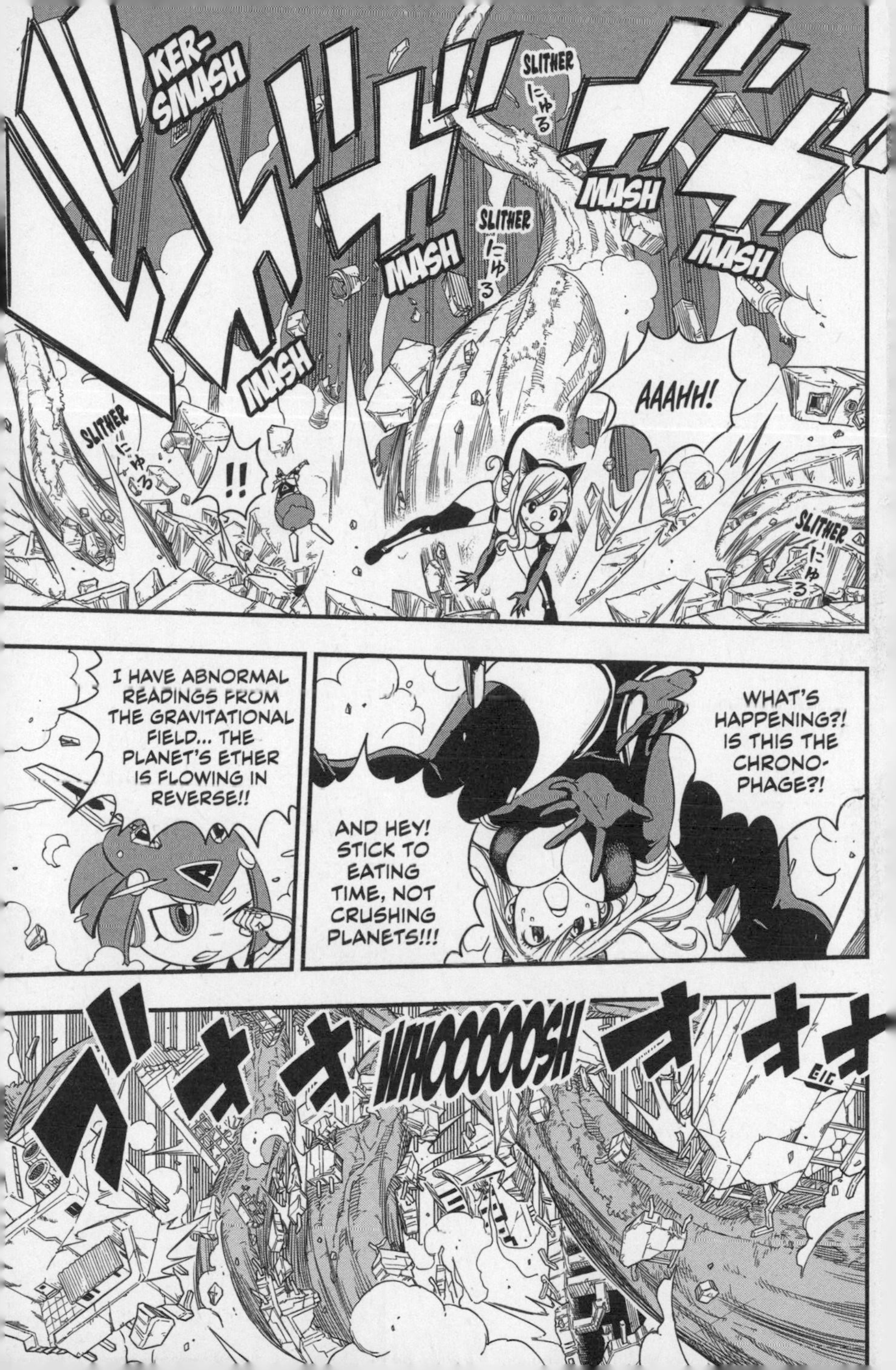
MASH
SLITHER
にゅる
MASH
AAAHH!
SLITHER
にゅる
MASH
SLITHER
にゅる
MASH
KER-SMASH
MASH
!!
SLITHER
にゅる
WHAT'S HAPPENING?! IS THIS THE CHRONO-PHAGE?!
AND HEY! STICK TO EATING TIME, NOT CRUSHING PLANETS!!!
I HAVE ABNORMAL READINGS FROM THE GRAVITATIONAL FIELD... THE PLANET'S ETHER IS FLOWING IN REVERSE!!
WHOOOOOOSH

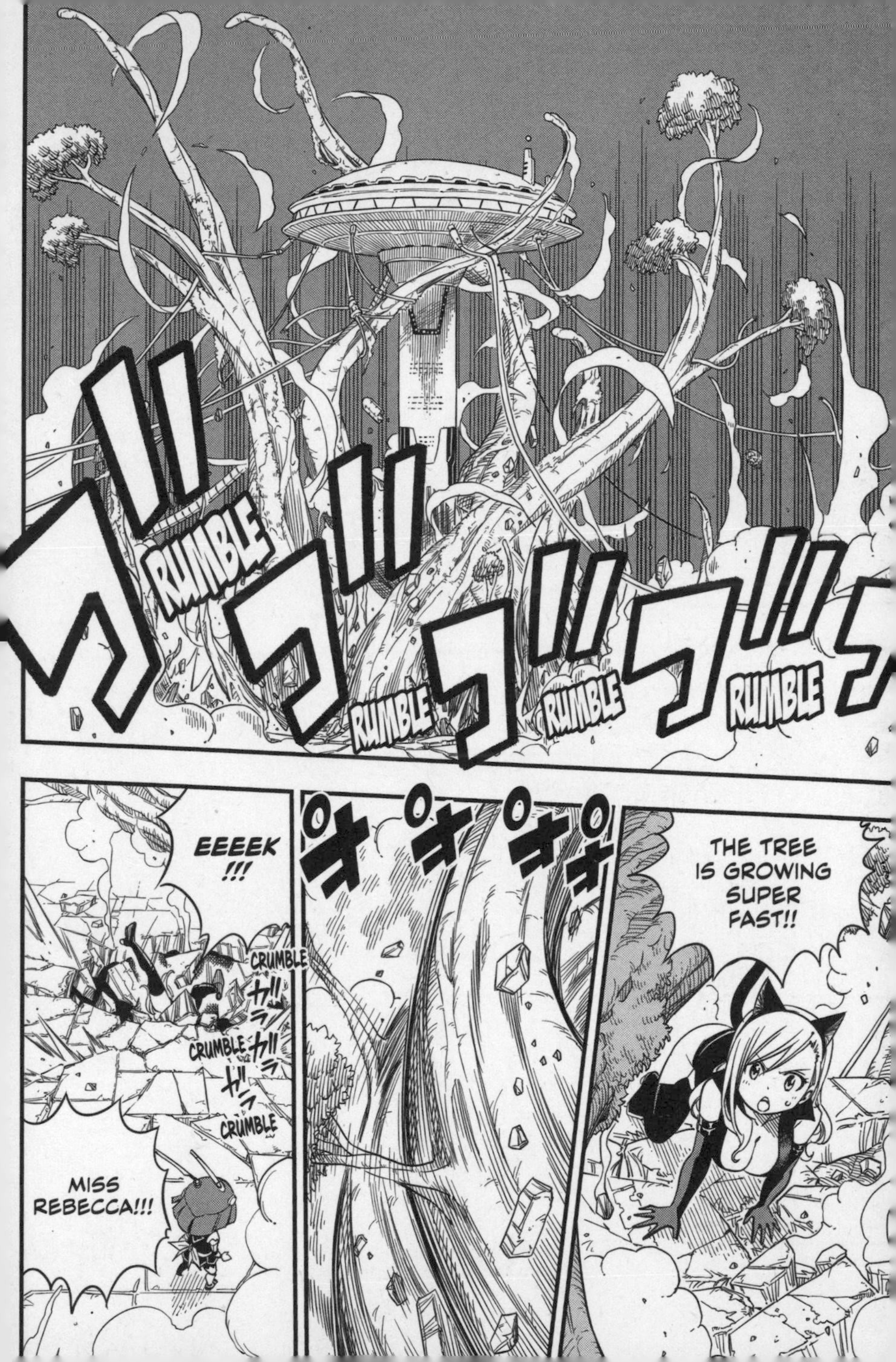
RUMBLE
RUMBLE
RUMBLE
RUMBLE
THE TREE IS GROWING SUPER FAST!!
EEEEK!!!
CRUMBLE
CRUMBLE
CRUMBLE
MISS REBECCA!!!

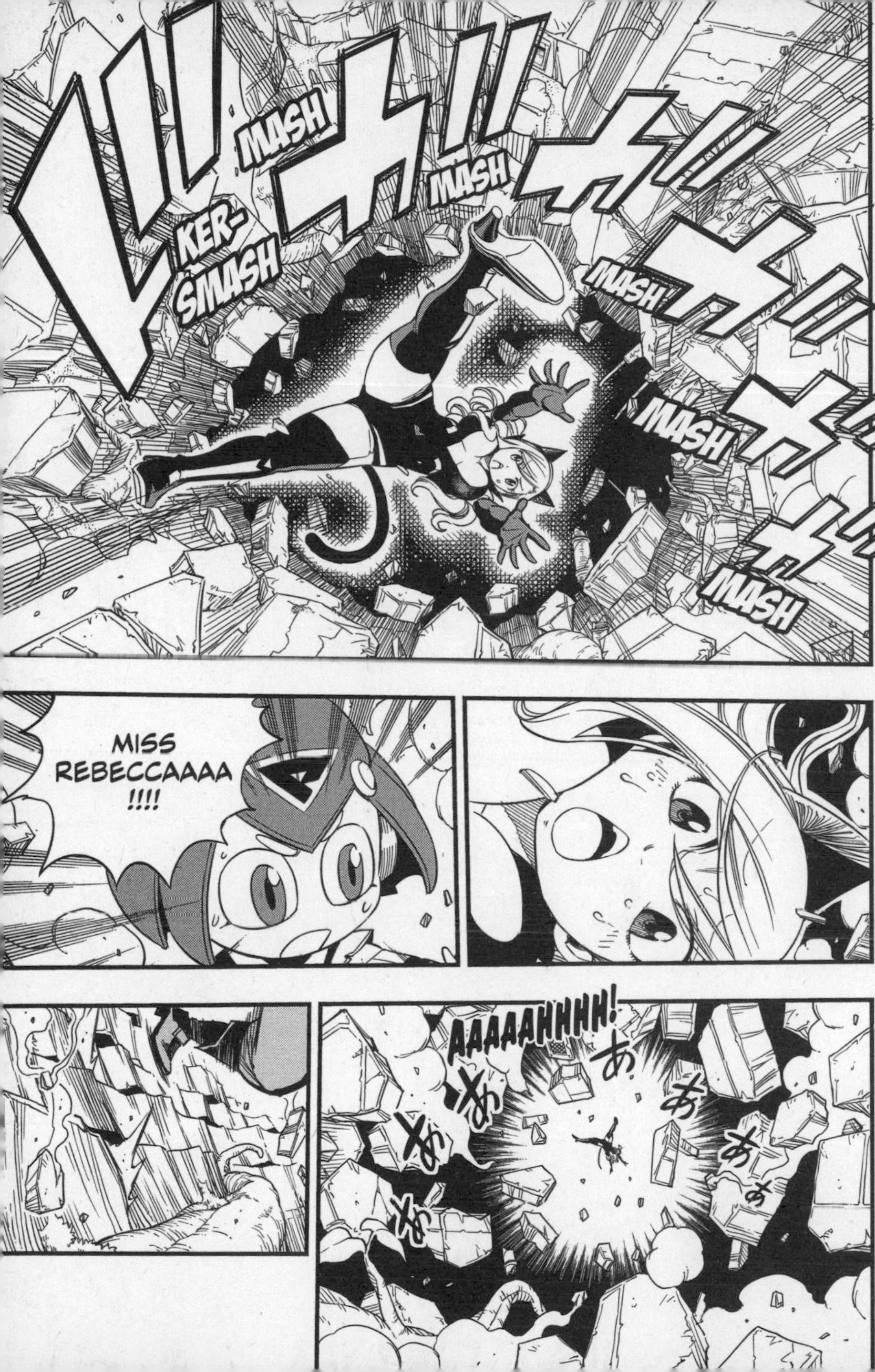
KER-SMASH
MASH
MASH
MASH
MASH
MASH
MISS REBECCAAAA !!!!
AAAAAHHHH!

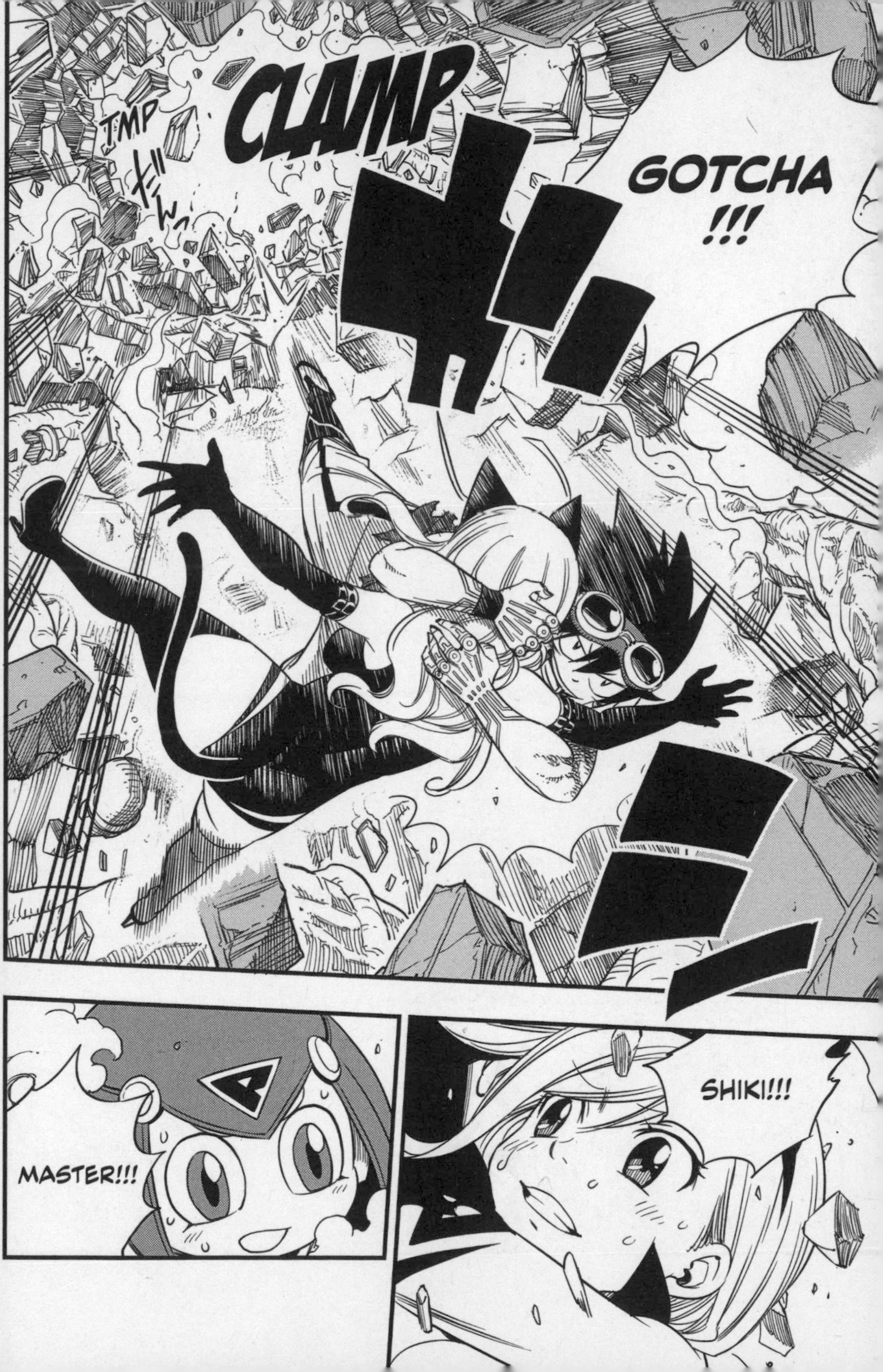
GOTCHA !!!
CLAMP
TMP
SHIKI!!!
MASTER!!!

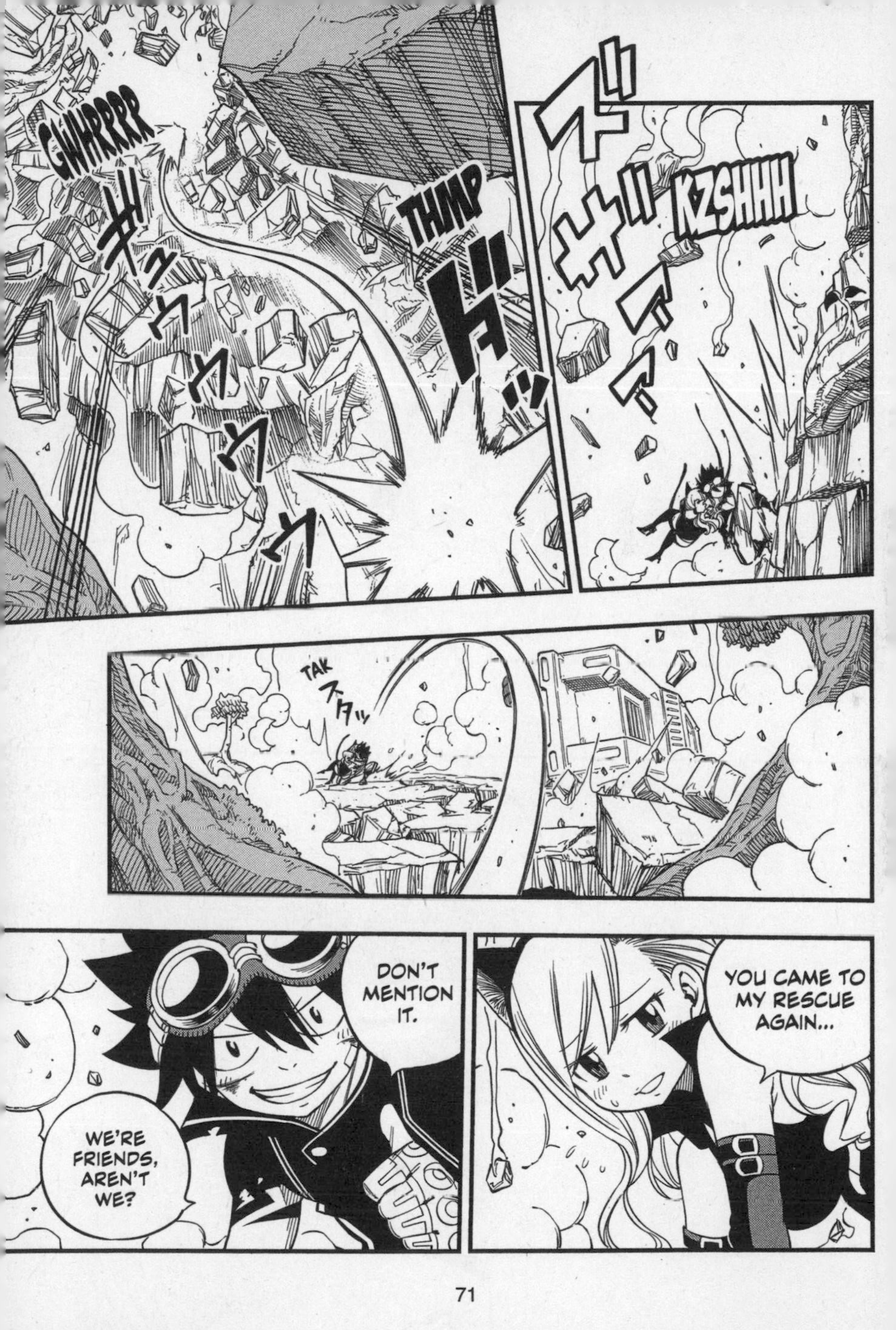

KZSHHH
GWHRRRR
THMP
TAK
スタッ
YOU CAME TO MY RESCUE AGAIN...
DON'T MENTION IT.
WE'RE FRIENDS, AREN'T WE?

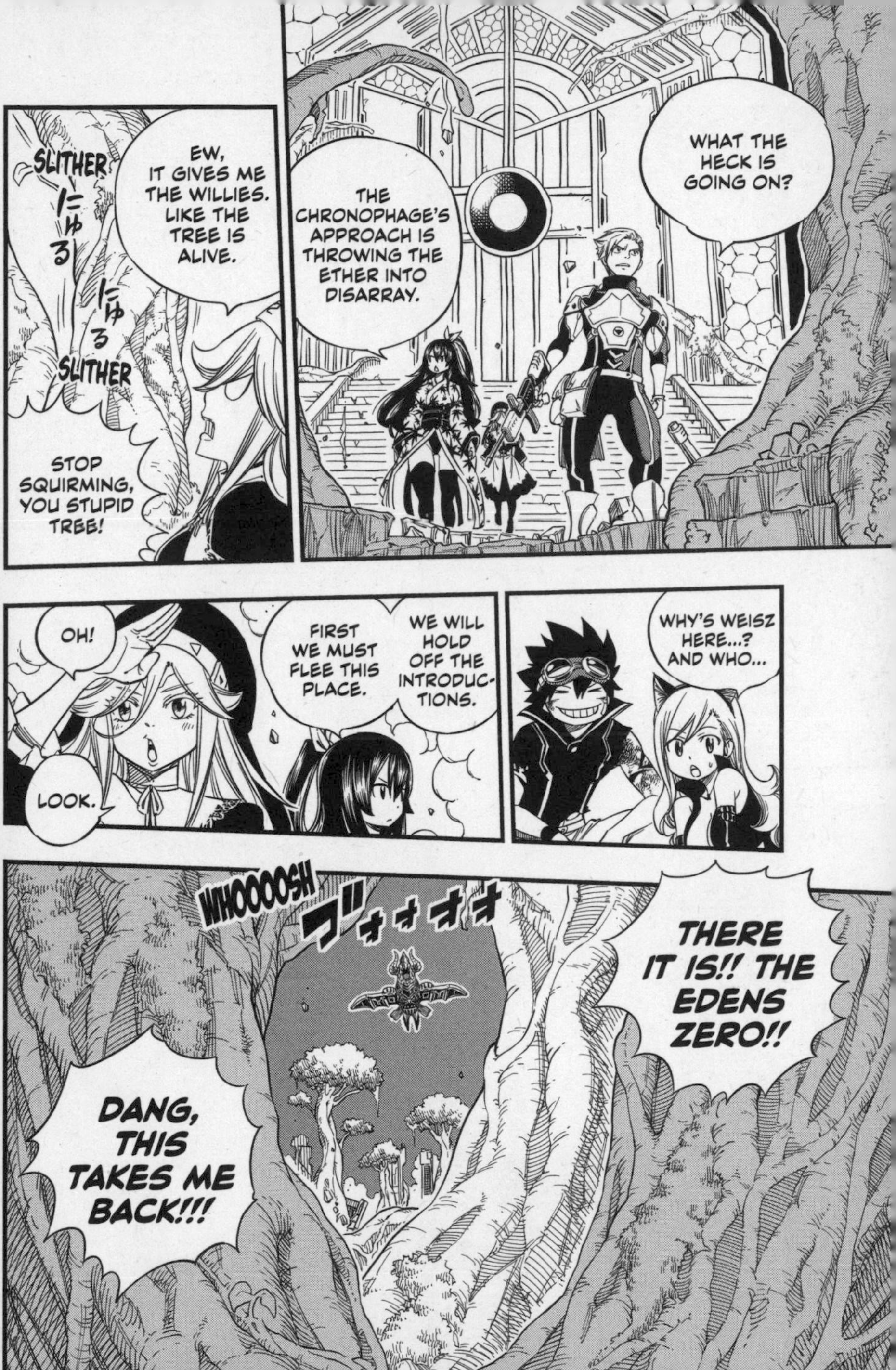
WHAT THE HECK IS GOING ON?
THE CHRONOPHAGE'S APPROACH IS THROWING THE ETHER INTO DISARRAY.
EW, IT GIVES ME THE WILLIES. LIKE THE TREE IS ALIVE.
SLITHER にゅる
にゅる SLITHER
STOP SQUIRMING, YOU STUPID TREE!
WHY'S WEISZ HERE...? AND WHO...
WE WILL HOLD OFF THE INTRODUCTIONS.
FIRST WE MUST FLEE THIS PLACE.
OH!
LOOK.
WHOOOOSH ブォォオオ
THERE IT IS!! THE EDENS ZERO!!
DANG, THIS TAKES ME BACK!!!

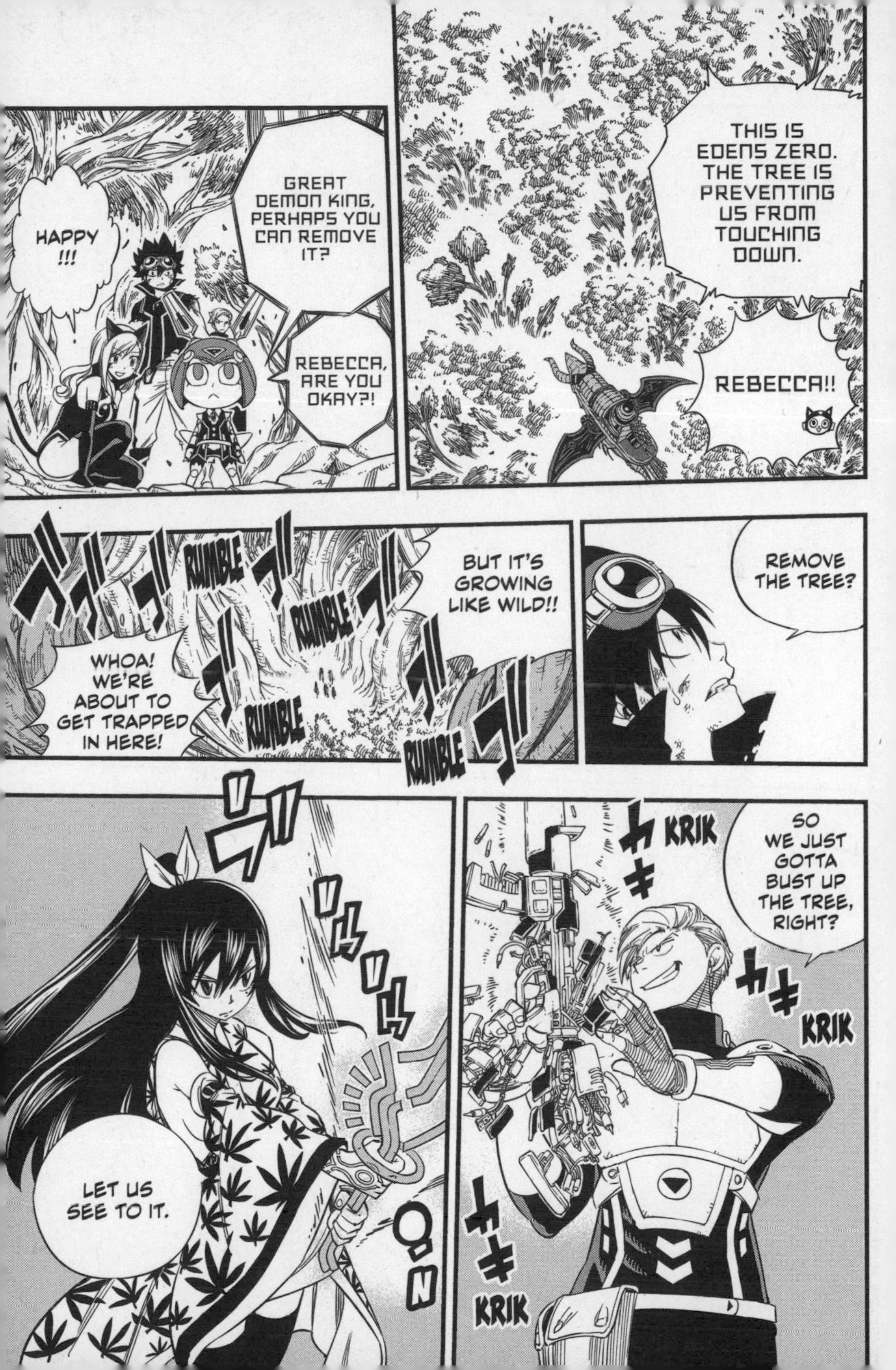
THIS IS EDENS ZERO. THE TREE IS PREVENTING US FROM TOUCHING DOWN.
REBECCA!!
GREAT DEMON KING, PERHAPS YOU CAN REMOVE IT?
HAPPY !!!
REBECCA, ARE YOU OKAY?!
REMOVE THE TREE?
BUT IT'S GROWING LIKE WILD!!
RUMBLE
RUMBLE
WHOA! WE'RE ABOUT TO GET TRAPPED IN HERE!
RUMBLE
RUMBLE
KRIK
SO WE JUST GOTTA BUST UP THE TREE, RIGHT?
KRIK
KRIK
LET US SEE TO IT.
N

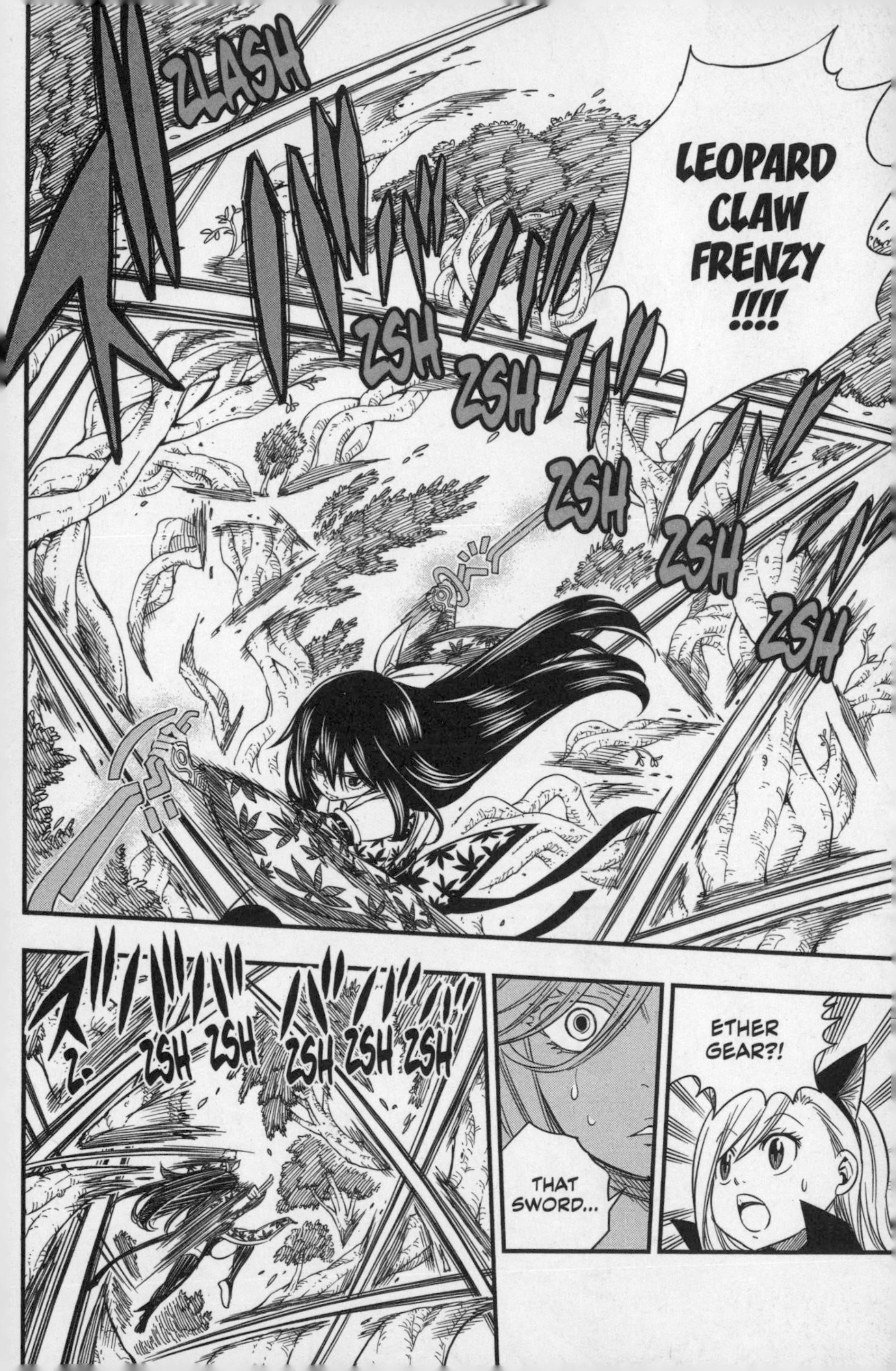
LEOPARD CLAW FRENZY!!!!
ZLASH
ZSH
ZSH
ZSH
ZSH
ZSH
ETHER GEAR?!
THAT SWORD...
ZSH ZSH ZSH ZSH ZSH
Z.

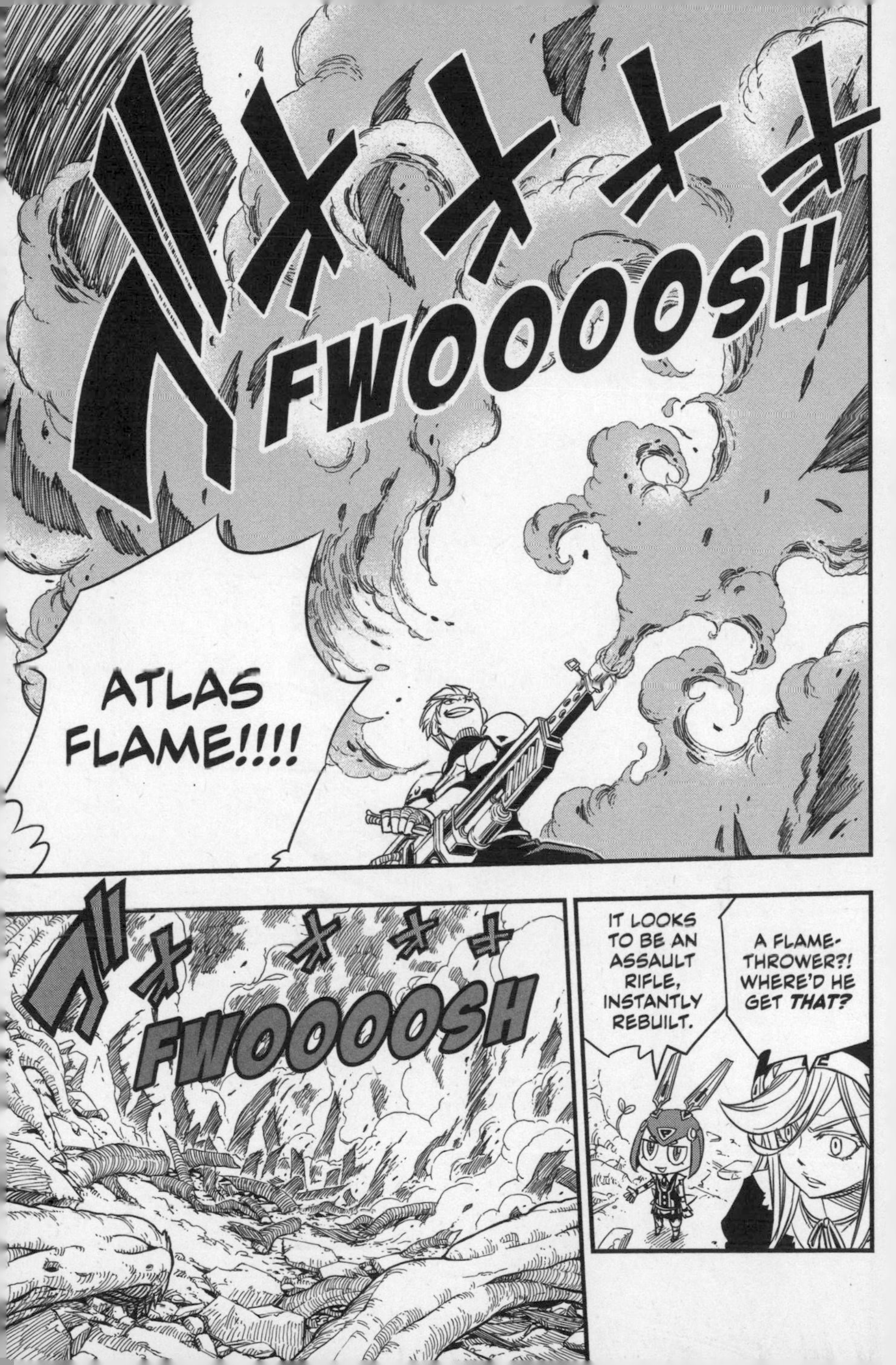
FWOOOOSH
ATLAS FLAME!!!!
A FLAME-THROWER?! WHERE'D HE GET *THAT?*
IT LOOKS TO BE AN ASSAULT RIFLE, INSTANTLY REBUILT.
FWOOOOSH

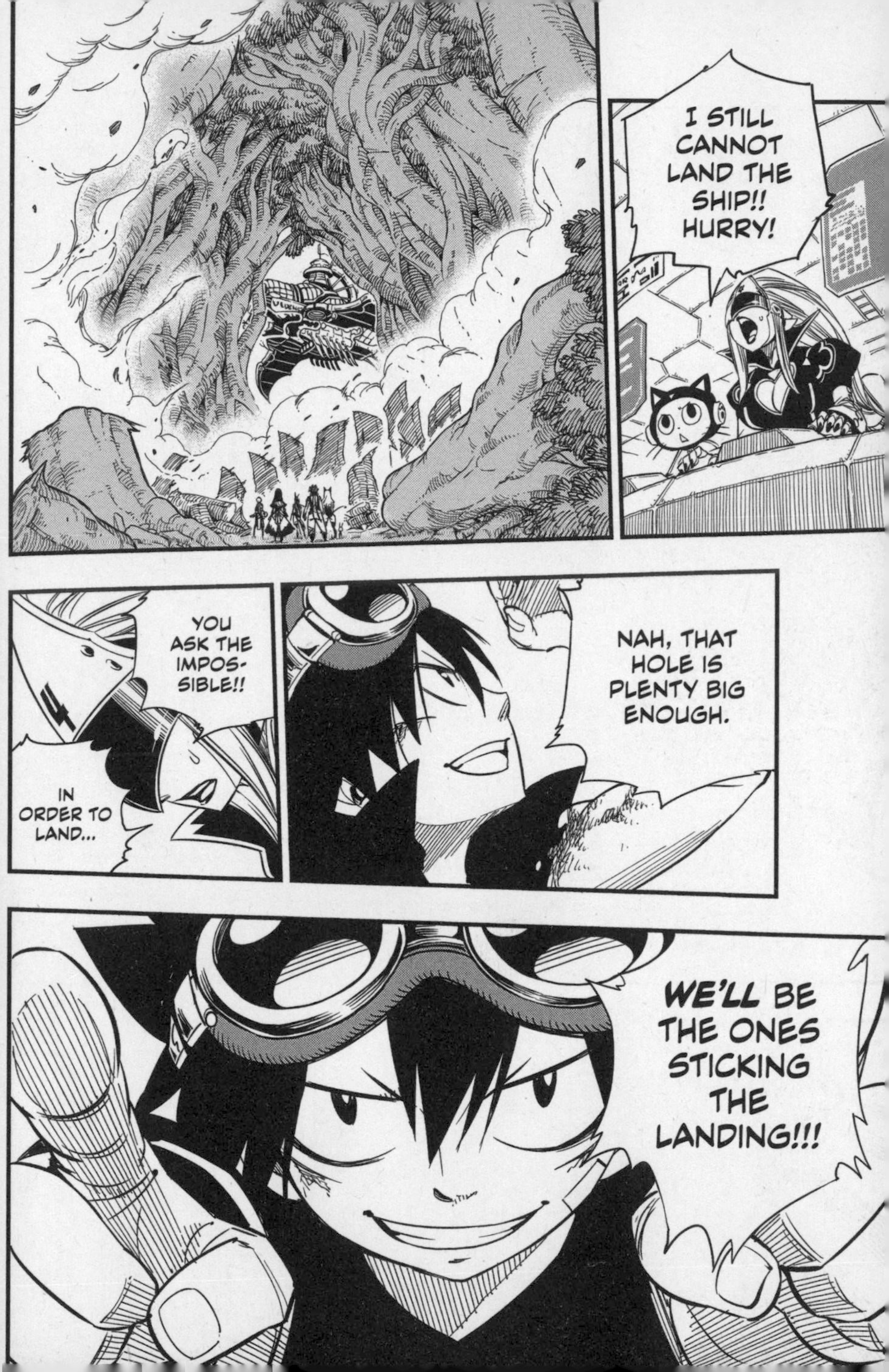
I STILL CANNOT LAND THE SHIP!! HURRY!
NAH, THAT HOLE IS PLENTY BIG ENOUGH.
YOU ASK THE IMPOSSIBLE!!
IN ORDER TO LAND...
WE'LL BE THE ONES STICKING THE LANDING!!!

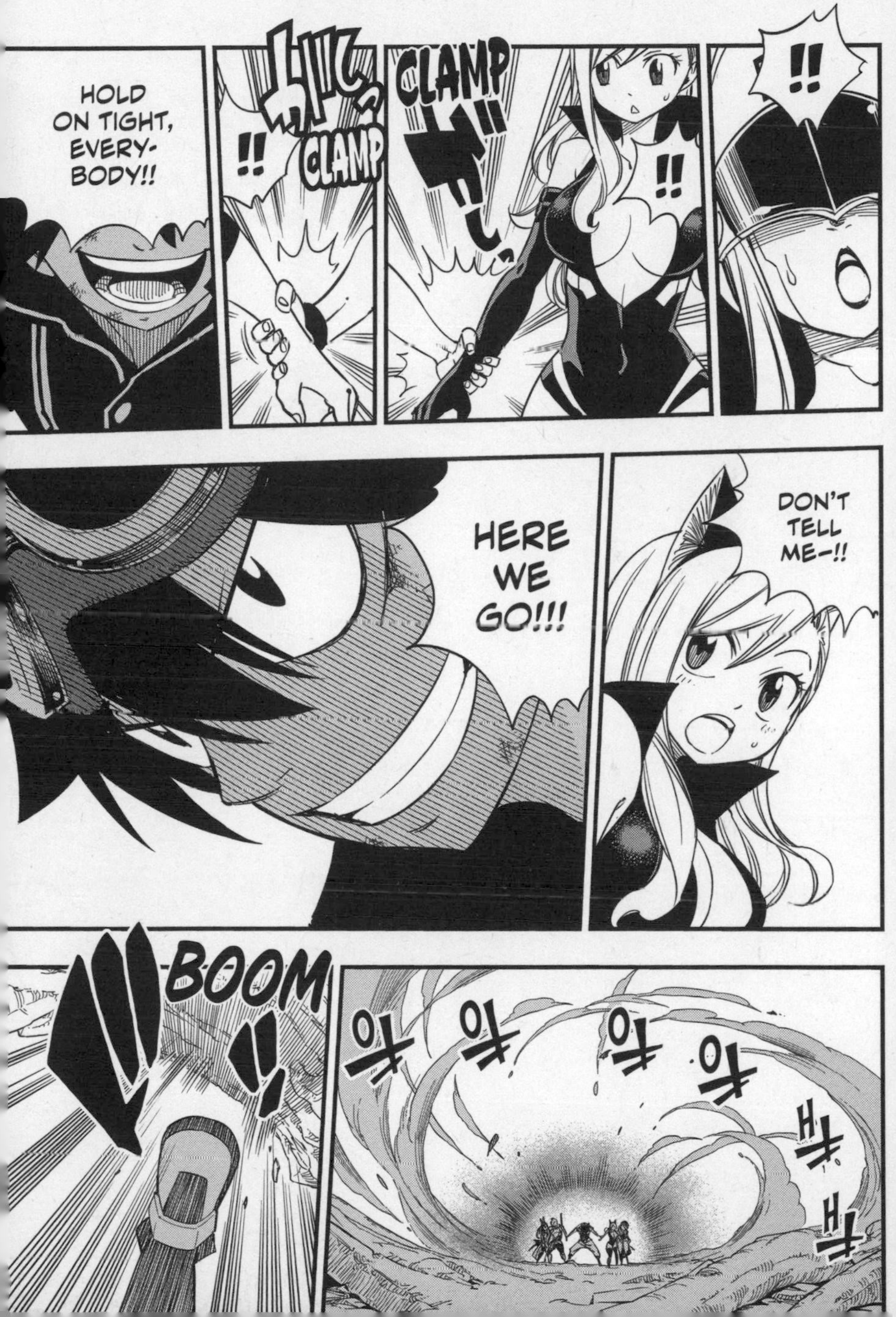
!!
CLAMP
!!
!!
CLAMP
HOLD ON TIGHT, EVERY-BODY!!
DON'T TELL ME-!!
HERE WE GO!!!
BOOM

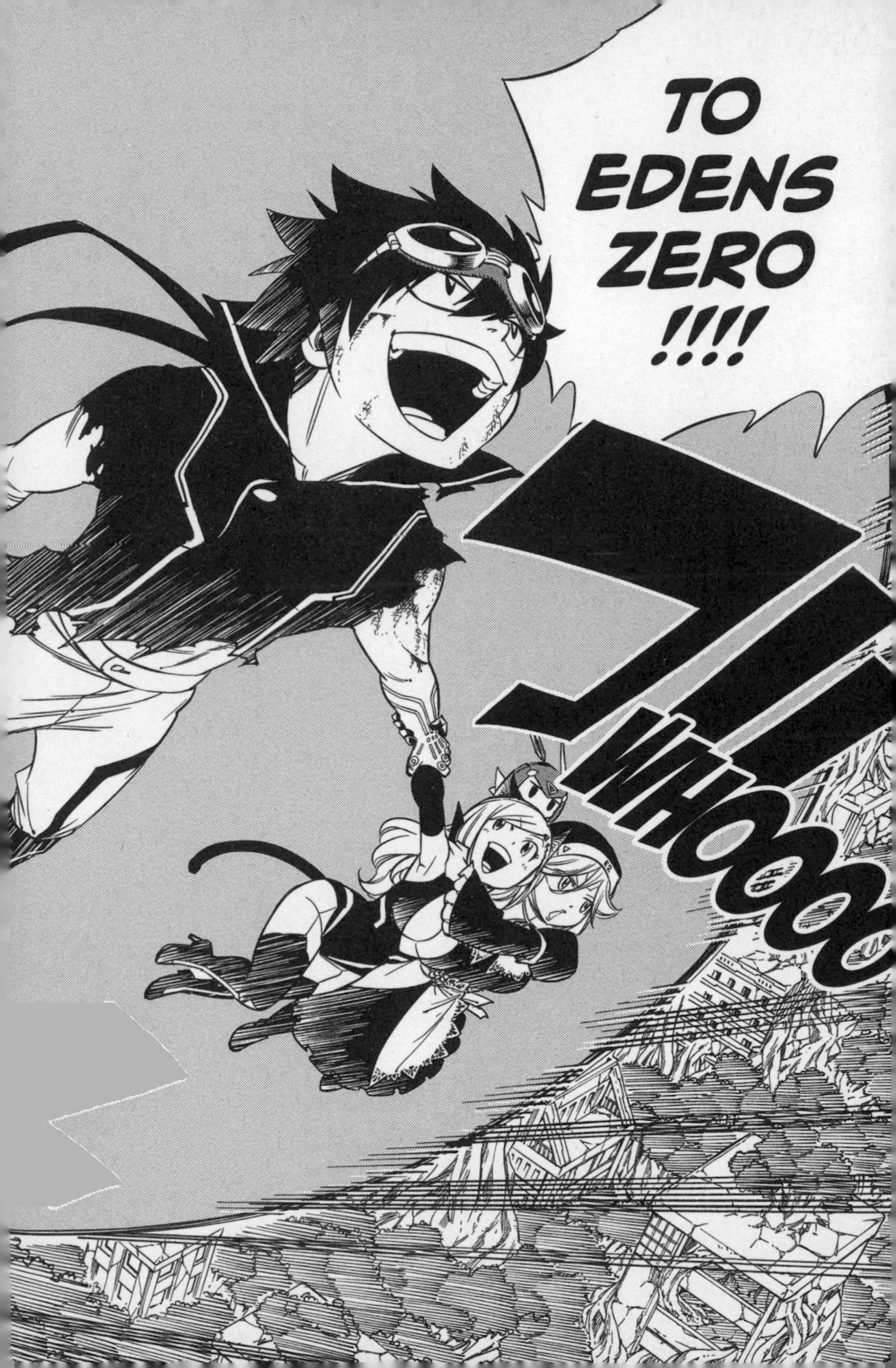
TO EDENS ZERO !!!!
WHOOOO

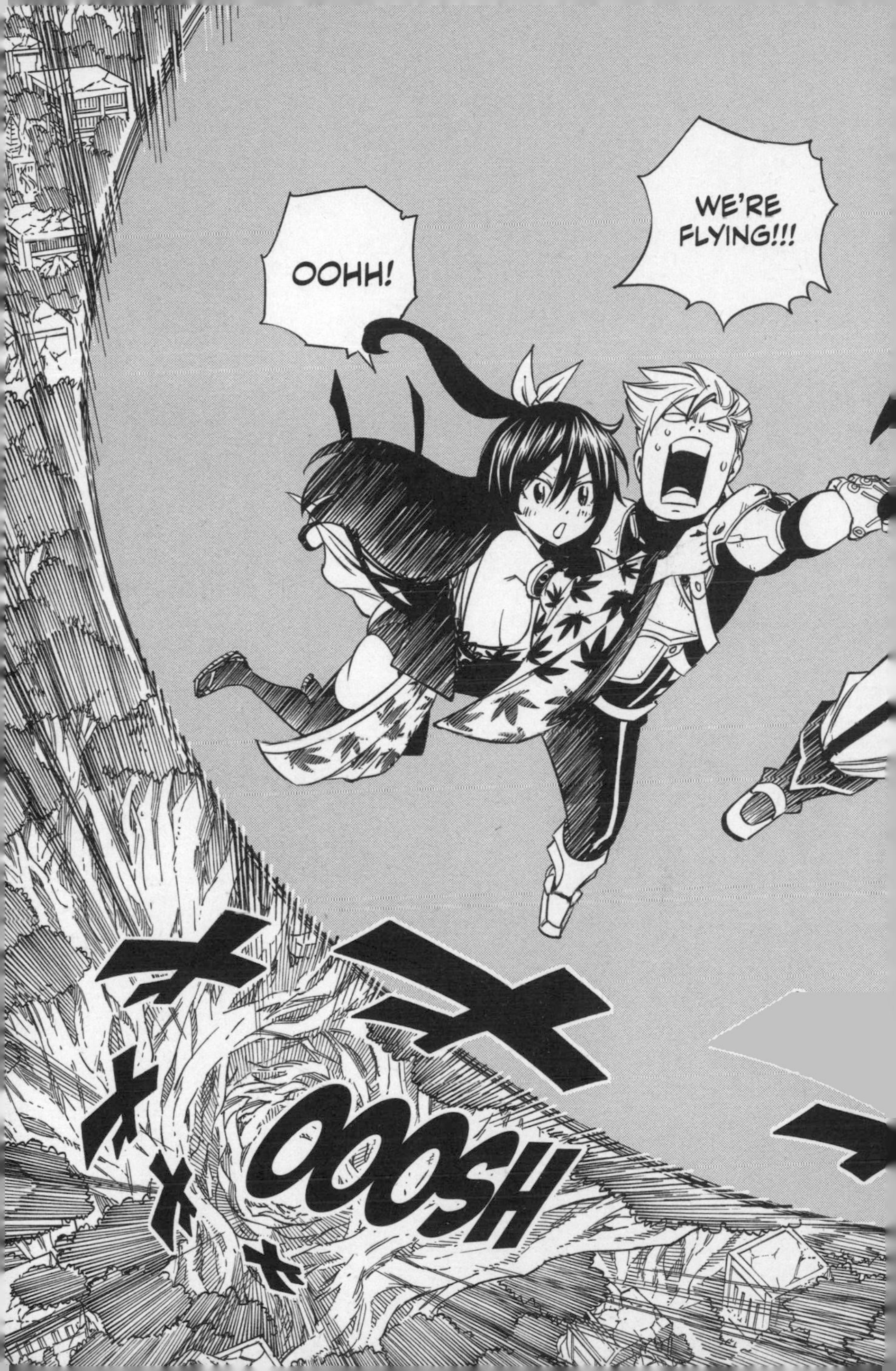
WE'RE FLYING!!!
OOHH!

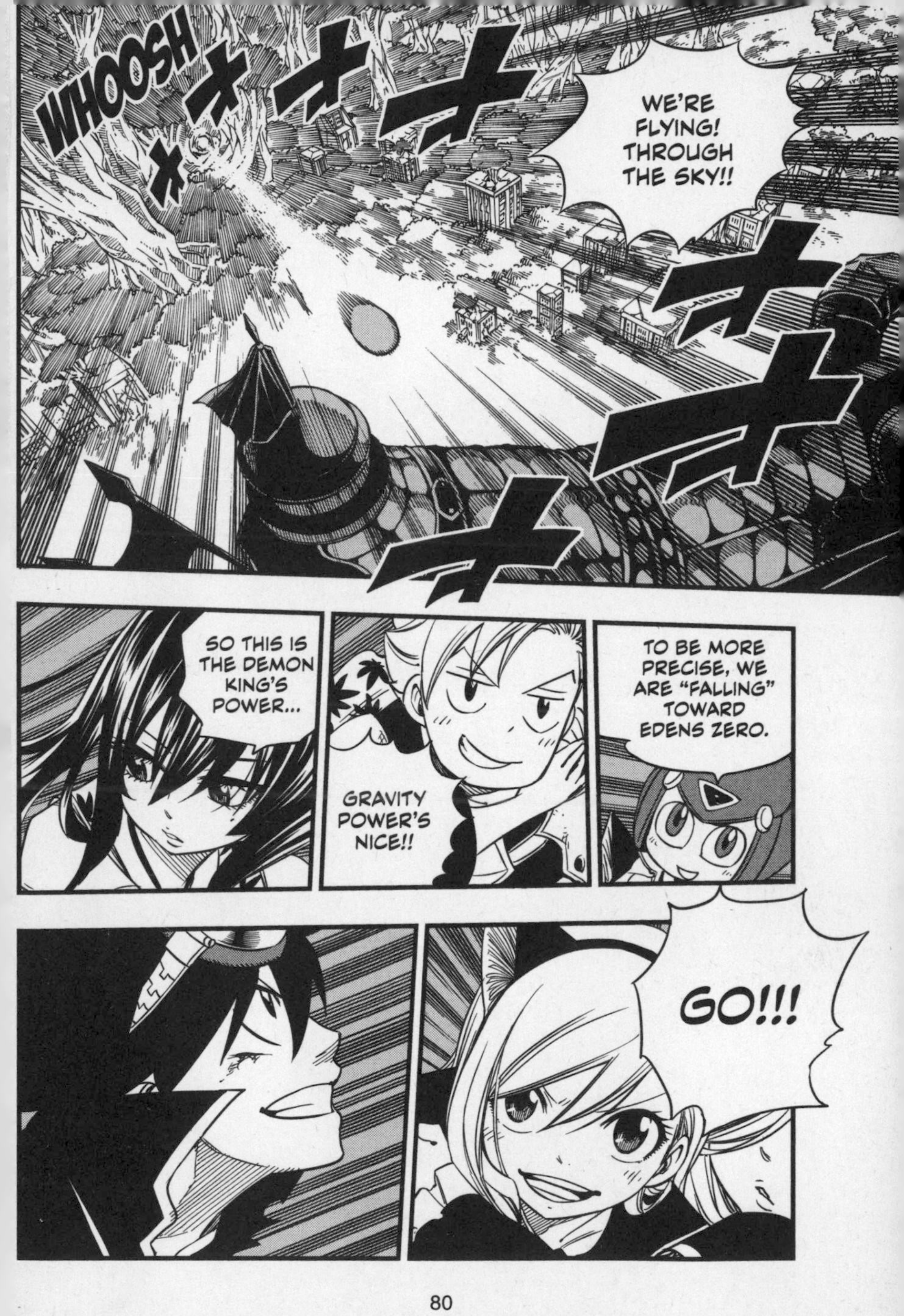
WE'RE FLYING! THROUGH THE SKY!!
WHOOSH
TO BE MORE PRECISE, WE ARE "FALLING" TOWARD EDENS ZERO.
GRAVITY POWER'S NICE!!
SO THIS IS THE DEMON KING'S POWER...
GO!!!

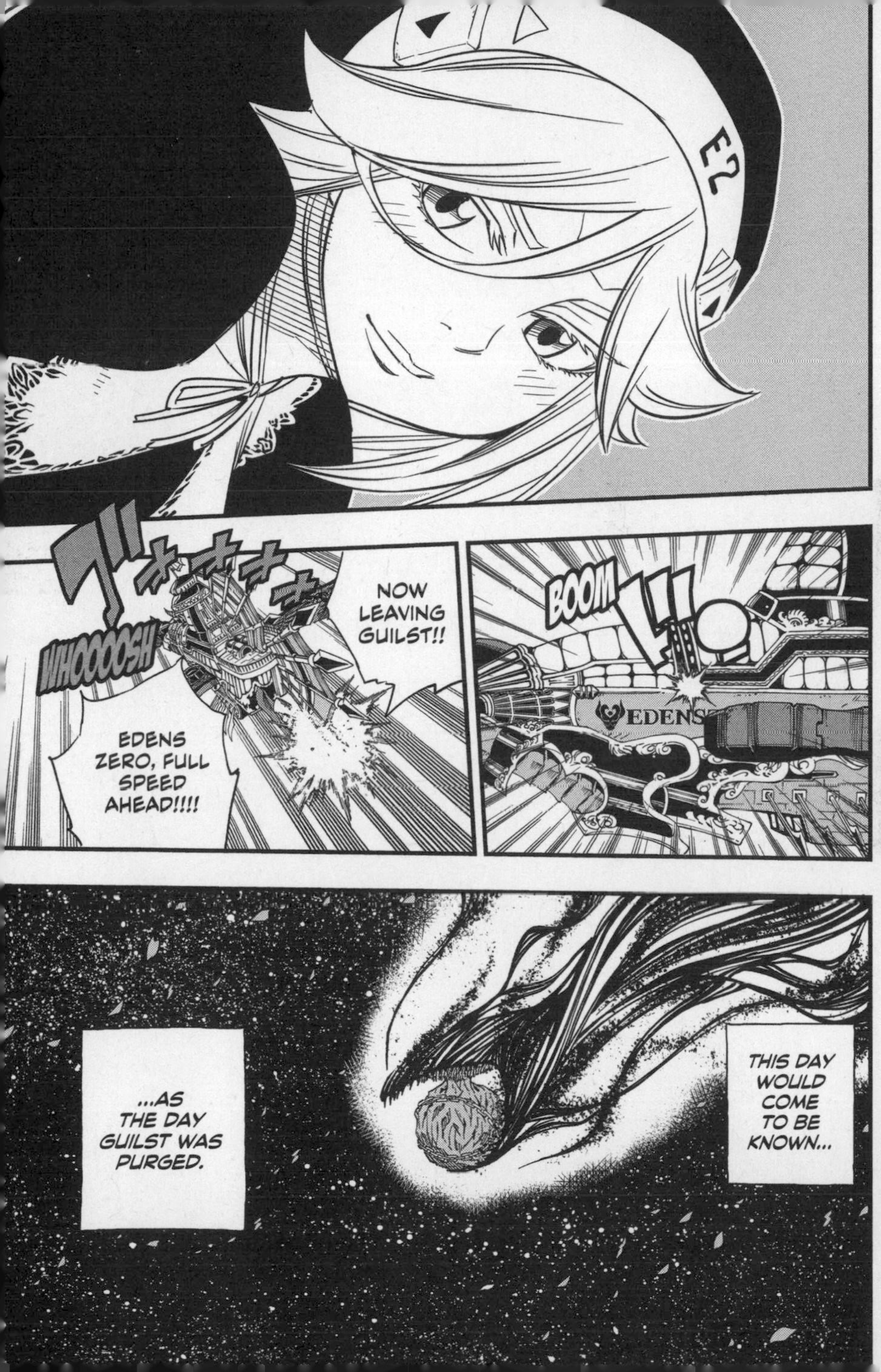
BOOM
EDENS
NOW LEAVING GUILST!!
WHOOOOSH
EDENS ZERO, FULL SPEED AHEAD!!!!
THIS DAY WOULD COME TO BE KNOWN...
...AS THE DAY GUILST WAS PURGED.

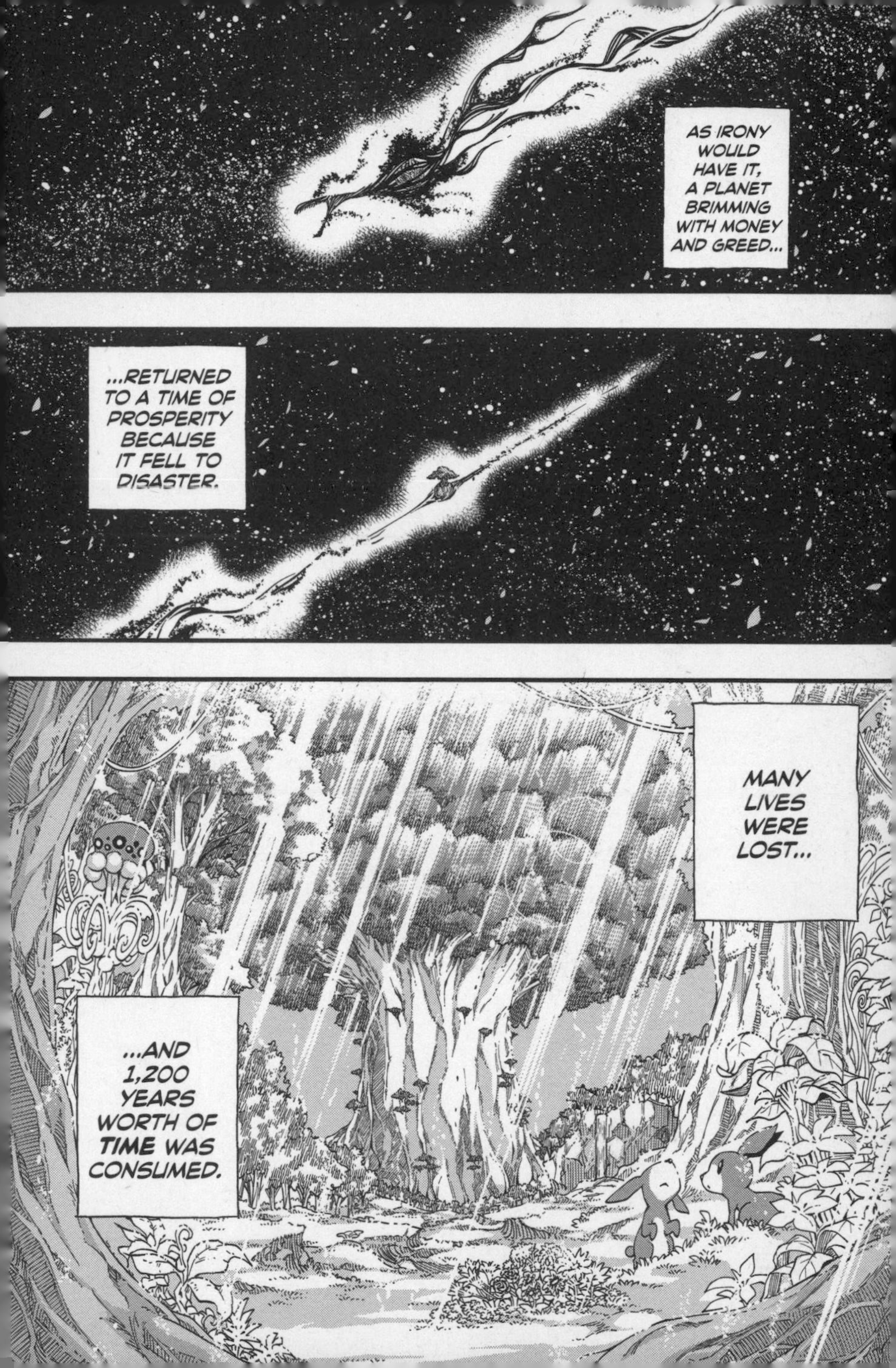
AS IRONY WOULD HAVE IT, A PLANET BRIMMING WITH MONEY AND GREED...
...RETURNED TO A TIME OF PROSPERITY BECAUSE IT FELL TO DISASTER.
MANY LIVES WERE LOST...
...AND 1,200 YEARS WORTH OF TIME WAS CONSUMED.

CHAPTER 28: NEW FRIENDS

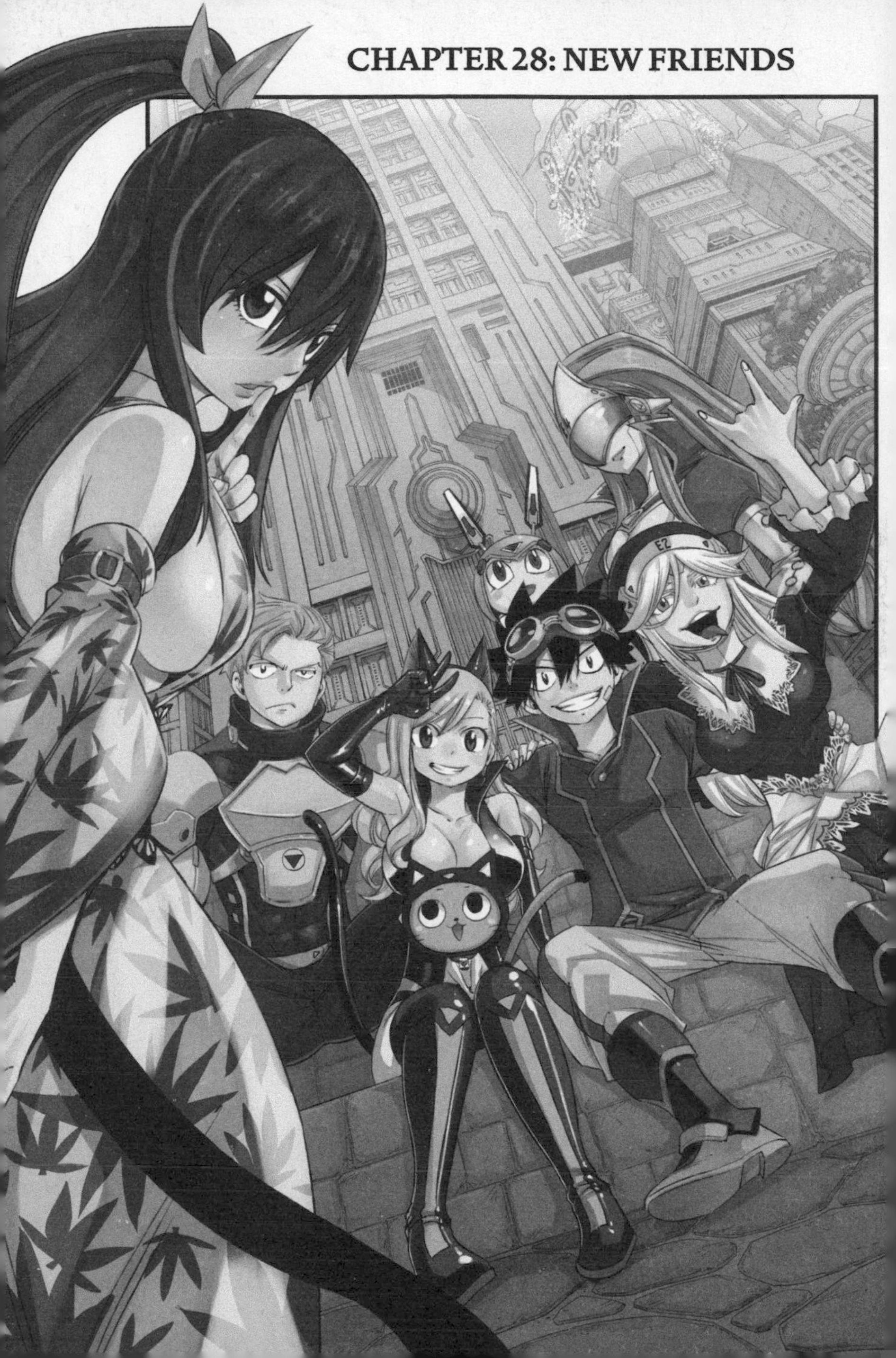

EDENSZERO

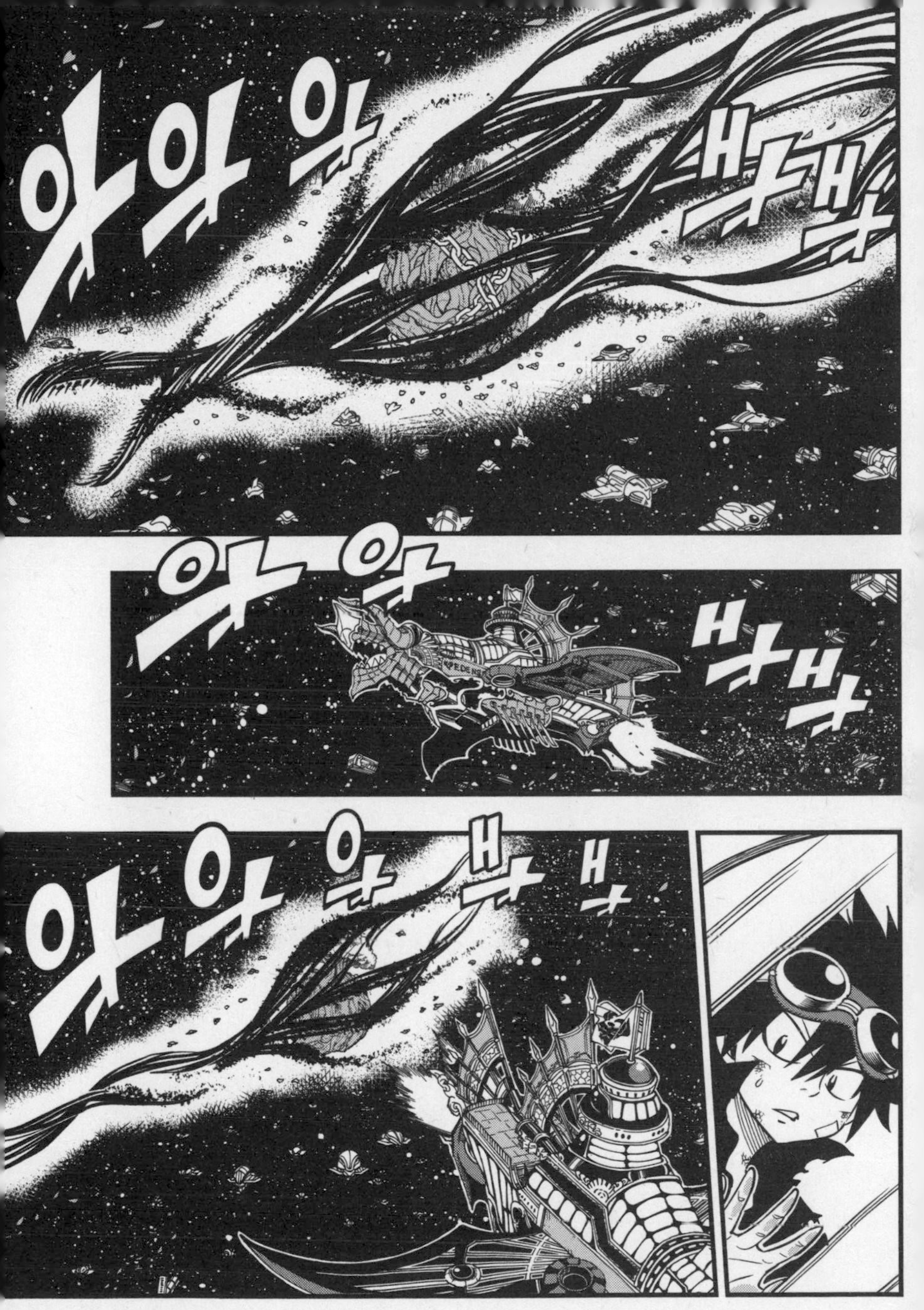

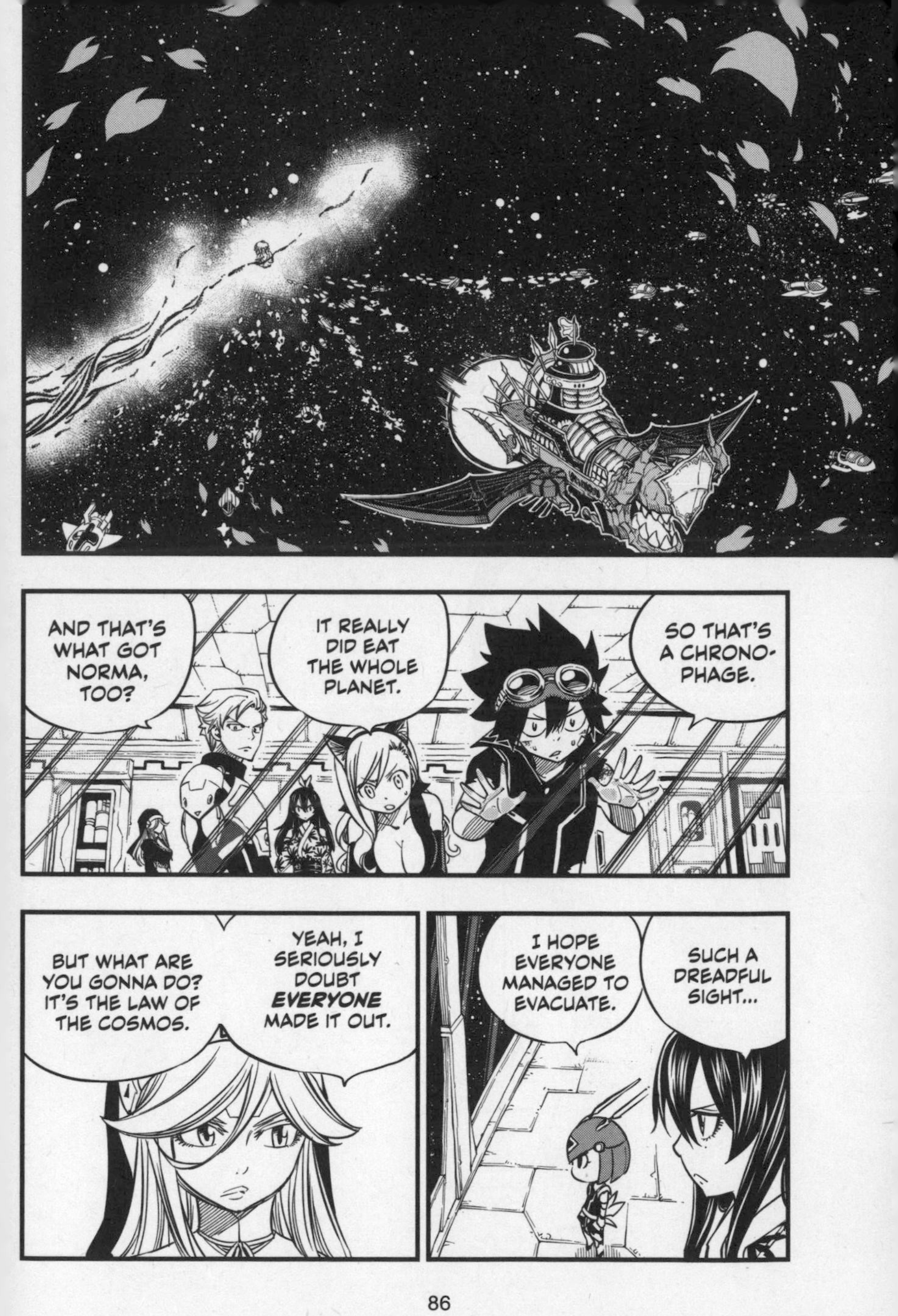
SO THAT'S A CHRONO-PHAGE.
IT REALLY DID EAT THE WHOLE PLANET.
AND THAT'S WHAT GOT NORMA, TOO?
SUCH A DREADFUL SIGHT...
I HOPE EVERYONE MANAGED TO EVACUATE.
YEAH, I SERIOUSLY DOUBT *EVERYONE* MADE IT OUT.
BUT WHAT ARE YOU GONNA DO? IT'S THE LAW OF THE COSMOS.

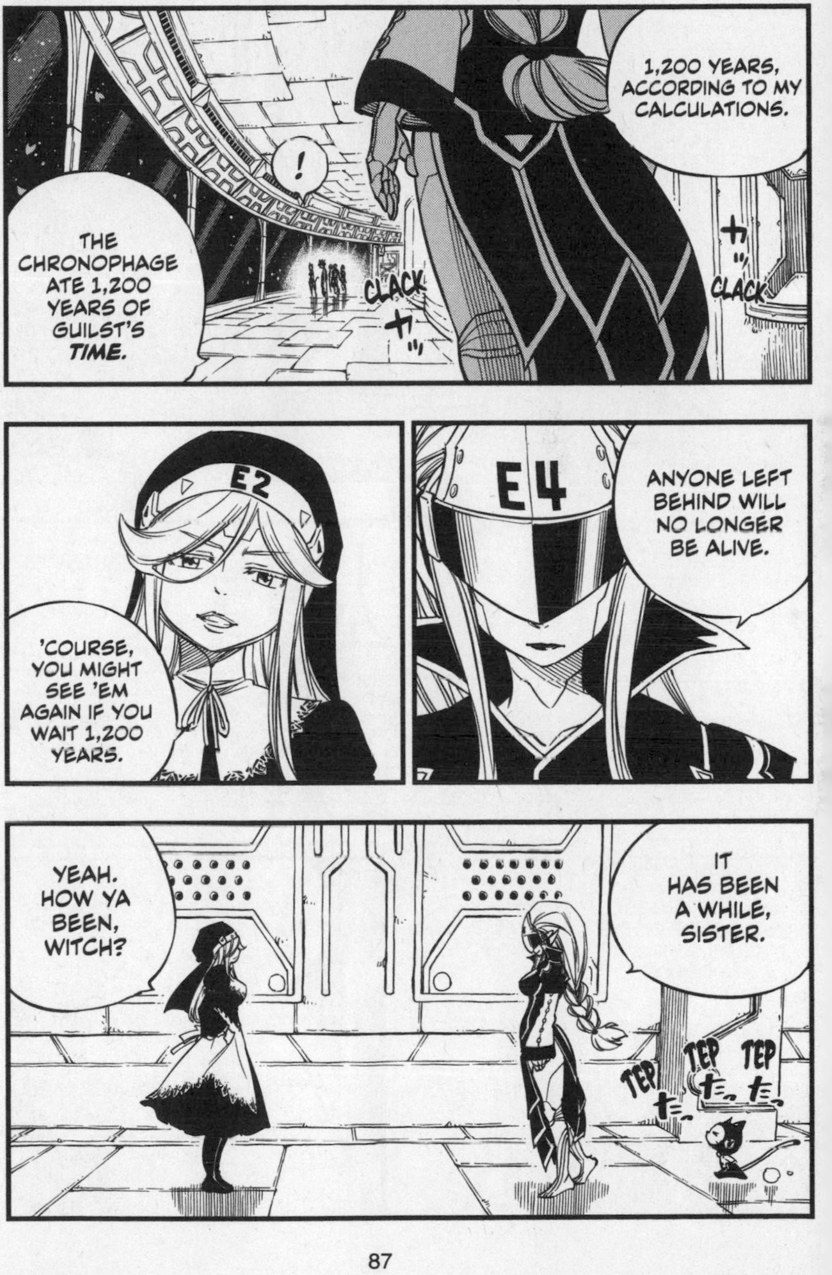
1,200 YEARS, ACCORDING TO MY CALCULATIONS.
!
CLACK
CLACK
THE CHRONOPHAGE ATE 1,200 YEARS OF GUILST'S *TIME*.
ANYONE LEFT BEHIND WILL NO LONGER BE ALIVE.
'COURSE, YOU MIGHT SEE 'EM AGAIN IF YOU WAIT 1,200 YEARS.
IT HAS BEEN A WHILE, SISTER.
TEP TEP TEP
YEAH. HOW YA BEEN, WITCH?

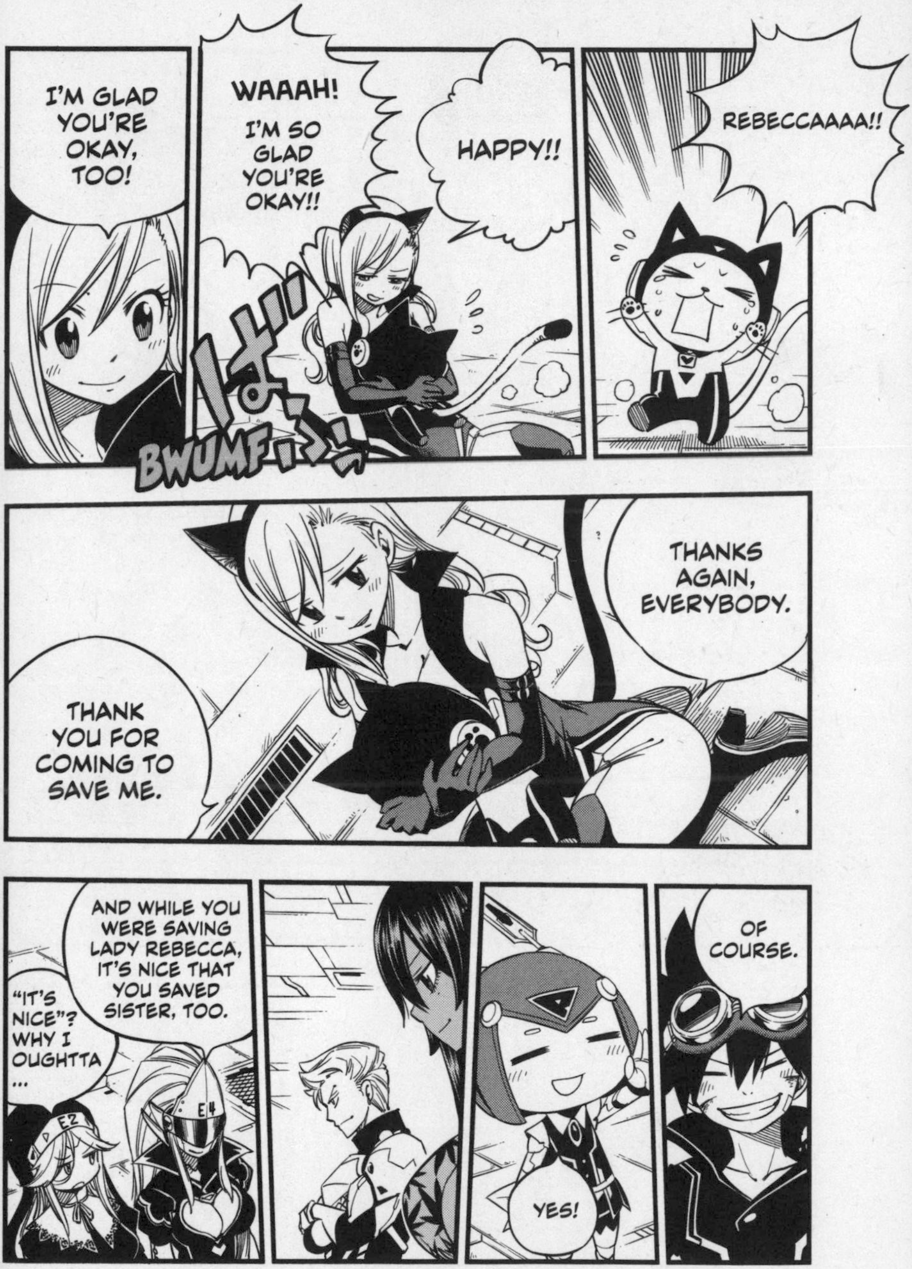
REBECCAAAA!!
HAPPY!!
WAAAH!
I'M SO GLAD YOU'RE OKAY!!
BWUMF
I'M GLAD YOU'RE OKAY, TOO!
THANKS AGAIN, EVERYBODY.
THANK YOU FOR COMING TO SAVE ME.
OF COURSE.
YES!
AND WHILE YOU WERE SAVING LADY REBECCA, IT'S NICE THAT YOU SAVED SISTER, TOO.
"IT'S NICE"? WHY I OUGHTTA ...

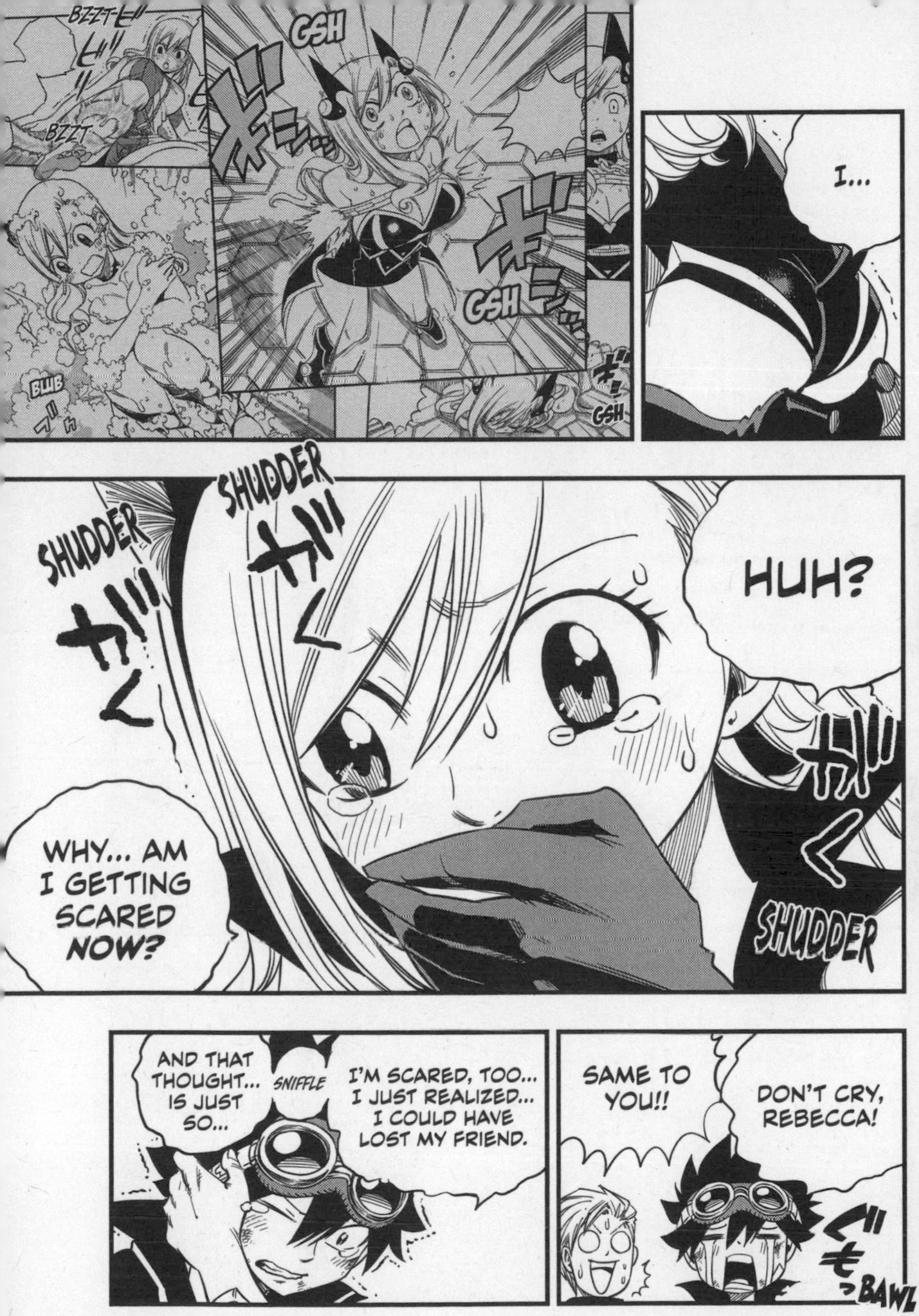
I...
GSH
GSH
GSH
BZZT
BZZT
BUB
HUH?
SHUDDER
SHUDDER
SHUDDER
WHY... AM I GETTING SCARED NOW?
DON'T CRY, REBECCA!
SAME TO YOU!!
BAWL
I'M SCARED, TOO... I JUST REALIZED... I COULD HAVE LOST MY FRIEND.
SNIFFLE
AND THAT THOUGHT... IS JUST SO...

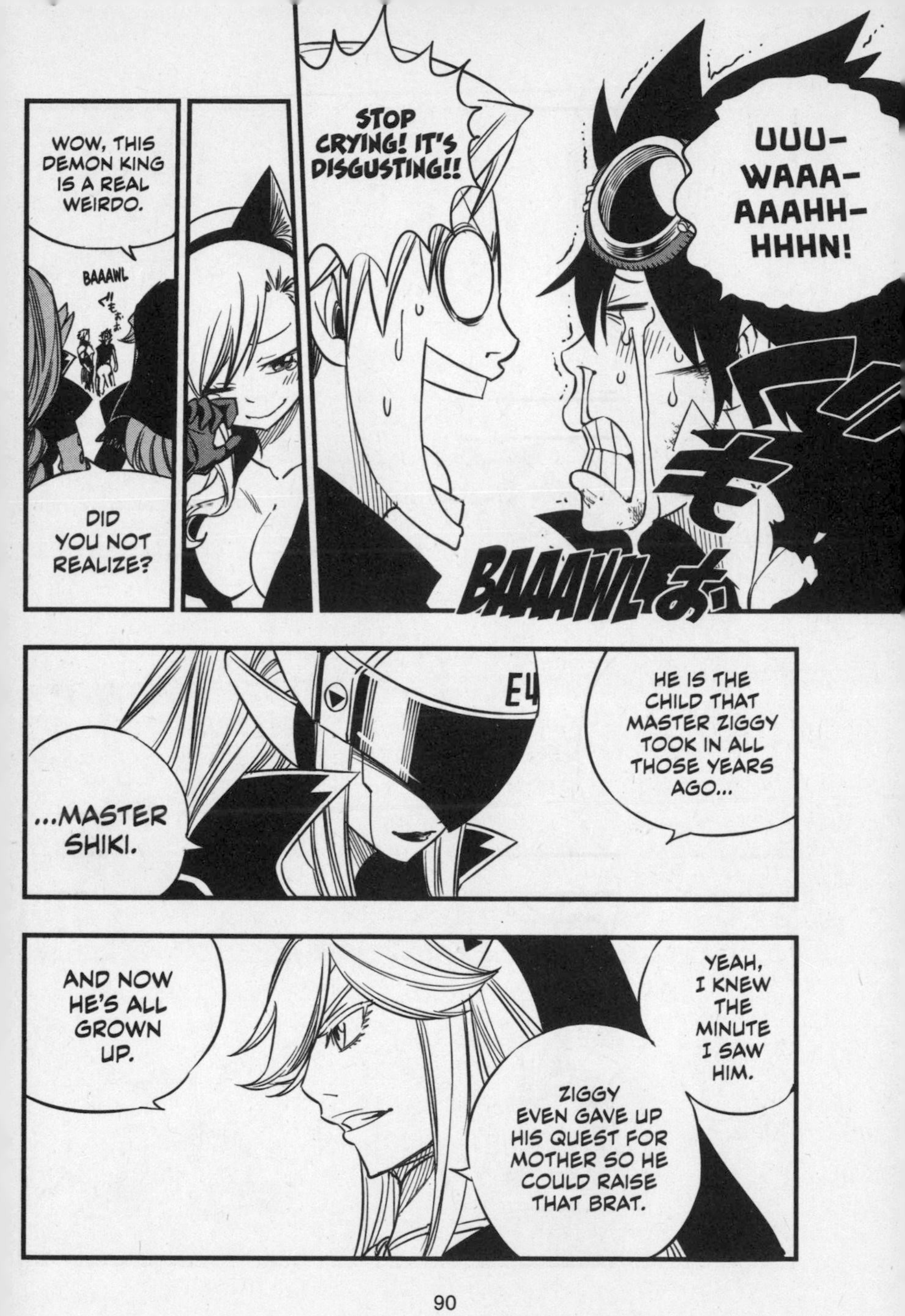
UUU-WAAA-AAAHH-HHHN!
BAAAWL
STOP CRYING! IT'S DISGUSTING!!
WOW, THIS DEMON KING IS A REAL WEIRDO.
BAAAWL
DID YOU NOT REALIZE?
HE IS THE CHILD THAT MASTER ZIGGY TOOK IN ALL THOSE YEARS AGO...
...MASTER SHIKI.
YEAH, I KNEW THE MINUTE I SAW HIM.
ZIGGY EVEN GAVE UP HIS QUEST FOR MOTHER SO HE COULD RAISE THAT BRAT.
AND NOW HE'S ALL GROWN UP.

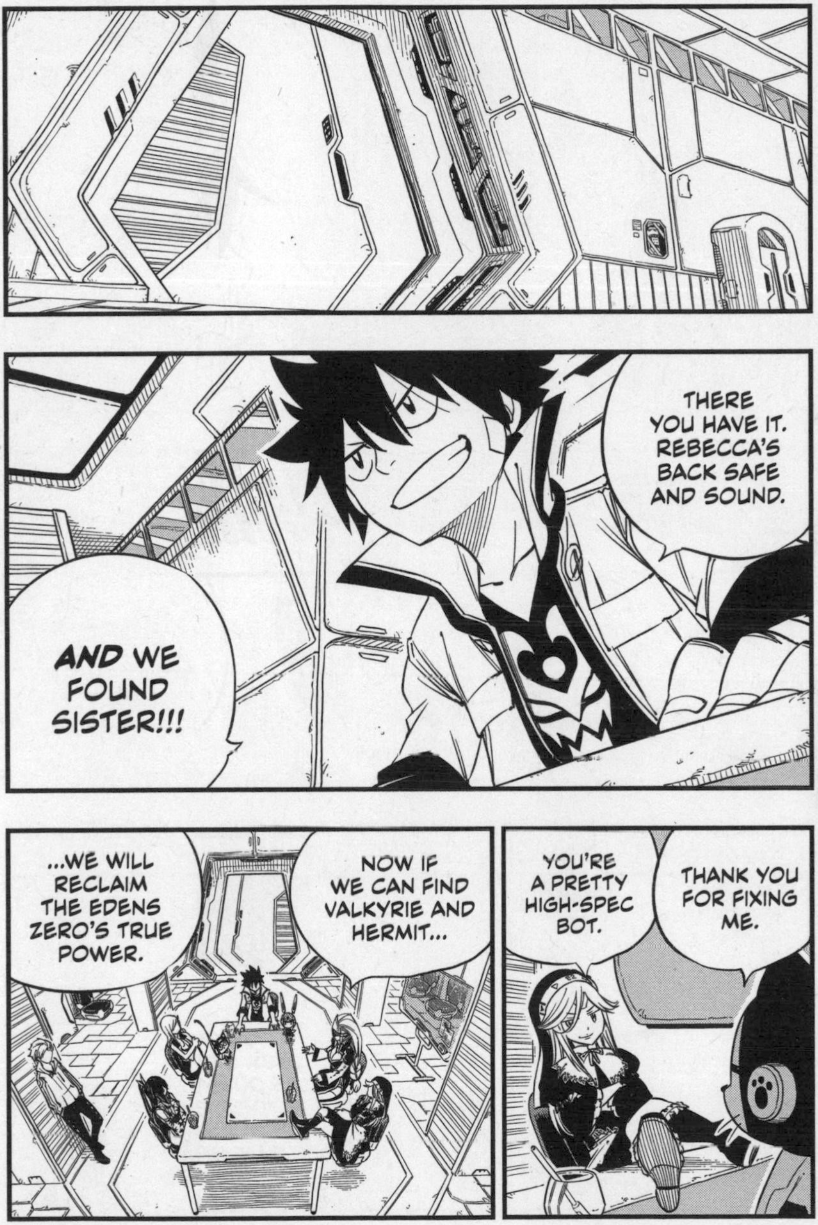
THERE YOU HAVE IT. REBECCA'S BACK SAFE AND SOUND.
AND WE FOUND SISTER!!!
THANK YOU FOR FIXING ME.
YOU'RE A PRETTY HIGH-SPEC BOT.
NOW IF WE CAN FIND VALKYRIE AND HERMIT...
...WE WILL RECLAIM THE EDENS ZERO'S TRUE POWER.

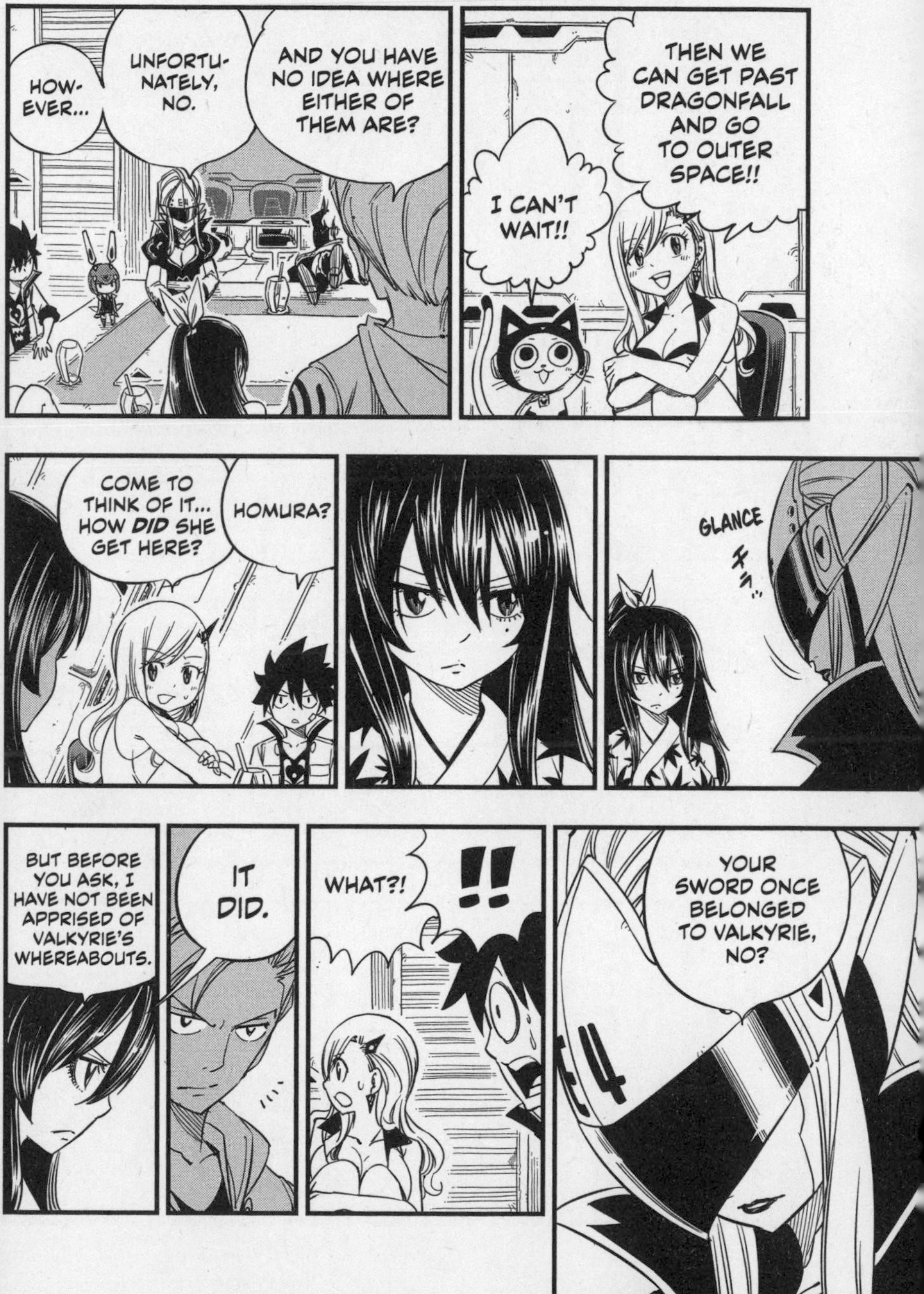
THEN WE CAN GET PAST DRAGONFALL AND GO TO OUTER SPACE!!
I CAN'T WAIT!!
AND YOU HAVE NO IDEA WHERE EITHER OF THEM ARE?
UNFORTU-NATELY, NO.
HOW-EVER...
GLANCE
チラッ
HOMURA?
COME TO THINK OF IT... HOW *DID* SHE GET HERE?
YOUR SWORD ONCE BELONGED TO VALKYRIE, NO?
!!
WHAT?!
IT DID.
BUT BEFORE YOU ASK, I HAVE NOT BEEN APPRISED OF VALKYRIE'S WHEREABOUTS.

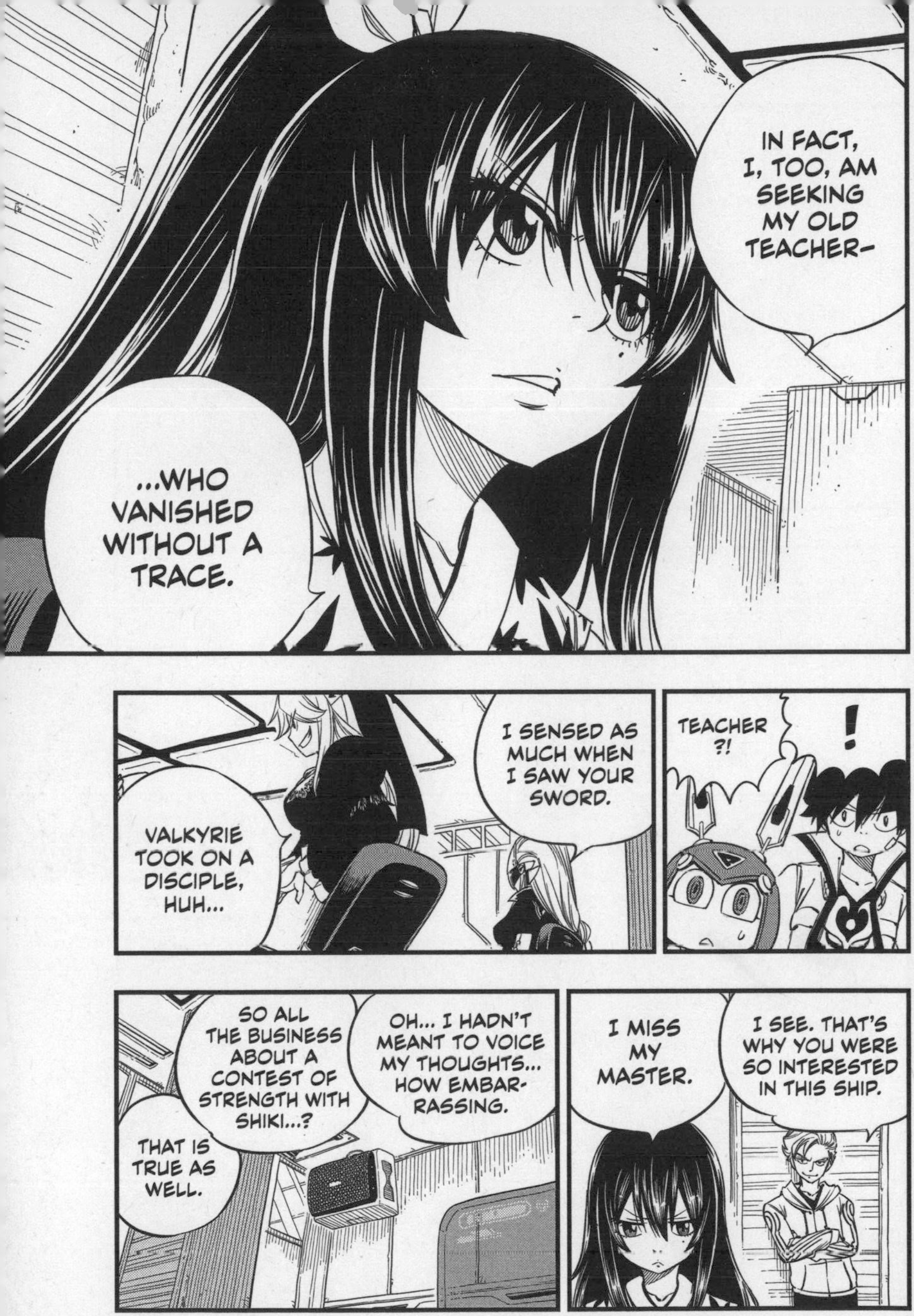
IN FACT, I, TOO, AM SEEKING MY OLD TEACHER—
...WHO VANISHED WITHOUT A TRACE.
TEACHER?!
!
I SENSED AS MUCH WHEN I SAW YOUR SWORD.
VALKYRIE TOOK ON A DISCIPLE, HUH...
I SEE. THAT'S WHY YOU WERE SO INTERESTED IN THIS SHIP.
I MISS MY MASTER.
OH... I HADN'T MEANT TO VOICE MY THOUGHTS... HOW EMBARRASSING.
SO ALL THE BUSINESS ABOUT A CONTEST OF STRENGTH WITH SHIKI...?
THAT IS TRUE AS WELL.

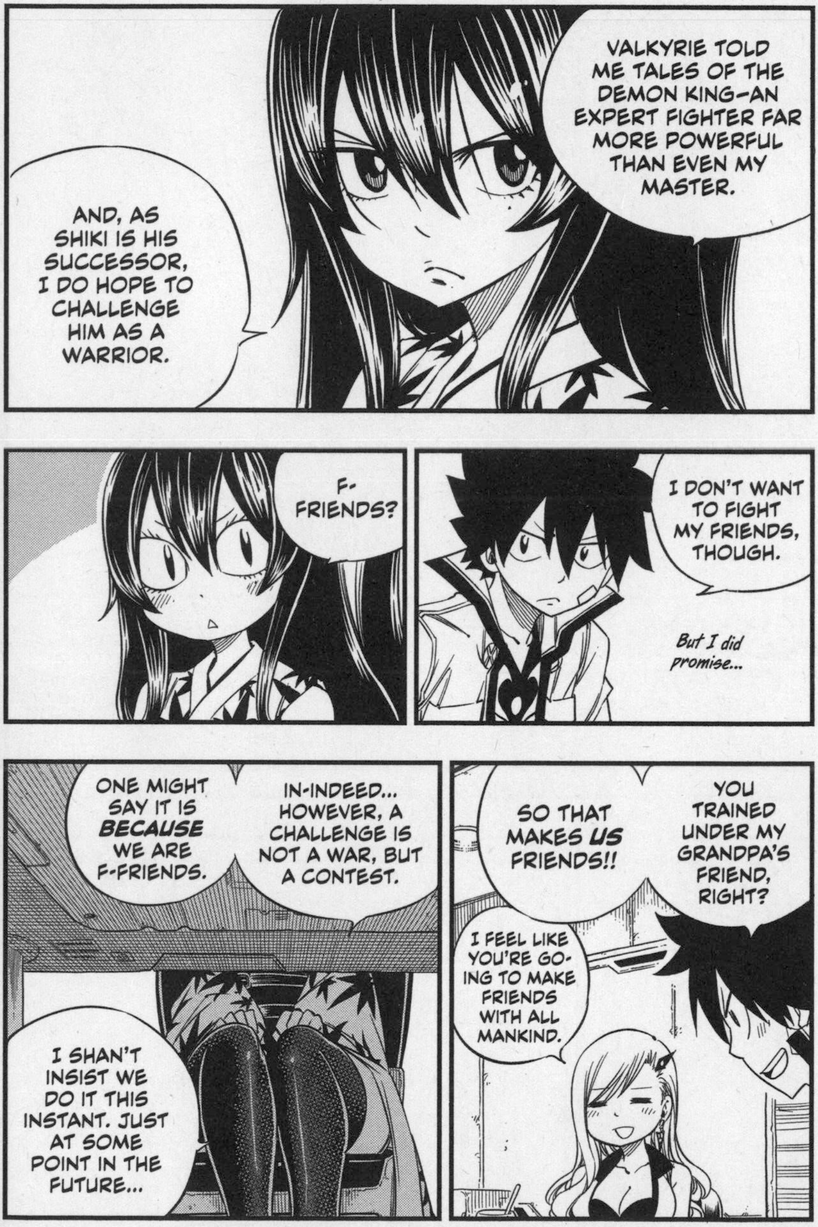
VALKYRIE TOLD ME TALES OF THE DEMON KING—AN EXPERT FIGHTER FAR MORE POWERFUL THAN EVEN MY MASTER.
AND, AS SHIKI IS HIS SUCCESSOR, I DO HOPE TO CHALLENGE HIM AS A WARRIOR.
I DON'T WANT TO FIGHT MY FRIENDS, THOUGH.
But I did promise...
F-FRIENDS?
YOU TRAINED UNDER MY GRANDPA'S FRIEND, RIGHT?
SO THAT MAKES US FRIENDS!!
I FEEL LIKE YOU'RE GO-ING TO MAKE FRIENDS WITH ALL MANKIND.
IN-INDEED... HOWEVER, A CHALLENGE IS NOT A WAR, BUT A CONTEST.
ONE MIGHT SAY IT IS BECAUSE WE ARE F-FRIENDS.
I SHAN'T INSIST WE DO IT THIS INSTANT. JUST AT SOME POINT IN THE FUTURE...

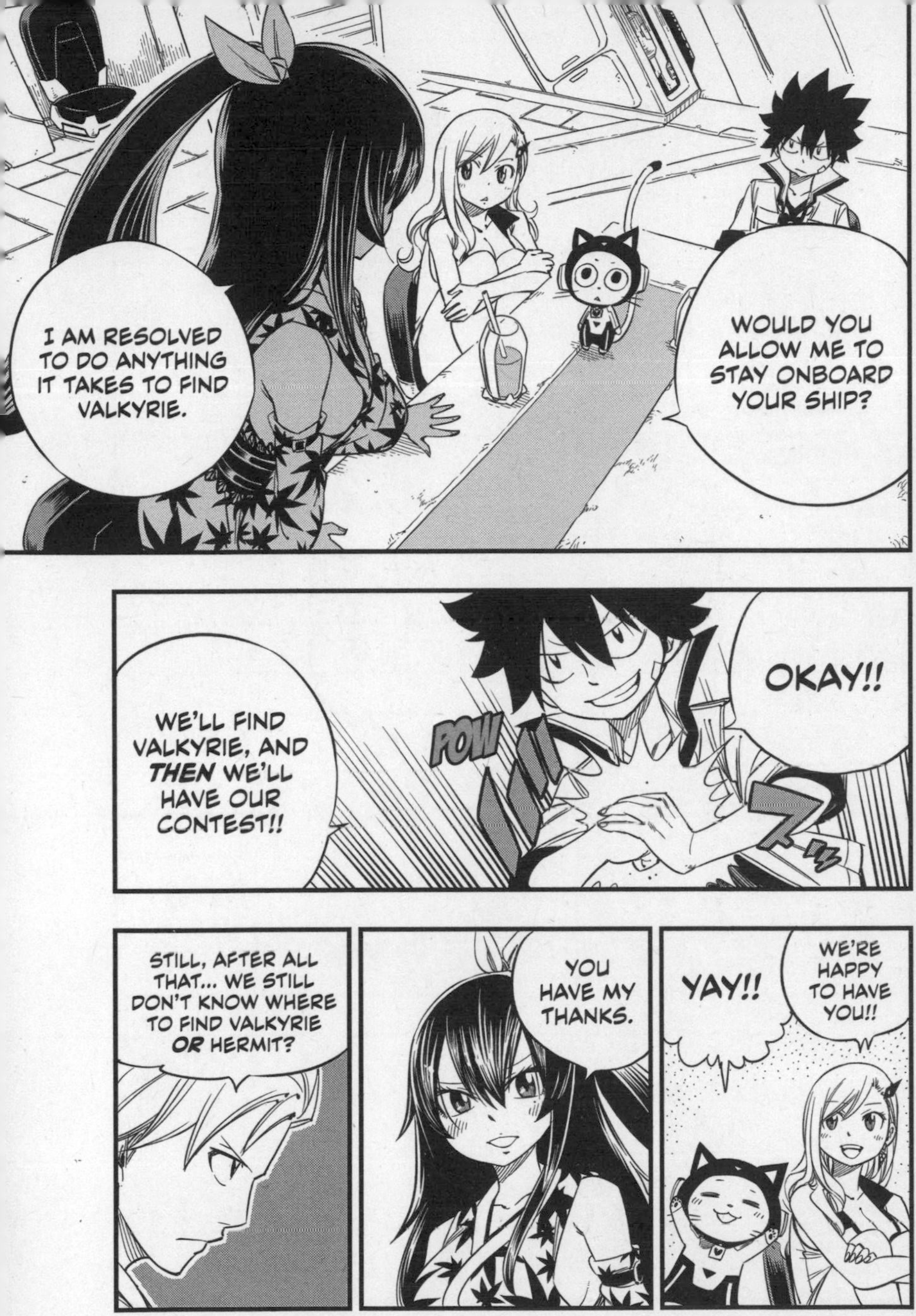
WOULD YOU ALLOW ME TO STAY ONBOARD YOUR SHIP?
I AM RESOLVED TO DO ANYTHING IT TAKES TO FIND VALKYRIE.
OKAY!!
POW
WE'LL FIND VALKYRIE, AND *THEN* WE'LL HAVE OUR CONTEST!!
WE'RE HAPPY TO HAVE YOU!!
YAY!!
YOU HAVE MY THANKS.
STILL, AFTER ALL THAT... WE STILL DON'T KNOW WHERE TO FIND VALKYRIE *OR* HERMIT?

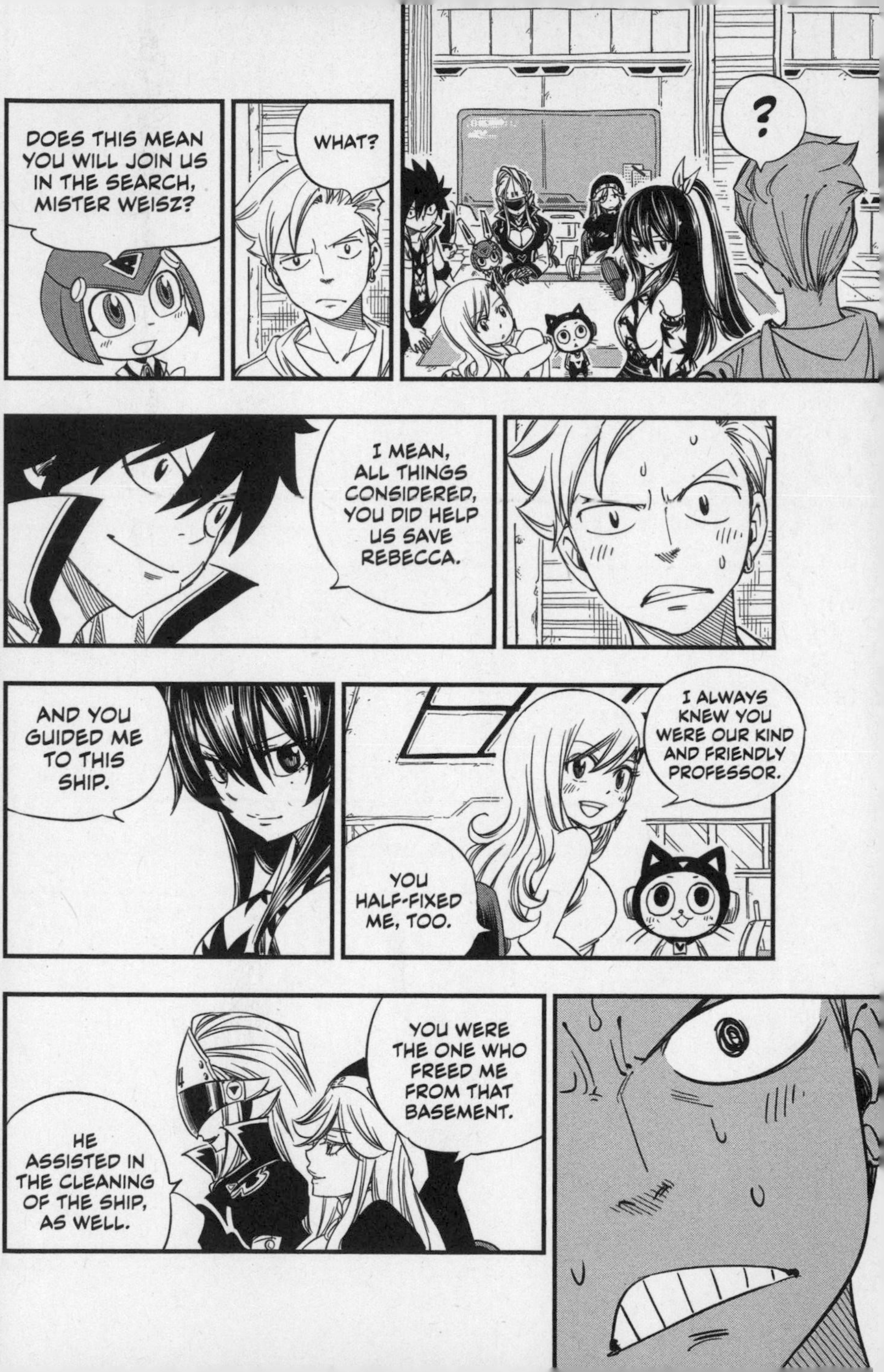
?
WHAT?
DOES THIS MEAN YOU WILL JOIN US IN THE SEARCH, MISTER WEISZ?
I MEAN, ALL THINGS CONSIDERED, YOU DID HELP US SAVE REBECCA.
I ALWAYS KNEW YOU WERE OUR KIND AND FRIENDLY PROFESSOR.
YOU HALF-FIXED ME, TOO.
AND YOU GUIDED ME TO THIS SHIP.
YOU WERE THE ONE WHO FREED ME FROM THAT BASEMENT.
HE ASSISTED IN THE CLEANING OF THE SHIP, AS WELL.

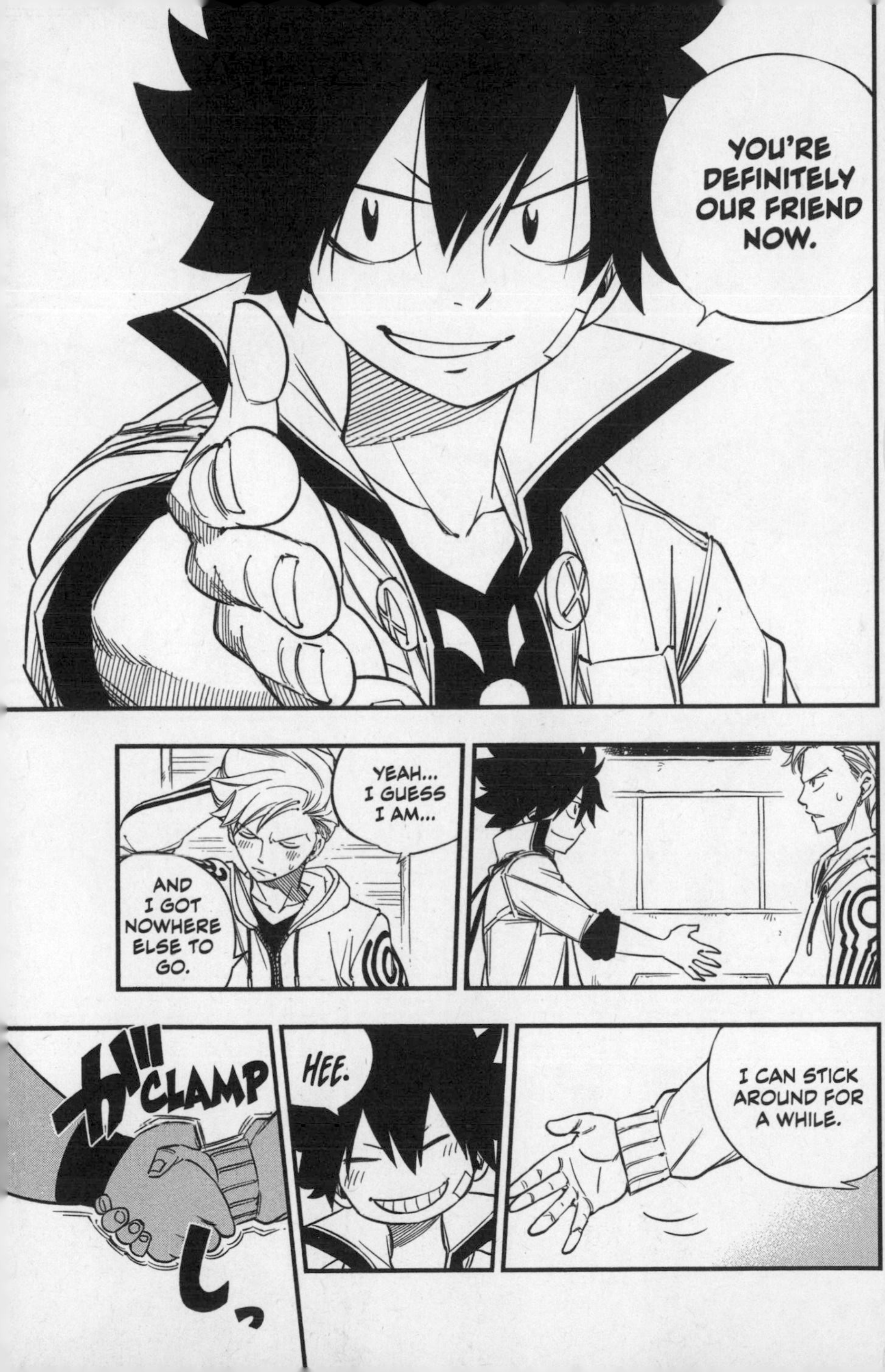
YOU'RE DEFINITELY OUR FRIEND NOW.
YEAH... I GUESS I AM...
AND I GOT NOWHERE ELSE TO GO.
I CAN STICK AROUND FOR A WHILE.
HEE.
CLAMP

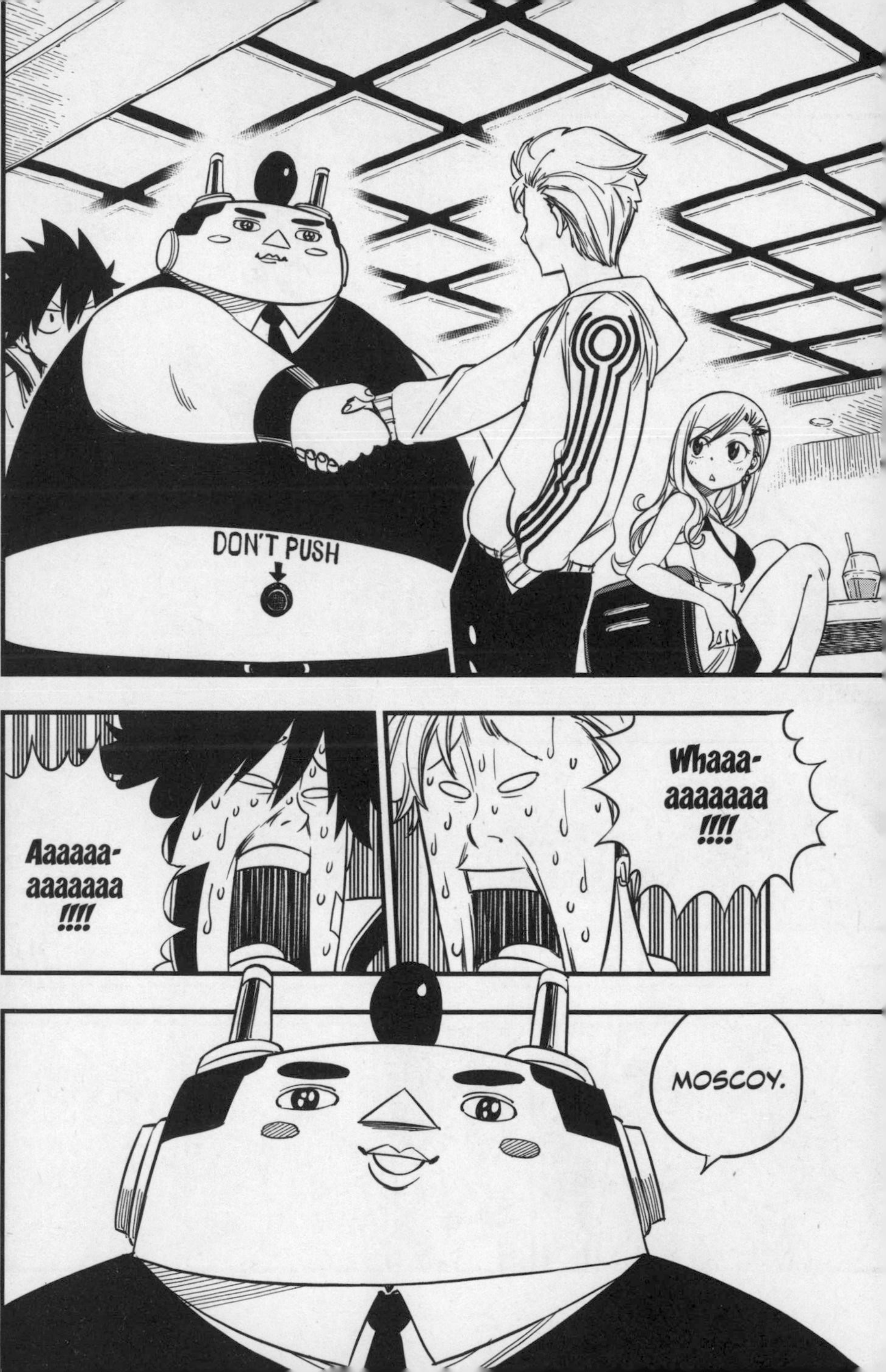
DON'T PUSH
Whaaa-aaaaaaa!!!!
Aaaaaa-aaaaaaa!!!!
MOSCOY.

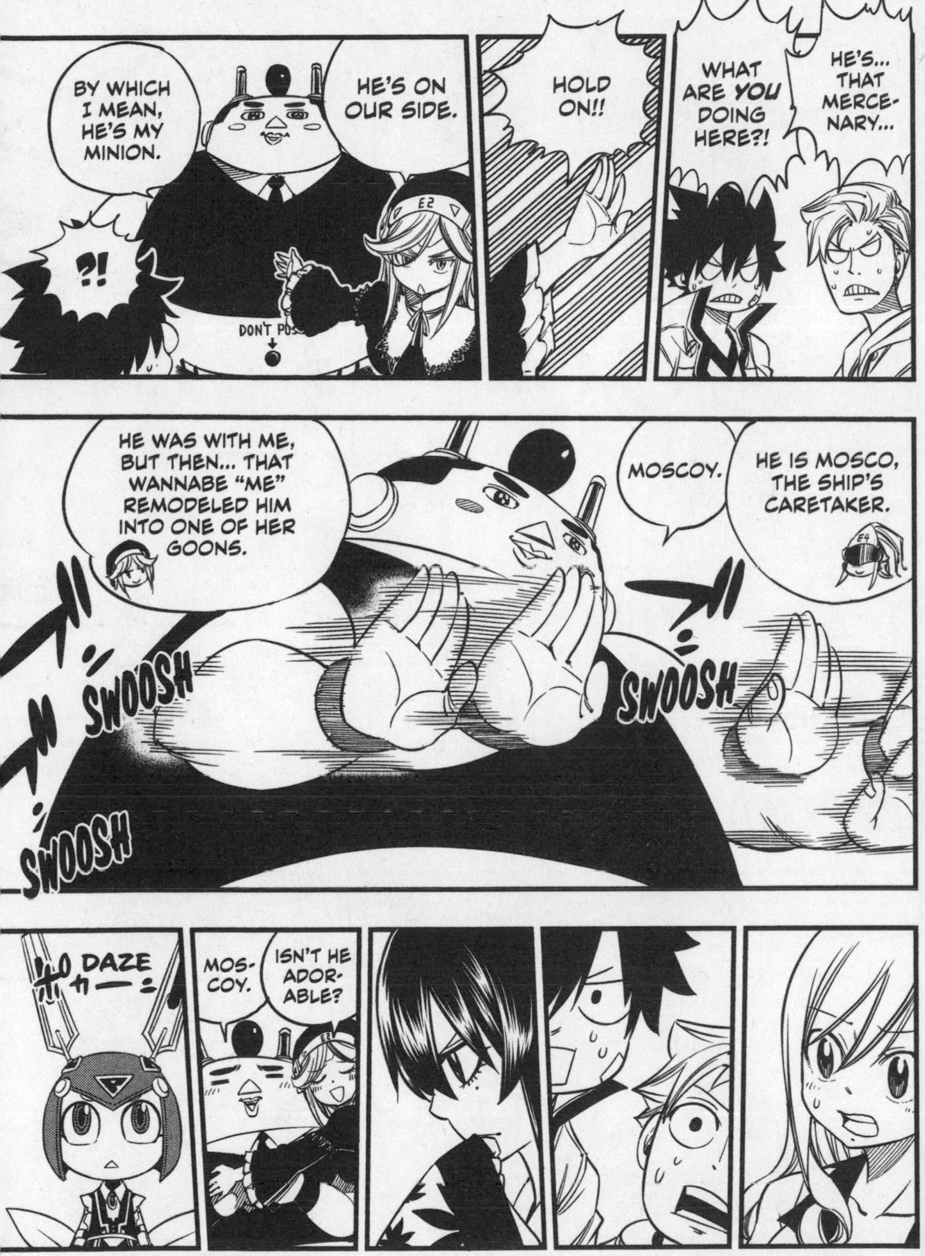
HE'S... THAT MERCE-NARY...
WHAT ARE YOU DOING HERE?!
HOLD ON!!
HE'S ON OUR SIDE.
BY WHICH I MEAN, HE'S MY MINION.
?!
DON'T PUS
HE IS MOSCO, THE SHIP'S CARETAKER.
MOSCOY.
HE WAS WITH ME, BUT THEN... THAT WANNABE "ME" REMODELED HIM INTO ONE OF HER GOONS.
SWOOSH
SWOOSH
SWOOSH
ISN'T HE ADOR-ABLE?
MOS-COY.
DAZE

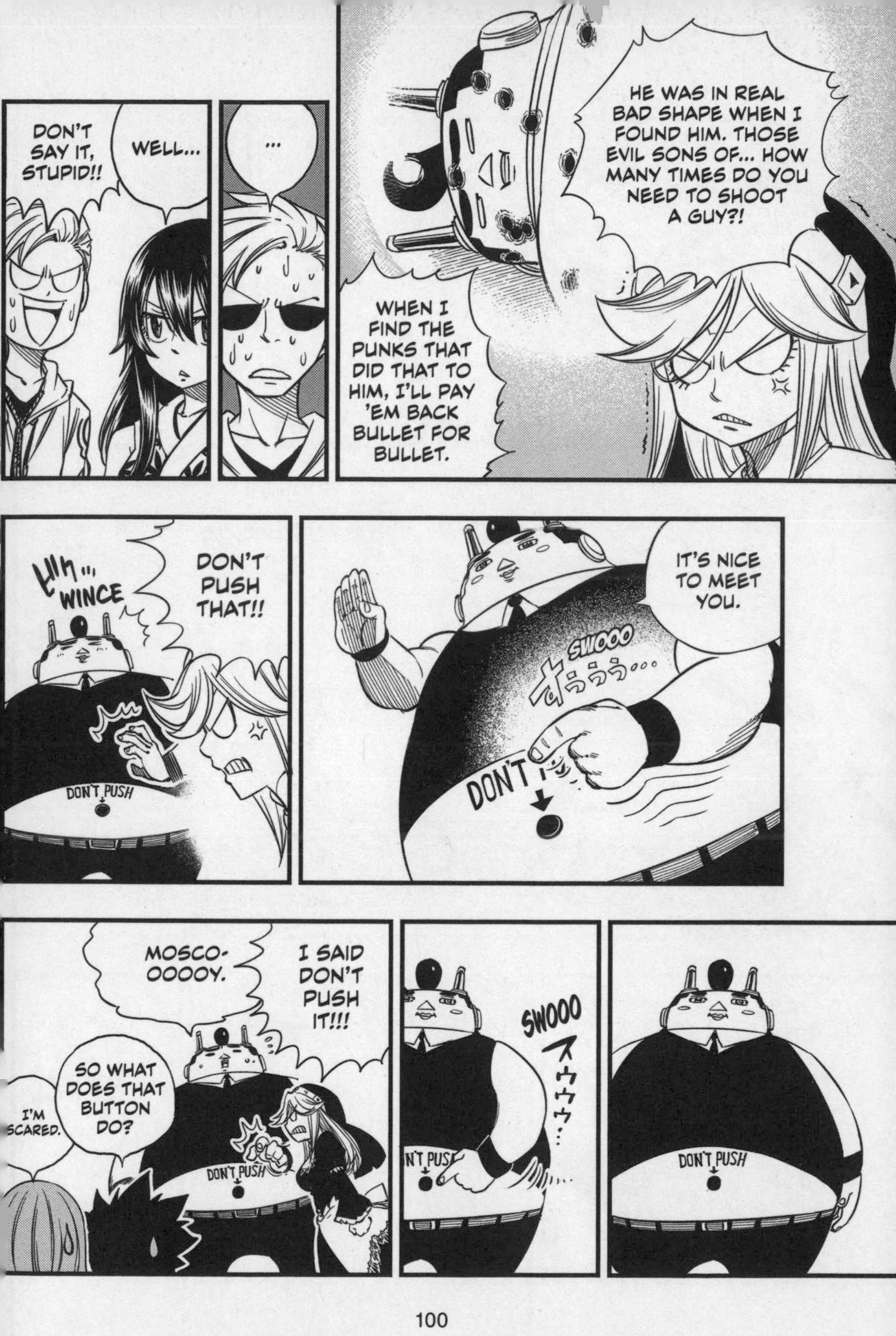
HE WAS IN REAL BAD SHAPE WHEN I FOUND HIM. THOSE EVIL SONS OF... HOW MANY TIMES DO YOU NEED TO SHOOT A GUY?!
WHEN I FIND THE PUNKS THAT DID THAT TO HIM, I'LL PAY 'EM BACK BULLET FOR BULLET.
...
WELL...
DON'T SAY IT, STUPID!!
IT'S NICE TO MEET YOU.
SWOOO
DON'T
DON'T PUSH THAT!!
WINCE
DON'T PUSH
DON'T PUSH
SWOOO
N'T PUSH
I SAID DON'T PUSH IT!!!
MOSCO-OOOOY.
SO WHAT DOES THAT BUTTON DO?
I'M SCARED.
DON'T PUSH

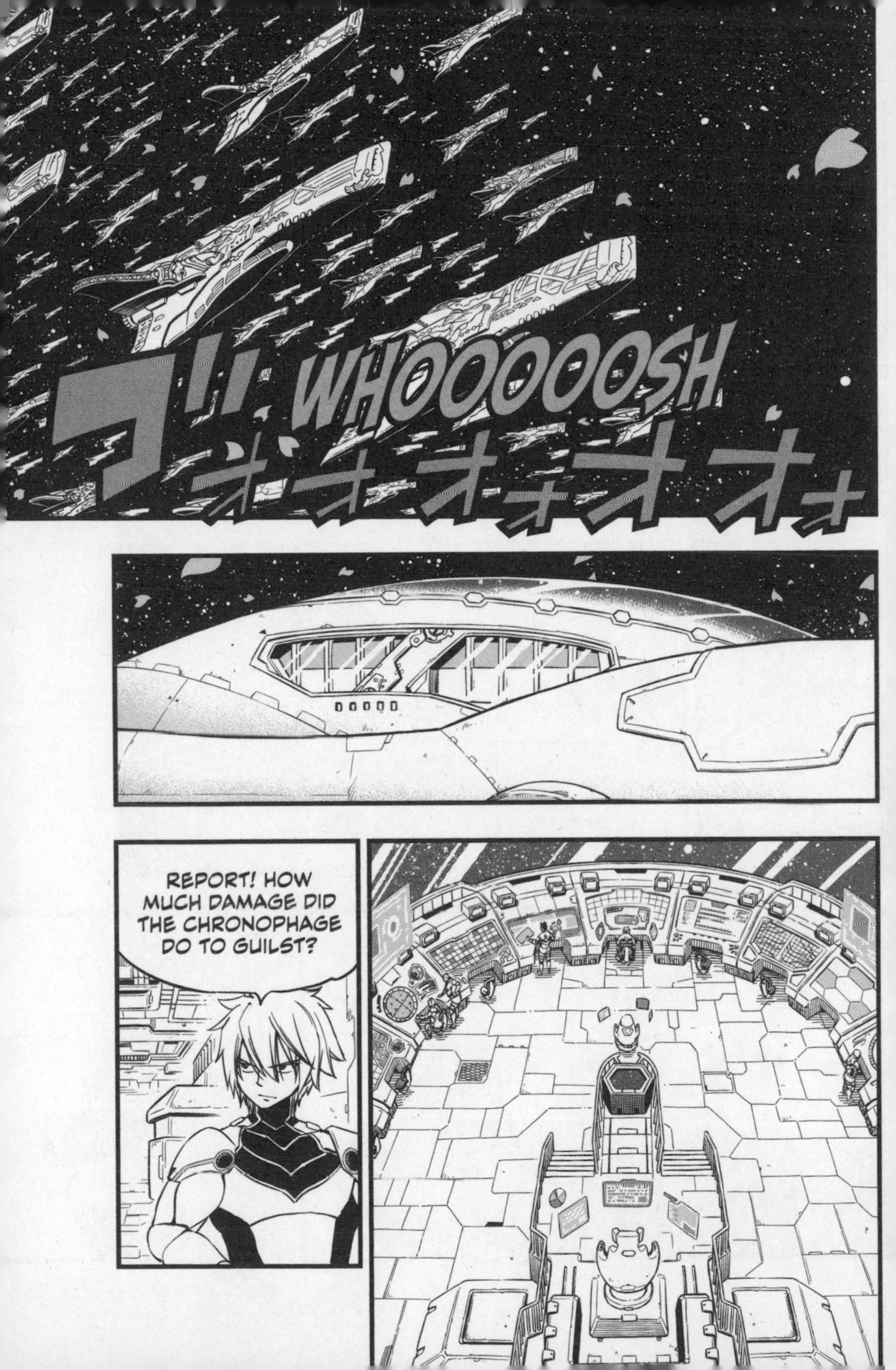
WHOOOOOSH
REPORT! HOW MUCH DAMAGE DID THE CHRONOPHAGE DO TO GUILST?

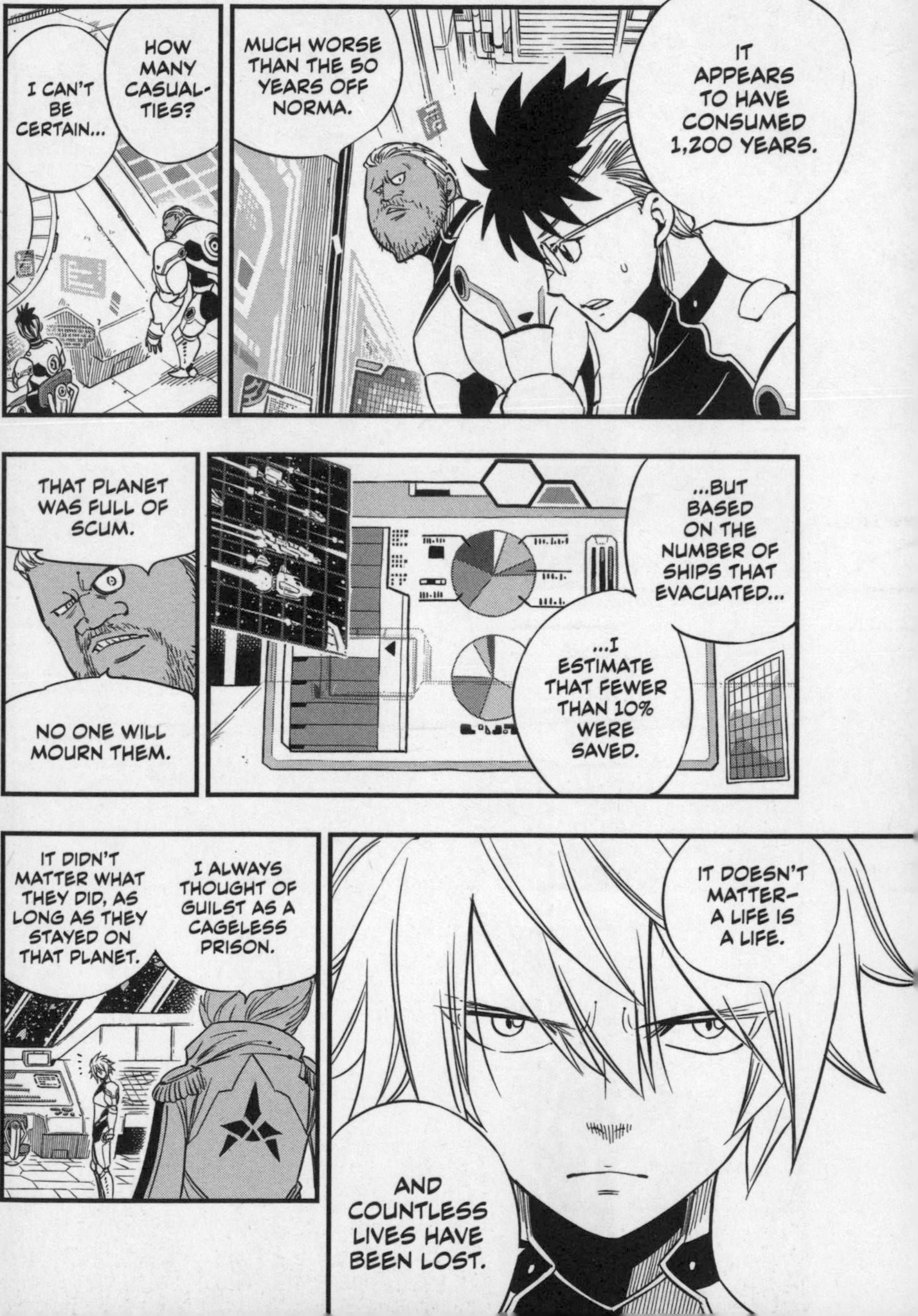
IT APPEARS TO HAVE CONSUMED 1,200 YEARS.
MUCH WORSE THAN THE 50 YEARS OFF NORMA.
HOW MANY CASUAL-TIES?
I CAN'T BE CERTAIN...
...BUT BASED ON THE NUMBER OF SHIPS THAT EVACUATED...
...I ESTIMATE THAT FEWER THAN 10% WERE SAVED.
THAT PLANET WAS FULL OF SCUM.
NO ONE WILL MOURN THEM.
IT DOESN'T MATTER– A LIFE IS A LIFE.
AND COUNTLESS LIVES HAVE BEEN LOST.
I ALWAYS THOUGHT OF GUILST AS A CAGELESS PRISON.
IT DIDN'T MATTER WHAT THEY DID, AS LONG AS THEY STAYED ON THAT PLANET.

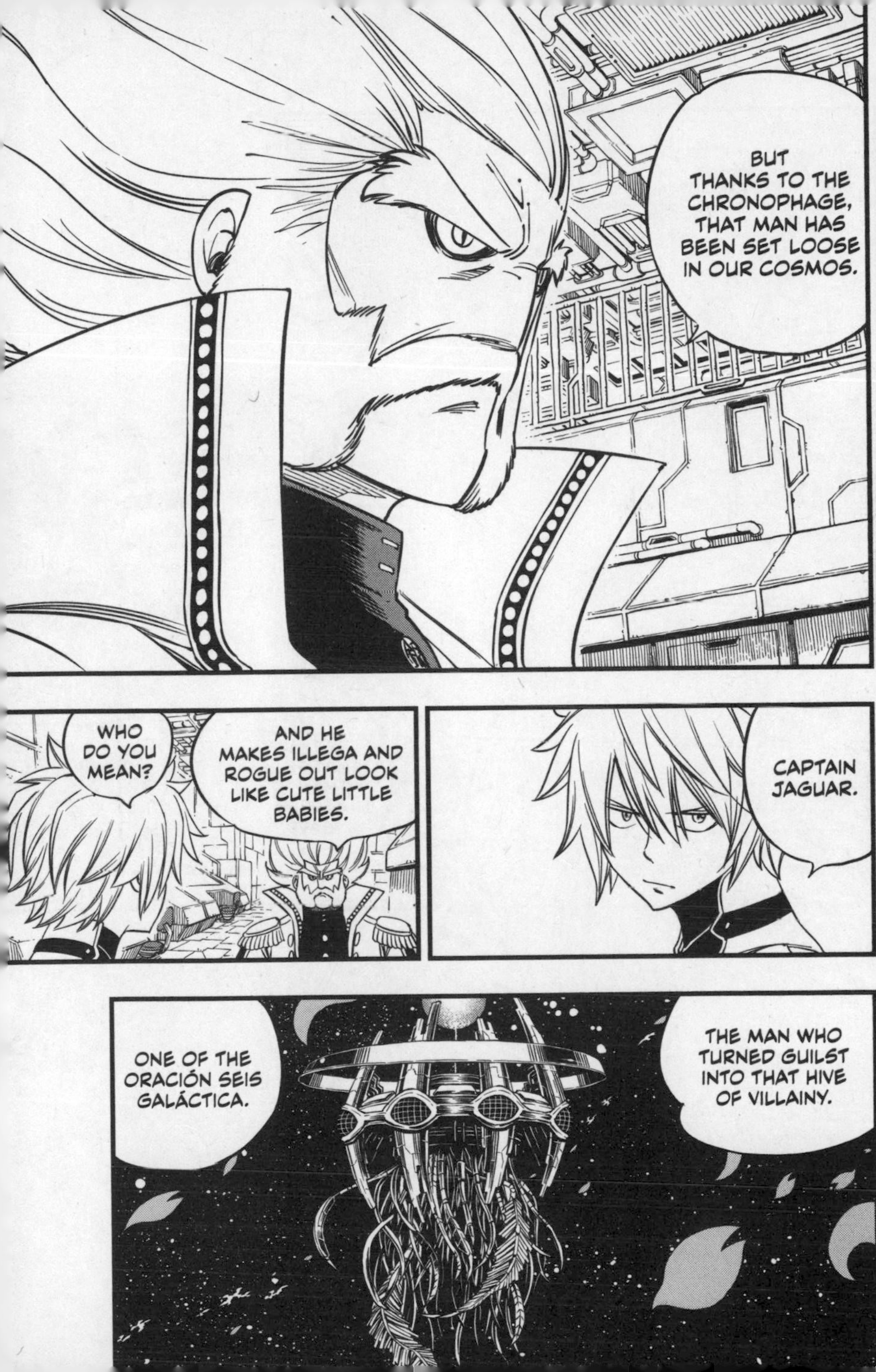
BUT THANKS TO THE CHRONOPHAGE, THAT MAN HAS BEEN SET LOOSE IN OUR COSMOS.
CAPTAIN JAGUAR.
AND HE MAKES ILLEGA AND ROGUE OUT LOOK LIKE CUTE LITTLE BABIES.
WHO DO YOU MEAN?
THE MAN WHO TURNED GUILST INTO THAT HIVE OF VILLAINY.
ONE OF THE ORACIÓN SEIS GALÁCTICA.

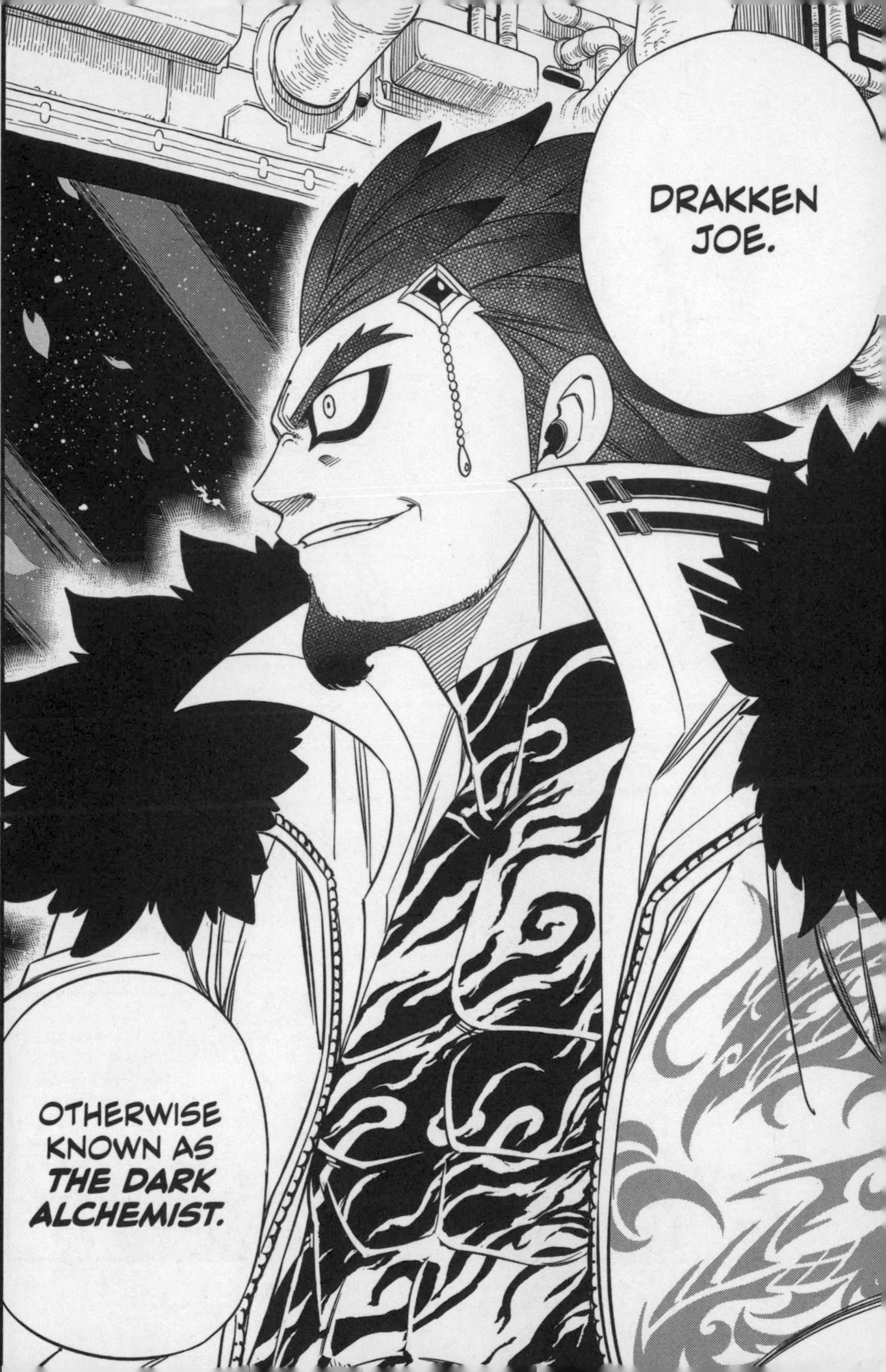
DRAKKEN JOE.
OTHERWISE KNOWN AS THE DARK ALCHEMIST.

EDENS ZERO

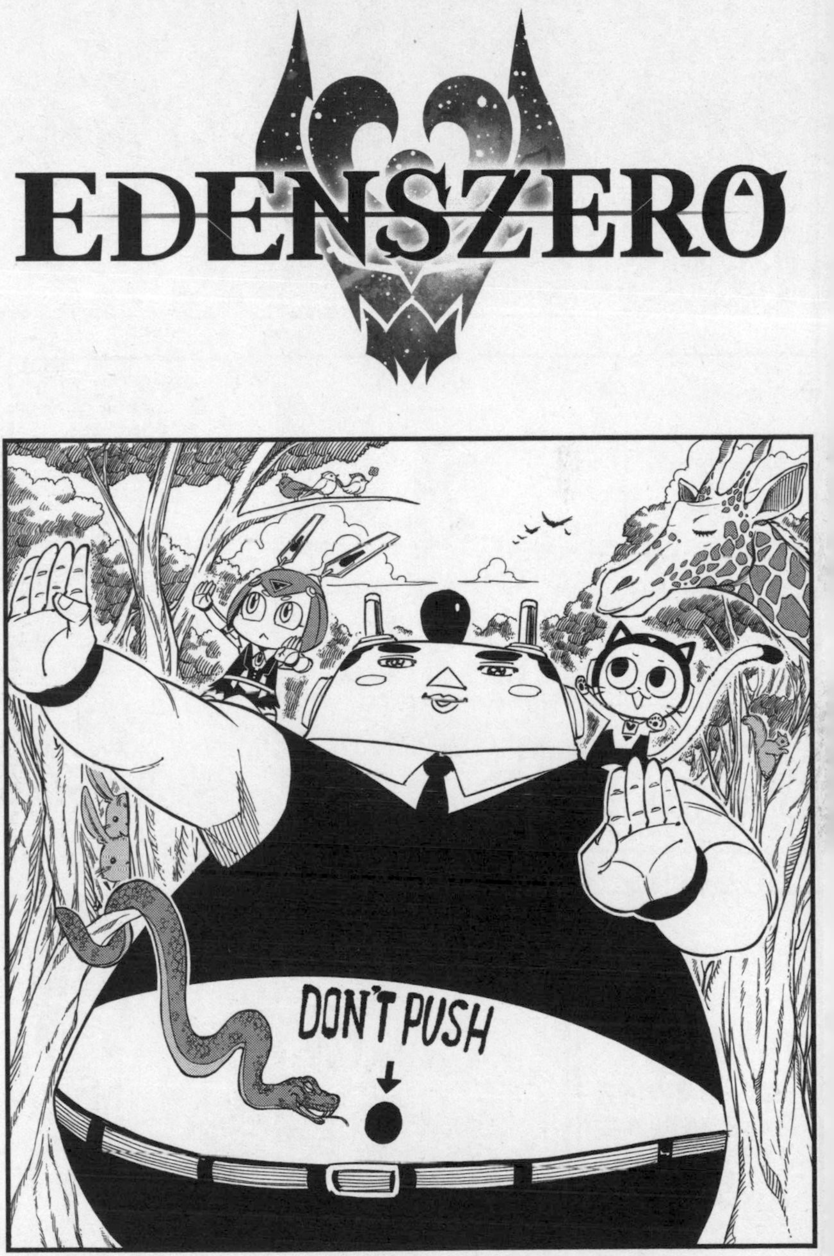
DON'T PUSH

CHAPTER 29: IRON HILL

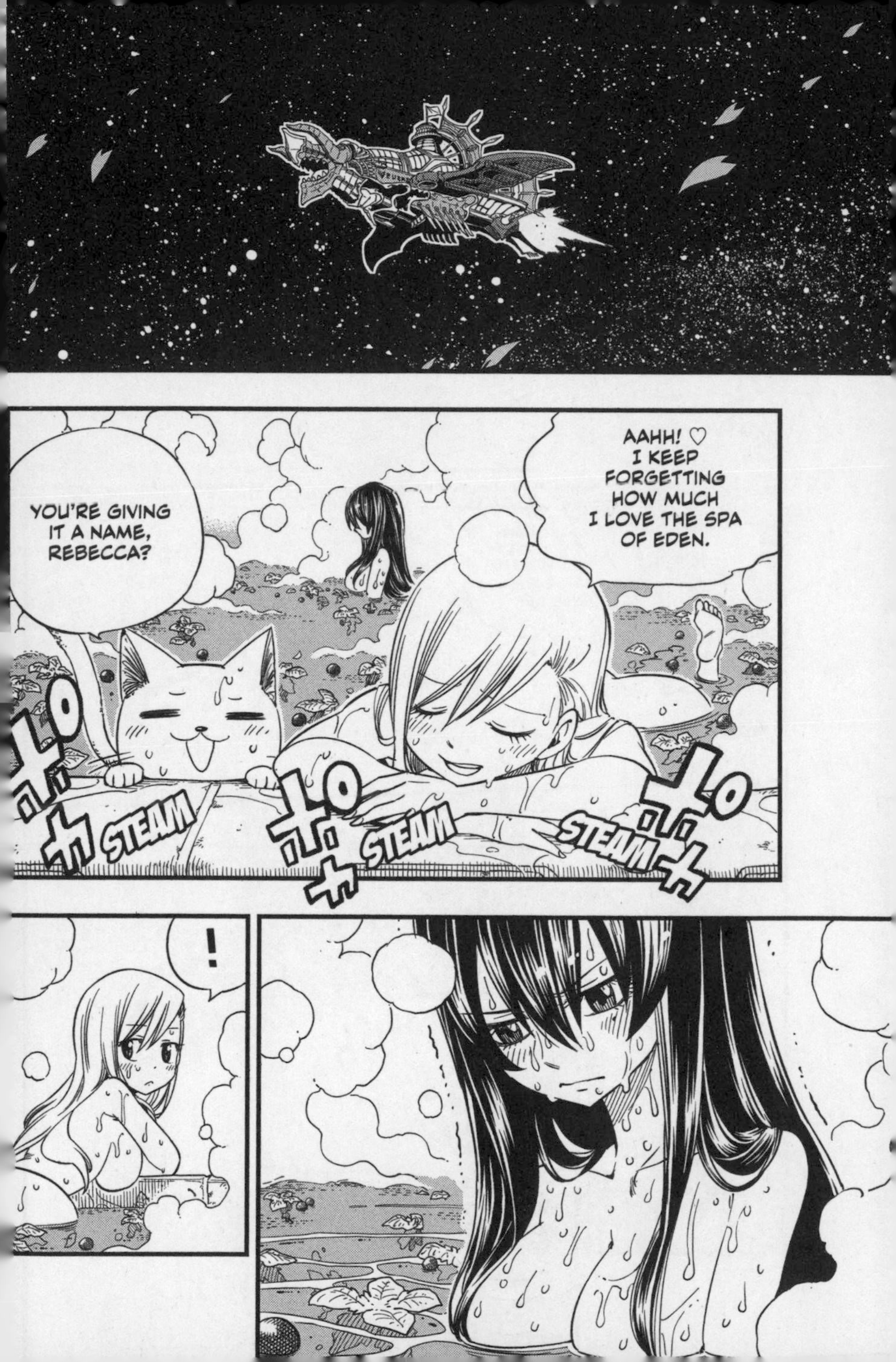
AAHH! ♡ I KEEP FORGETTING HOW MUCH I LOVE THE SPA OF EDEN.
YOU'RE GIVING IT A NAME, REBECCA?
STEAM
STEAM
STEAM
!

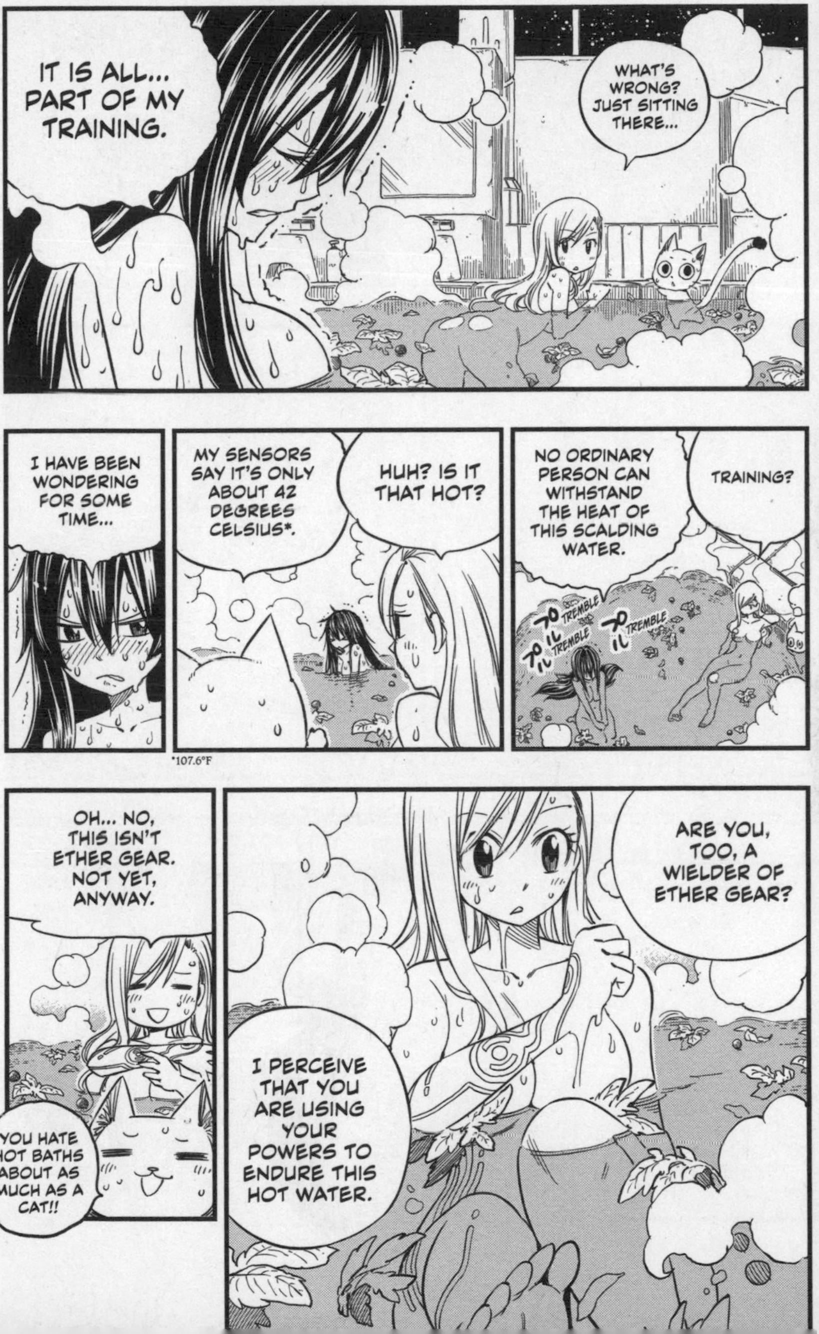
WHAT'S WRONG? JUST SITTING THERE...
IT IS ALL... PART OF MY TRAINING.
TRAINING?
NO ORDINARY PERSON CAN WITHSTAND THE HEAT OF THIS SCALDING WATER.
TREMBLE TREMBLE TREMBLE TREMBLE
HUH? IS IT THAT HOT?
MY SENSORS SAY IT'S ONLY ABOUT 42 DEGREES CELSIUS*.
I HAVE BEEN WONDERING FOR SOME TIME...
ARE YOU, TOO, A WIELDER OF ETHER GEAR?
I PERCEIVE THAT YOU ARE USING YOUR POWERS TO ENDURE THIS HOT WATER.
OH... NO, THIS ISN'T ETHER GEAR. NOT YET, ANYWAY.
YOU HATE HOT BATHS ABOUT AS MUCH AS A CAT!!
*107.6°F

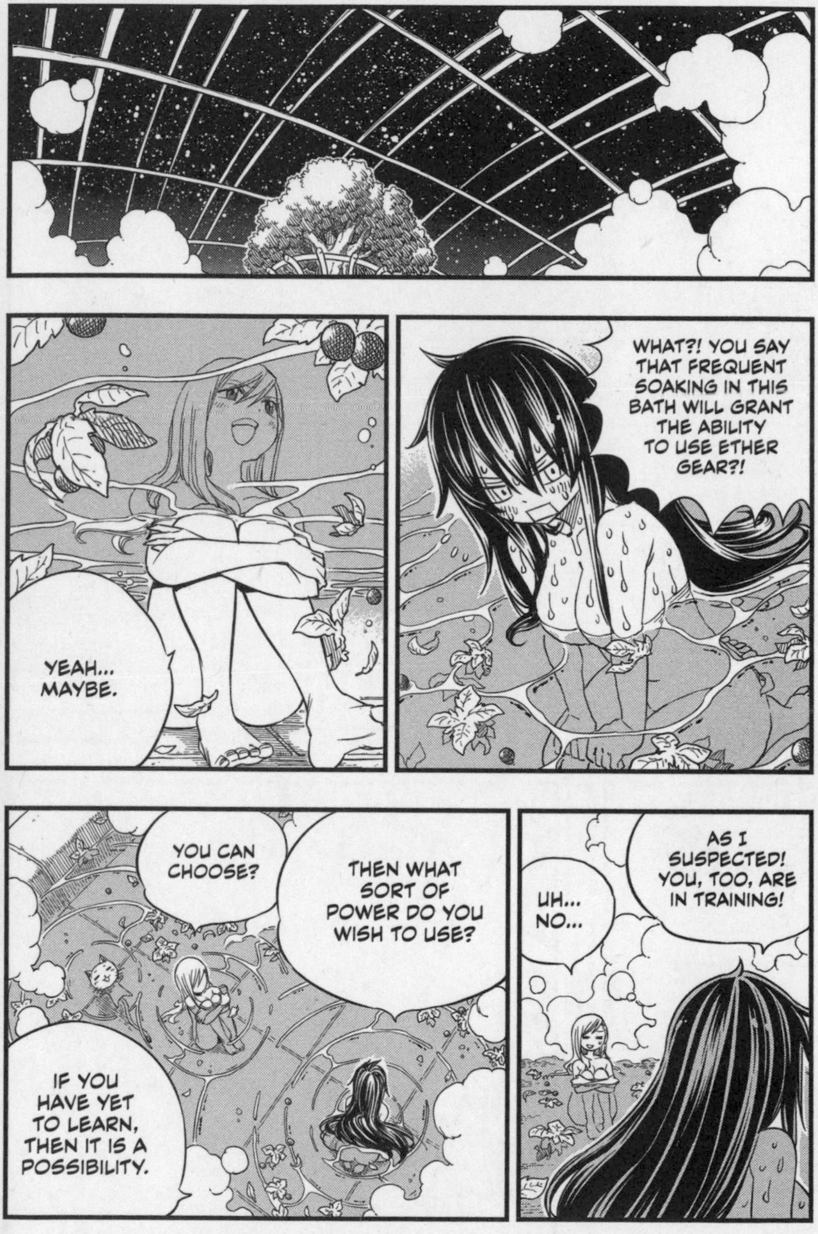
WHAT?! YOU SAY THAT FREQUENT SOAKING IN THIS BATH WILL GRANT THE ABILITY TO USE ETHER GEAR?!
YEAH... MAYBE.
AS I SUSPECTED! YOU, TOO, ARE IN TRAINING!
UH... NO...
YOU CAN CHOOSE?
THEN WHAT SORT OF POWER DO YOU WISH TO USE?
IF YOU HAVE YET TO LEARN, THEN IT IS A POSSIBILITY.

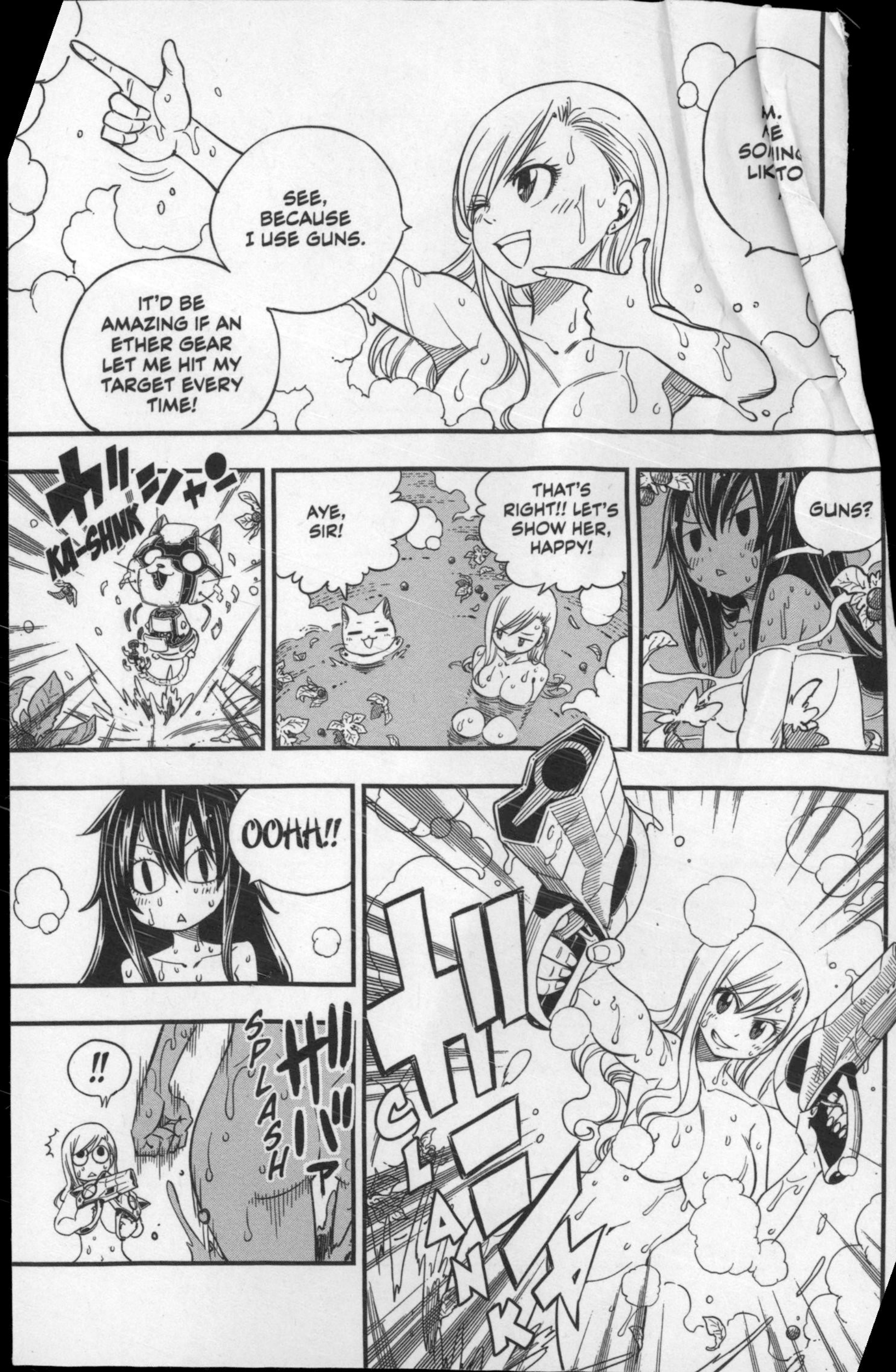
SEE, BECAUSE I USE GUNS.
IT'D BE AMAZING IF AN ETHER GEAR LET ME HIT MY TARGET EVERY TIME!
GUNS?
THAT'S RIGHT!! LET'S SHOW HER, HAPPY!
AYE, SIR!
KA-SHNK
CLANK
OOHH!!
!!
SPLASH

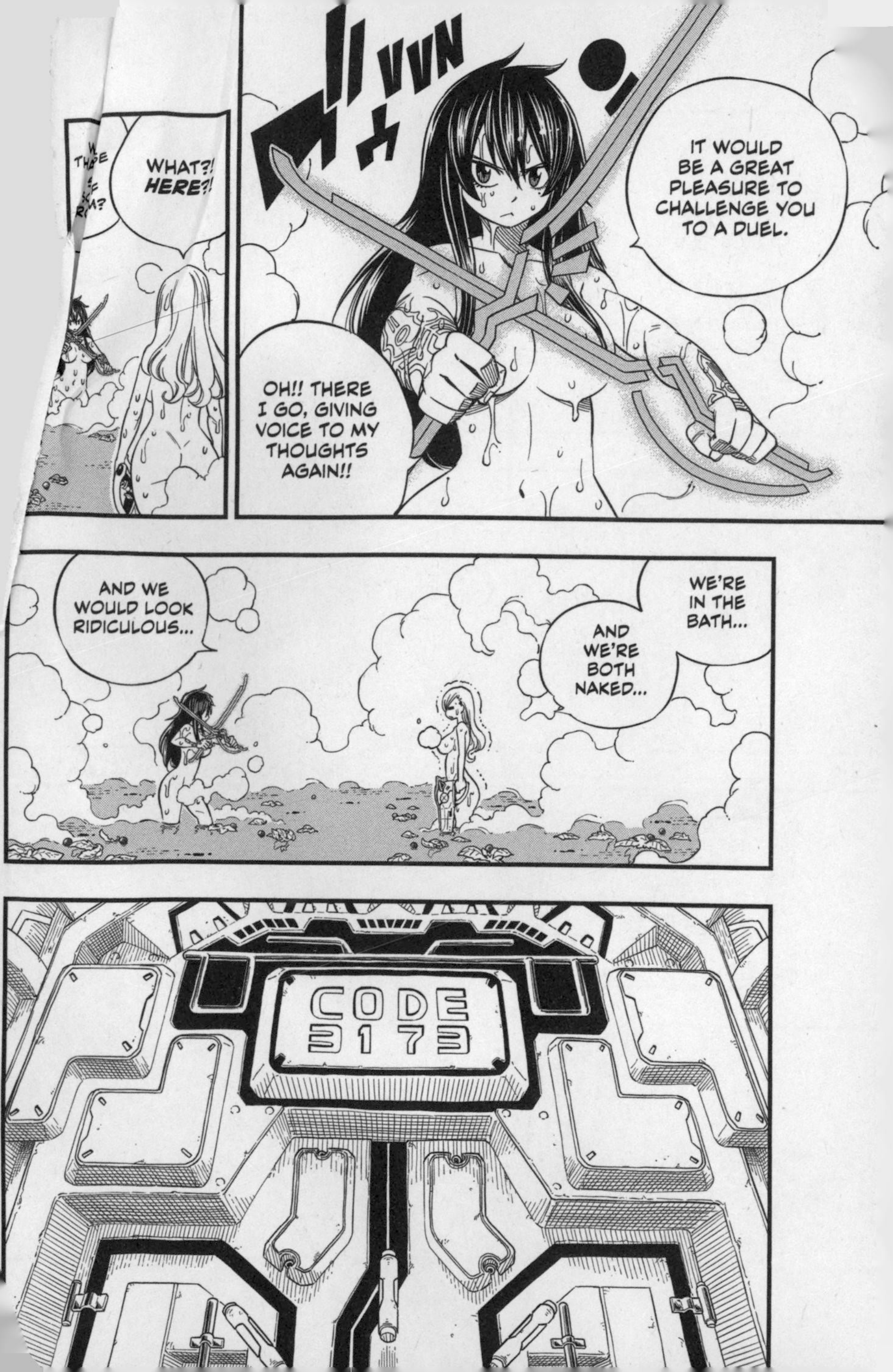
VVN
IT WOULD BE A GREAT PLEASURE TO CHALLENGE YOU TO A DUEL.
OH!! THERE I GO, GIVING VOICE TO MY THOUGHTS AGAIN!!
WHAT?! *HERE*?!
WE'RE IN THE BATH...
AND WE'RE BOTH NAKED...
AND WE WOULD LOOK RIDICULOUS...
CODE 3173

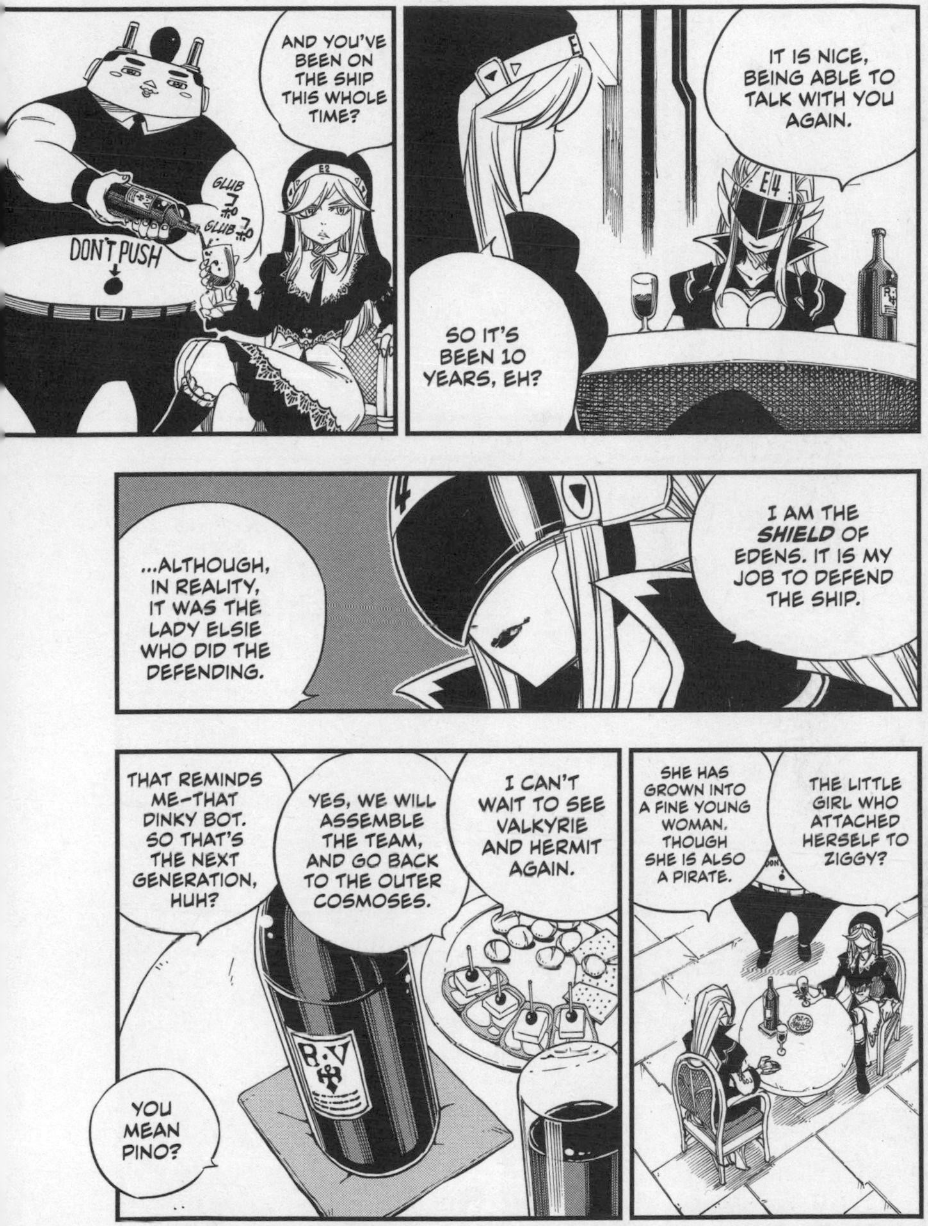
IT IS NICE, BEING ABLE TO TALK WITH YOU AGAIN.
SO IT'S BEEN 10 YEARS, EH?
AND YOU'VE BEEN ON THE SHIP THIS WHOLE TIME?
GLUB
GLUB
DON'T PUSH
I AM THE SHIELD OF EDENS. IT IS MY JOB TO DEFEND THE SHIP.
...ALTHOUGH, IN REALITY, IT WAS THE LADY ELSIE WHO DID THE DEFENDING.
THE LITTLE GIRL WHO ATTACHED HERSELF TO ZIGGY?
SHE HAS GROWN INTO A FINE YOUNG WOMAN. THOUGH SHE IS ALSO A PIRATE.
I CAN'T WAIT TO SEE VALKYRIE AND HERMIT AGAIN.
YES, WE WILL ASSEMBLE THE TEAM, AND GO BACK TO THE OUTER COSMOSES.
THAT REMINDS ME—THAT DINKY BOT. SO THAT'S THE NEXT GENERATION, HUH?
YOU MEAN PINO?

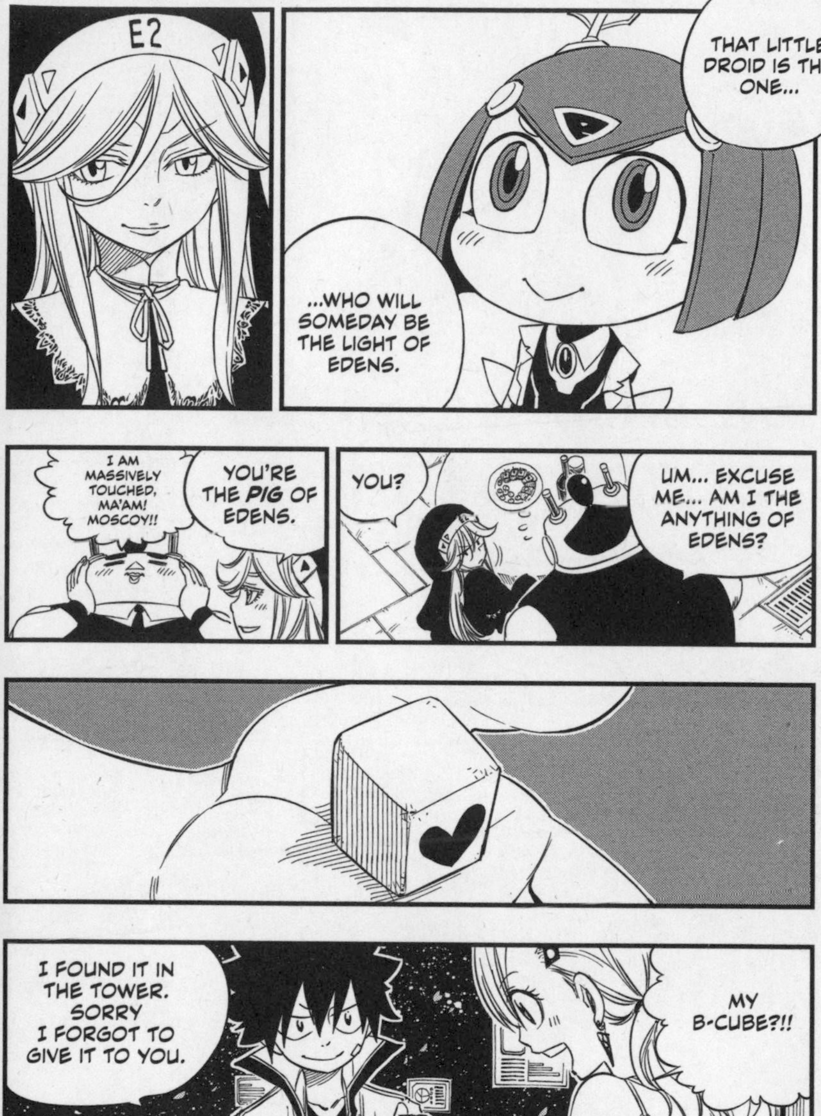
THAT LITTLE DROID IS THE ONE...
...WHO WILL SOMEDAY BE THE LIGHT OF EDENS.
UM... EXCUSE ME... AM I THE ANYTHING OF EDENS?
YOU?
YOU'RE THE *PIG* OF EDENS.
I AM MASSIVELY TOUCHED, MA'AM! MOSCOY!!
MY B-CUBE?!!
I FOUND IT IN THE TOWER. SORRY I FORGOT TO GIVE IT TO YOU.

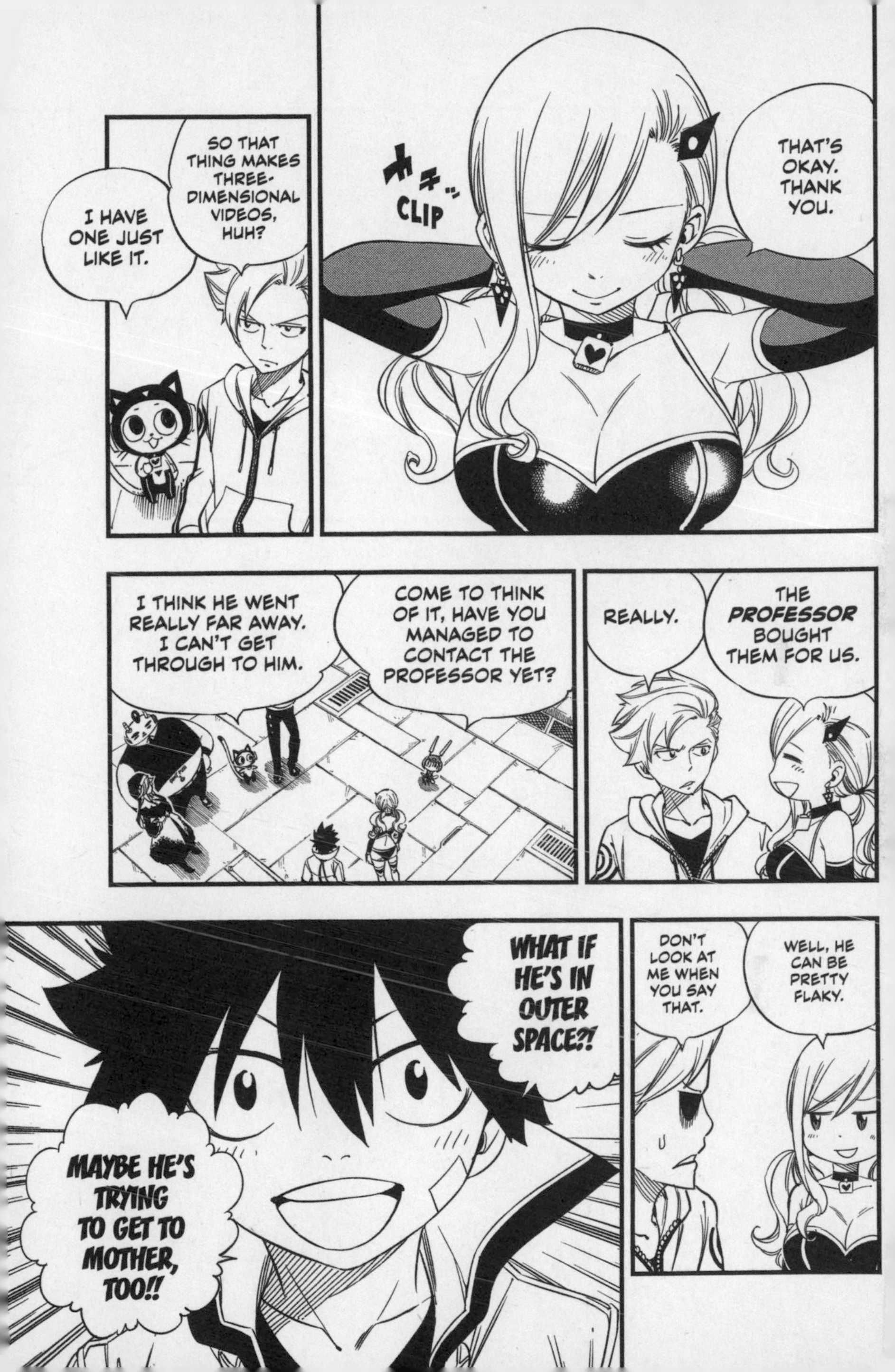
THAT'S OKAY. THANK YOU.
CLIP
SO THAT THING MAKES THREE-DIMENSIONAL VIDEOS, HUH?
I HAVE ONE JUST LIKE IT.
THE *PROFESSOR* BOUGHT THEM FOR US.
REALLY.
COME TO THINK OF IT, HAVE YOU MANAGED TO CONTACT THE PROFESSOR YET?
I THINK HE WENT REALLY FAR AWAY. I CAN'T GET THROUGH TO HIM.
WELL, HE CAN BE PRETTY FLAKY.
DON'T LOOK AT ME WHEN YOU SAY THAT.
WHAT IF HE'S IN OUTER SPACE?!
MAYBE HE'S TRYING TO GET TO MOTHER, TOO!!

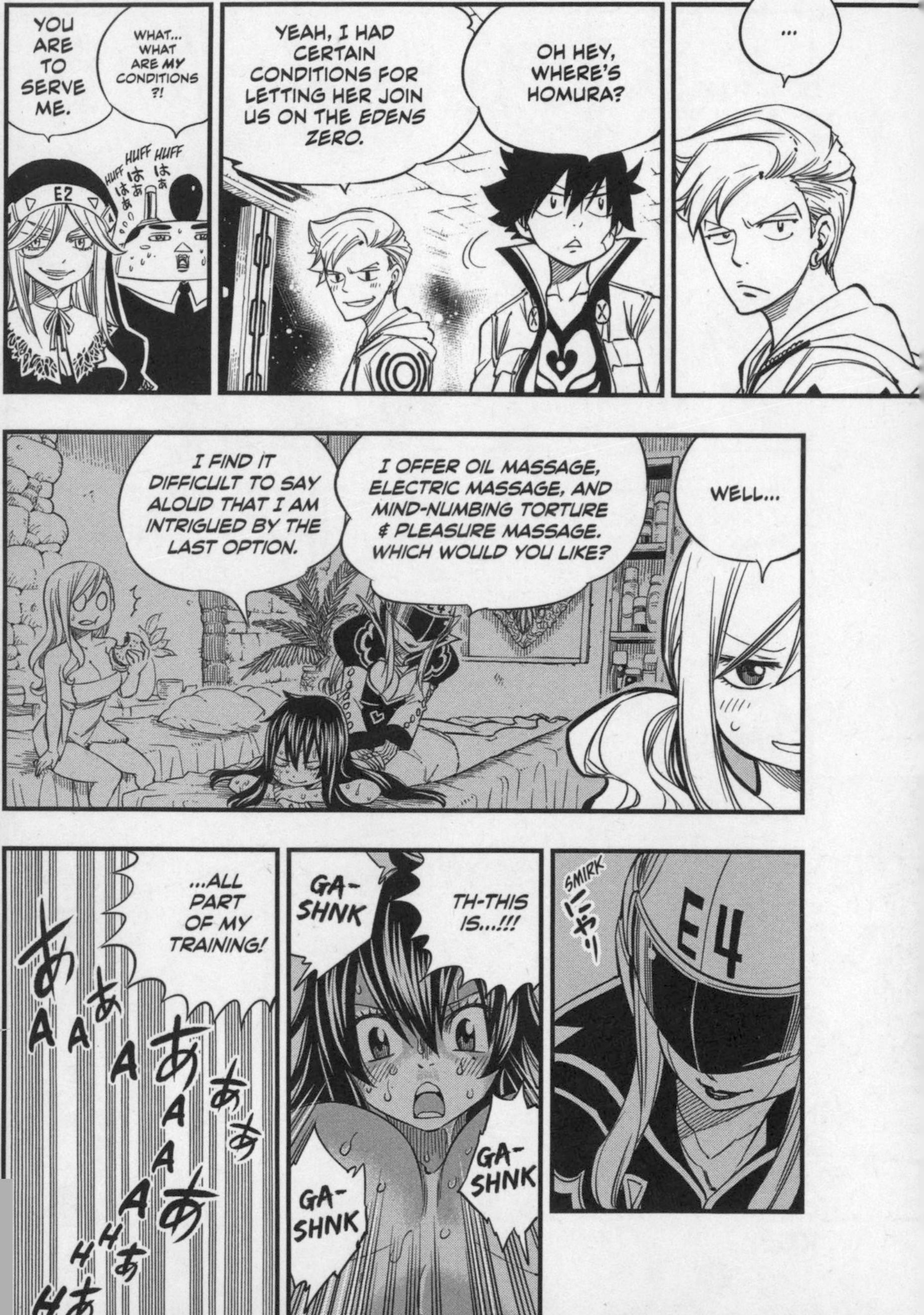
...
OH HEY, WHERE'S HOMURA?
YEAH, I HAD CERTAIN CONDITIONS FOR LETTING HER JOIN US ON THE EDENS ZERO.
WHAT... WHAT ARE MY CONDITIONS?!
HUFF はぁ HUFF はぁ HUFF はぁ
YOU ARE TO SERVE ME.
WELL...
I OFFER OIL MASSAGE, ELECTRIC MASSAGE, AND MIND-NUMBING TORTURE & PLEASURE MASSAGE. WHICH WOULD YOU LIKE?
I FIND IT DIFFICULT TO SAY ALOUD THAT I AM INTRIGUED BY THE LAST OPTION.
SMIRK にやり
TH-THIS IS...!!!
GA-SHNK
GA-SHNK
GA-SHNK
...ALL PART OF MY TRAINING!
AAAAAAAHHH

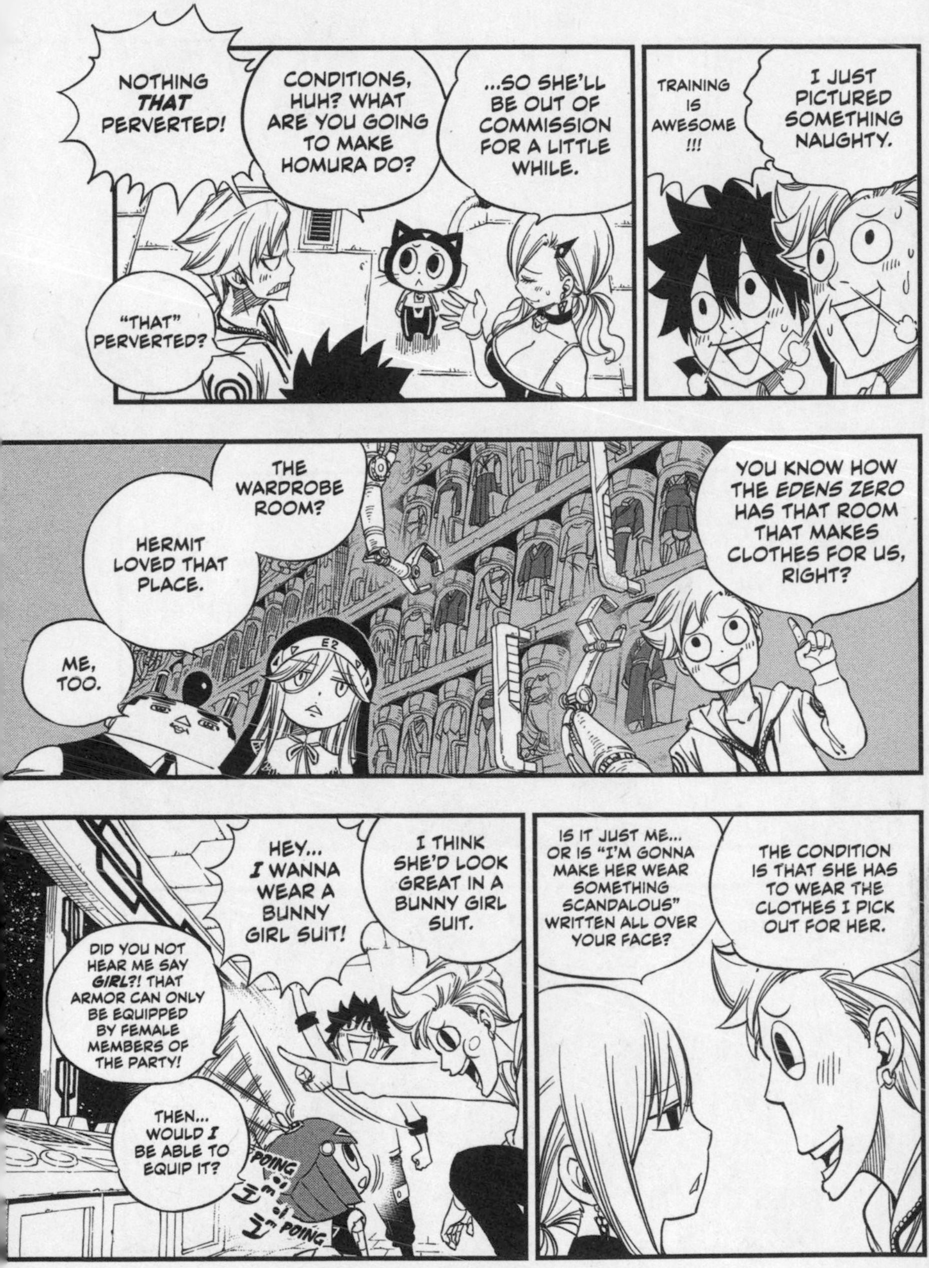

I JUST PICTURED SOMETHING NAUGHTY.
TRAINING IS AWESOME!!!
...SO SHE'LL BE OUT OF COMMISSION FOR A LITTLE WHILE.
CONDITIONS, HUH? WHAT ARE YOU GOING TO MAKE HOMURA DO?
NOTHING *THAT* PERVERTED!
"THAT" PERVERTED?
YOU KNOW HOW THE *EDENS ZERO* HAS THAT ROOM THAT MAKES CLOTHES FOR US, RIGHT?
THE WARDROBE ROOM?
HERMIT LOVED THAT PLACE.
ME, TOO.
THE CONDITION IS THAT SHE HAS TO WEAR THE CLOTHES I PICK OUT FOR HER.
IS IT JUST ME... OR IS "I'M GONNA MAKE HER WEAR SOMETHING SCANDALOUS" WRITTEN ALL OVER YOUR FACE?
I THINK SHE'D LOOK GREAT IN A BUNNY GIRL SUIT.
HEY... *I* WANNA WEAR A BUNNY GIRL SUIT!
DID YOU NOT HEAR ME SAY *GIRL*?! THAT ARMOR CAN ONLY BE EQUIPPED BY FEMALE MEMBERS OF THE PARTY!
THEN... WOULD *I* BE ABLE TO EQUIP IT?
POING
POING

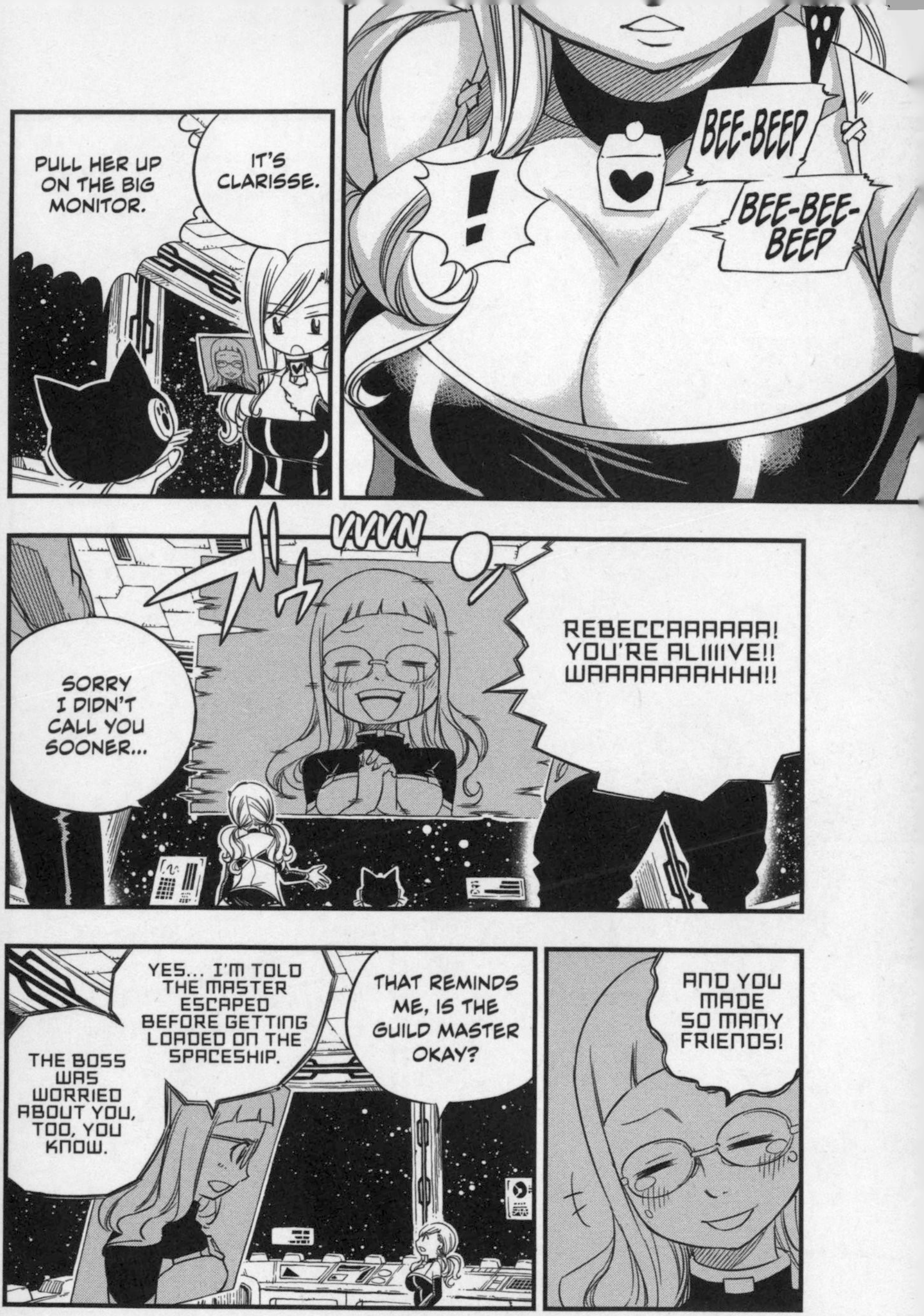
BEE-BEEP
BEE-BEE-BEEP
!
IT'S CLARISSE.
PULL HER UP ON THE BIG MONITOR.
VVVN
REBECCAAAAAA! YOU'RE ALIIIIVE!! WAAAAAAAHHH!!
SORRY I DIDN'T CALL YOU SOONER...
AND YOU MADE SO MANY FRIENDS!
THAT REMINDS ME, IS THE GUILD MASTER OKAY?
YES... I'M TOLD THE MASTER ESCAPED BEFORE GETTING LOADED ON THE SPACESHIP.
THE BOSS WAS WORRIED ABOUT YOU, TOO, YOU KNOW.

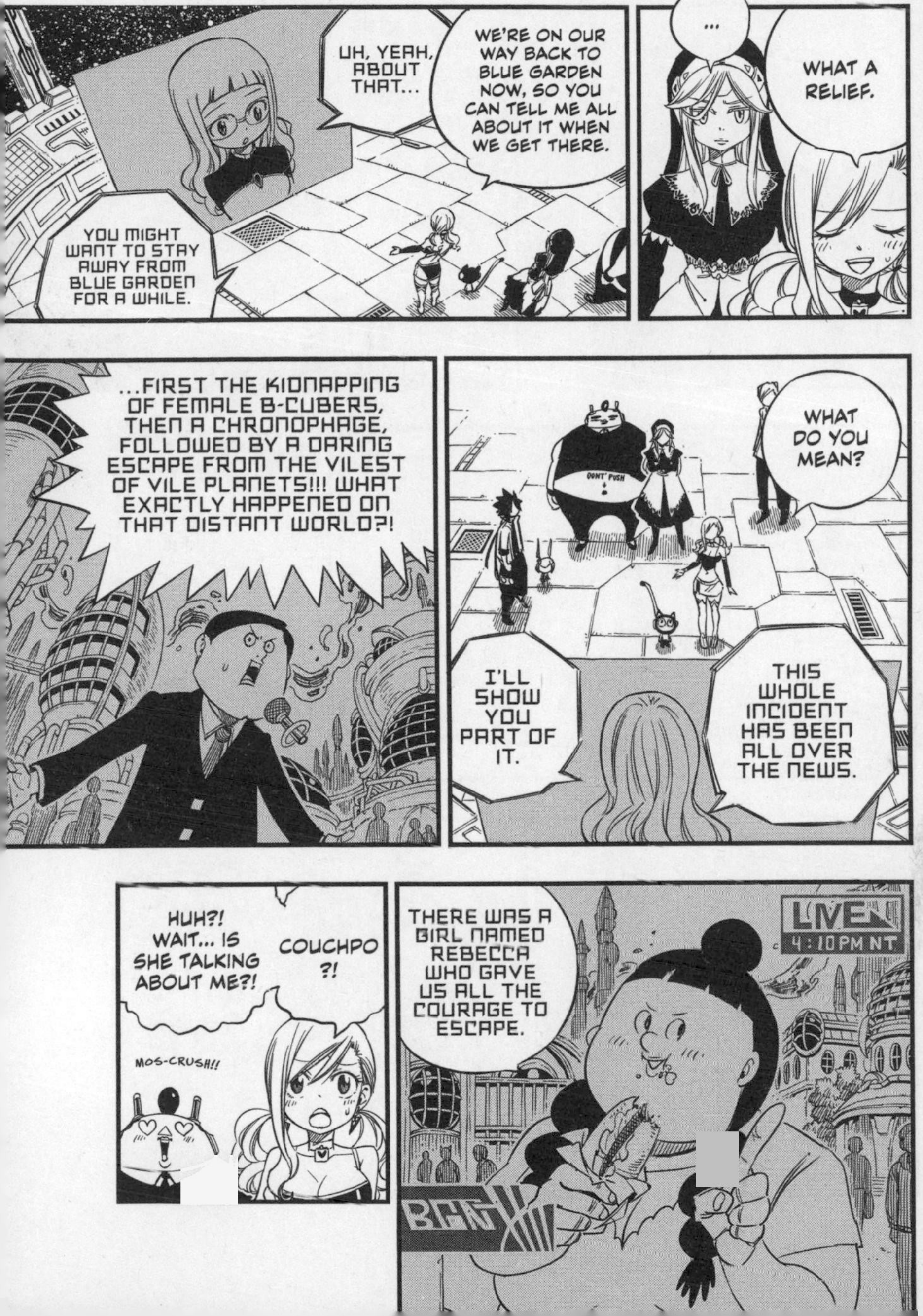

...
WHAT A RELIEF.
WE'RE ON OUR WAY BACK TO BLUE GARDEN NOW, SO YOU CAN TELL ME ALL ABOUT IT WHEN WE GET THERE.
UH, YEAH, ABOUT THAT...
YOU MIGHT WANT TO STAY AWAY FROM BLUE GARDEN FOR A WHILE.
WHAT DO YOU MEAN?
THIS WHOLE INCIDENT HAS BEEN ALL OVER THE NEWS.
I'LL SHOW YOU PART OF IT.
...FIRST THE KIDNAPPING OF FEMALE B-CUBERS, THEN A CHRONOPHAGE, FOLLOWED BY A DARING ESCAPE FROM THE VILEST OF VILE PLANETS!!! WHAT EXACTLY HAPPENED ON THAT DISTANT WORLD?!
LIVE
4:10PM NT
THERE WAS A GIRL NAMED REBECCA WHO GAVE US ALL THE COURAGE TO ESCAPE.
COUCHPO ?!
HUH?! WAIT... IS SHE TALKING ABOUT ME?!
MOS-CRUSH!!

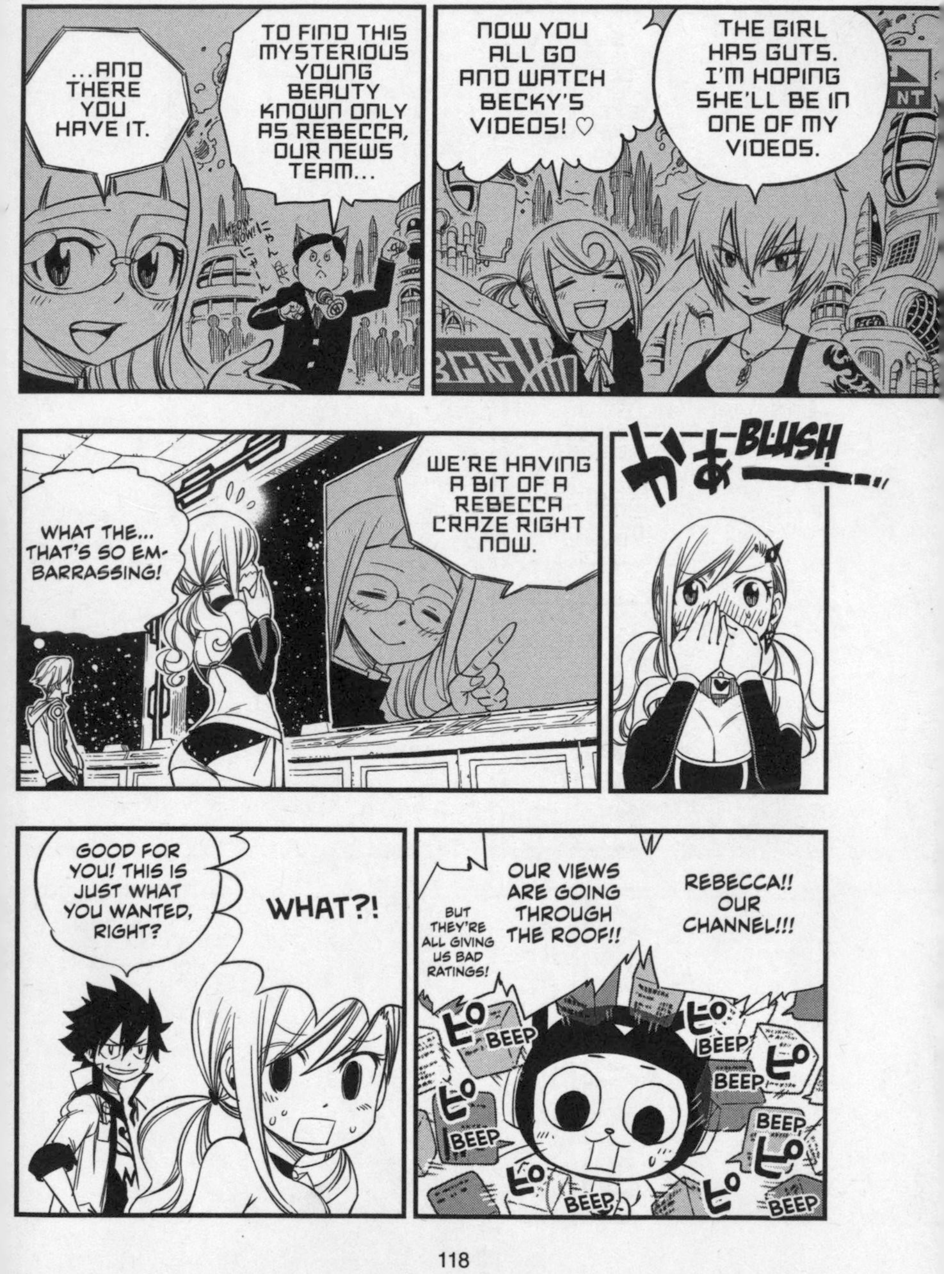
THE GIRL HAS GUTS. I'M HOPING SHE'LL BE IN ONE OF MY VIDEOS.
NOW YOU ALL GO AND WATCH BECKY'S VIDEOS! ♡
TO FIND THIS MYSTERIOUS YOUNG BEAUTY KNOWN ONLY AS REBECCA, OUR NEWS TEAM...
MEOW-MEOW! にゃんにゃーん
...AND THERE YOU HAVE IT.
かあーー BLUSH
WE'RE HAVING A BIT OF A REBECCA CRAZE RIGHT NOW.
WHAT THE... THAT'S SO EM-BARRASSING!
REBECCA!! OUR CHANNEL!!!
OUR VIEWS ARE GOING THROUGH THE ROOF!!
BUT THEY'RE ALL GIVING US BAD RATINGS!
ピ BEEP ピ BEEP ピ BEEP ピ BEEP ピ BEEP ピ BEEP ピ BEEP ピ BEEP
WHAT?!
GOOD FOR YOU! THIS IS JUST WHAT YOU WANTED, RIGHT?

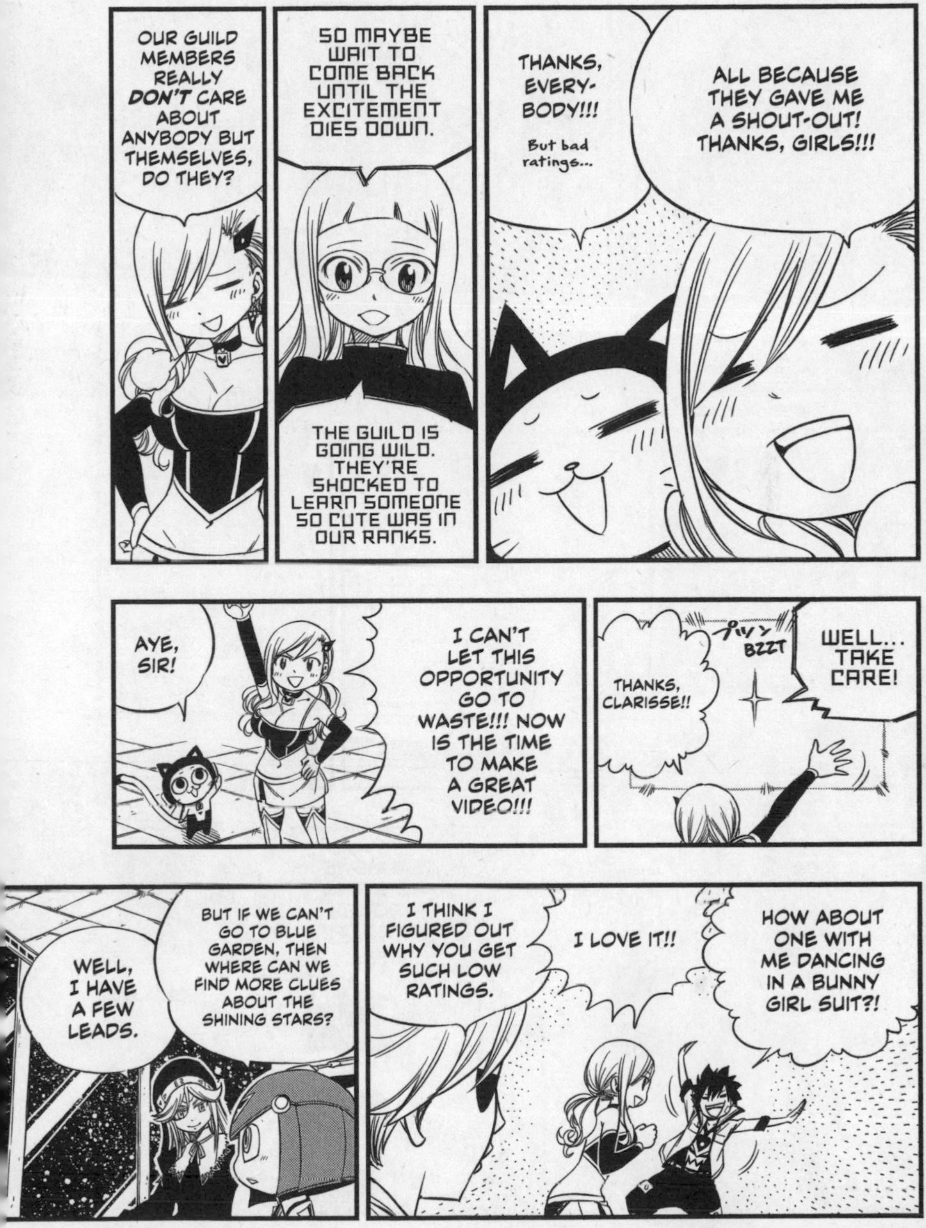
ALL BECAUSE THEY GAVE ME A SHOUT-OUT! THANKS, GIRLS!!!
THANKS, EVERY-BODY!!!
But bad ratings...
SO MAYBE WAIT TO COME BACK UNTIL THE EXCITEMENT DIES DOWN.
THE GUILD IS GOING WILD. THEY'RE SHOCKED TO LEARN SOMEONE SO CUTE WAS IN OUR RANKS.
OUR GUILD MEMBERS REALLY *DON'T* CARE ABOUT ANYBODY BUT THEMSELVES, DO THEY?
WELL... TAKE CARE!
BZZT
THANKS, CLARISSE!!
I CAN'T LET THIS OPPORTUNITY GO TO WASTE!!! NOW IS THE TIME TO MAKE A GREAT VIDEO!!!
AYE, SIR!
HOW ABOUT ONE WITH ME DANCING IN A BUNNY GIRL SUIT?!
I LOVE IT!!
I THINK I FIGURED OUT WHY YOU GET SUCH LOW RATINGS.
BUT IF WE CAN'T GO TO BLUE GARDEN, THEN WHERE CAN WE FIND MORE CLUES ABOUT THE SHINING STARS?
WELL, I HAVE A FEW LEADS.

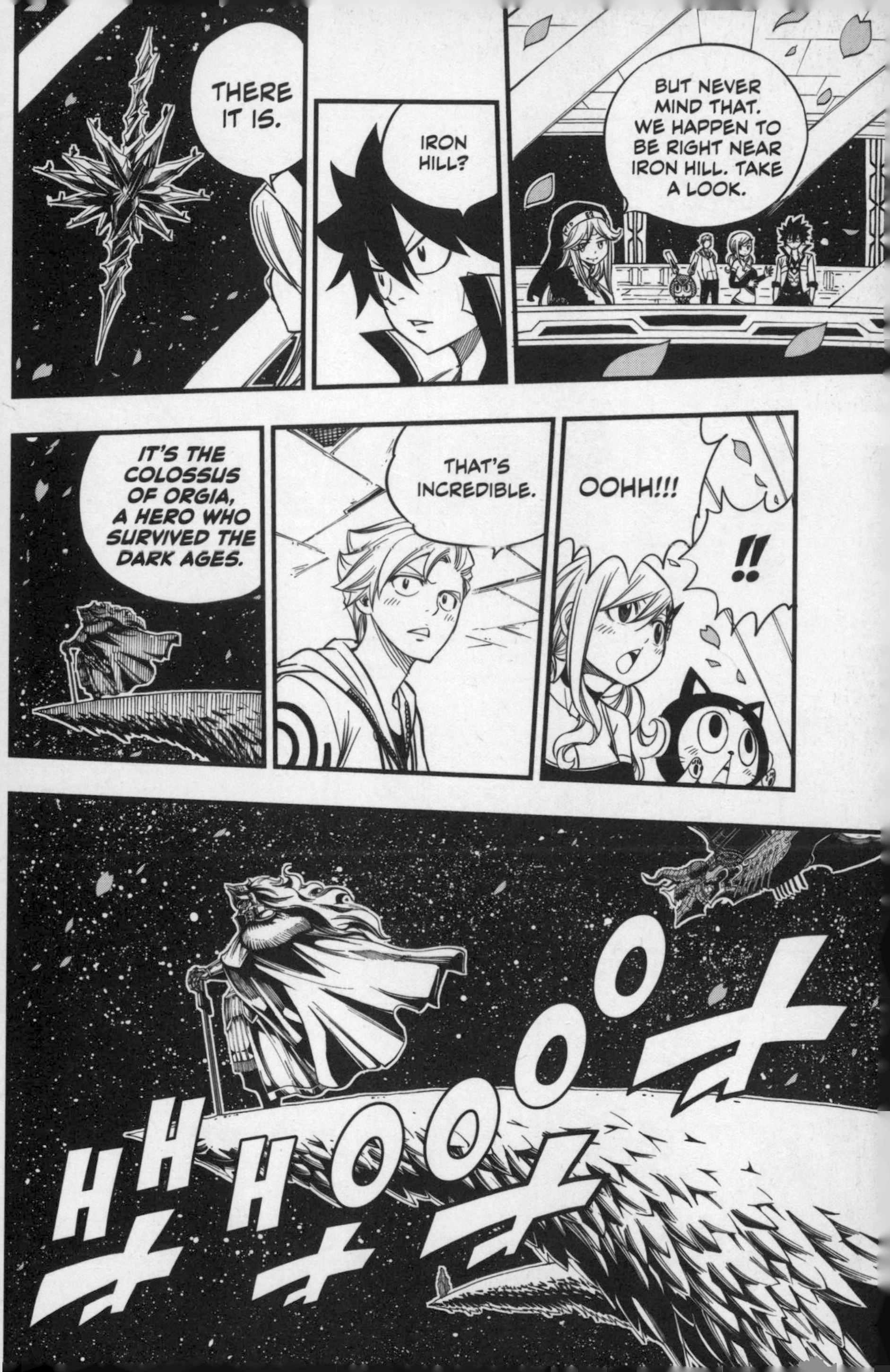
BUT NEVER MIND THAT. WE HAPPEN TO BE RIGHT NEAR IRON HILL. TAKE A LOOK.
IRON HILL?
THERE IT IS.
OOHH!!!
!!
THAT'S INCREDIBLE.
IT'S THE COLOSSUS OF ORGIA, A HERO WHO SURVIVED THE DARK AGES.
HHHOOOO

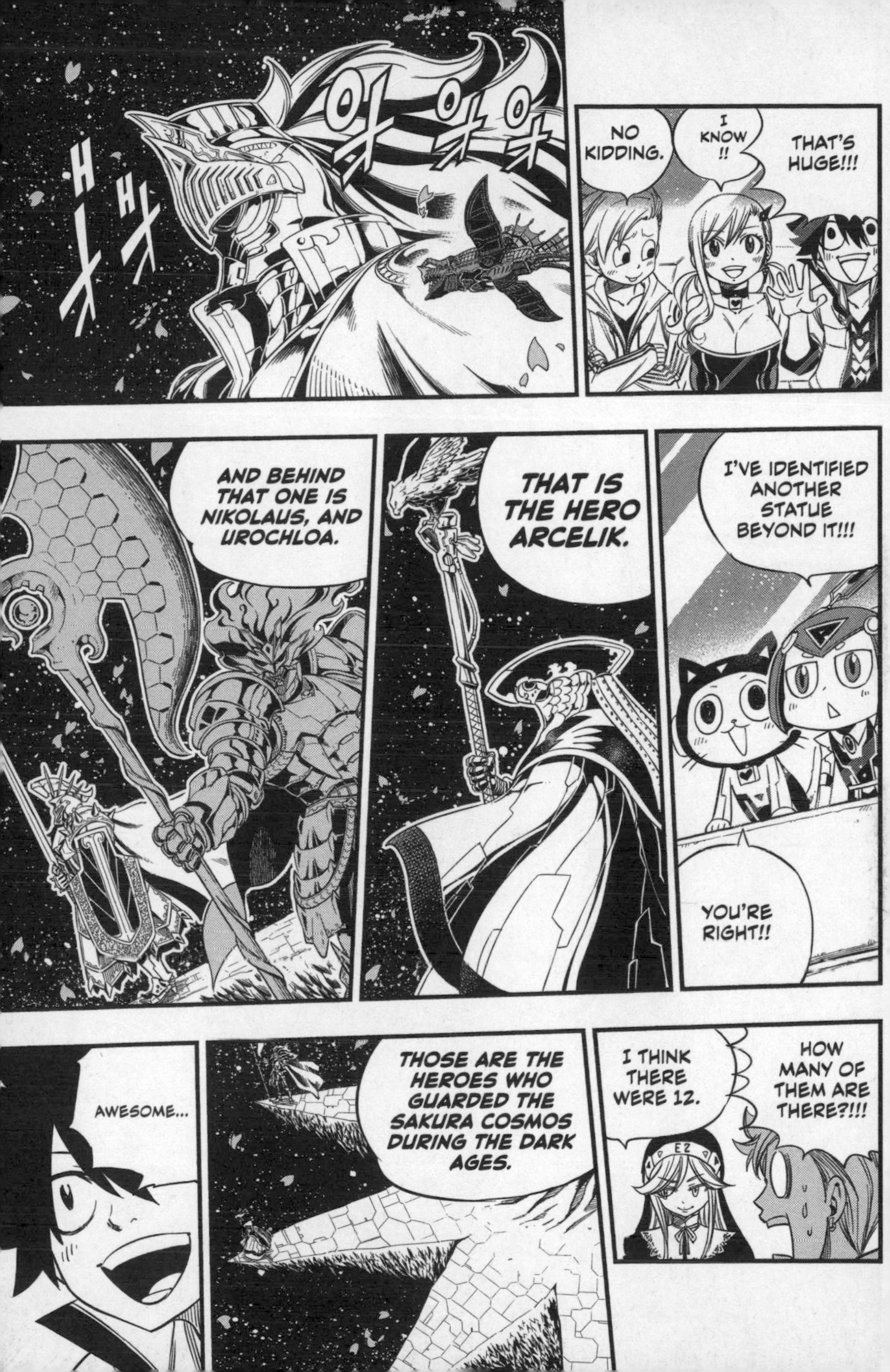
THAT'S HUGE!!!
I KNOW!!
NO KIDDING.
I'VE IDENTIFIED ANOTHER STATUE BEYOND IT!!!
YOU'RE RIGHT!!
THAT IS THE HERO ARCELIK.
AND BEHIND THAT ONE IS NIKOLAUS, AND UROCHLOA.
HOW MANY OF THEM ARE THERE?!!!
I THINK THERE WERE 12.
THOSE ARE THE HEROES WHO GUARDED THE SAKURA COSMOS DURING THE DARK AGES.
AWESOME...

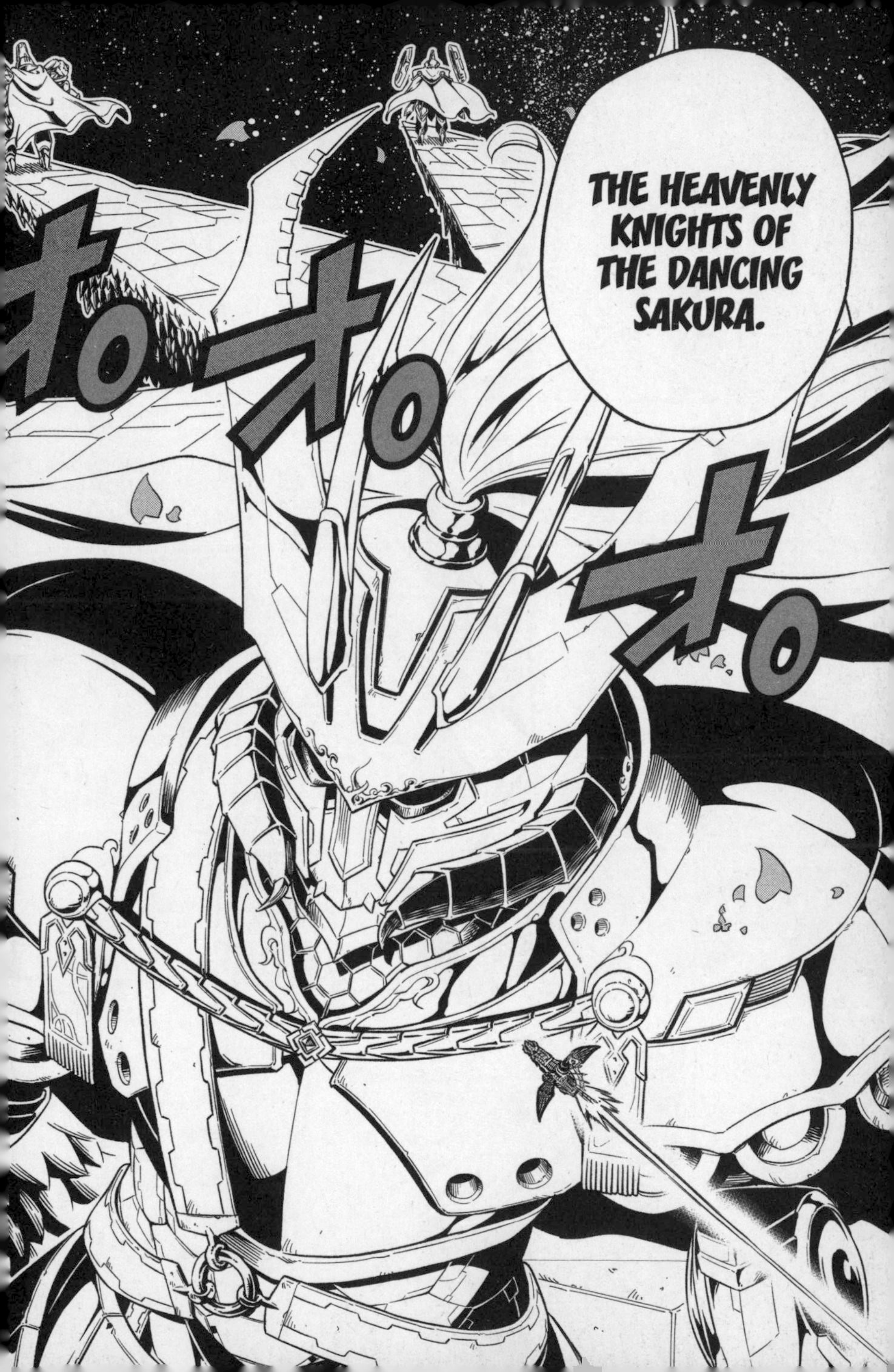
THE HEAVENLY KNIGHTS OF THE DANCING SAKURA.

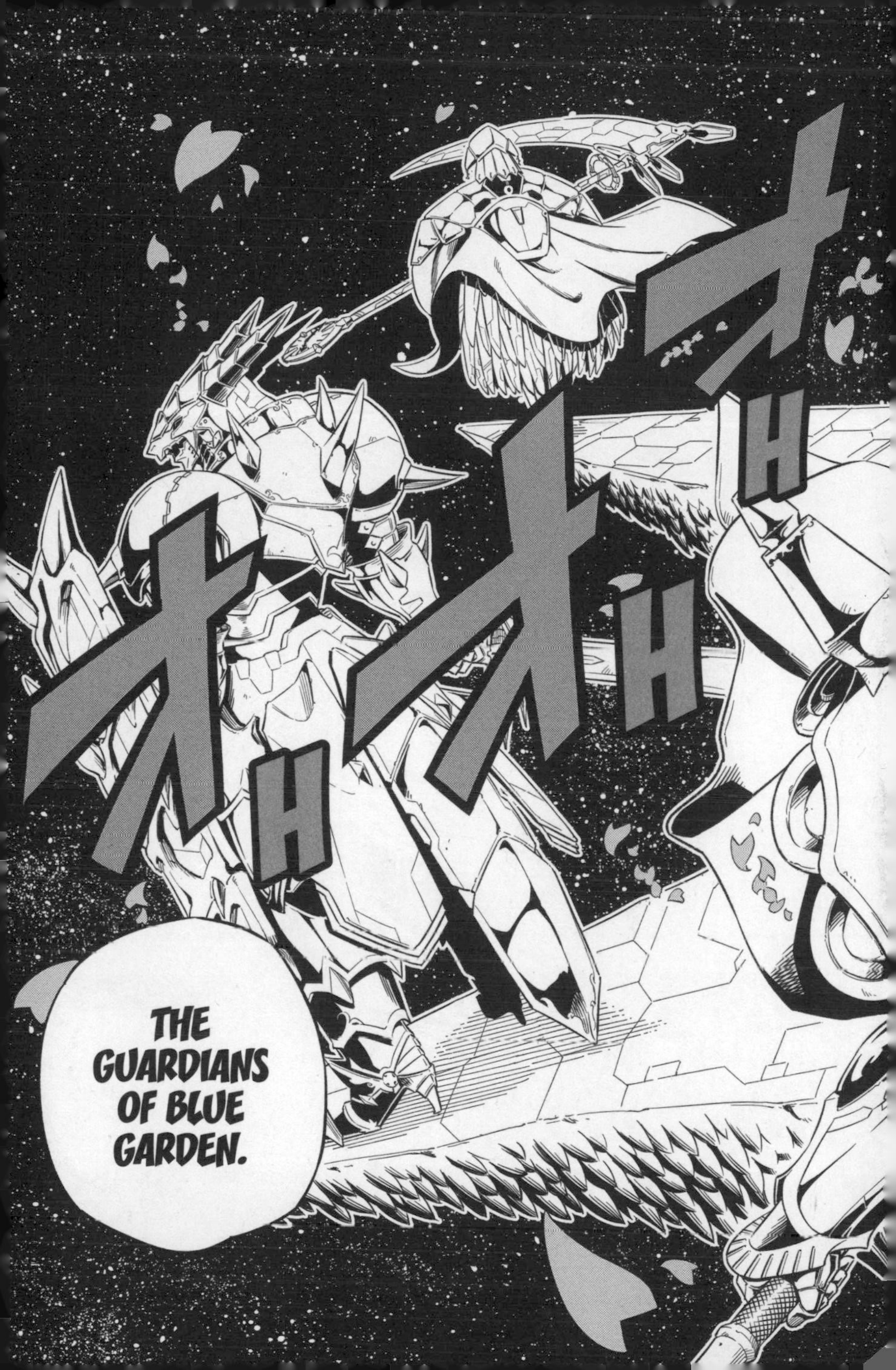
オオオ
HHHH
THE GUARDIANS OF BLUE GARDEN.

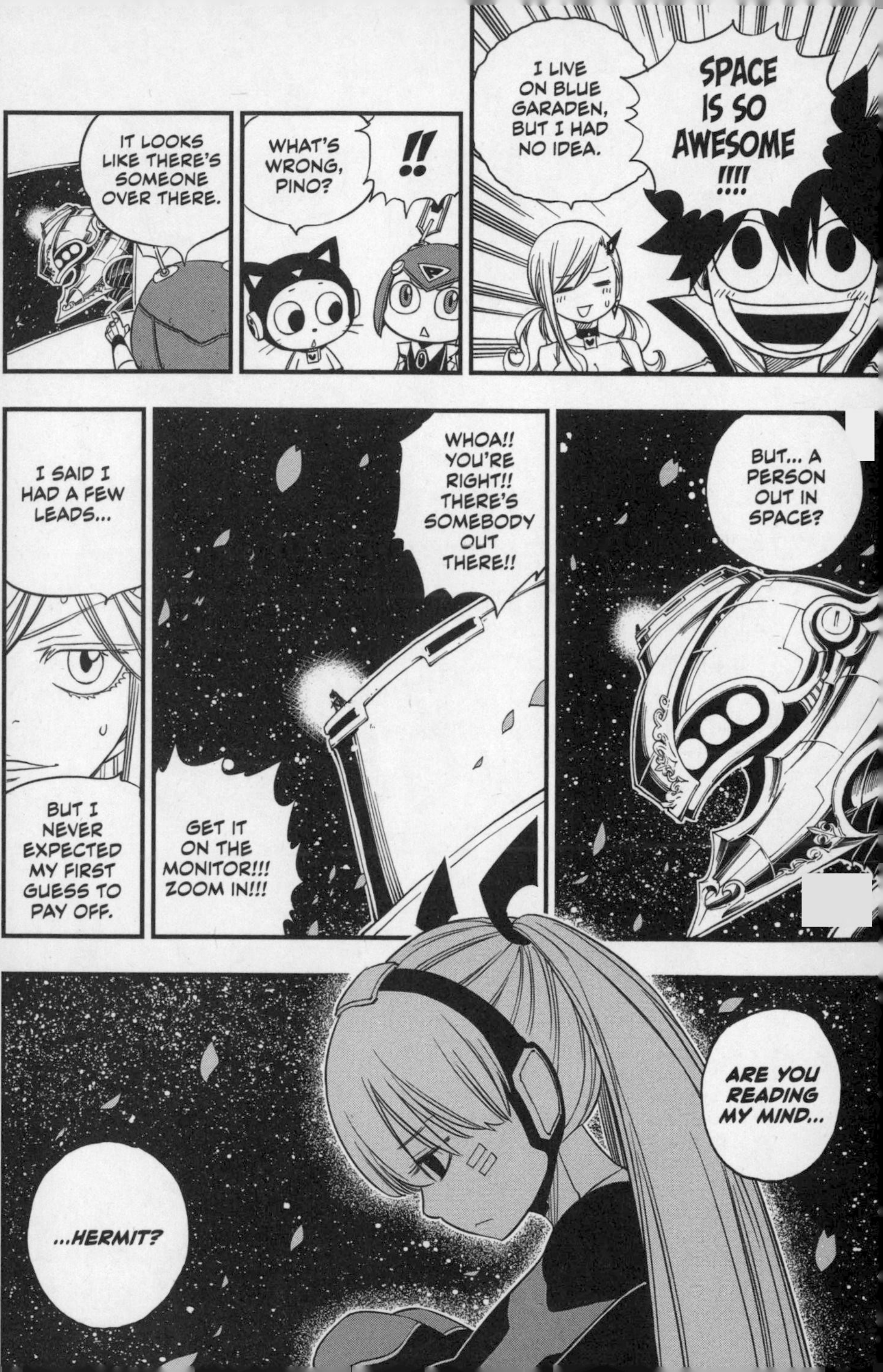
SPACE IS SO AWESOME!!!!
I LIVE ON BLUE GARADEN, BUT I HAD NO IDEA.
!!
WHAT'S WRONG, PINO?
IT LOOKS LIKE THERE'S SOMEONE OVER THERE.
BUT... A PERSON OUT IN SPACE?
WHOA!! YOU'RE RIGHT!! THERE'S SOMEBODY OUT THERE!!
GET IT ON THE MONITOR!!! ZOOM IN!!!
I SAID I HAD A FEW LEADS...
BUT I NEVER EXPECTED MY FIRST GUESS TO PAY OFF.
ARE YOU READING MY MIND...
...HERMIT?

CHAPTER 30: THE SUPER VIRTUAL PLANET

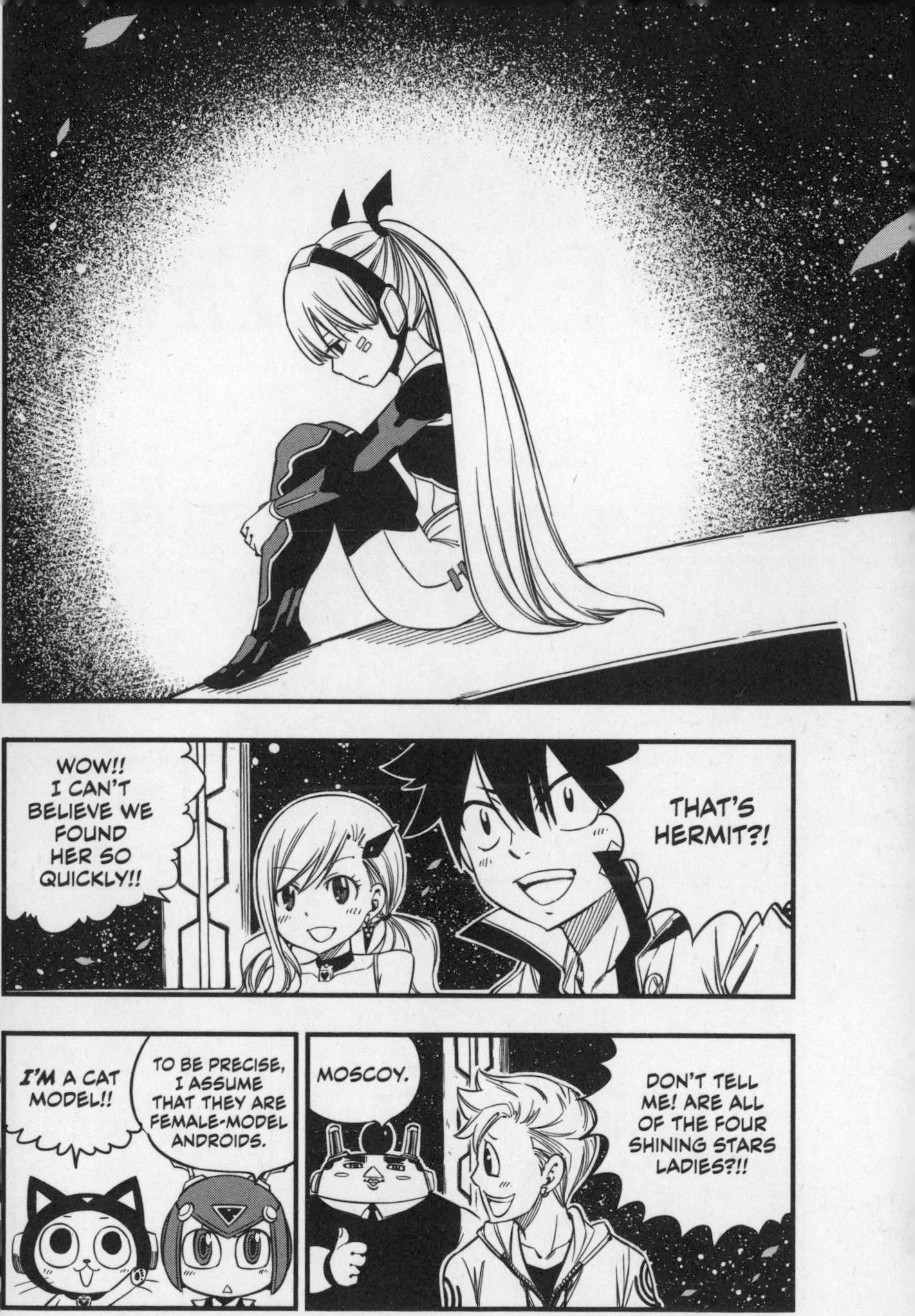
THAT'S HERMIT?!
WOW!! I CAN'T BELIEVE WE FOUND HER SO QUICKLY!!
DON'T TELL ME! ARE ALL OF THE FOUR SHINING STARS LADIES?!!
MOSCOY.
TO BE PRECISE, I ASSUME THAT THEY ARE FEMALE-MODEL ANDROIDS.
I'M A CAT MODEL!!

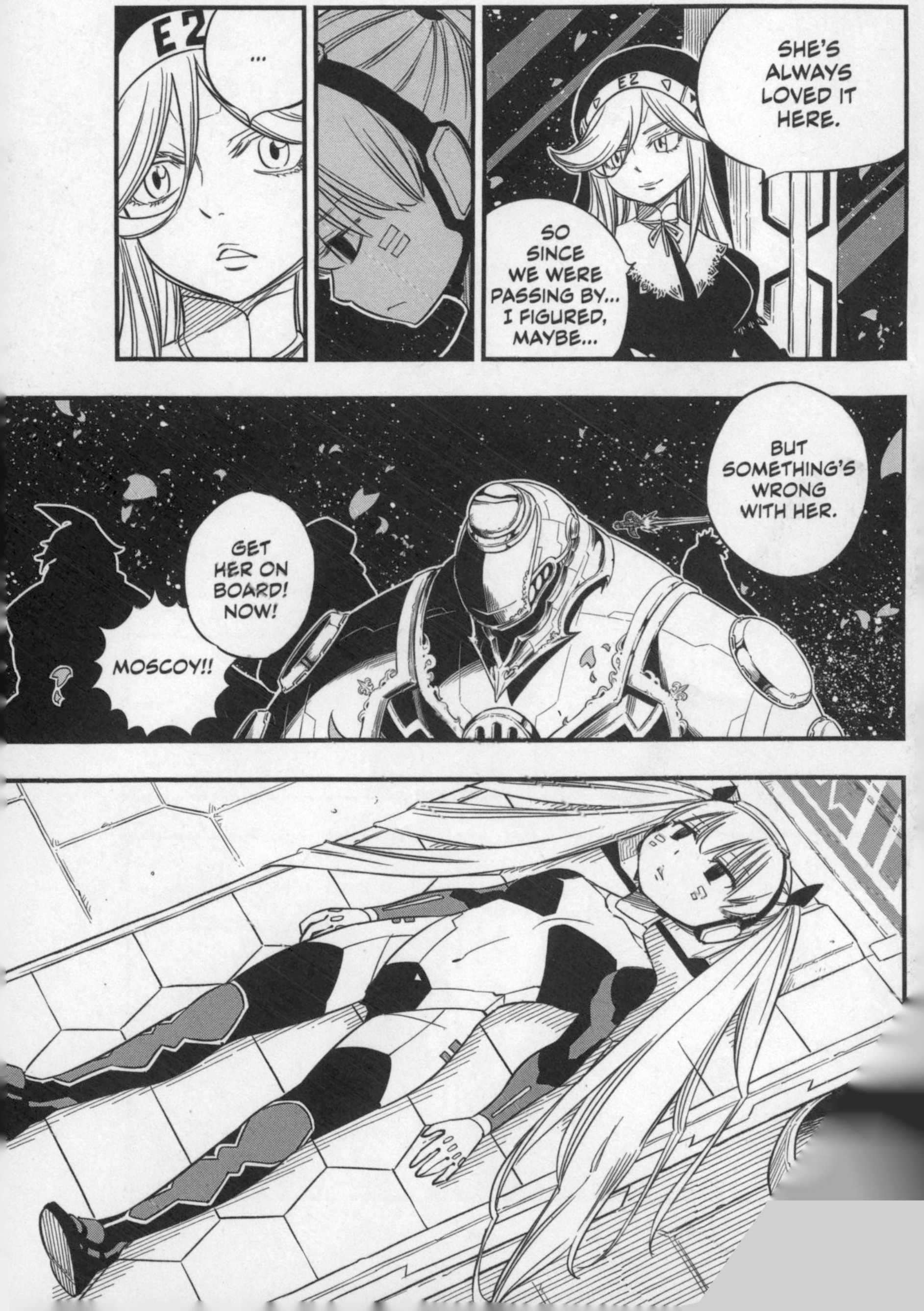
SHE'S ALWAYS LOVED IT HERE.
SO SINCE WE WERE PASSING BY... I FIGURED, MAYBE...
...
BUT SOMETHING'S WRONG WITH HER.
GET HER ON BOARD! NOW!
MOSCOY!!

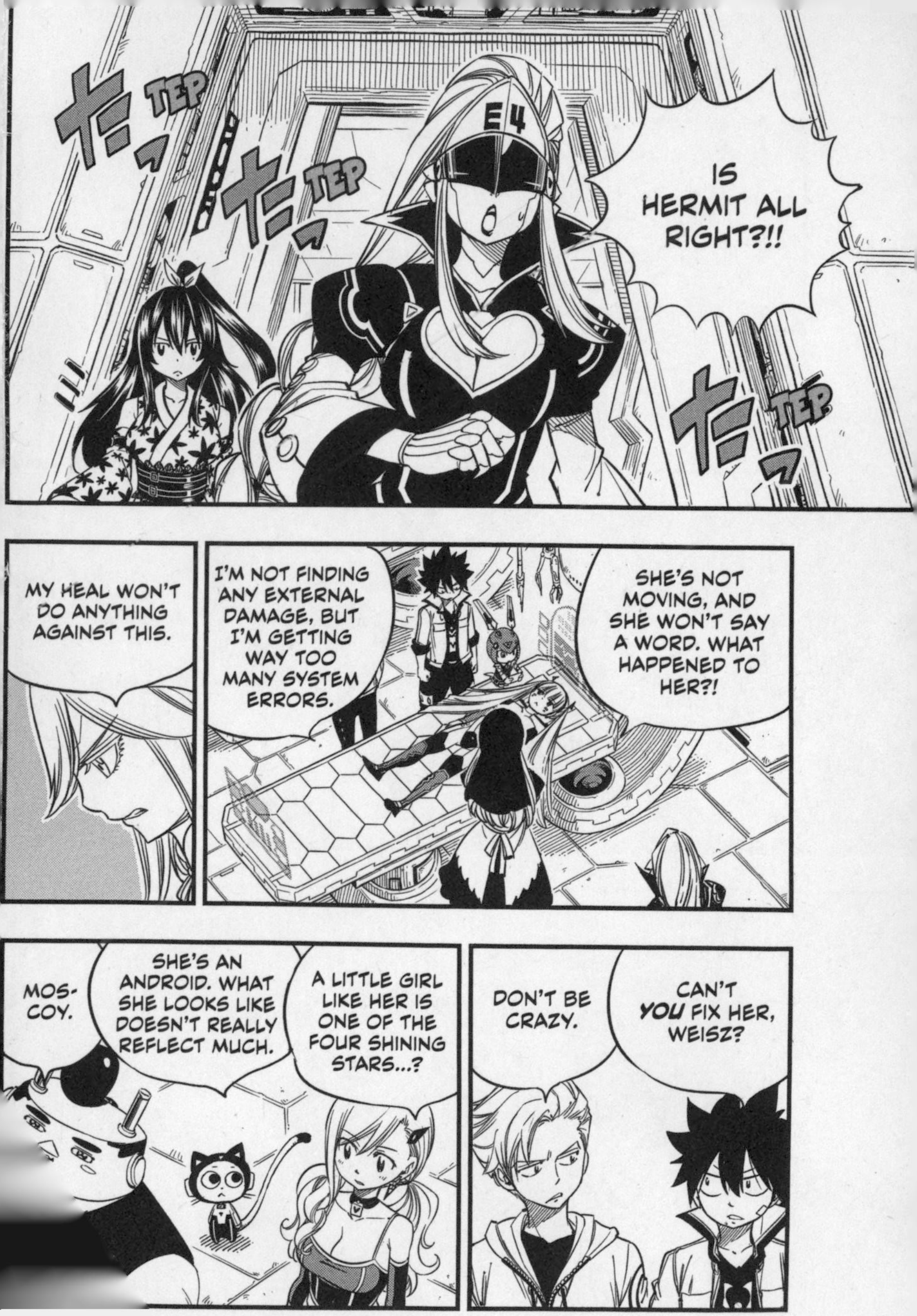
IS HERMIT ALL RIGHT?!!
TEP
TEP
TEP
SHE'S NOT MOVING, AND SHE WON'T SAY A WORD. WHAT HAPPENED TO HER?!
I'M NOT FINDING ANY EXTERNAL DAMAGE, BUT I'M GETTING WAY TOO MANY SYSTEM ERRORS.
MY HEAL WON'T DO ANYTHING AGAINST THIS.
CAN'T *YOU* FIX HER, WEISZ?
DON'T BE CRAZY.
A LITTLE GIRL LIKE HER IS ONE OF THE FOUR SHINING STARS...?
SHE'S AN ANDROID. WHAT SHE LOOKS LIKE DOESN'T REALLY REFLECT MUCH.
MOS-COY.

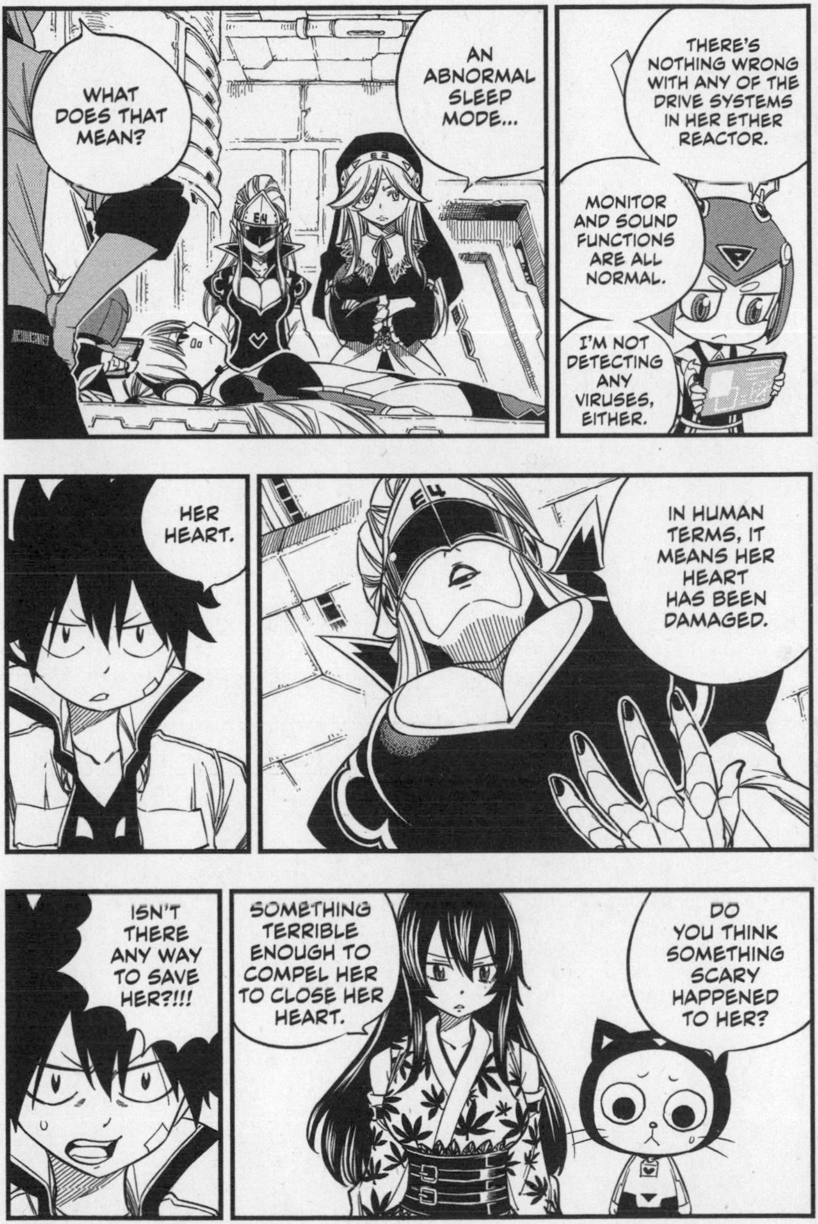
THERE'S NOTHING WRONG WITH ANY OF THE DRIVE SYSTEMS IN HER ETHER REACTOR.
MONITOR AND SOUND FUNCTIONS ARE ALL NORMAL.
I'M NOT DETECTING ANY VIRUSES, EITHER.
AN ABNORMAL SLEEP MODE...
WHAT DOES THAT MEAN?
IN HUMAN TERMS, IT MEANS HER HEART HAS BEEN DAMAGED.
HER HEART.
DO YOU THINK SOMETHING SCARY HAPPENED TO HER?
SOMETHING TERRIBLE ENOUGH TO COMPEL HER TO CLOSE HER HEART.
ISN'T THERE ANY WAY TO SAVE HER?!!!

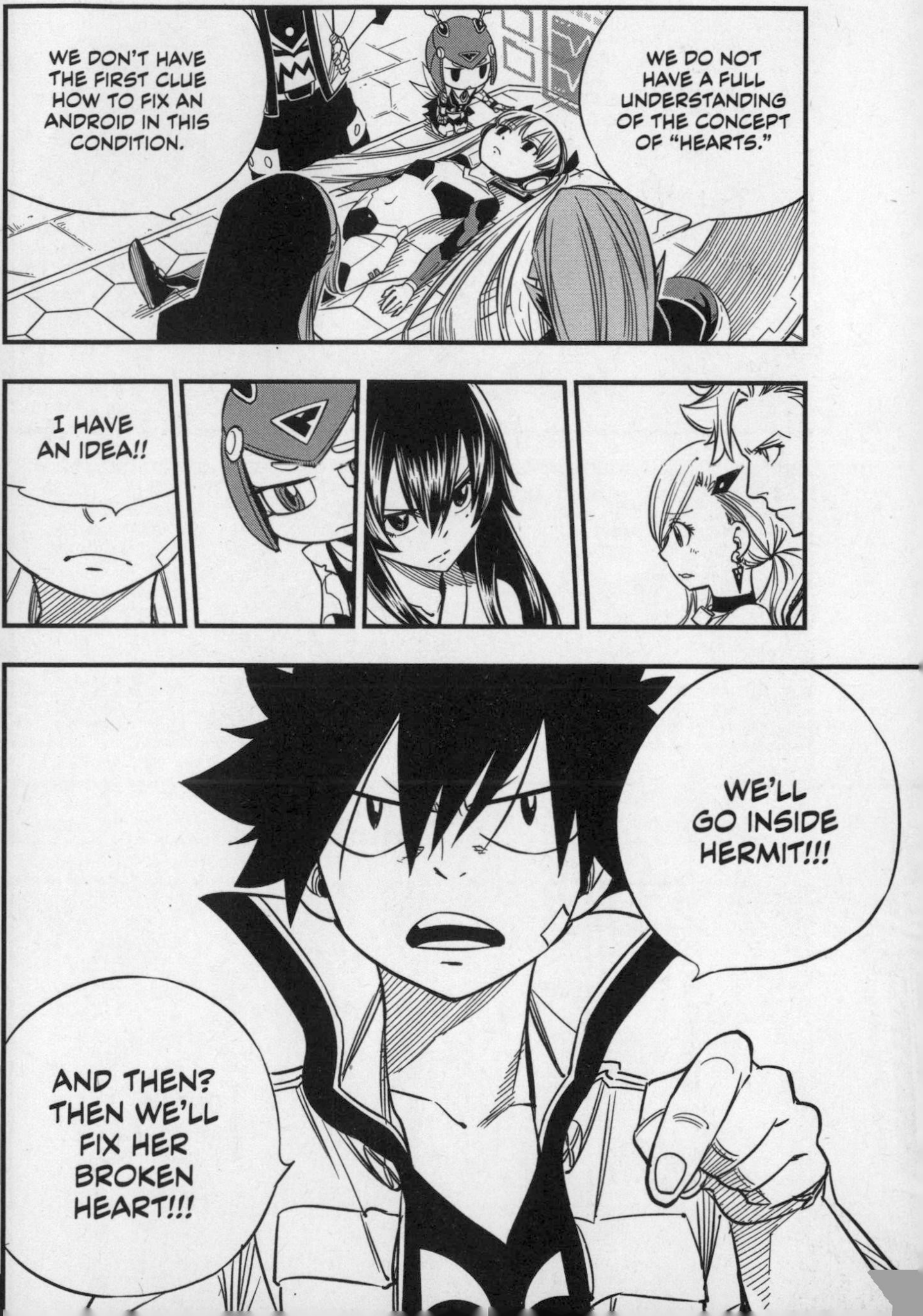
WE DO NOT HAVE A FULL UNDERSTANDING OF THE CONCEPT OF "HEARTS."
WE DON'T HAVE THE FIRST CLUE HOW TO FIX AN ANDROID IN THIS CONDITION.
I HAVE AN IDEA!!
WE'LL GO INSIDE HERMIT!!!
AND THEN? THEN WE'LL FIX HER BROKEN HEART!!!

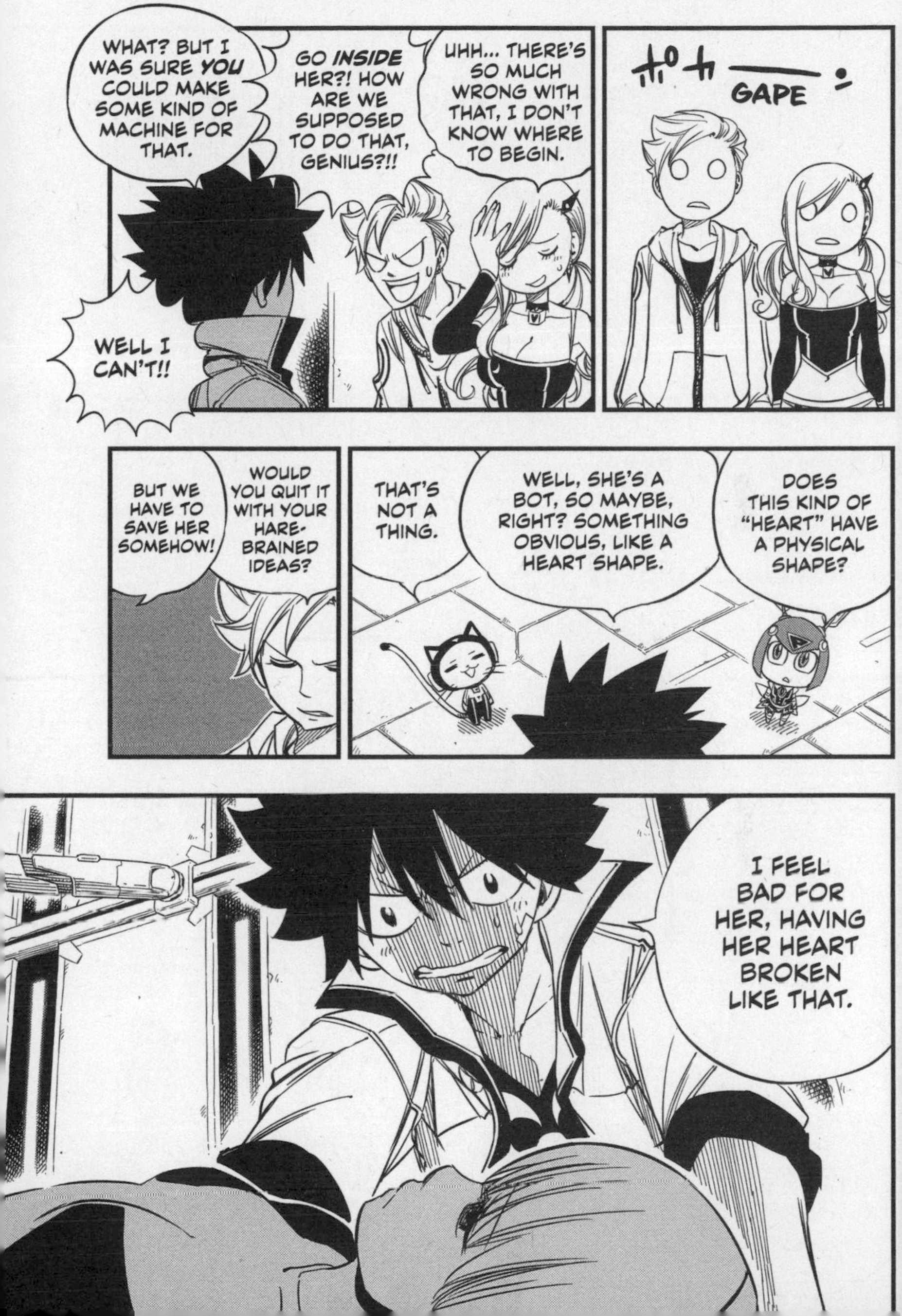
GAPE
UHH... THERE'S SO MUCH WRONG WITH THAT, I DON'T KNOW WHERE TO BEGIN.
GO INSIDE HER?! HOW ARE WE SUPPOSED TO DO THAT, GENIUS?!!
WHAT? BUT I WAS SURE YOU COULD MAKE SOME KIND OF MACHINE FOR THAT.
WELL I CAN'T!!
DOES THIS KIND OF "HEART" HAVE A PHYSICAL SHAPE?
WELL, SHE'S A BOT, SO MAYBE, RIGHT? SOMETHING OBVIOUS, LIKE A HEART SHAPE.
THAT'S NOT A THING.
WOULD YOU QUIT IT WITH YOUR HARE-BRAINED IDEAS?
BUT WE HAVE TO SAVE HER SOMEHOW!
I FEEL BAD FOR HER, HAVING HER HEART BROKEN LIKE THAT.

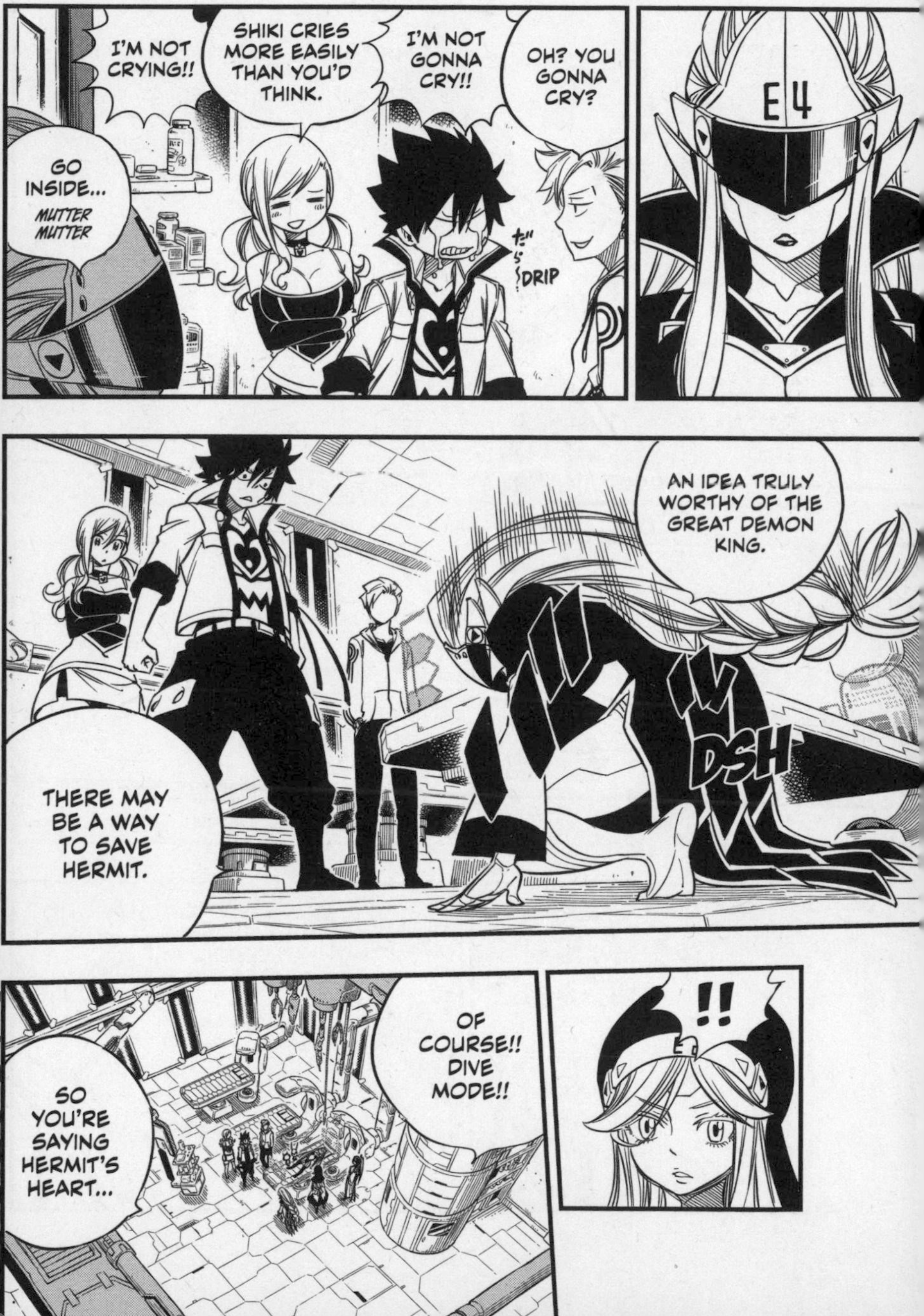
OH? YOU GONNA CRY?
I'M NOT GONNA CRY!!
SHIKI CRIES MORE EASILY THAN YOU'D THINK.
I'M NOT CRYING!!
GO INSIDE...
MUTTER MUTTER
DRIP
AN IDEA TRULY WORTHY OF THE GREAT DEMON KING.
DSH
THERE MAY BE A WAY TO SAVE HERMIT.
!!
SO YOU'RE SAYING HERMIT'S HEART...
OF COURSE!! DIVE MODE!!

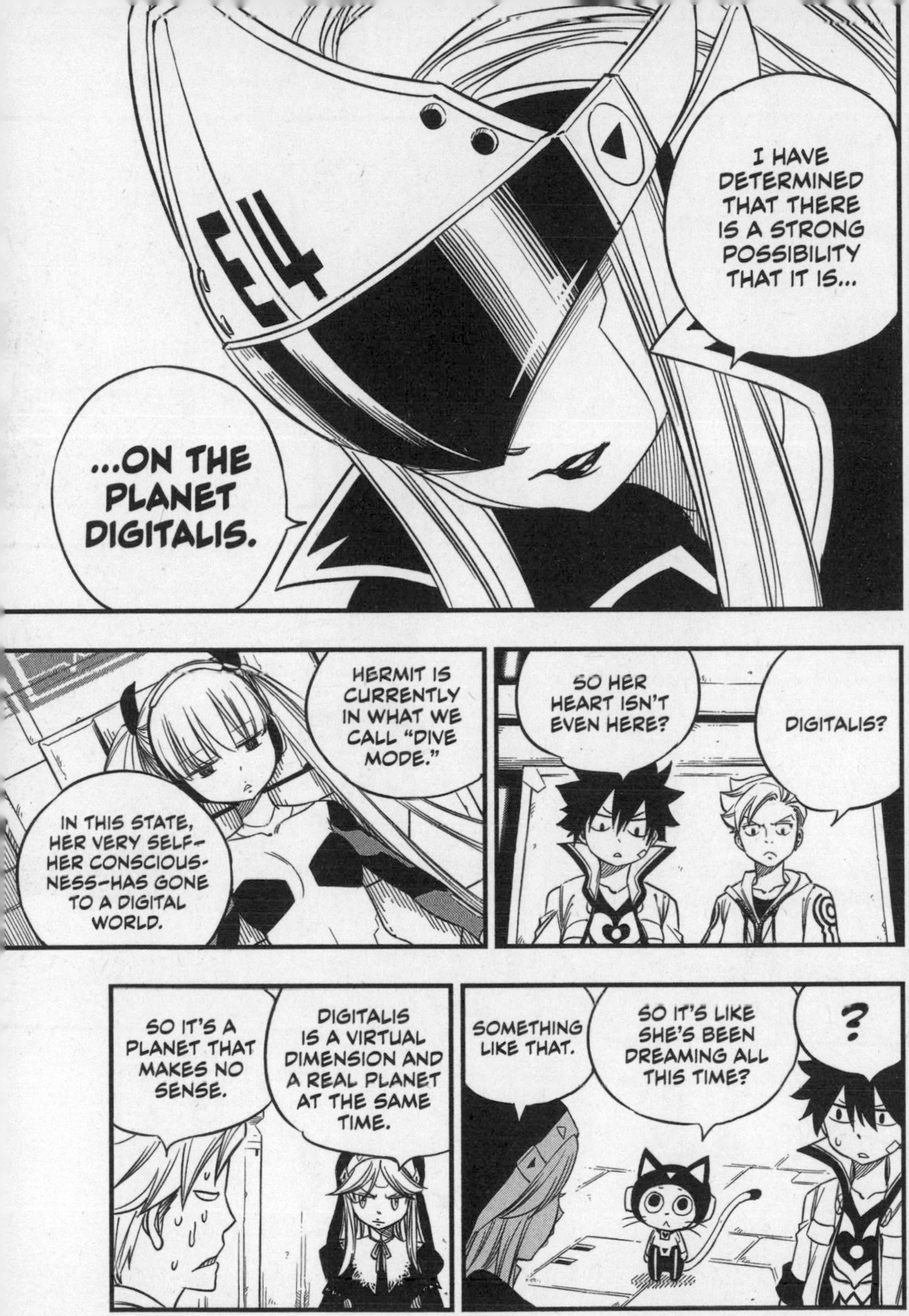
I HAVE DETERMINED THAT THERE IS A STRONG POSSIBILITY THAT IT IS...
...ON THE PLANET DIGITALIS.
DIGITALIS?
SO HER HEART ISN'T EVEN HERE?
HERMIT IS CURRENTLY IN WHAT WE CALL "DIVE MODE."
IN THIS STATE, HER VERY SELF—HER CONSCIOUSNESS—HAS GONE TO A DIGITAL WORLD.
?
SO IT'S LIKE SHE'S BEEN DREAMING ALL THIS TIME?
SOMETHING LIKE THAT.
DIGITALIS IS A VIRTUAL DIMENSION AND A REAL PLANET AT THE SAME TIME.
SO IT'S A PLANET THAT MAKES NO SENSE.

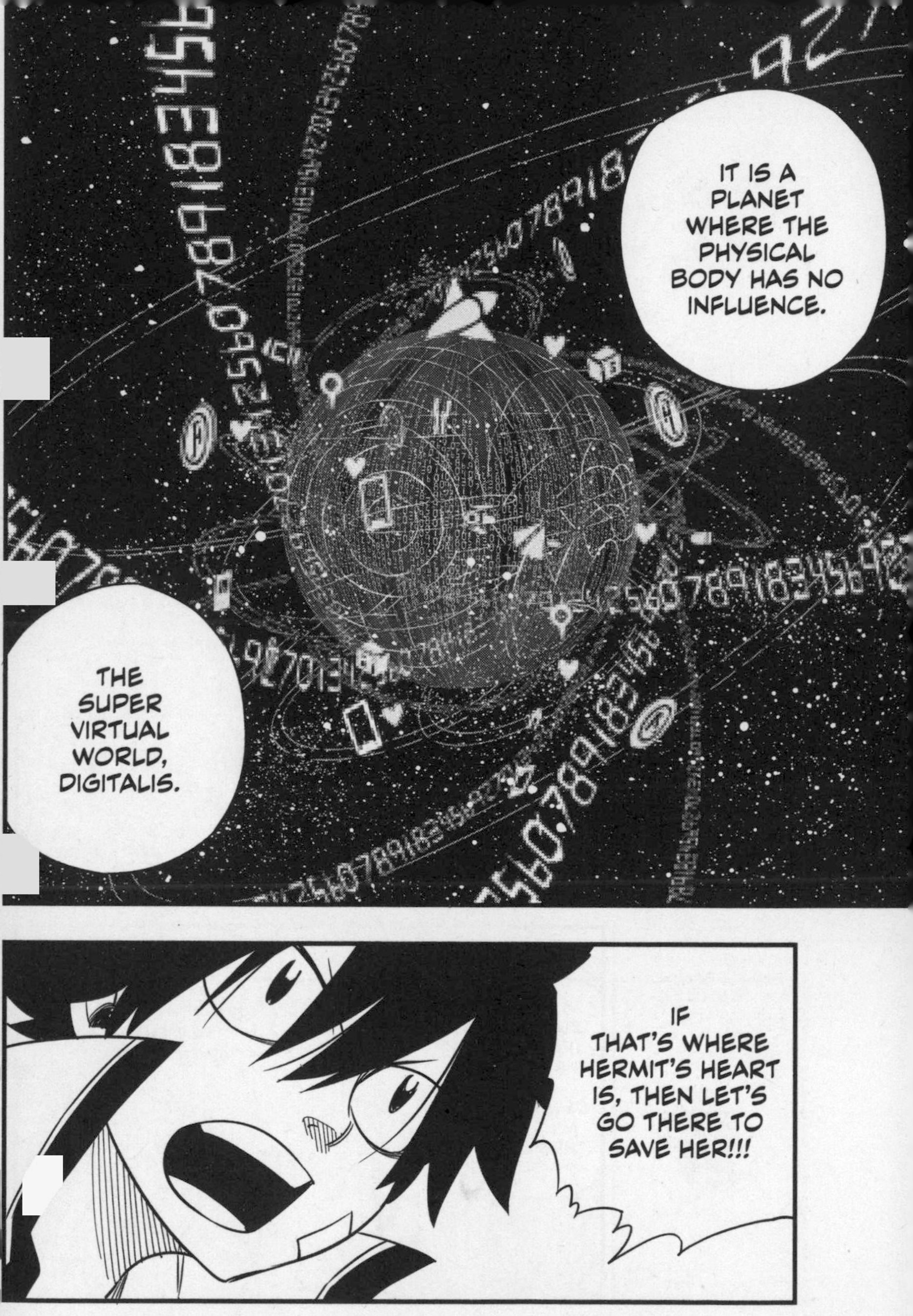
IT IS A PLANET WHERE THE PHYSICAL BODY HAS NO INFLUENCE.
THE SUPER VIRTUAL WORLD, DIGITALIS.
IF THAT'S WHERE HERMIT'S HEART IS, THEN LET'S GO THERE TO SAVE HER!!!

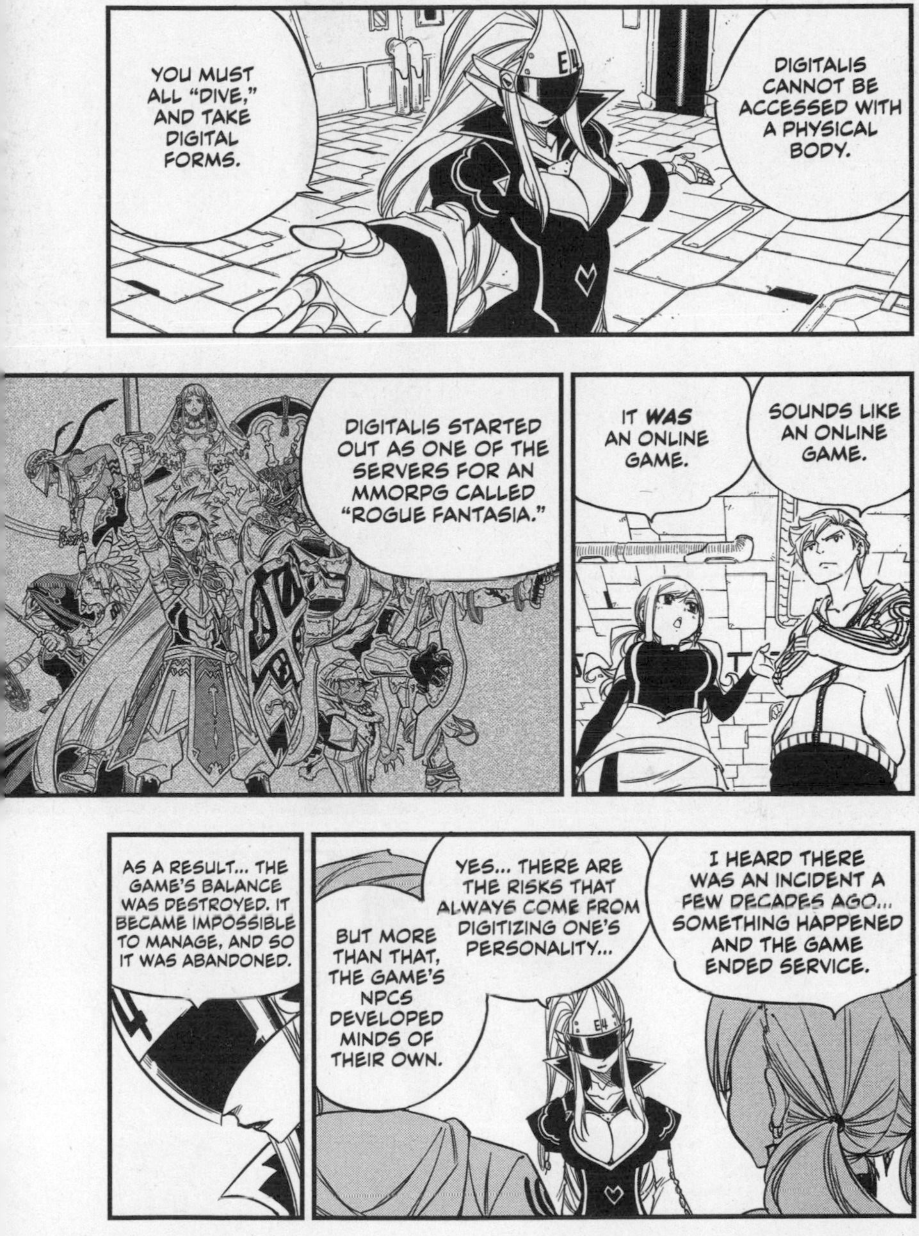
DIGITALIS CANNOT BE ACCESSED WITH A PHYSICAL BODY.
YOU MUST ALL "DIVE," AND TAKE DIGITAL FORMS.
SOUNDS LIKE AN ONLINE GAME.
IT *WAS* AN ONLINE GAME.
DIGITALIS STARTED OUT AS ONE OF THE SERVERS FOR AN MMORPG CALLED "ROGUE FANTASIA."
I HEARD THERE WAS AN INCIDENT A FEW DECADES AGO... SOMETHING HAPPENED AND THE GAME ENDED SERVICE.
YES... THERE ARE THE RISKS THAT ALWAYS COME FROM DIGITIZING ONE'S PERSONALITY...
BUT MORE THAN THAT, THE GAME'S NPCS DEVELOPED MINDS OF THEIR OWN.
AS A RESULT... THE GAME'S BALANCE WAS DESTROYED. IT BECAME IMPOSSIBLE TO MANAGE, AND SO IT WAS ABANDONED.

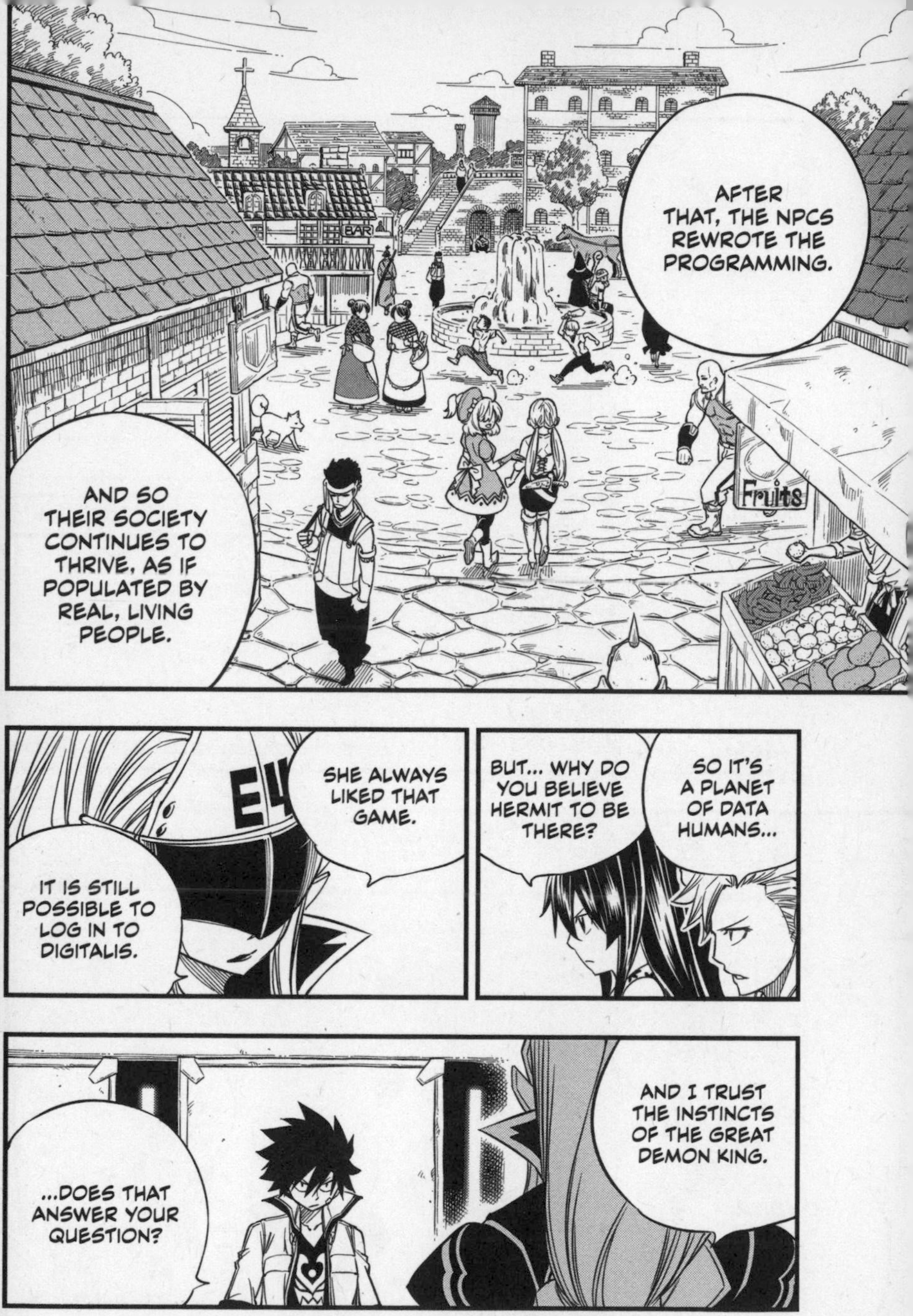
AFTER THAT, THE NPCS REWROTE THE PROGRAMMING.
BAR
Fruits
AND SO THEIR SOCIETY CONTINUES TO THRIVE, AS IF POPULATED BY REAL, LIVING PEOPLE.
SO IT'S A PLANET OF DATA HUMANS...
BUT... WHY DO YOU BELIEVE HERMIT TO BE THERE?
SHE ALWAYS LIKED THAT GAME.
IT IS STILL POSSIBLE TO LOG IN TO DIGITALIS.
AND I TRUST THE INSTINCTS OF THE GREAT DEMON KING.
...DOES THAT ANSWER YOUR QUESTION?

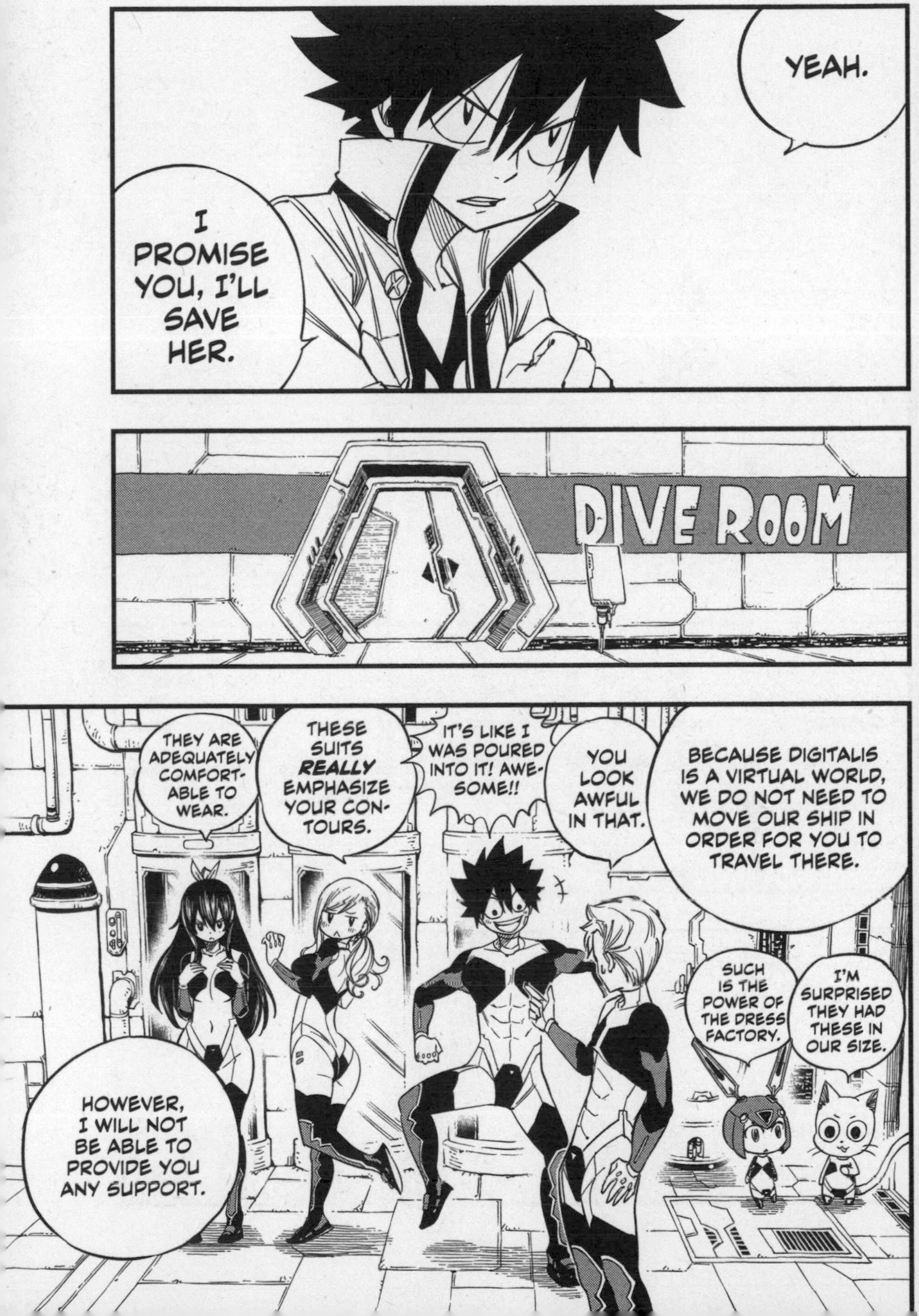
YEAH.
I PROMISE YOU, I'LL SAVE HER.
DIVE ROOM
BECAUSE DIGITALIS IS A VIRTUAL WORLD, WE DO NOT NEED TO MOVE OUR SHIP IN ORDER FOR YOU TO TRAVEL THERE.
YOU LOOK AWFUL IN THAT.
IT'S LIKE I WAS POURED INTO IT! AWE-SOME!!
THESE SUITS *REALLY* EMPHASIZE YOUR CON-TOURS.
THEY ARE ADEQUATELY COMFORT-ABLE TO WEAR.
I'M SURPRISED THEY HAD THESE IN OUR SIZE.
SUCH IS THE POWER OF THE DRESS FACTORY.
HOWEVER, I WILL NOT BE ABLE TO PROVIDE YOU ANY SUPPORT.

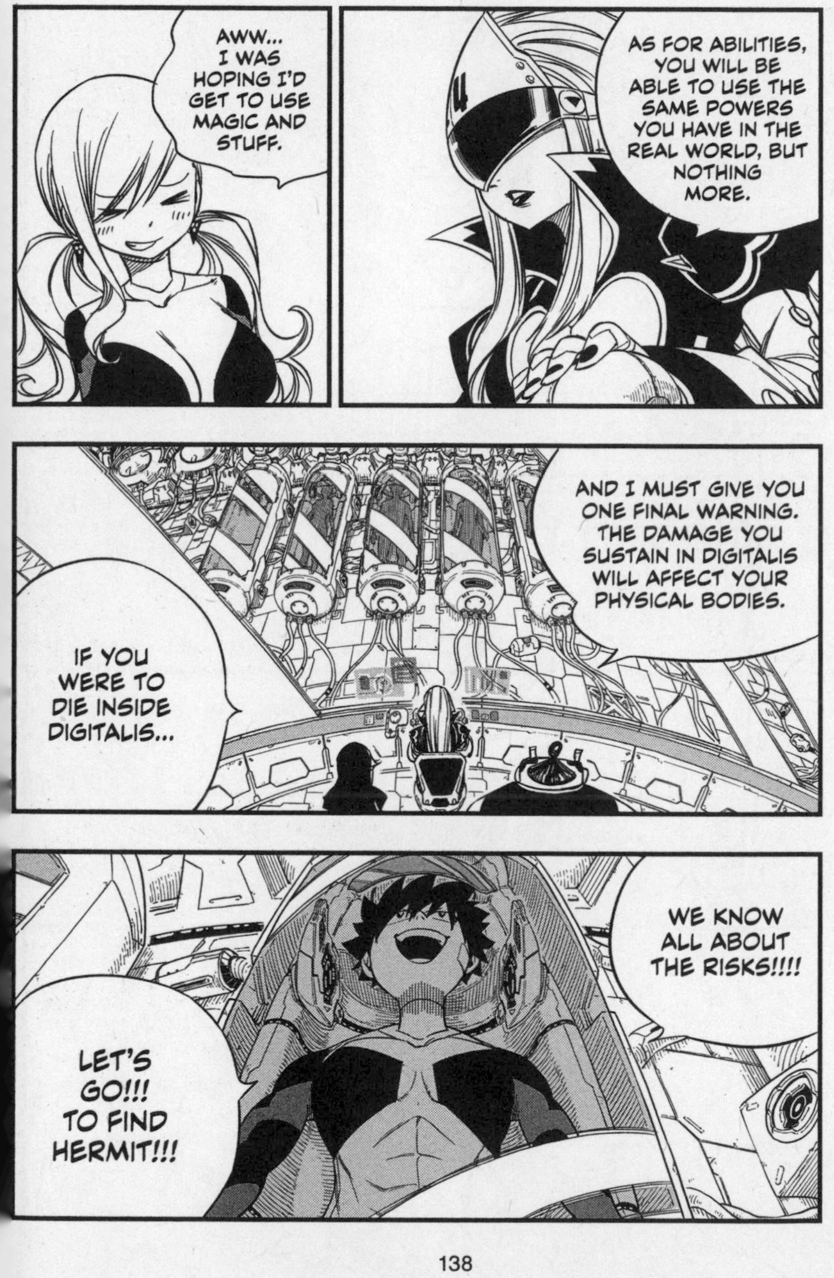
AS FOR ABILITIES, YOU WILL BE ABLE TO USE THE SAME POWERS YOU HAVE IN THE REAL WORLD, BUT NOTHING MORE.
AWW... I WAS HOPING I'D GET TO USE MAGIC AND STUFF.
AND I MUST GIVE YOU ONE FINAL WARNING. THE DAMAGE YOU SUSTAIN IN DIGITALIS WILL AFFECT YOUR PHYSICAL BODIES.
IF YOU WERE TO DIE INSIDE DIGITALIS...
WE KNOW ALL ABOUT THE RISKS!!!!
LET'S GO!!! TO FIND HERMIT!!!

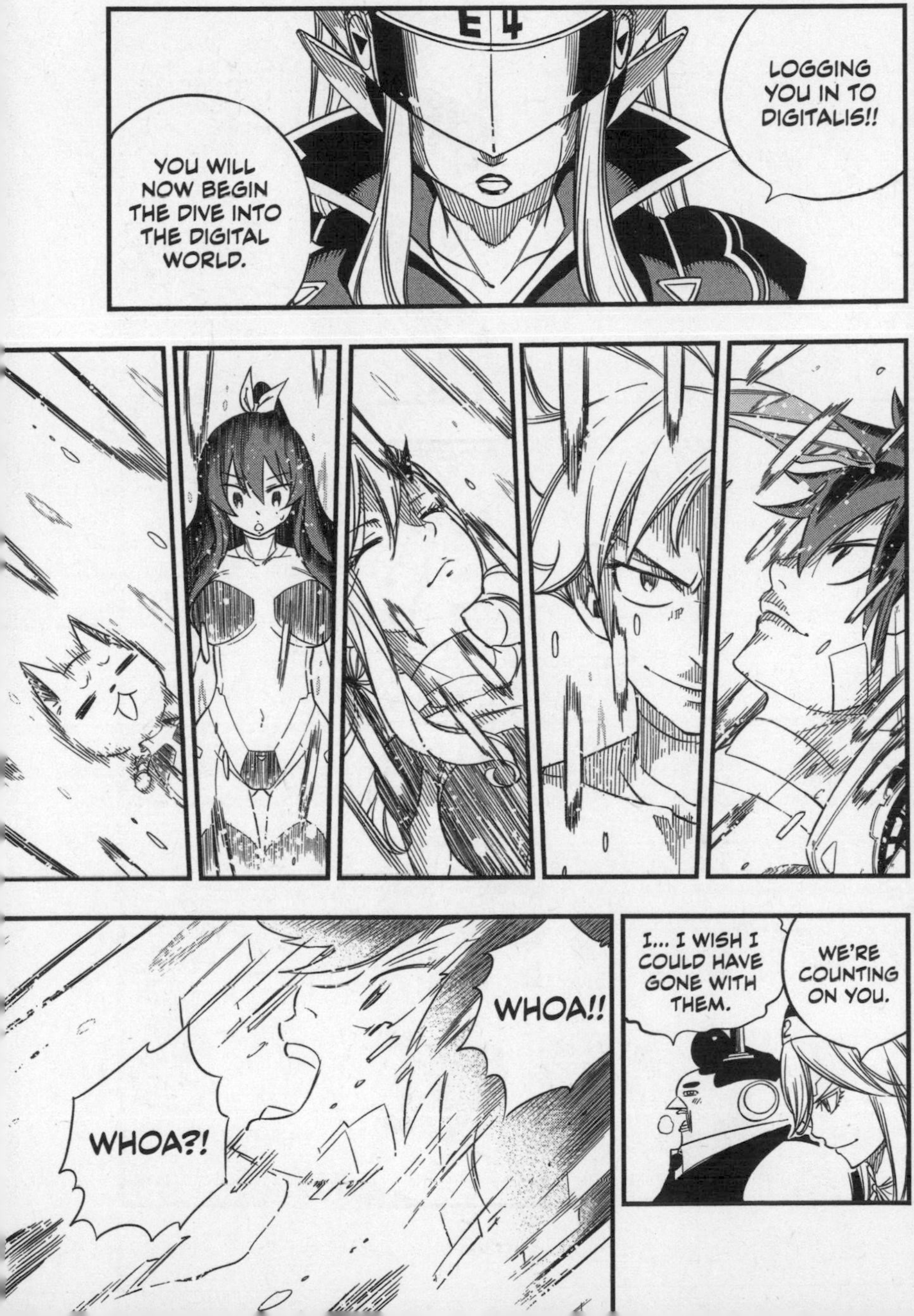
LOGGING YOU IN TO DIGITALIS!!
YOU WILL NOW BEGIN THE DIVE INTO THE DIGITAL WORLD.
WE'RE COUNTING ON YOU.
I... I WISH I COULD HAVE GONE WITH THEM.
WHOA!!
WHOA?!

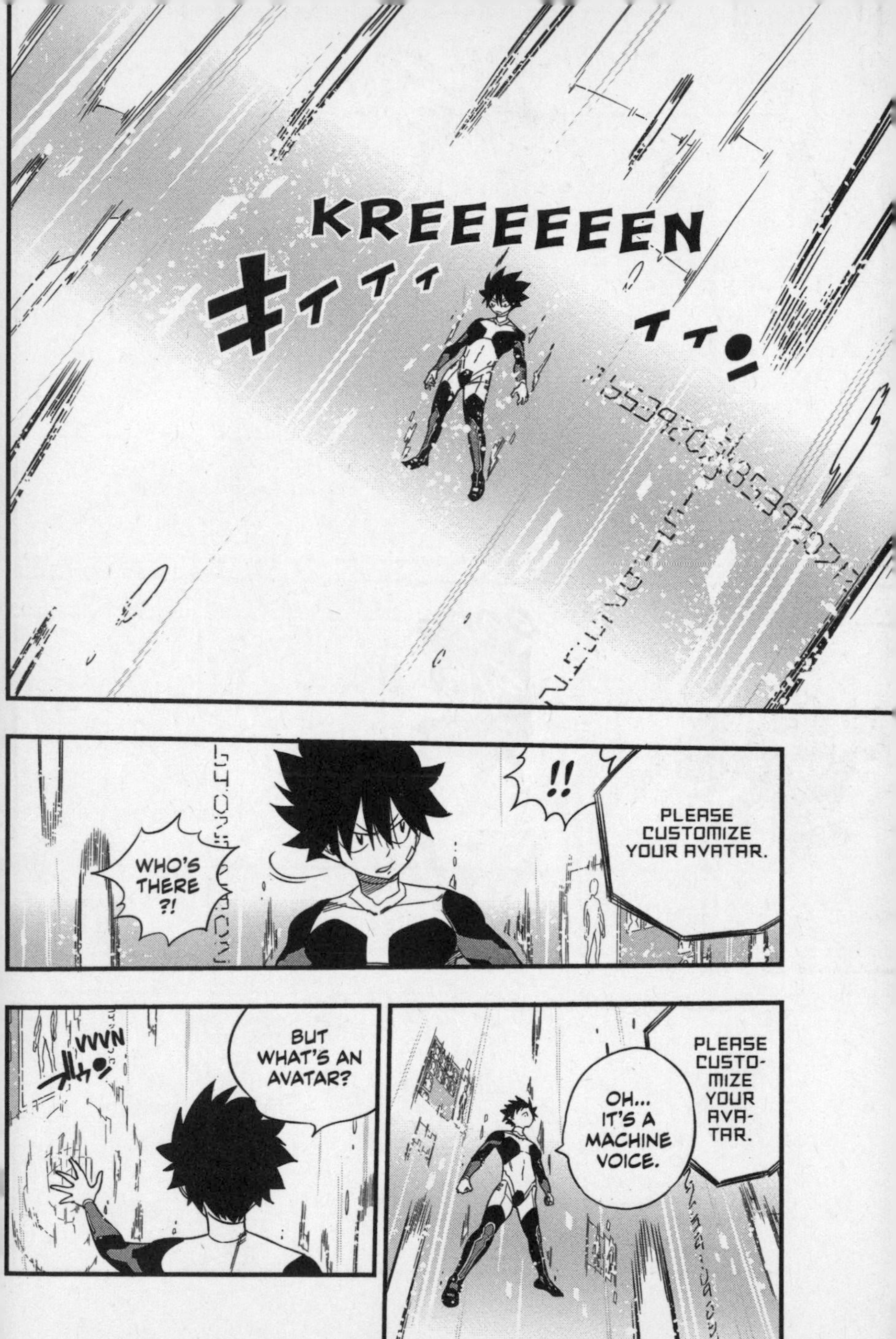
KREEEEEEN
キィィィ
ィィン
PLEASE CUSTOMIZE YOUR AVATAR.
!!
WHO'S THERE ?!
PLEASE CUSTO-MIZE YOUR AVA-TAR.
OH... IT'S A MACHINE VOICE.
VVVN
BUT WHAT'S AN AVATAR?

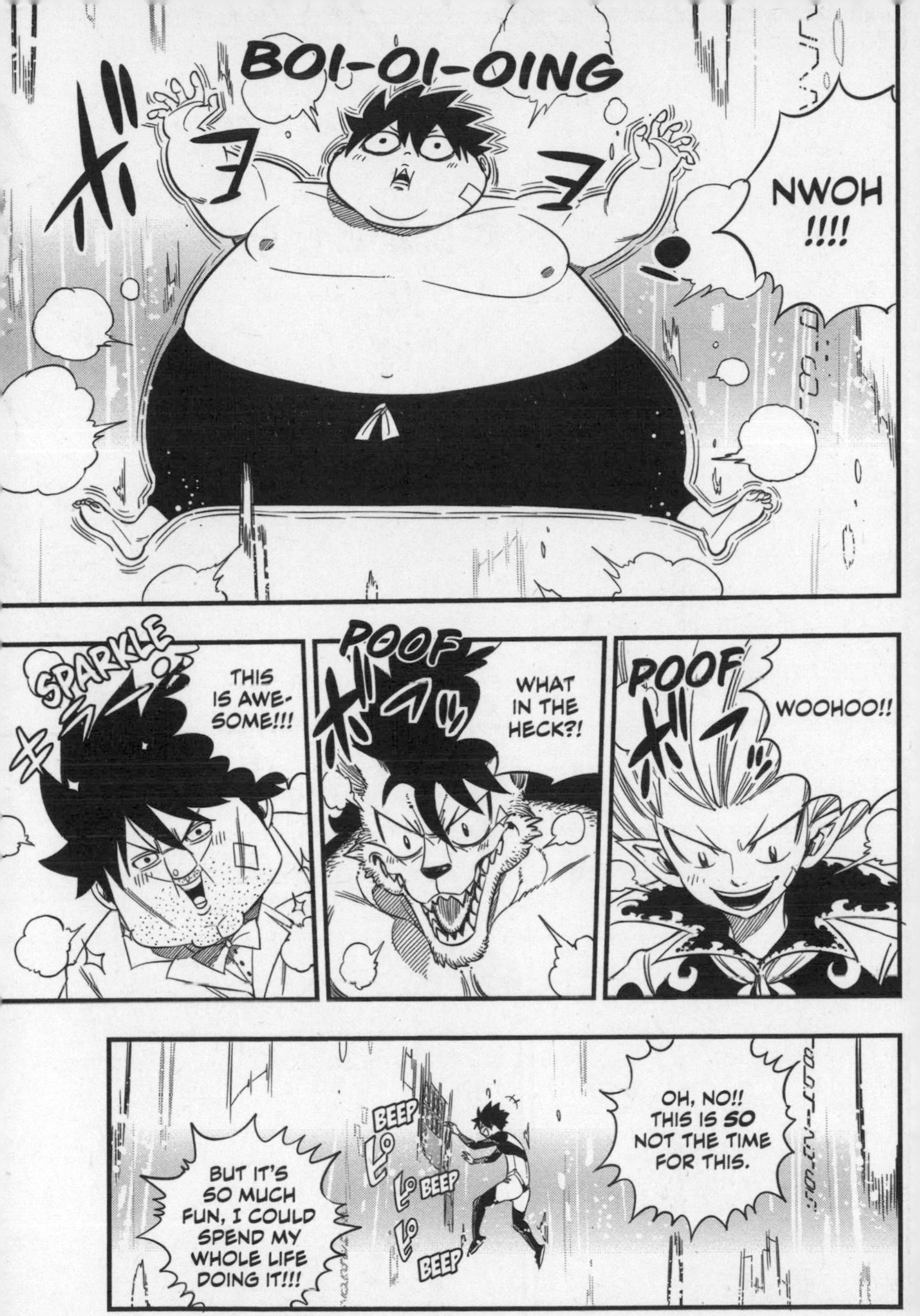

BOI-OI-OING
NWOH !!!!
POOF
WOOHOO!!
POOF
WHAT IN THE HECK?!
SPARKLE
THIS IS AWESOME!!!
OH, NO!! THIS IS SO NOT THE TIME FOR THIS.
BEEP
BEEP
BEEP
BEEP
BUT IT'S SO MUCH FUN, I COULD SPEND MY WHOLE LIFE DOING IT!!!

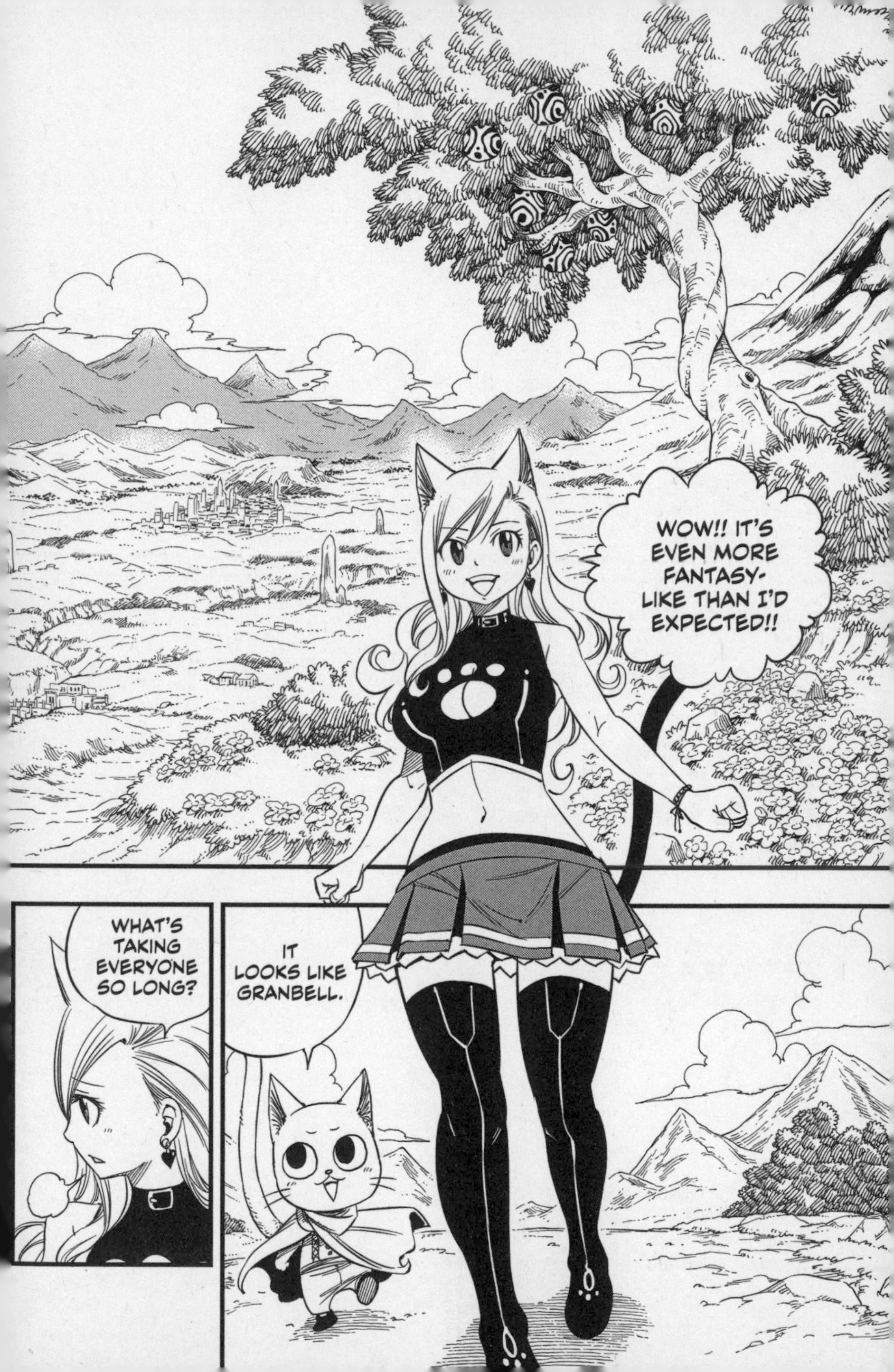
WOW!! IT'S EVEN MORE FANTASY-LIKE THAN I'D EXPECTED!!
IT LOOKS LIKE GRANBELL.
WHAT'S TAKING EVERYONE SO LONG?

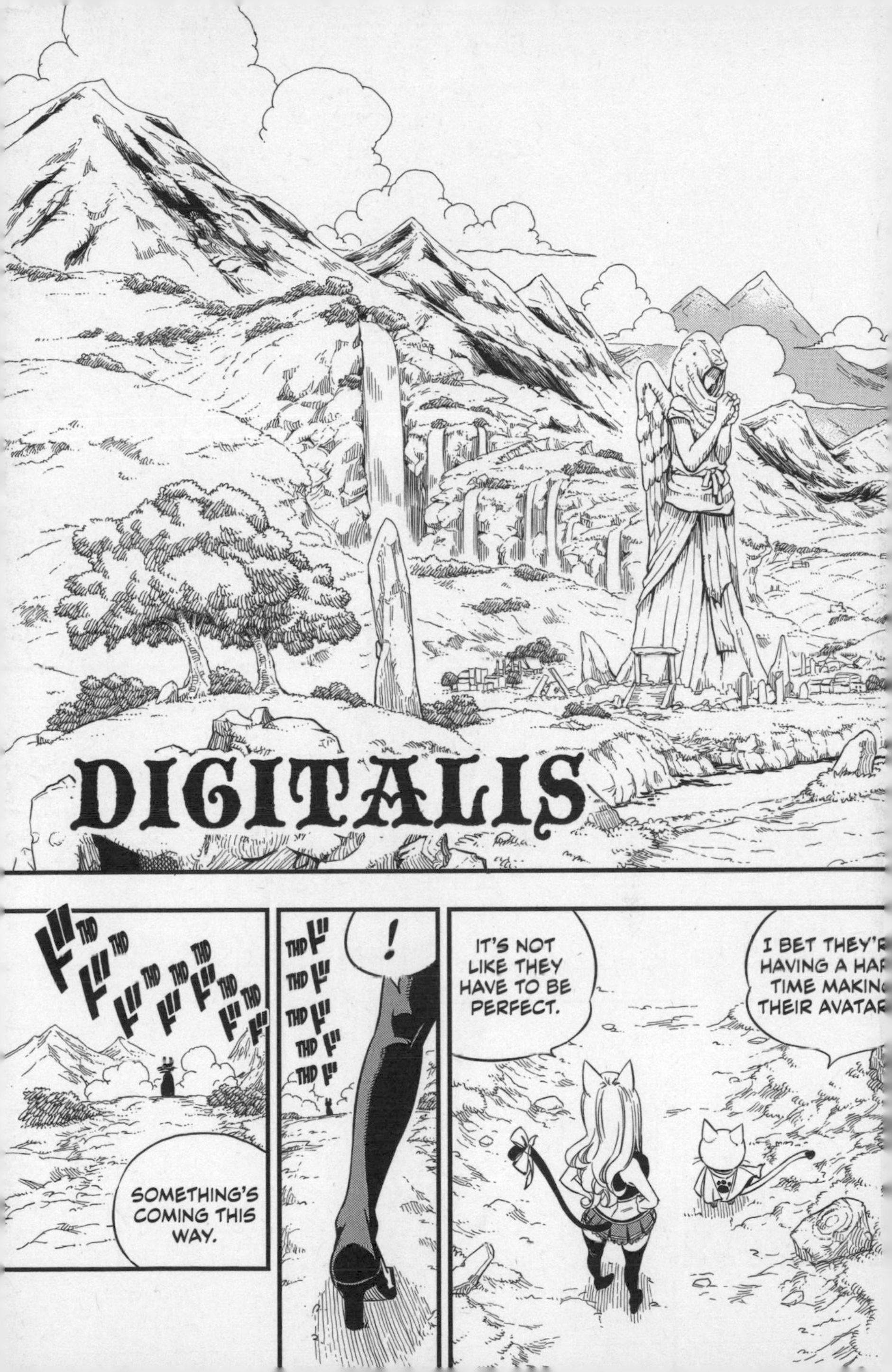
DIGITALIS
I BET THEY'R HAVING A HAR TIME MAKIN THEIR AVATAR
IT'S NOT LIKE THEY HAVE TO BE PERFECT.
!
ド THD ド THD ド THD ド THD ド THD
ド THD ド THD ド THD ド THD ド THD ド THD ド THD
SOMETHING'S COMING THIS WAY.

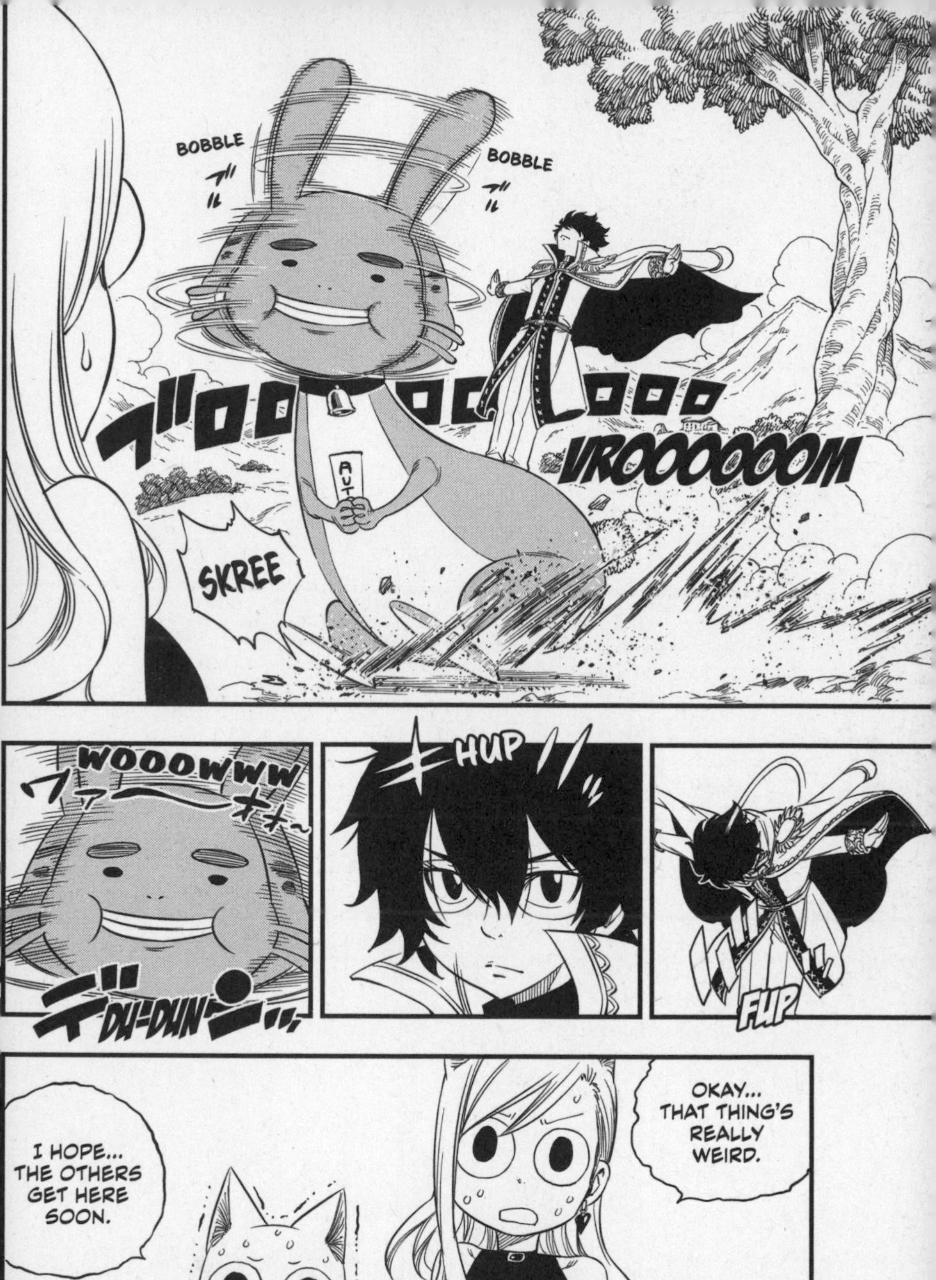
BOBBLE
BOBBLE
VROOOOOOM
SKREE
FUP
HUP
WOOOWWW
DU-DUN
OKAY... THAT THING'S REALLY WEIRD.
I HOPE... THE OTHERS GET HERE SOON.

CHAPTER 31: THE PEOPLE OF DIGITALIS

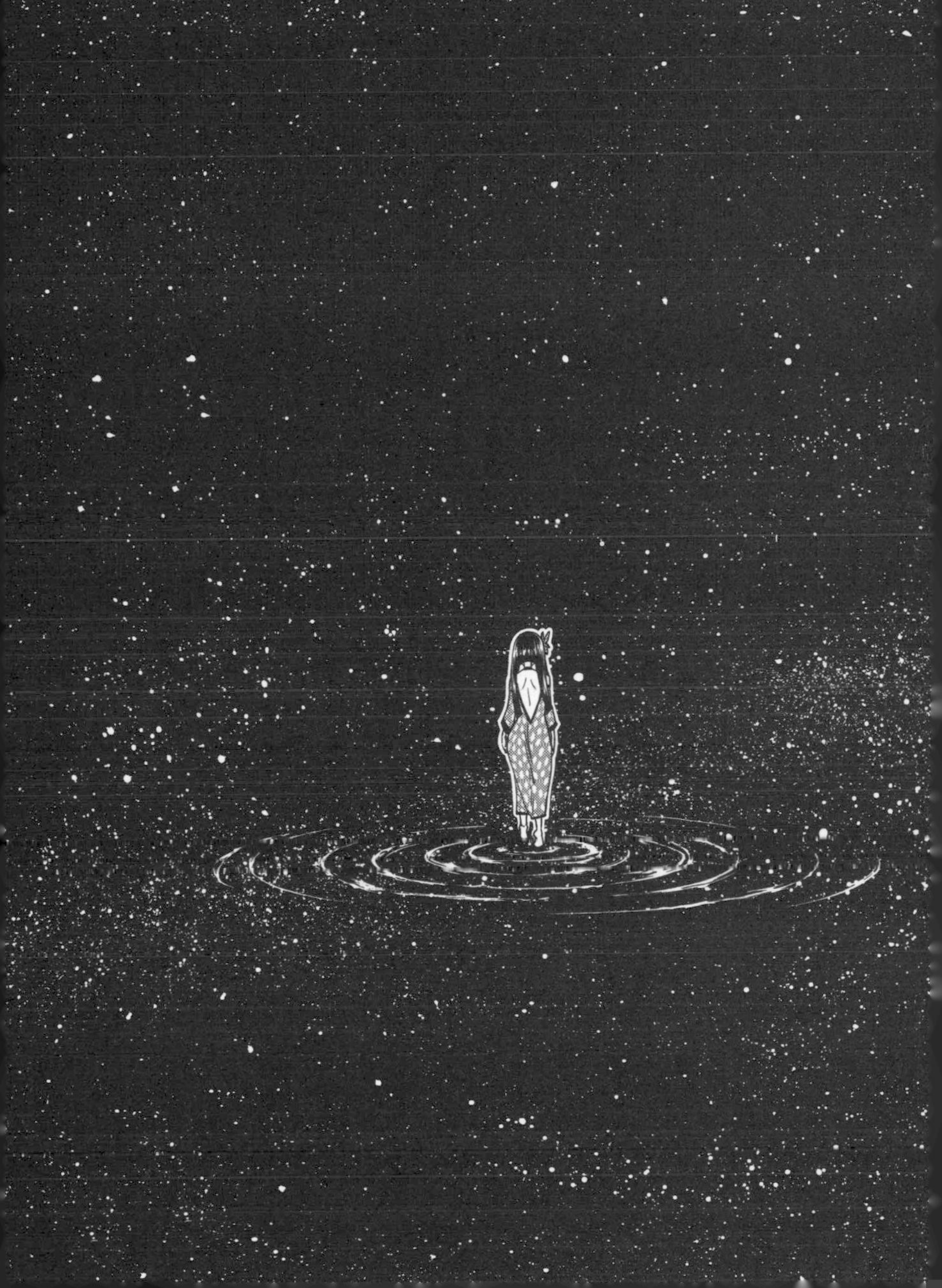

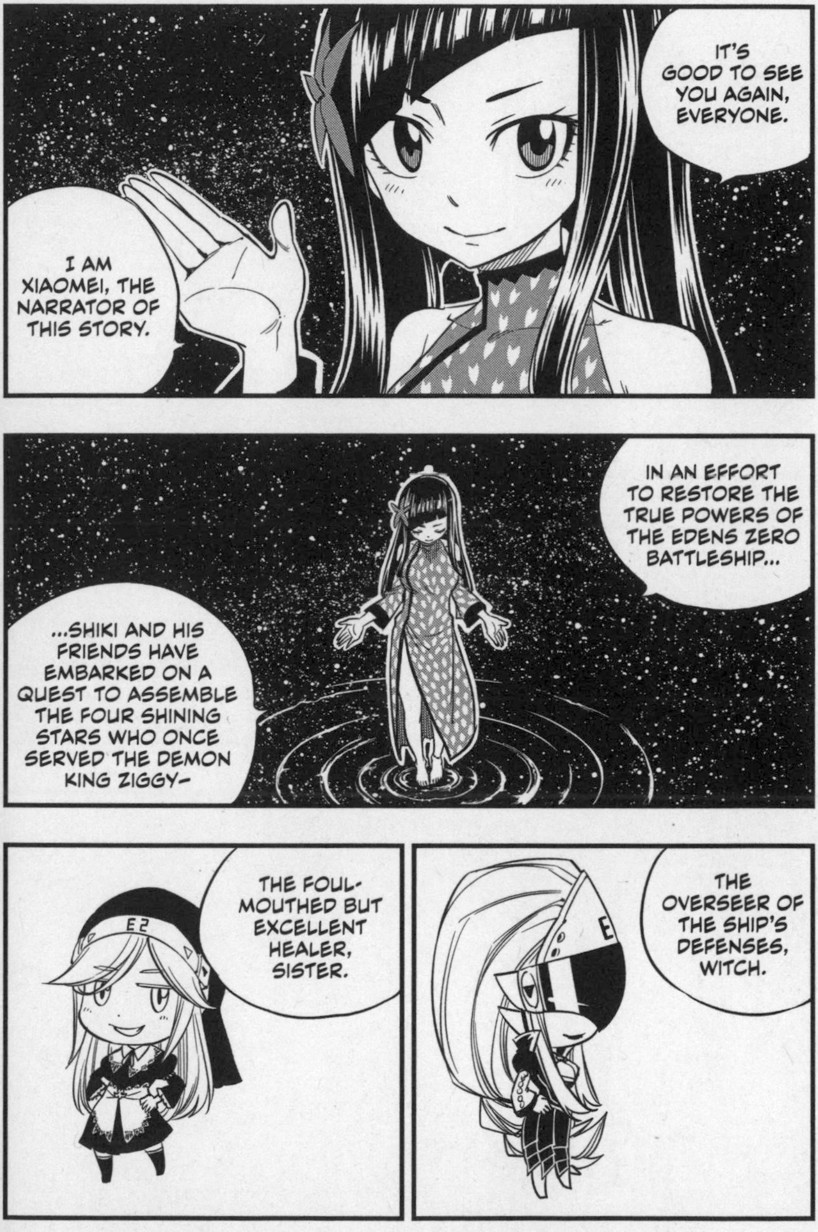
IT'S GOOD TO SEE YOU AGAIN, EVERYONE.
I AM XIAOMEI, THE NARRATOR OF THIS STORY.
IN AN EFFORT TO RESTORE THE TRUE POWERS OF THE EDENS ZERO BATTLESHIP...
...SHIKI AND HIS FRIENDS HAVE EMBARKED ON A QUEST TO ASSEMBLE THE FOUR SHINING STARS WHO ONCE SERVED THE DEMON KING ZIGGY–
THE OVERSEER OF THE SHIP'S DEFENSES, WITCH.
THE FOUL-MOUTHED BUT EXCELLENT HEALER, SISTER.

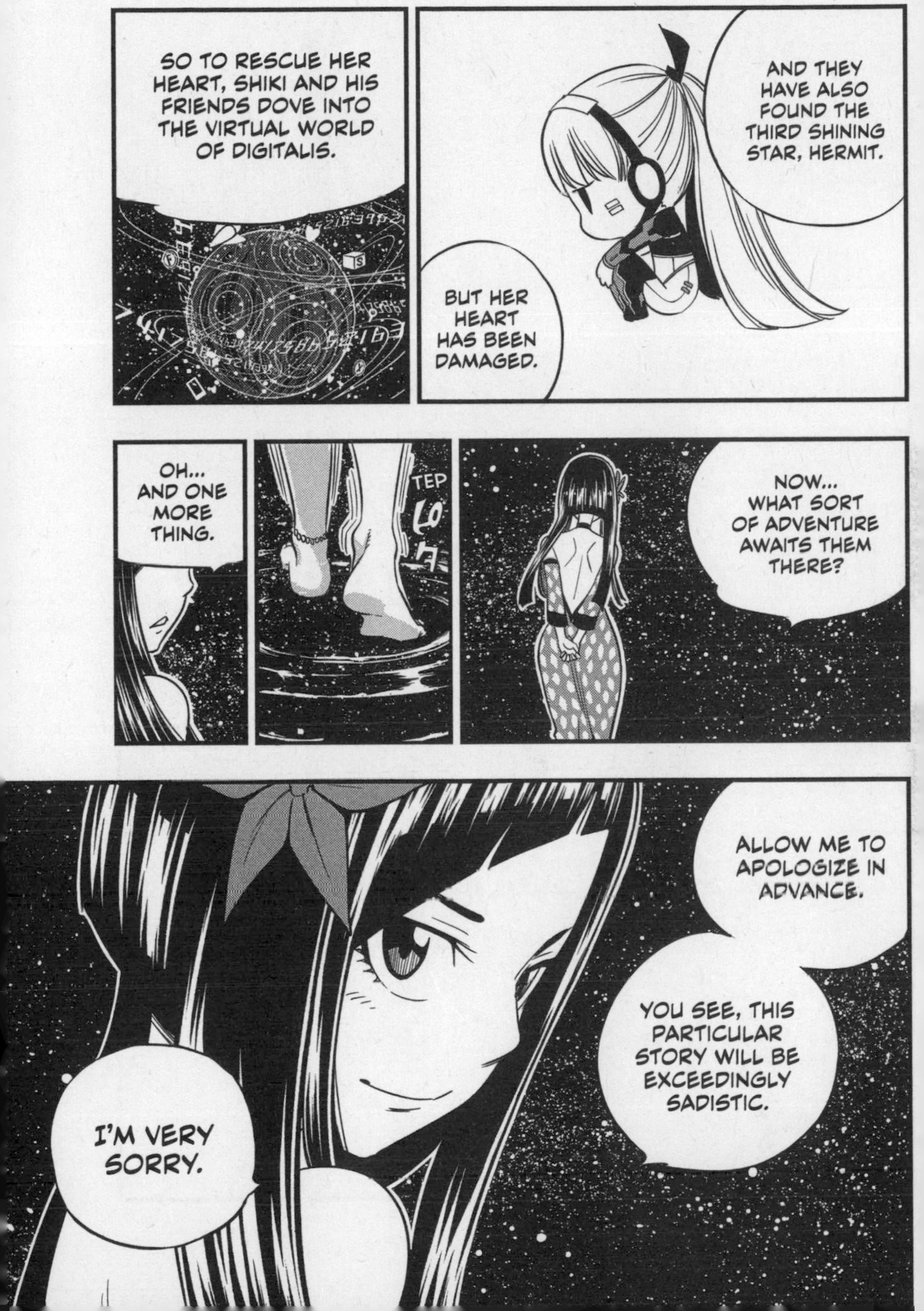
AND THEY HAVE ALSO FOUND THE THIRD SHINING STAR, HERMIT.
BUT HER HEART HAS BEEN DAMAGED.
SO TO RESCUE HER HEART, SHIKI AND HIS FRIENDS DOVE INTO THE VIRTUAL WORLD OF DIGITALIS.
NOW... WHAT SORT OF ADVENTURE AWAITS THEM THERE?
TEP
OH... AND ONE MORE THING.
ALLOW ME TO APOLOGIZE IN ADVANCE.
YOU SEE, THIS PARTICULAR STORY WILL BE EXCEEDINGLY SADISTIC.
I'M VERY SORRY.

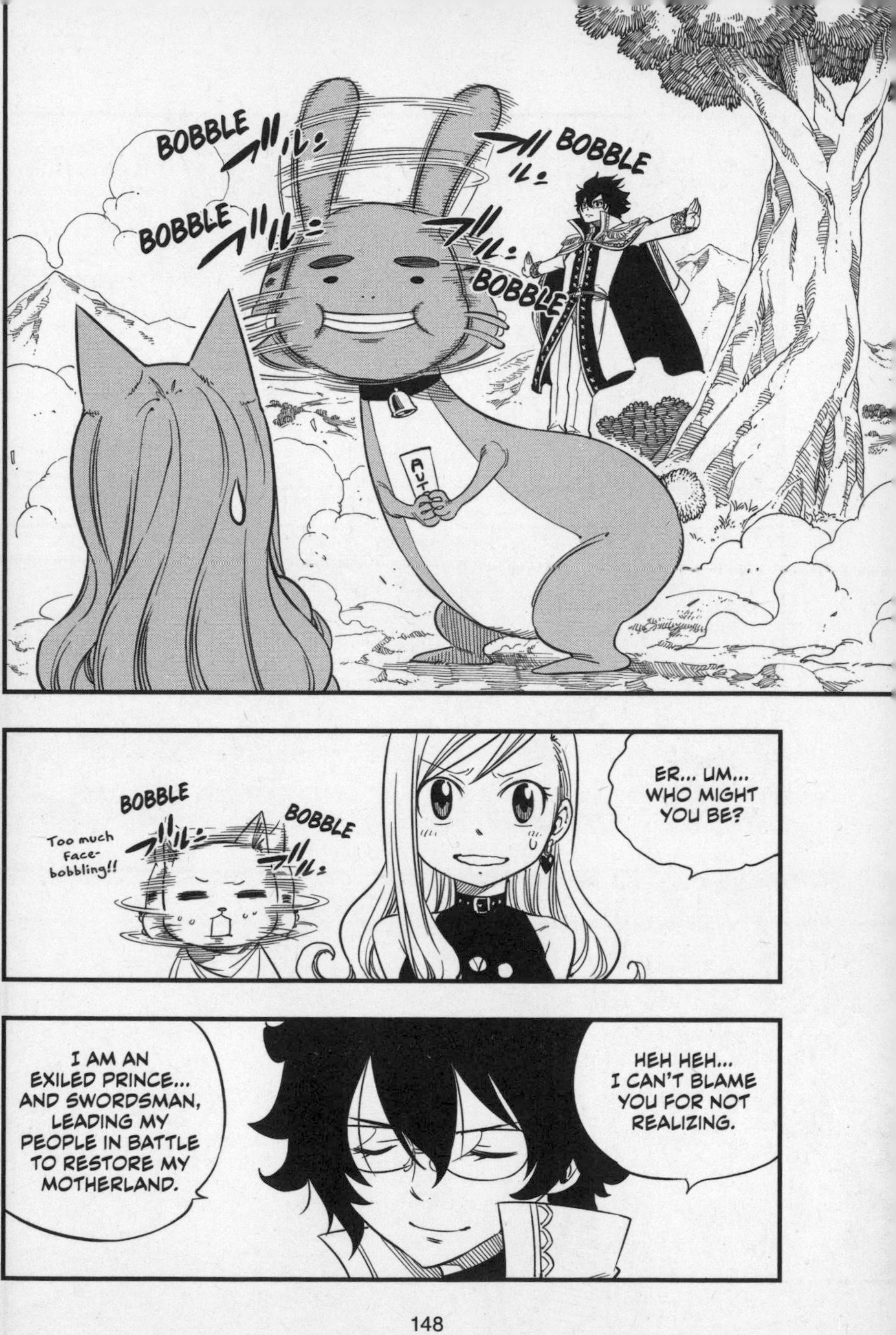
BOBBLE
BOBBLE
BOBBLE
BOBBLE
ER... UM... WHO MIGHT YOU BE?
BOBBLE
BOBBLE
Too much Face-bobbling!!
HEH HEH... I CAN'T BLAME YOU FOR NOT REALIZING.
I AM AN EXILED PRINCE... AND SWORDSMAN, LEADING MY PEOPLE IN BATTLE TO RESTORE MY MOTHERLAND.

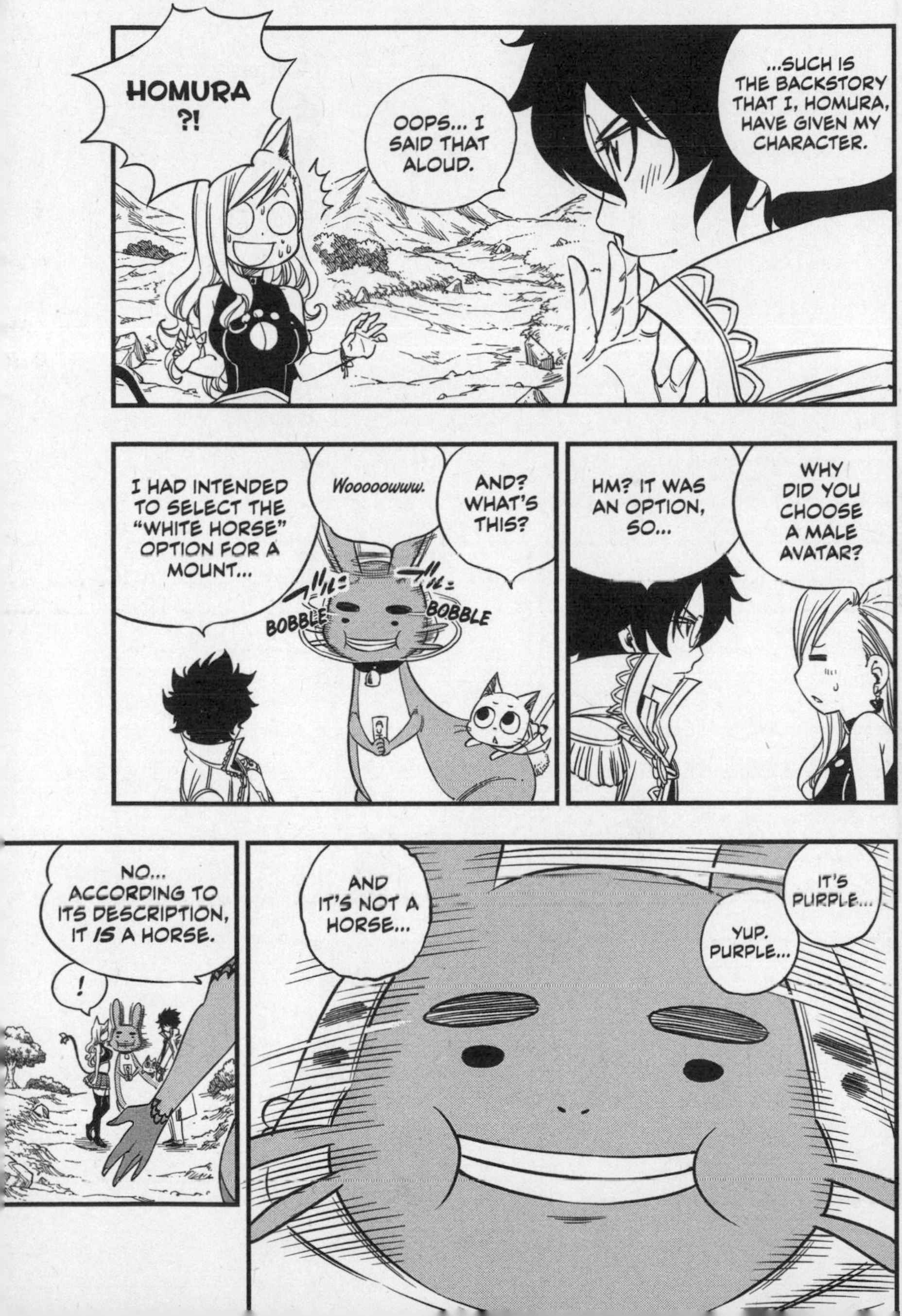
...SUCH IS THE BACKSTORY THAT I, HOMURA, HAVE GIVEN MY CHARACTER.
OOPS... I SAID THAT ALOUD.
HOMURA ?!
WHY DID YOU CHOOSE A MALE AVATAR?
HM? IT WAS AN OPTION, SO...
AND? WHAT'S THIS?
Wooooowww.
BOBBLE
BOBBLE
I HAD INTENDED TO SELECT THE "WHITE HORSE" OPTION FOR A MOUNT...
IT'S PURPLE...
YUP. PURPLE...
AND IT'S NOT A HORSE...
NO... ACCORDING TO ITS DESCRIPTION, IT *IS* A HORSE.
!

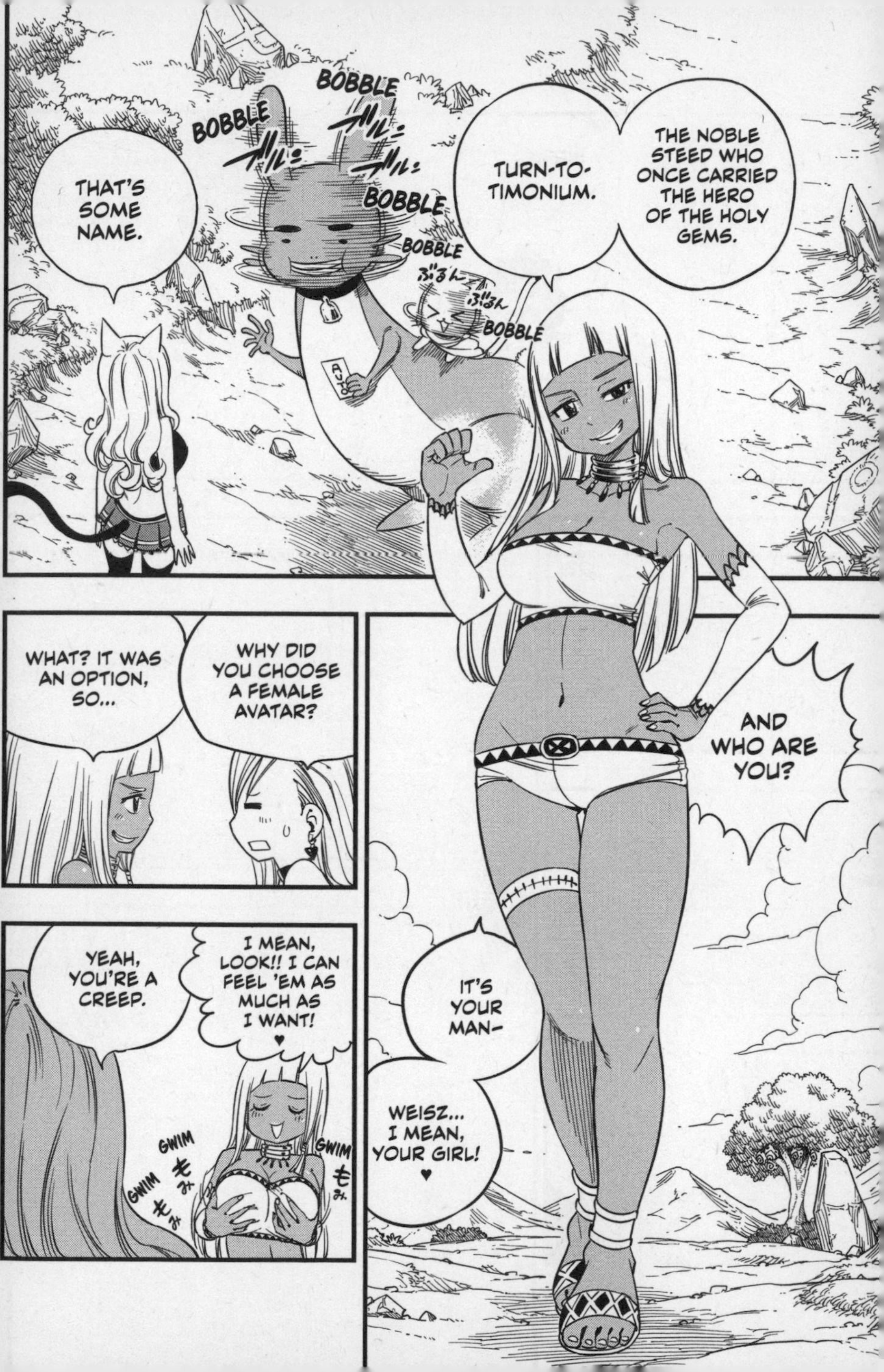
THE NOBLE STEED WHO ONCE CARRIED THE HERO OF THE HOLY GEMS.
TURN-TO-TIMONIUM.
BOBBLE BOBBLE BOBBLE BOBBLE BOBBLE
ぶるん ぶるん
AUTO
THAT'S SOME NAME.
AND WHO ARE YOU?
IT'S YOUR MAN-
WEISZ... I MEAN, YOUR GIRL! ♥
WHY DID YOU CHOOSE A FEMALE AVATAR?
WHAT? IT WAS AN OPTION, SO...
I MEAN, LOOK!! I CAN FEEL 'EM AS MUCH AS I WANT! ♥
GWIM GWIM GWIM
もみ もみ もみ
YEAH, YOU'RE A CREEP.

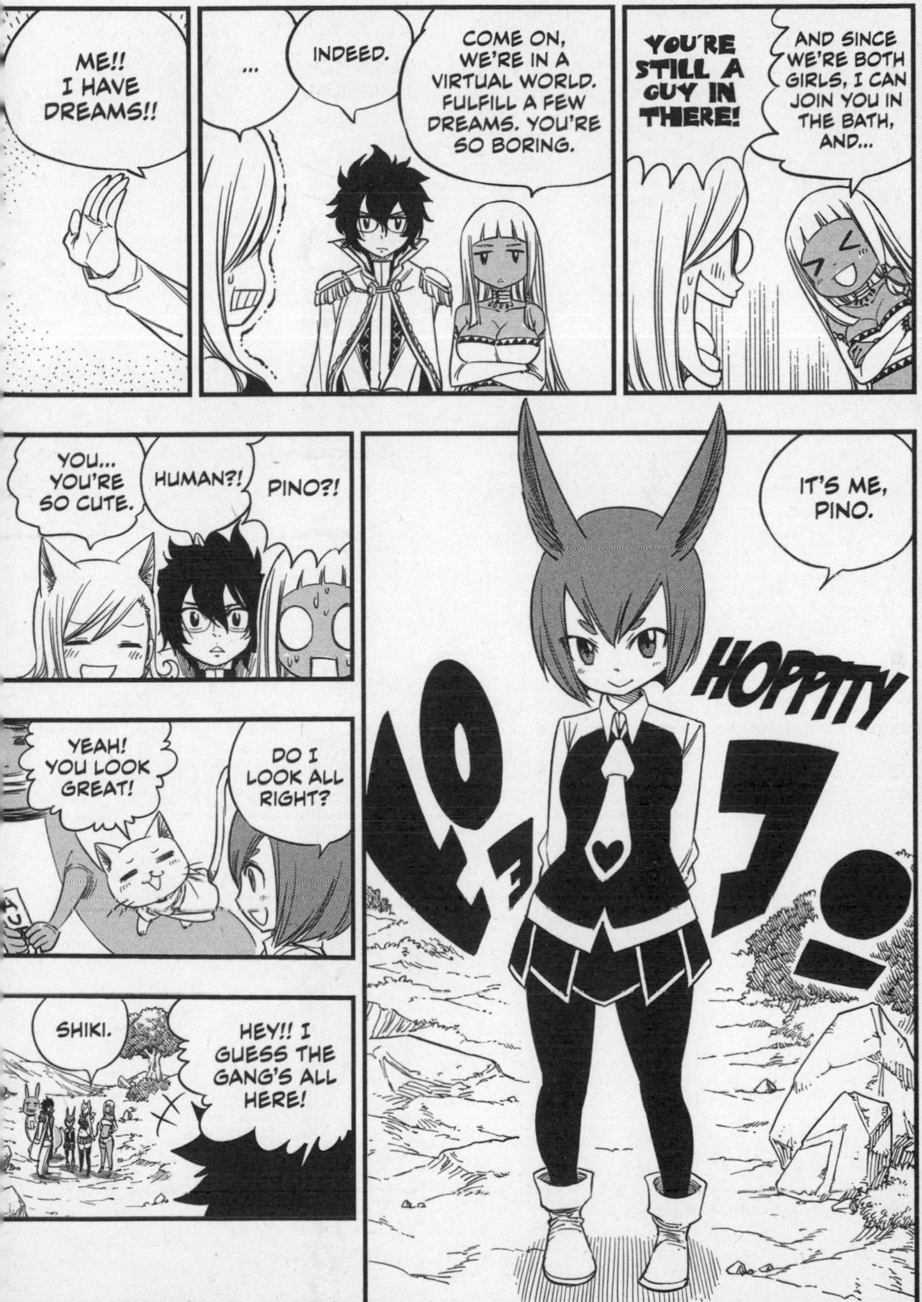
AND SINCE WE'RE BOTH GIRLS, I CAN JOIN YOU IN THE BATH, AND...
YOU'RE STILL A GUY IN THERE!
COME ON, WE'RE IN A VIRTUAL WORLD. FULFILL A FEW DREAMS. YOU'RE SO BORING.
INDEED.
...
ME!! I HAVE DREAMS!!
IT'S ME, PINO.
HOPPITY
PINO?!
HUMAN?!
YOU... YOU'RE SO CUTE.
DO I LOOK ALL RIGHT?
YEAH! YOU LOOK GREAT!
HEY!! I GUESS THE GANG'S ALL HERE!
SHIKI.

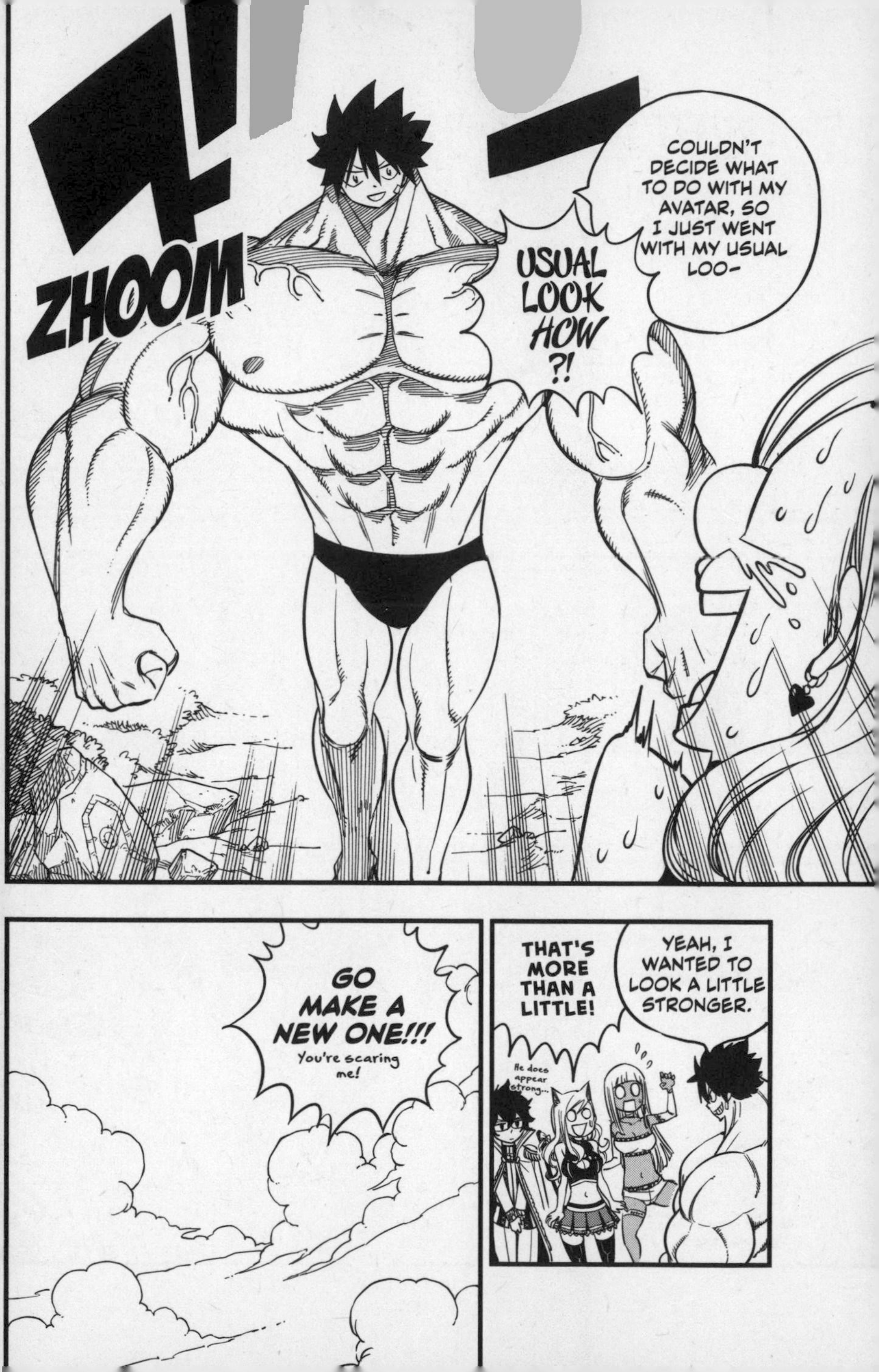
COULDN'T DECIDE WHAT TO DO WITH MY AVATAR, SO I JUST WENT WITH MY USUAL LOO-
USUAL LOOK HOW ?!
ZHOOM
YEAH, I WANTED TO LOOK A LITTLE STRONGER.
THAT'S MORE THAN A LITTLE!
He does appear strong...
GO MAKE A NEW ONE!!!
You're scaring me!

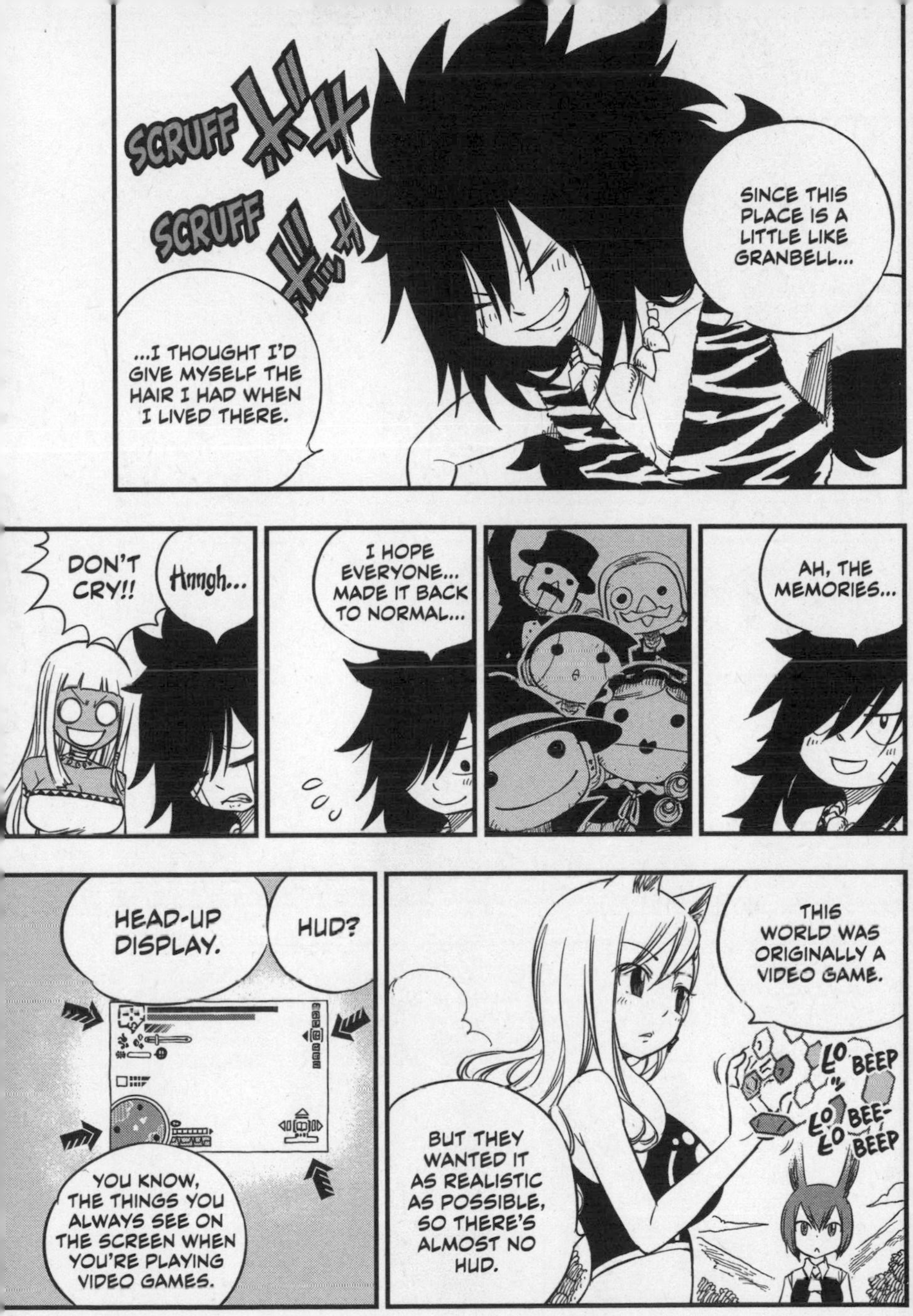
SINCE THIS PLACE IS A LITTLE LIKE GRANBELL...
SCRUFF
SCRUFF
...I THOUGHT I'D GIVE MYSELF THE HAIR I HAD WHEN I LIVED THERE.
AH, THE MEMORIES...
I HOPE EVERYONE... MADE IT BACK TO NORMAL...
Hnngh...
DON'T CRY!!
THIS WORLD WAS ORIGINALLY A VIDEO GAME.
BEEP
BEE-BEEP
BUT THEY WANTED IT AS REALISTIC AS POSSIBLE, SO THERE'S ALMOST NO HUD.
HUD?
HEAD-UP DISPLAY.
YOU KNOW, THE THINGS YOU ALWAYS SEE ON THE SCREEN WHEN YOU'RE PLAYING VIDEO GAMES.

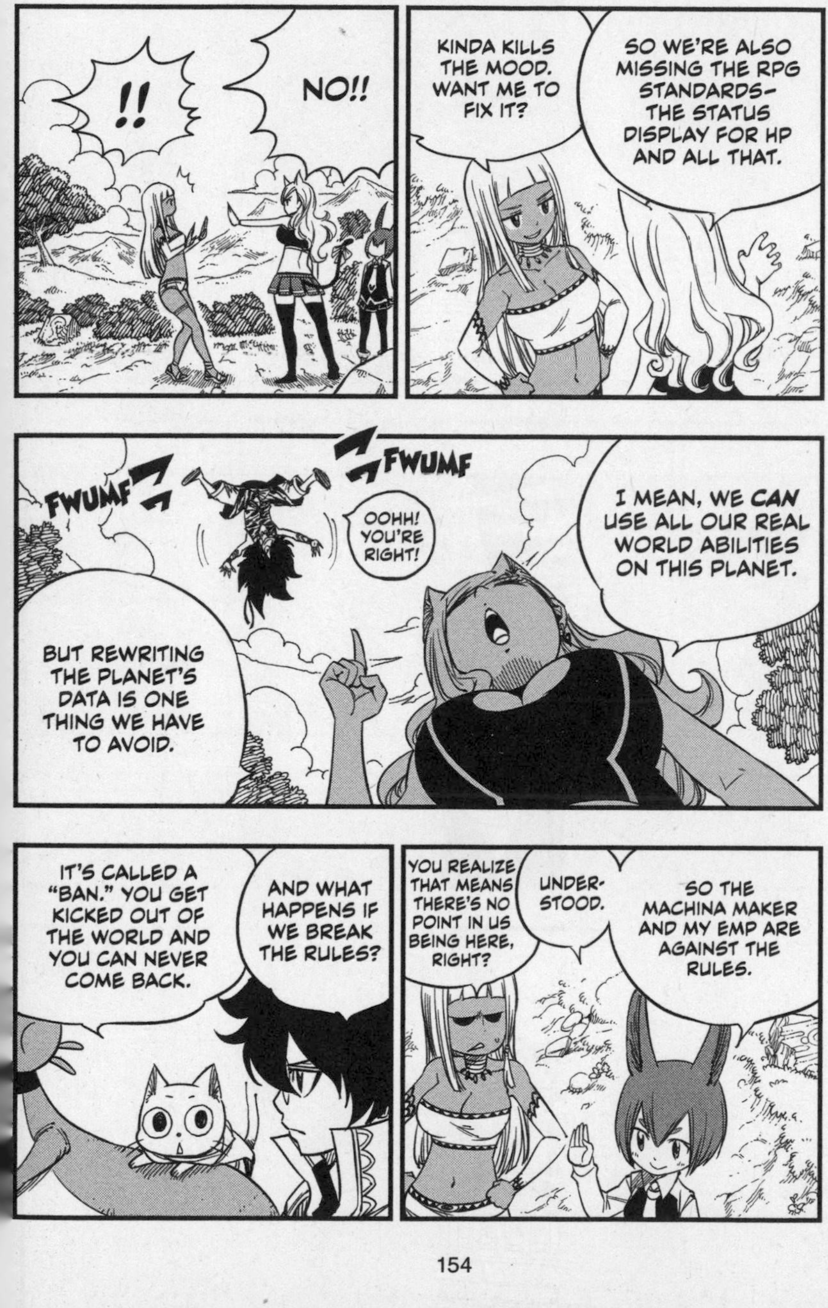
SO WE'RE ALSO MISSING THE RPG STANDARDS–THE STATUS DISPLAY FOR HP AND ALL THAT.
KINDA KILLS THE MOOD. WANT ME TO FIX IT?
NO!!
!!
I MEAN, WE CAN USE ALL OUR REAL WORLD ABILITIES ON THIS PLANET.
FWUMF
OOHH! YOU'RE RIGHT!
FWUMF
BUT REWRITING THE PLANET'S DATA IS ONE THING WE HAVE TO AVOID.
SO THE MACHINA MAKER AND MY EMP ARE AGAINST THE RULES.
UNDER-STOOD.
YOU REALIZE THAT MEANS THERE'S NO POINT IN US BEING HERE, RIGHT?
AND WHAT HAPPENS IF WE BREAK THE RULES?
IT'S CALLED A "BAN." YOU GET KICKED OUT OF THE WORLD AND YOU CAN NEVER COME BACK.

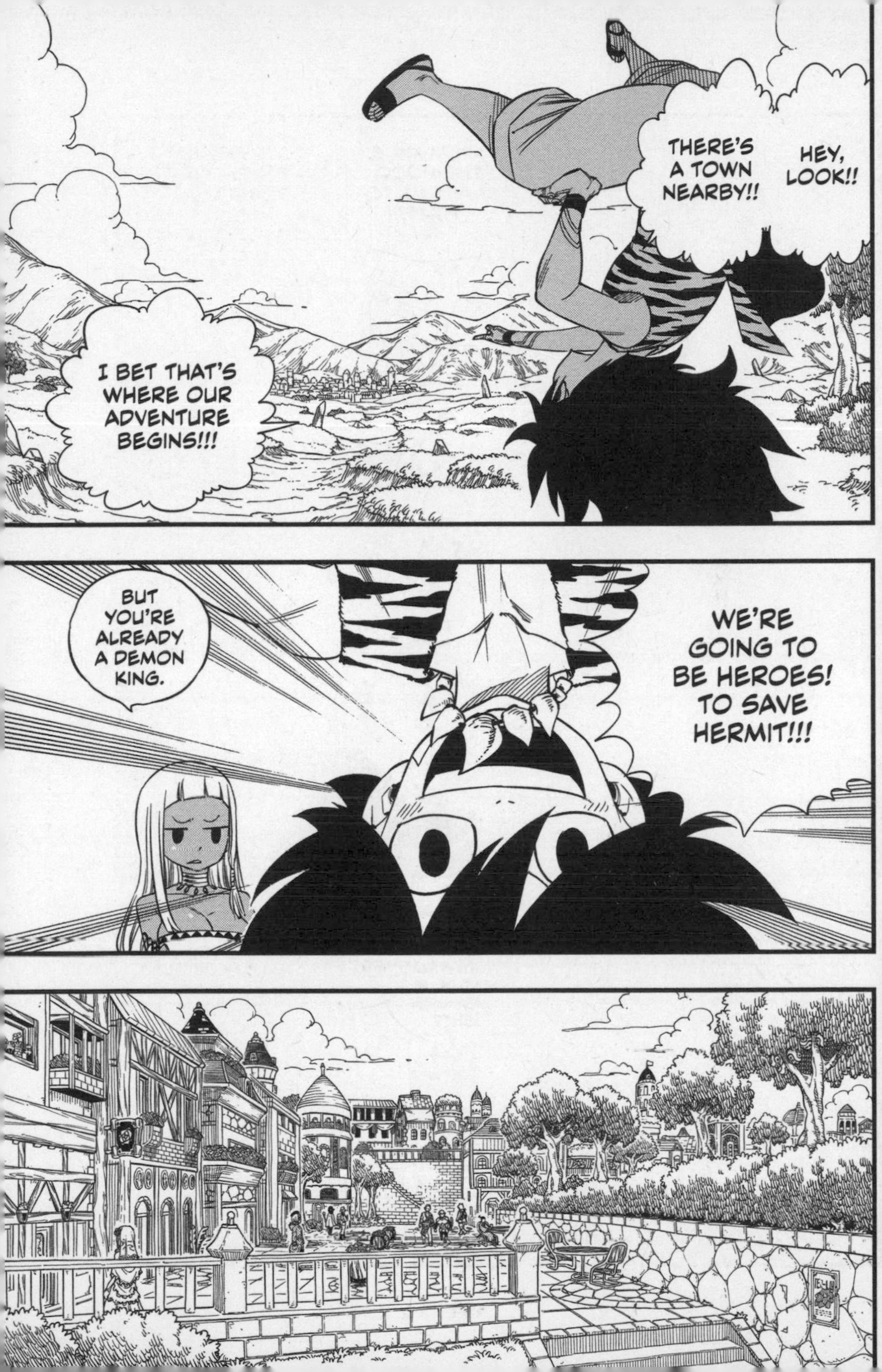
HEY, LOOK!!
THERE'S A TOWN NEARBY!!
I BET THAT'S WHERE OUR ADVENTURE BEGINS!!!
WE'RE GOING TO BE HEROES! TO SAVE HERMIT!!!
BUT YOU'RE ALREADY A DEMON KING.

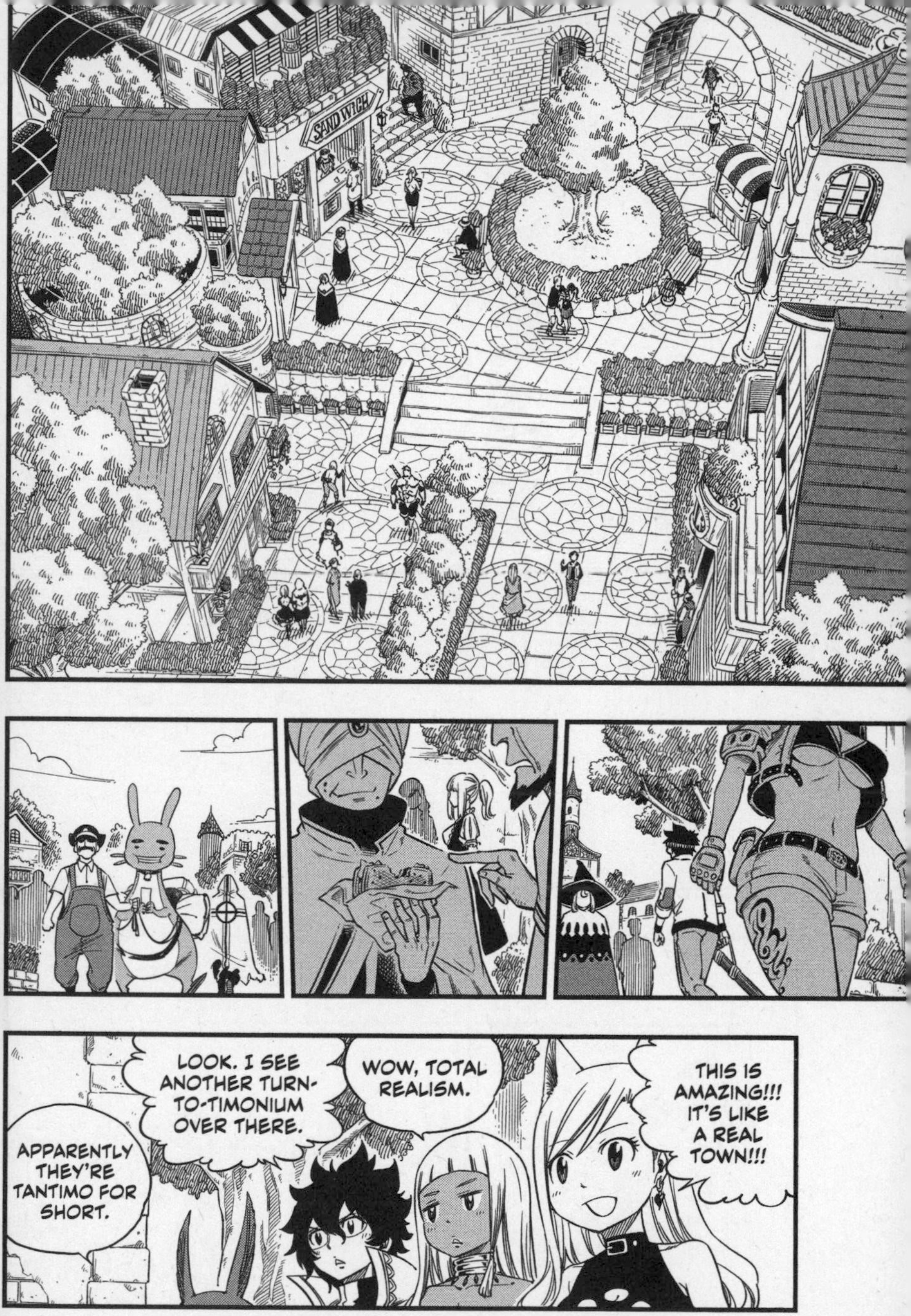
SAND WICH
THIS IS AMAZING!!! IT'S LIKE A REAL TOWN!!!
WOW, TOTAL REALISM.
LOOK. I SEE ANOTHER TURN-TO-TIMONIUM OVER THERE.
APPARENTLY THEY'RE TANTIMO FOR SHORT.

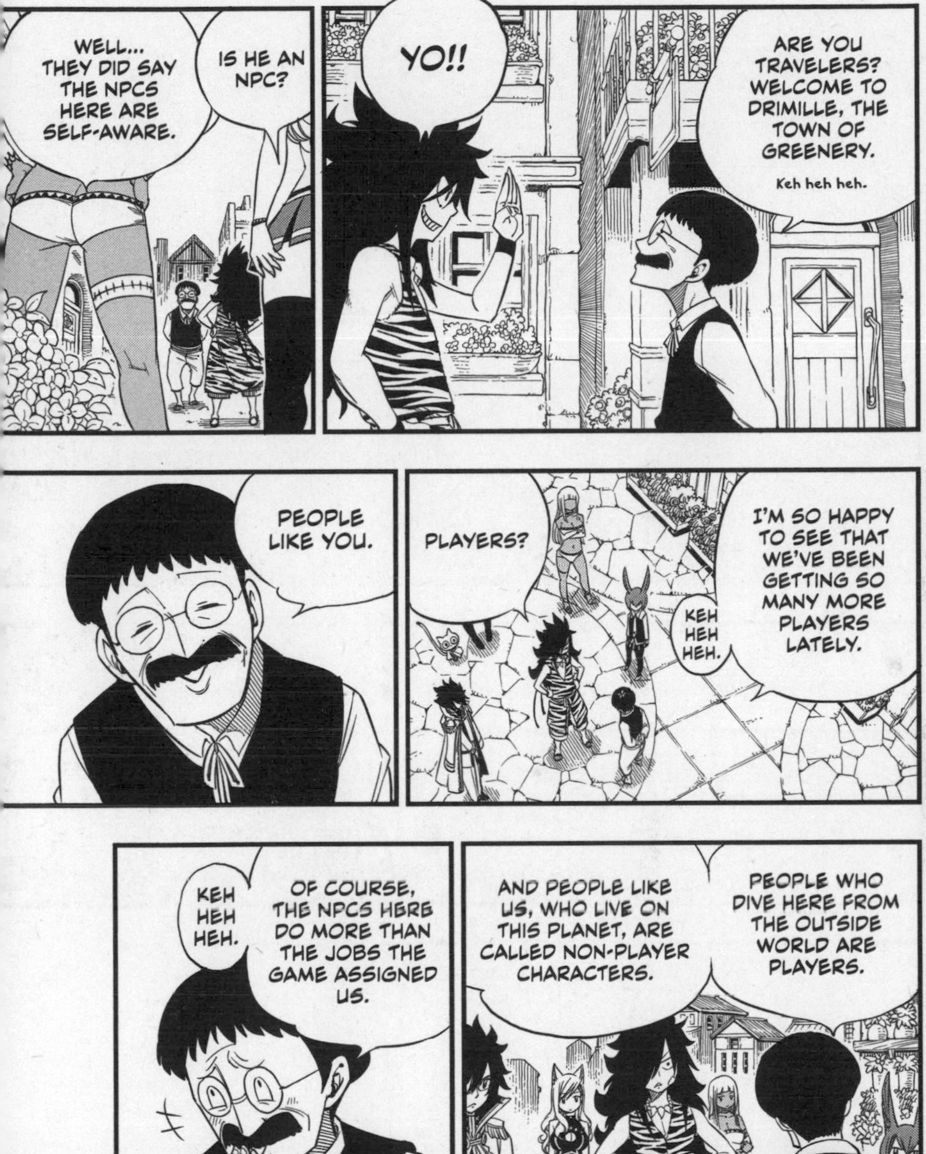
ARE YOU TRAVELERS? WELCOME TO DRIMILLE, THE TOWN OF GREENERY.
Keh heh heh.
YO!!
IS HE AN NPC?
WELL... THEY DID SAY THE NPCS HERE ARE SELF-AWARE.
I'M SO HAPPY TO SEE THAT WE'VE BEEN GETTING SO MANY MORE PLAYERS LATELY.
KEH HEH HEH.
PLAYERS?
PEOPLE LIKE YOU.
PEOPLE WHO DIVE HERE FROM THE OUTSIDE WORLD ARE PLAYERS.
AND PEOPLE LIKE US, WHO LIVE ON THIS PLANET, ARE CALLED NON-PLAYER CHARACTERS.
OF COURSE, THE NPCS HERE DO MORE THAN THE JOBS THE GAME ASSIGNED US.
KEH HEH HEH.

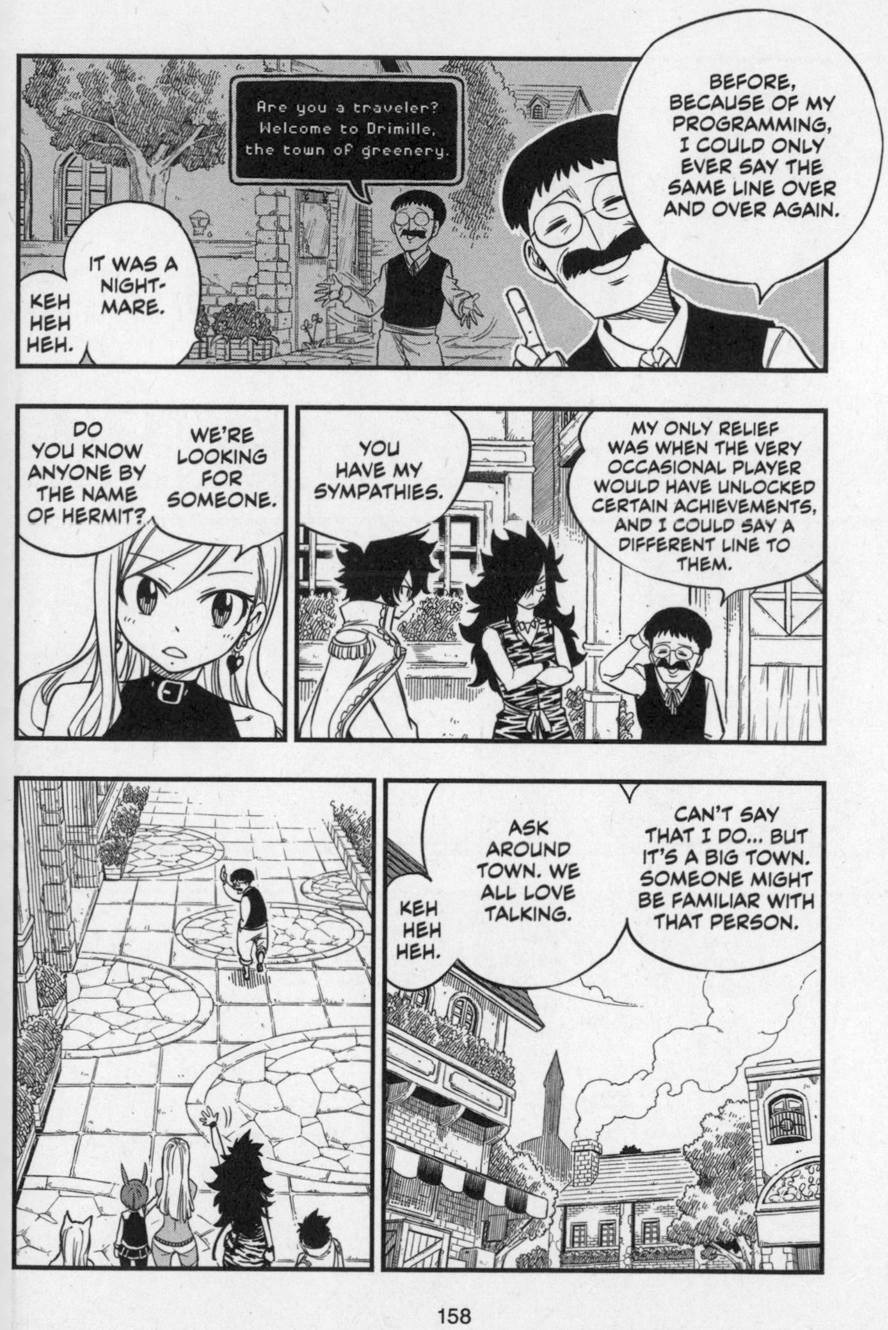
BEFORE, BECAUSE OF MY PROGRAMMING, I COULD ONLY EVER SAY THE SAME LINE OVER AND OVER AGAIN.
Are you a traveler? Welcome to Drimille, the town of greenery.
IT WAS A NIGHT-MARE.
KEH HEH HEH.
MY ONLY RELIEF WAS WHEN THE VERY OCCASIONAL PLAYER WOULD HAVE UNLOCKED CERTAIN ACHIEVEMENTS, AND I COULD SAY A DIFFERENT LINE TO THEM.
YOU HAVE MY SYMPATHIES.
WE'RE LOOKING FOR SOMEONE.
DO YOU KNOW ANYONE BY THE NAME OF HERMIT?
CAN'T SAY THAT I DO... BUT IT'S A BIG TOWN. SOMEONE MIGHT BE FAMILIAR WITH THAT PERSON.
ASK AROUND TOWN. WE ALL LOVE TALKING.
KEH HEH HEH.

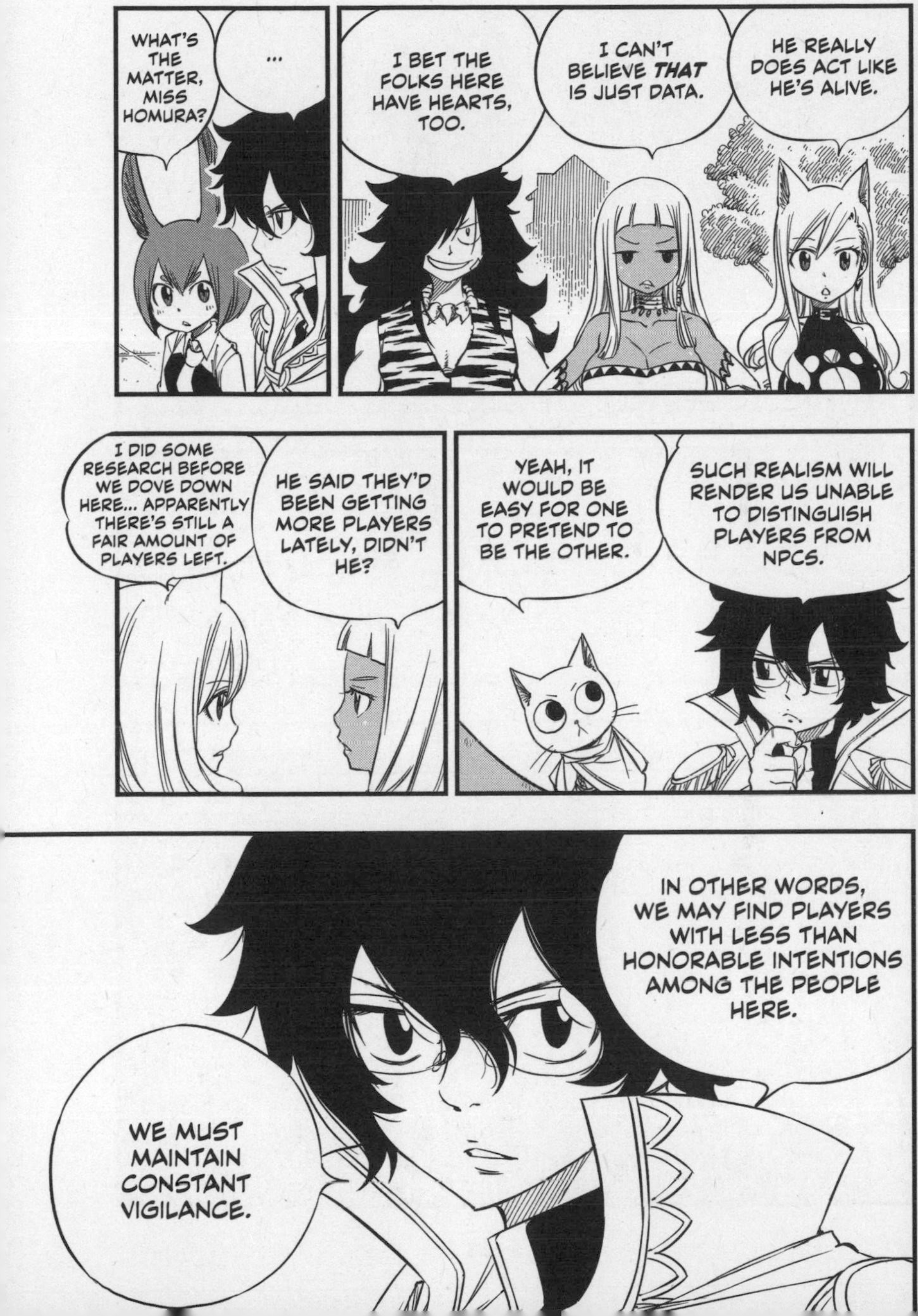
HE REALLY DOES ACT LIKE HE'S ALIVE.
I CAN'T BELIEVE *THAT* IS JUST DATA.
I BET THE FOLKS HERE HAVE HEARTS, TOO.
...
WHAT'S THE MATTER, MISS HOMURA?
SUCH REALISM WILL RENDER US UNABLE TO DISTINGUISH PLAYERS FROM NPCS.
YEAH, IT WOULD BE EASY FOR ONE TO PRETEND TO BE THE OTHER.
HE SAID THEY'D BEEN GETTING MORE PLAYERS LATELY, DIDN'T HE?
I DID SOME RESEARCH BEFORE WE DOVE DOWN HERE... APPARENTLY THERE'S STILL A FAIR AMOUNT OF PLAYERS LEFT.
IN OTHER WORDS, WE MAY FIND PLAYERS WITH LESS THAN HONORABLE INTENTIONS AMONG THE PEOPLE HERE.
WE MUST MAINTAIN CONSTANT VIGILANCE.

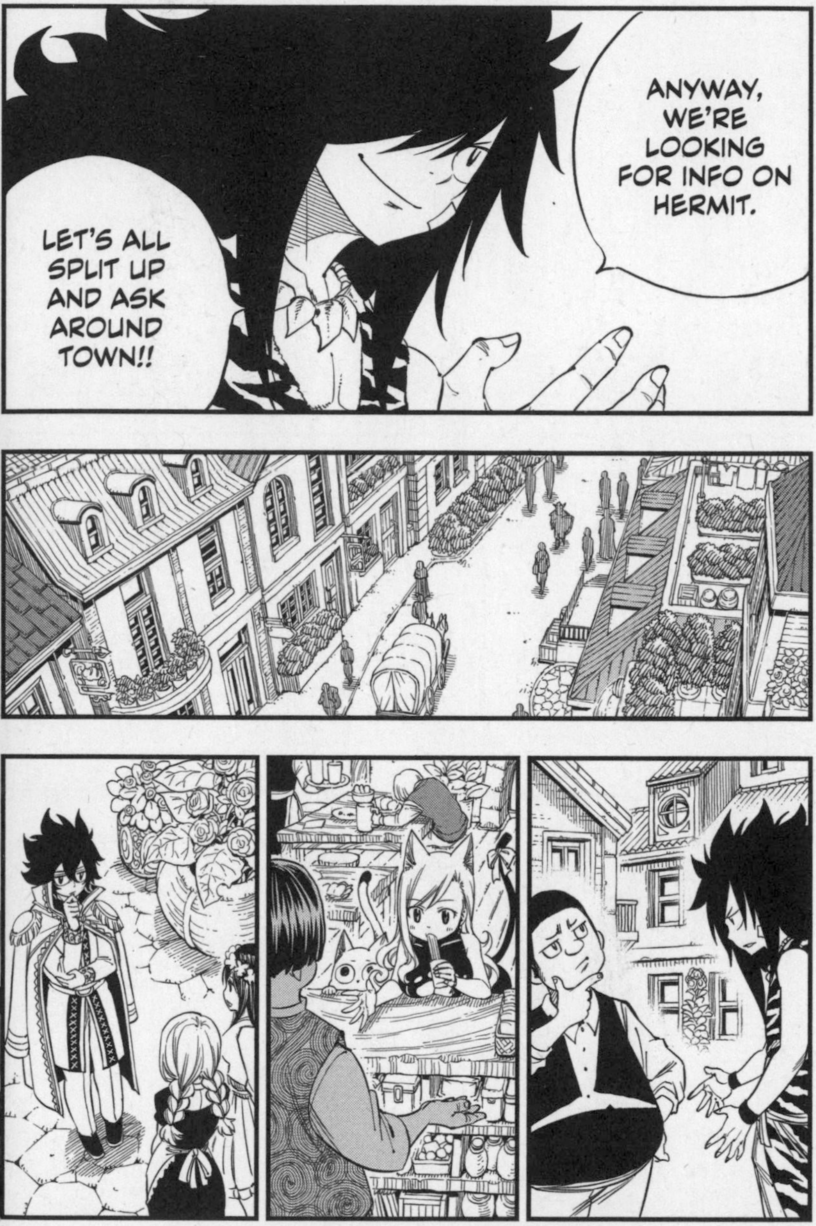
ANYWAY, WE'RE LOOKING FOR INFO ON HERMIT.
LET'S ALL SPLIT UP AND ASK AROUND TOWN!!

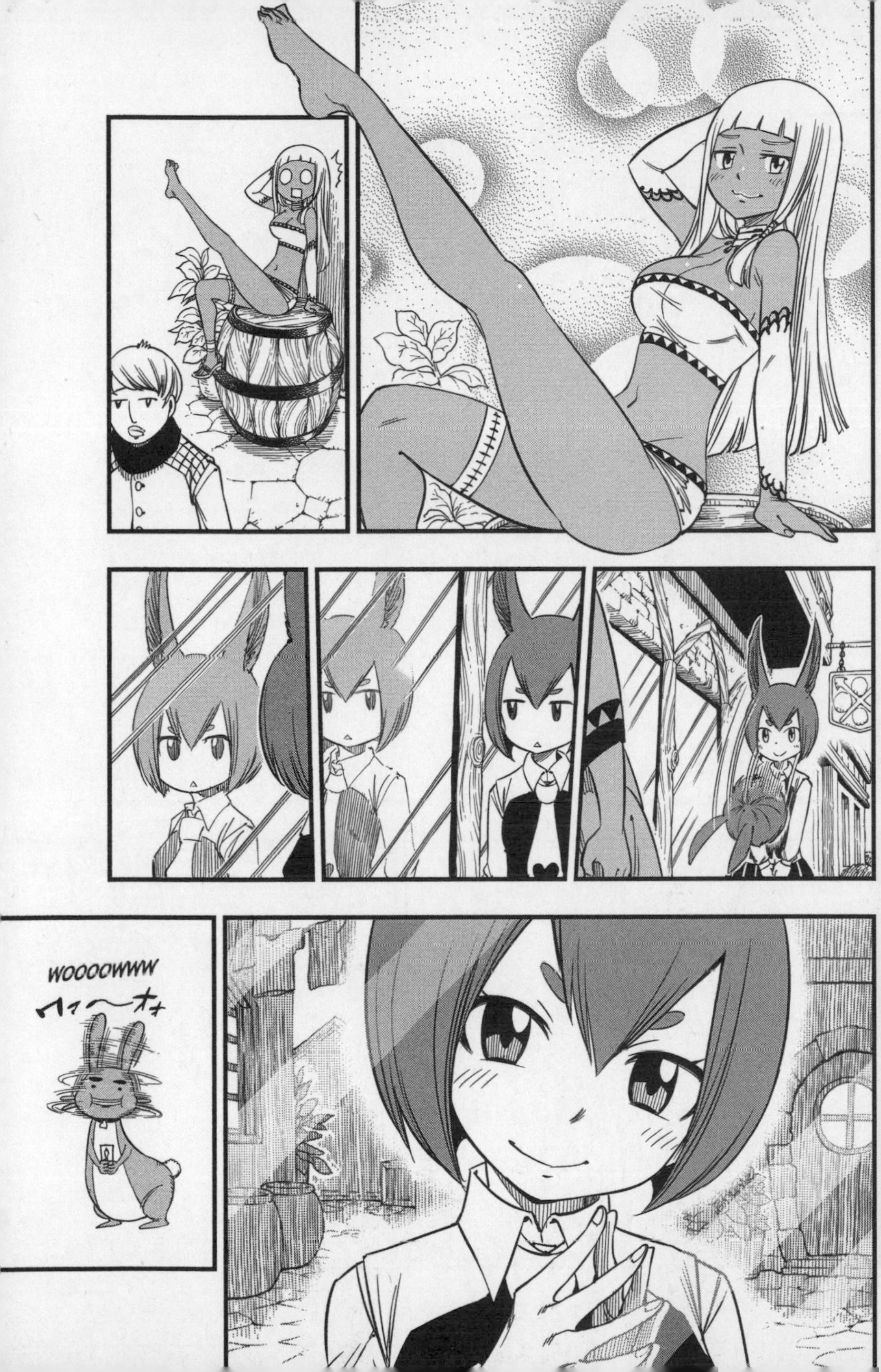
WOOOOWWW
ワァ〜オォ

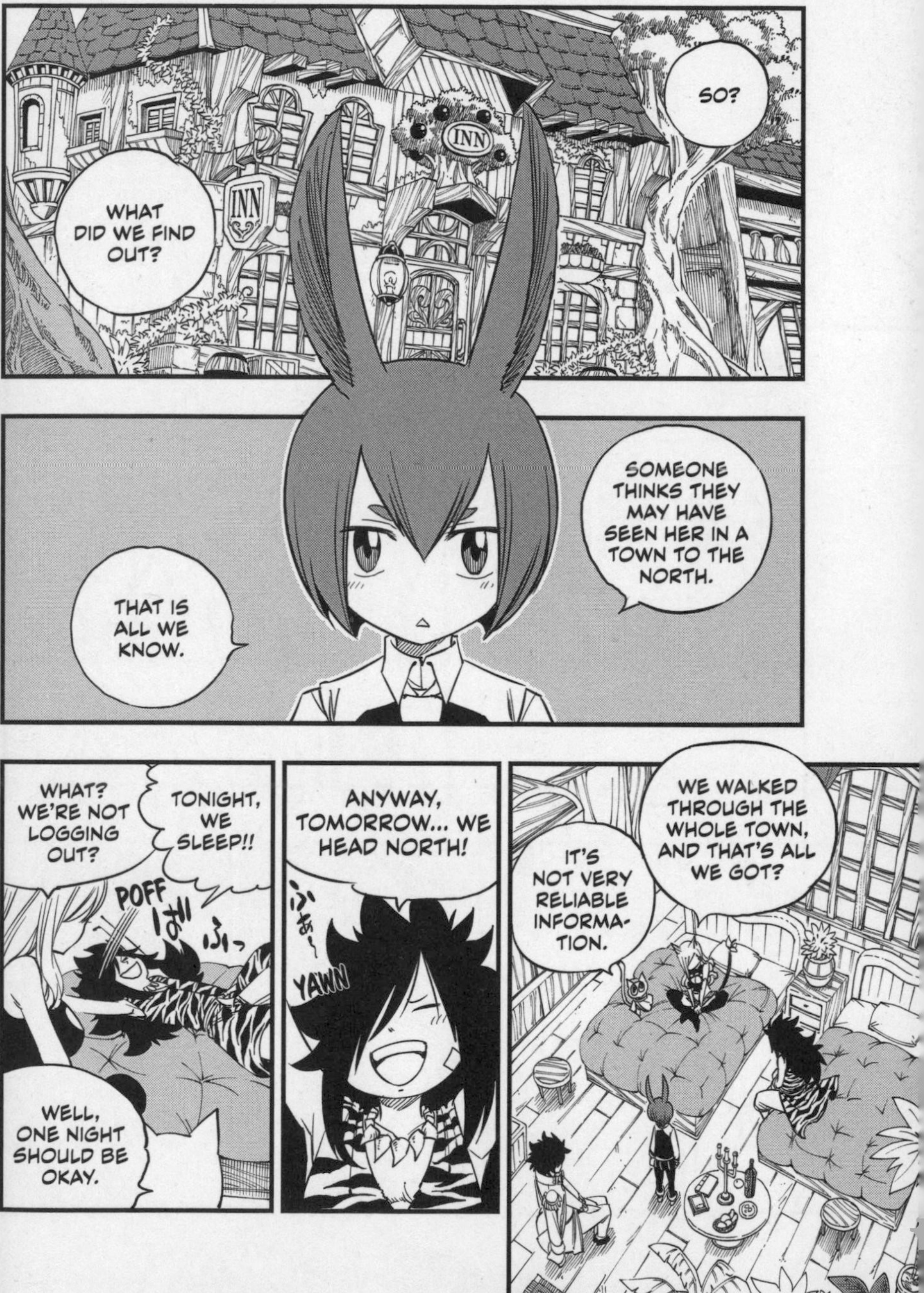
SO?
WHAT DID WE FIND OUT?
INN
INN
SOMEONE THINKS THEY MAY HAVE SEEN HER IN A TOWN TO THE NORTH.
THAT IS ALL WE KNOW.
WE WALKED THROUGH THE WHOLE TOWN, AND THAT'S ALL WE GOT?
IT'S NOT VERY RELIABLE INFORMATION.
ANYWAY, TOMORROW... WE HEAD NORTH!
ふあ~
YAWN
TONIGHT, WE SLEEP!!
WHAT? WE'RE NOT LOGGING OUT?
POFF
ふっ
WELL, ONE NIGHT SHOULD BE OKAY.

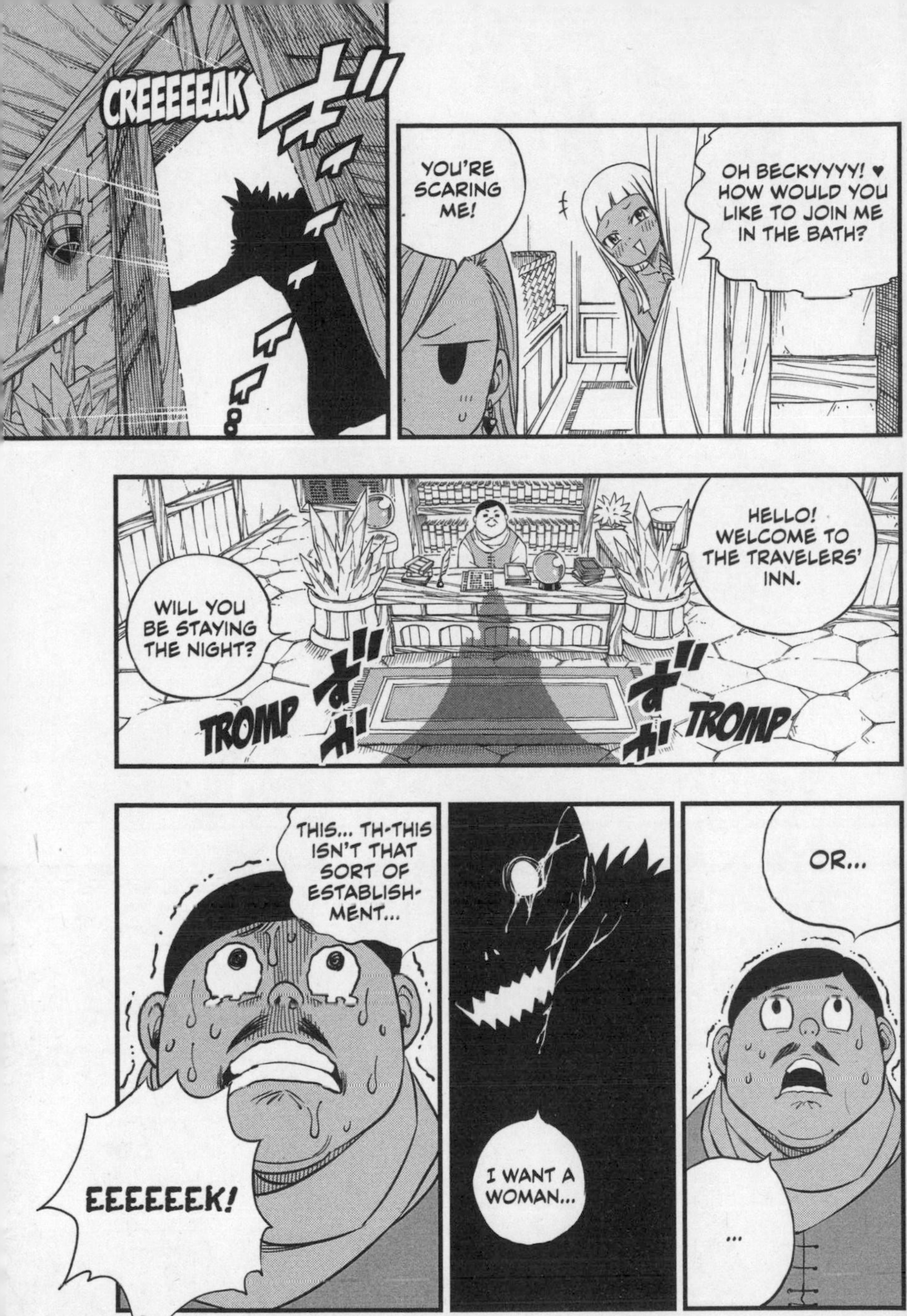

OH BECKYYYY! ♥ HOW WOULD YOU LIKE TO JOIN ME IN THE BATH?
YOU'RE SCARING ME!
CREEEEEAK
HELLO! WELCOME TO THE TRAVELERS' INN.
WILL YOU BE STAYING THE NIGHT?
TROMP
TROMP
OR...
...
I WANT A WOMAN...
THIS... TH-THIS ISN'T THAT SORT OF ESTABLISHMENT...
EEEEEEK!

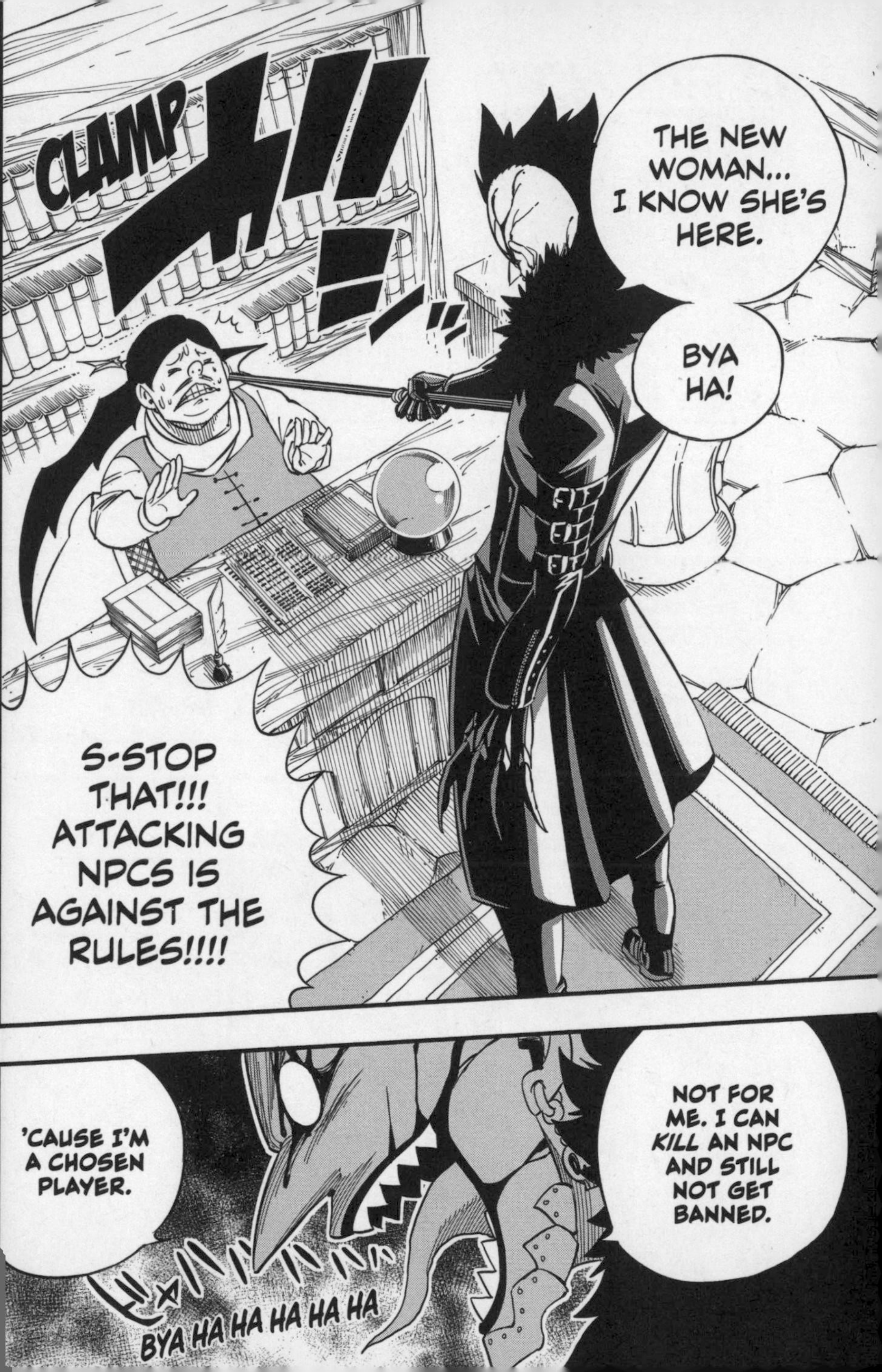
THE NEW WOMAN... I KNOW SHE'S HERE.
BYA HA!
CLAMP
S-STOP THAT!!! ATTACKING NPCS IS AGAINST THE RULES!!!!
NOT FOR ME. I CAN *KILL* AN NPC AND STILL NOT GET BANNED.
'CAUSE I'M A CHOSEN PLAYER.
BYA HA HA HA HA HA

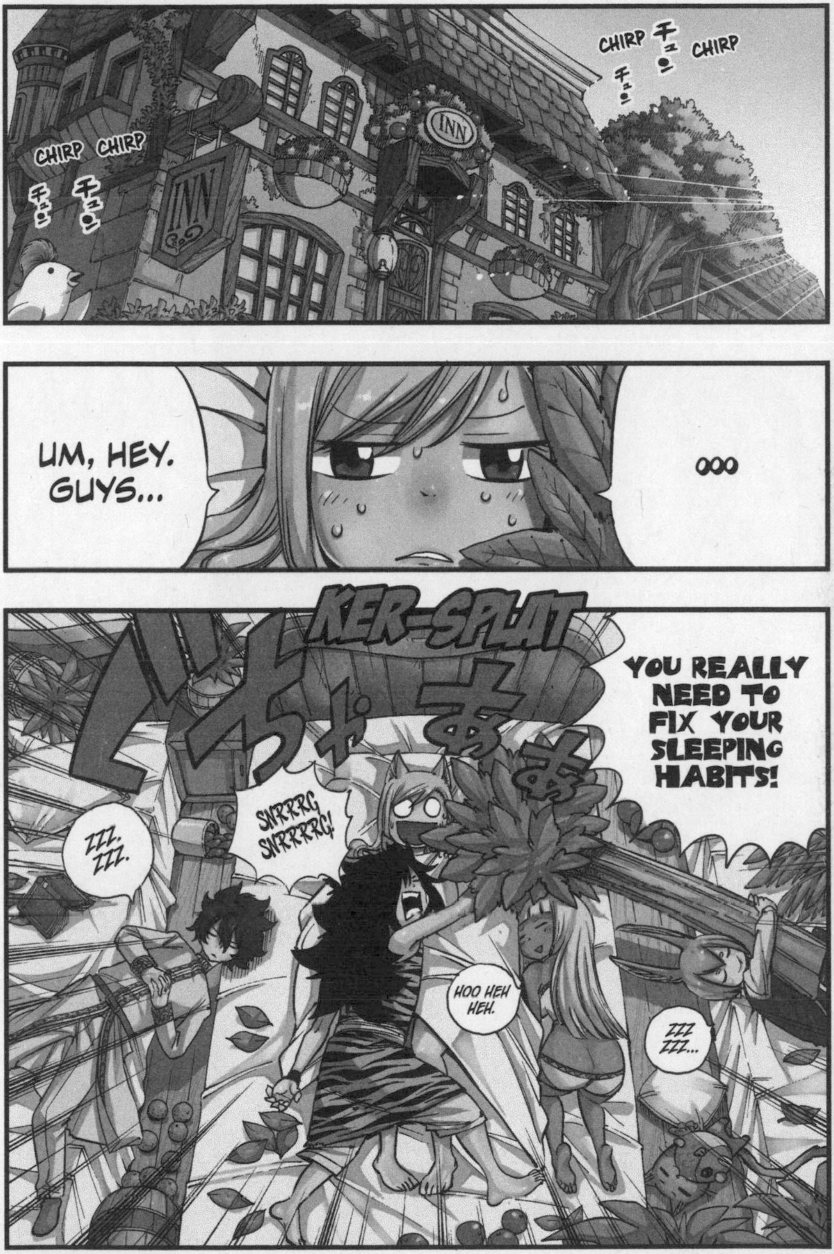
CHIRP
チュン
CHIRP
チュン
CHIRP
CHIRP
チュン
チュン
ooo
UM, HEY. GUYS...
KER-SPLAT
YOU REALLY NEED TO FIX YOUR SLEEPING HABITS!
SNRRRG SNRRRRG!
ZZZ. ZZZ.
HOO HEH HEH.
ZZZ ZZZ...

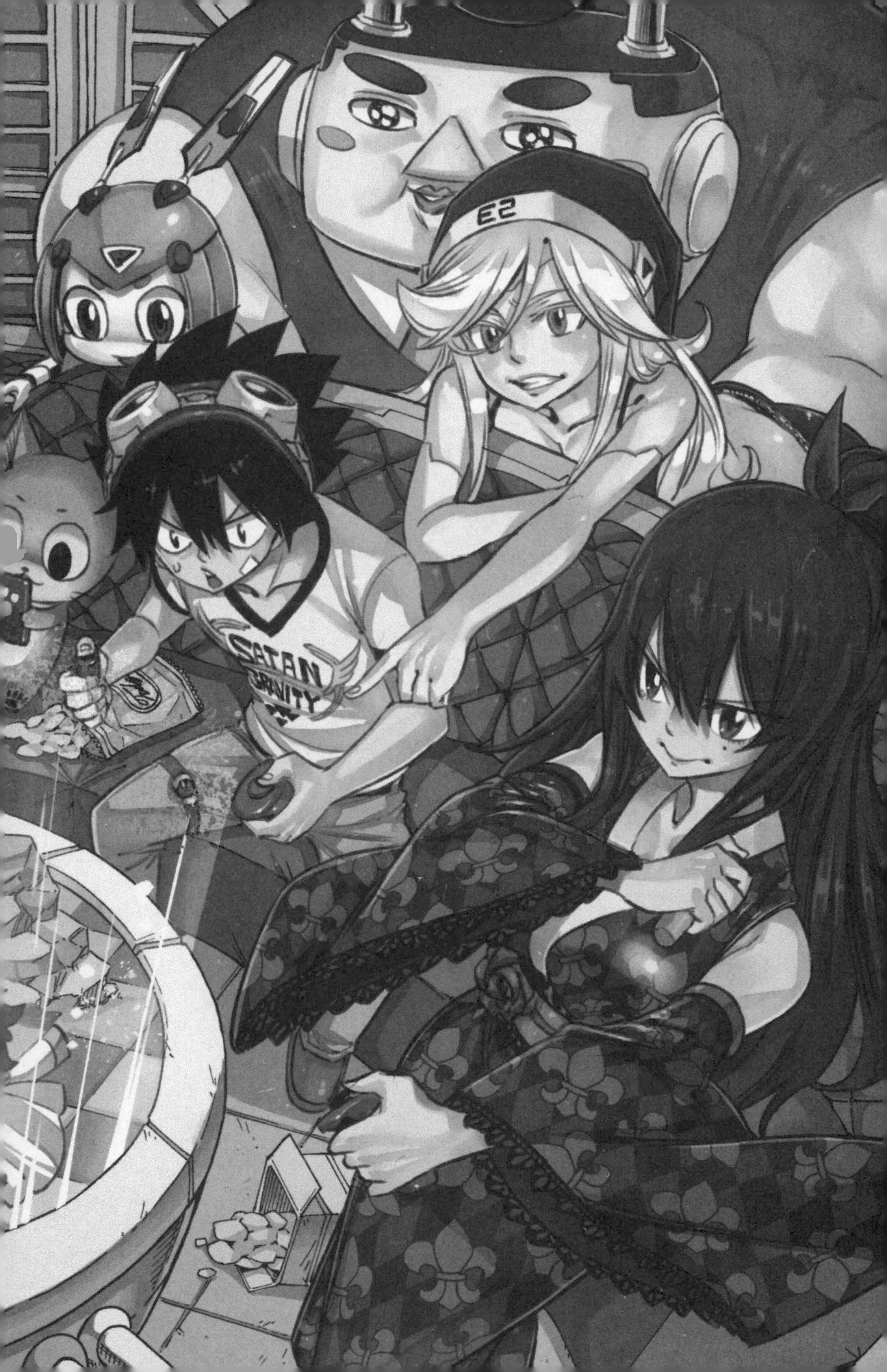
SATAN

CHAPTER 32: MASS MURDERER JAMILOV

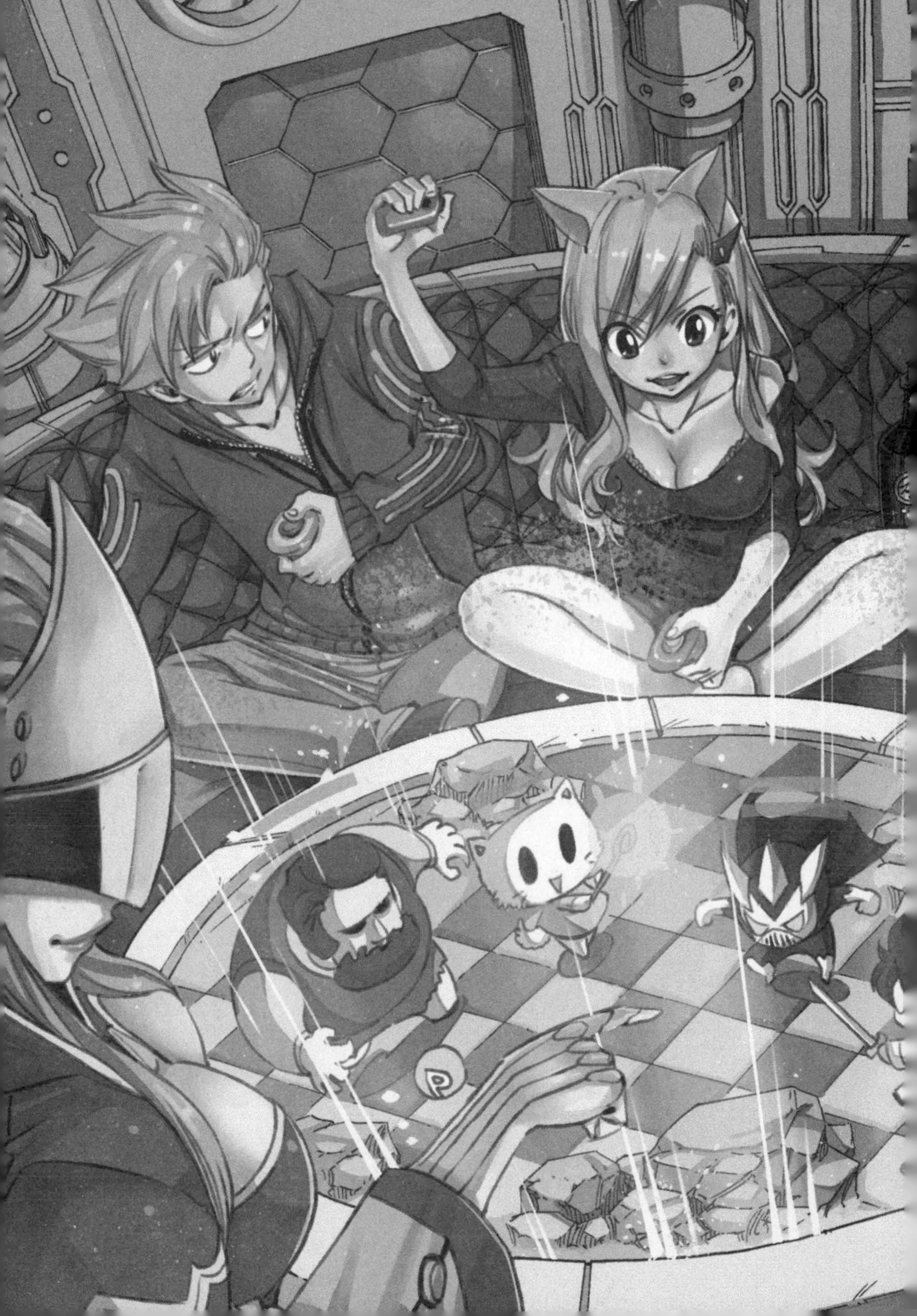

EZ DRAWING

IT'S TIME TO PRESENT OUR SECOND BATCH OF FAN DRAWINGS!

(NEMUKO-SAN, SAITAMA)

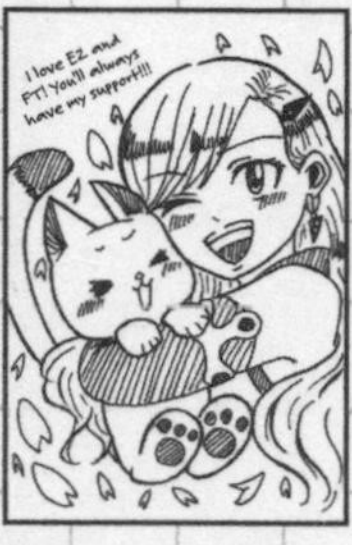
I love EZ and FT! You'll always have my support!!!

◀ EACH OF THEM USED TO BE ALONE. THAT'S EXACTLY WHY THEIR BOND IS FOREVER.

(TSUGUMI-SAN, SHIZUOKA)

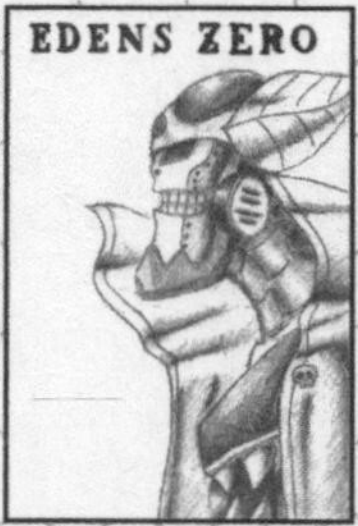
EDENS ZERO

◀ SHIKI'S GRANDPA, DEMON KING ZIGGY. WHAT DID HE SEE IN SHIKI'S FUTURE?

(ZEKI-SAN, GIFU)

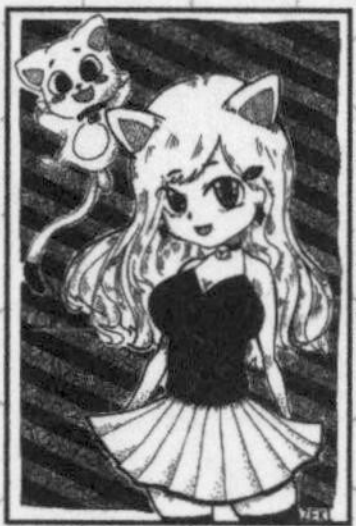

◀ THE SECRET WORD IS "MEOW-WOW!" EVERYBODY WATCH AONEKO CHANNEL, MEOW!

(BANWOLF-SAN, KANAGAWA)

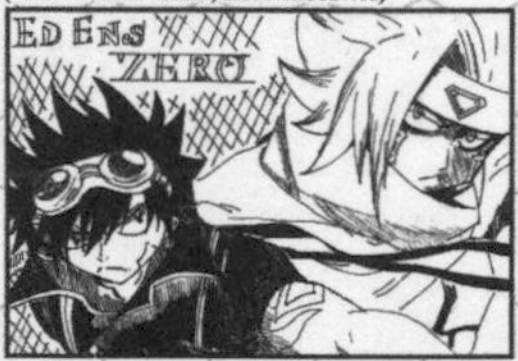
EDENS ZERO

▲ MAGIMECH VS. SKYMECH! DO I FORESEE A FATED RIVALRY?!

(TAMAGO PAN-SAN, TOKYO)

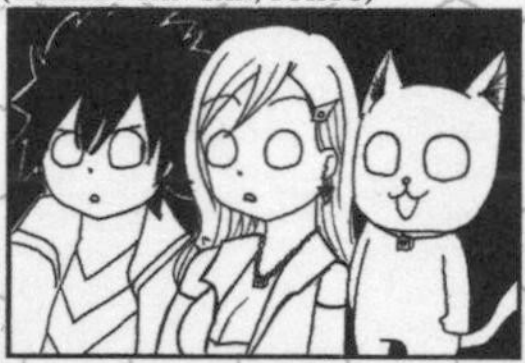

▲ WHAT DID THEY SEE?! WHAT HAPPENED?! I'M DYING TO KNOW!

(RIRAN-SAN, HIROSHIMA)

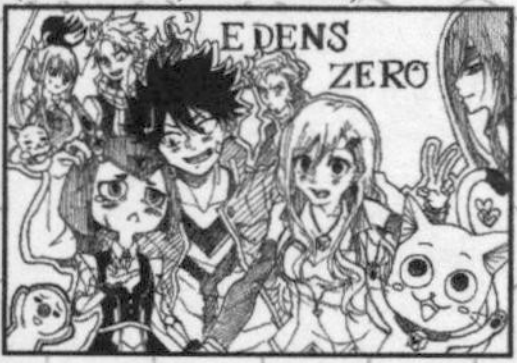
EDENS ZERO

▲ I WANT LOTS, *LOTS* MORE FRIENDS—SO MANY, YOU CAN'T COUNT 'EM.

(MOMONE AIZAWA-SAN, MIYAGI)

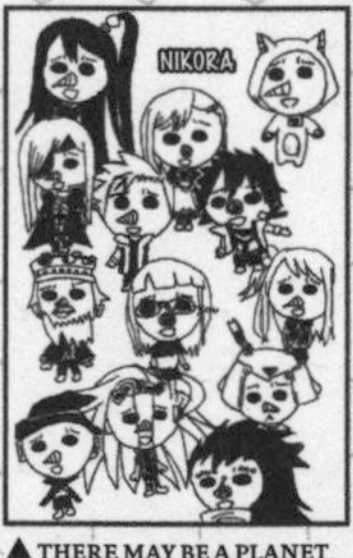
NIKORA

▲ THERE MAY BE A PLANET FULL OF THESE "DOGS," SOMEWHERE IN THE VAST REACHES OF SPACE.

(SAE INOGAMI-SAN, AICHI)

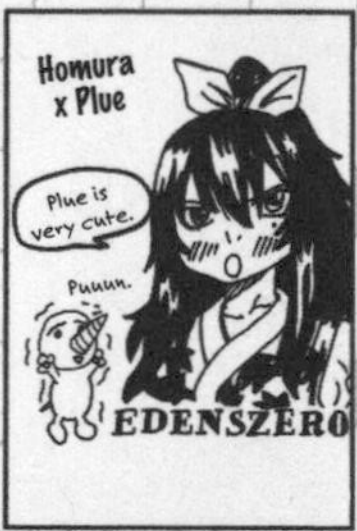
Homura x Plue
Plue is very cute.
Puuun.
EDENSZERO

▲ I ASSURE YOU I HAVE NO DESIRE TO ENCOUNTER SUCH A CREATURE.

(♦HIKANYAKO♦-SAN, MIE)

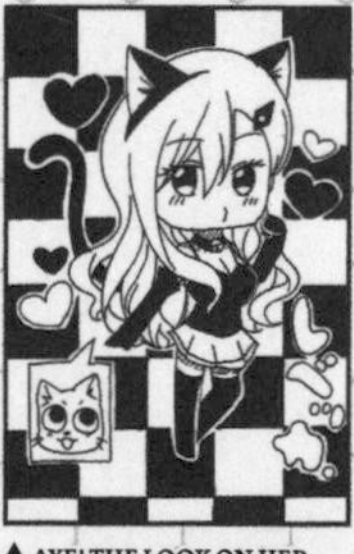

▲ AYE! THE LOOK ON HER FACE SAYS SOMETHING GOOD JUST HAPPENED.

(AKIHITO SHIMIZU-SAN, CHIBA)

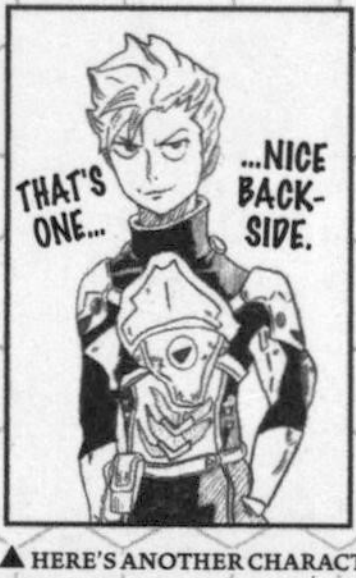
...NICE BACKSIDE.
THAT'S ONE...

▲ HERE'S ANOTHER CHARACTER WHO CAN'T HELP SAYING WHATEVER'S ON HIS MIND.

EDITOR'S NOTE: DRAWING SUBMISSIONS LIMITED TO JAPAN.

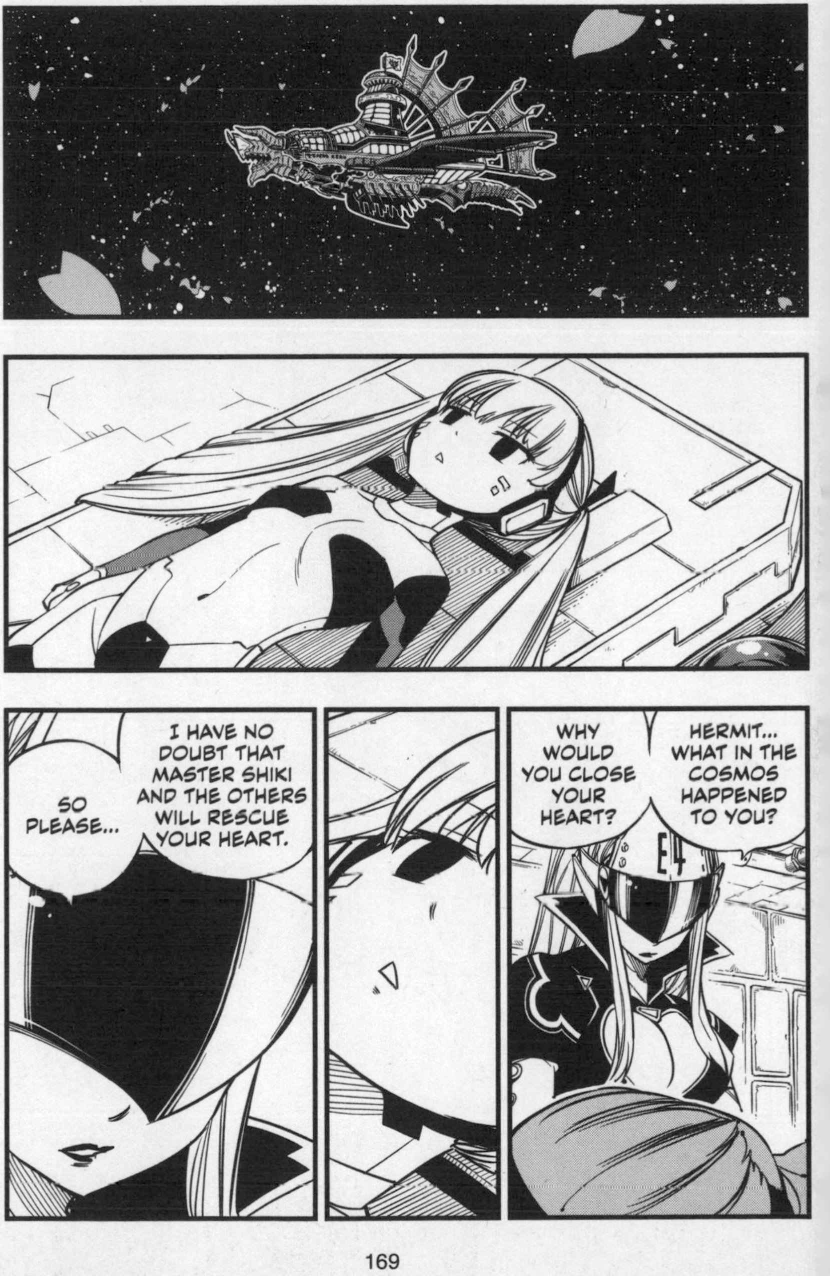
HERMIT... WHAT IN THE COSMOS HAPPENED TO YOU?
WHY WOULD YOU CLOSE YOUR HEART?
I HAVE NO DOUBT THAT MASTER SHIKI AND THE OTHERS WILL RESCUE YOUR HEART.
SO PLEASE...

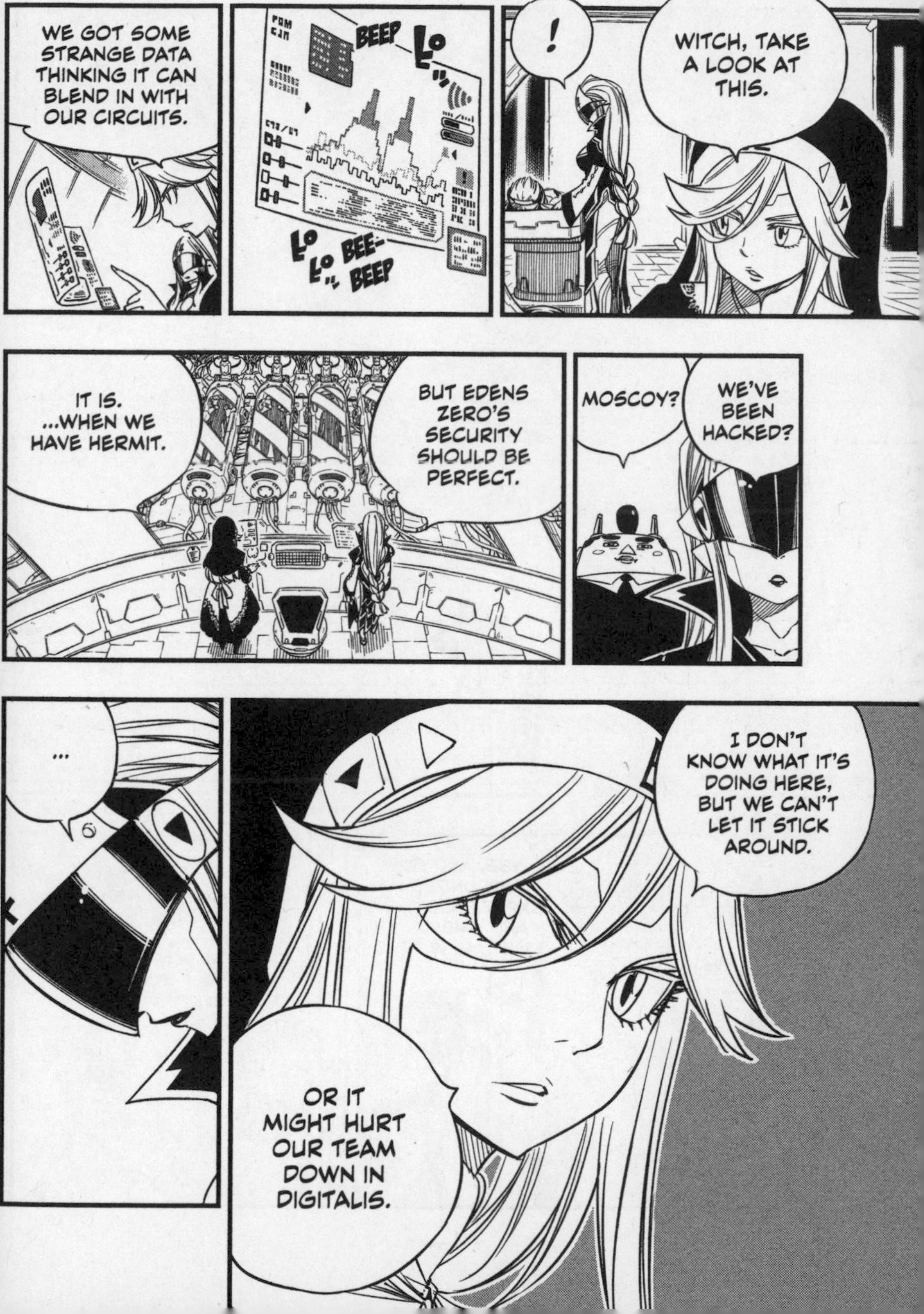
WITCH, TAKE A LOOK AT THIS.
!
BEEP
BEE- BEEP
WE GOT SOME STRANGE DATA THINKING IT CAN BLEND IN WITH OUR CIRCUITS.
WE'VE BEEN HACKED?
MOSCOY?
BUT EDENS ZERO'S SECURITY SHOULD BE PERFECT.
IT IS. ...WHEN WE HAVE HERMIT.
I DON'T KNOW WHAT IT'S DOING HERE, BUT WE CAN'T LET IT STICK AROUND.
OR IT MIGHT HURT OUR TEAM DOWN IN DIGITALIS.
...

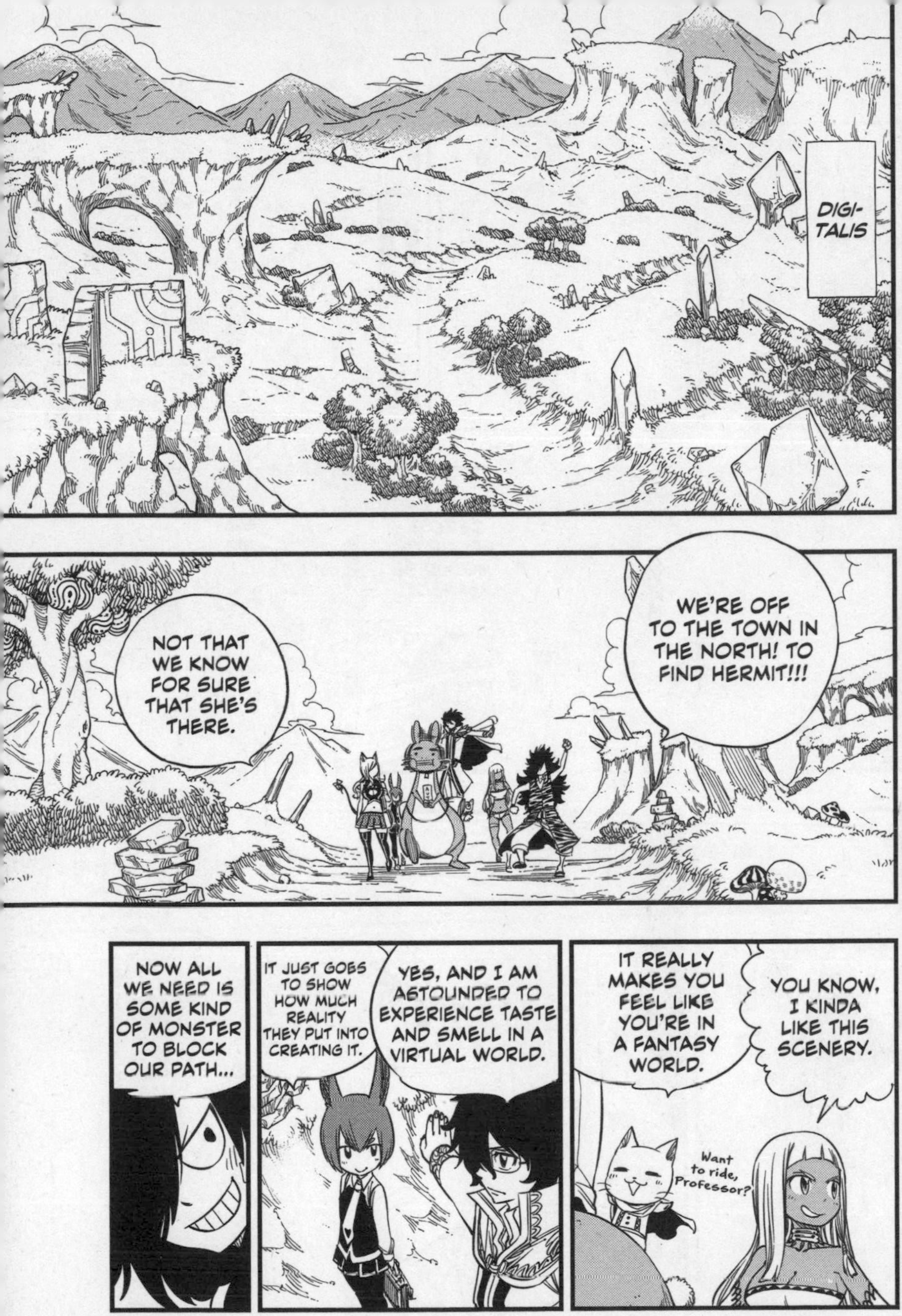
DIGI-TALIS
WE'RE OFF TO THE TOWN IN THE NORTH! TO FIND HERMIT!!!
NOT THAT WE KNOW FOR SURE THAT SHE'S THERE.
YOU KNOW, I KINDA LIKE THIS SCENERY.
IT REALLY MAKES YOU FEEL LIKE YOU'RE IN A FANTASY WORLD.
Want to ride, Professor?
YES, AND I AM ASTOUNDED TO EXPERIENCE TASTE AND SMELL IN A VIRTUAL WORLD.
IT JUST GOES TO SHOW HOW MUCH REALITY THEY PUT INTO CREATING IT.
NOW ALL WE NEED IS SOME KIND OF MONSTER TO BLOCK OUR PATH...

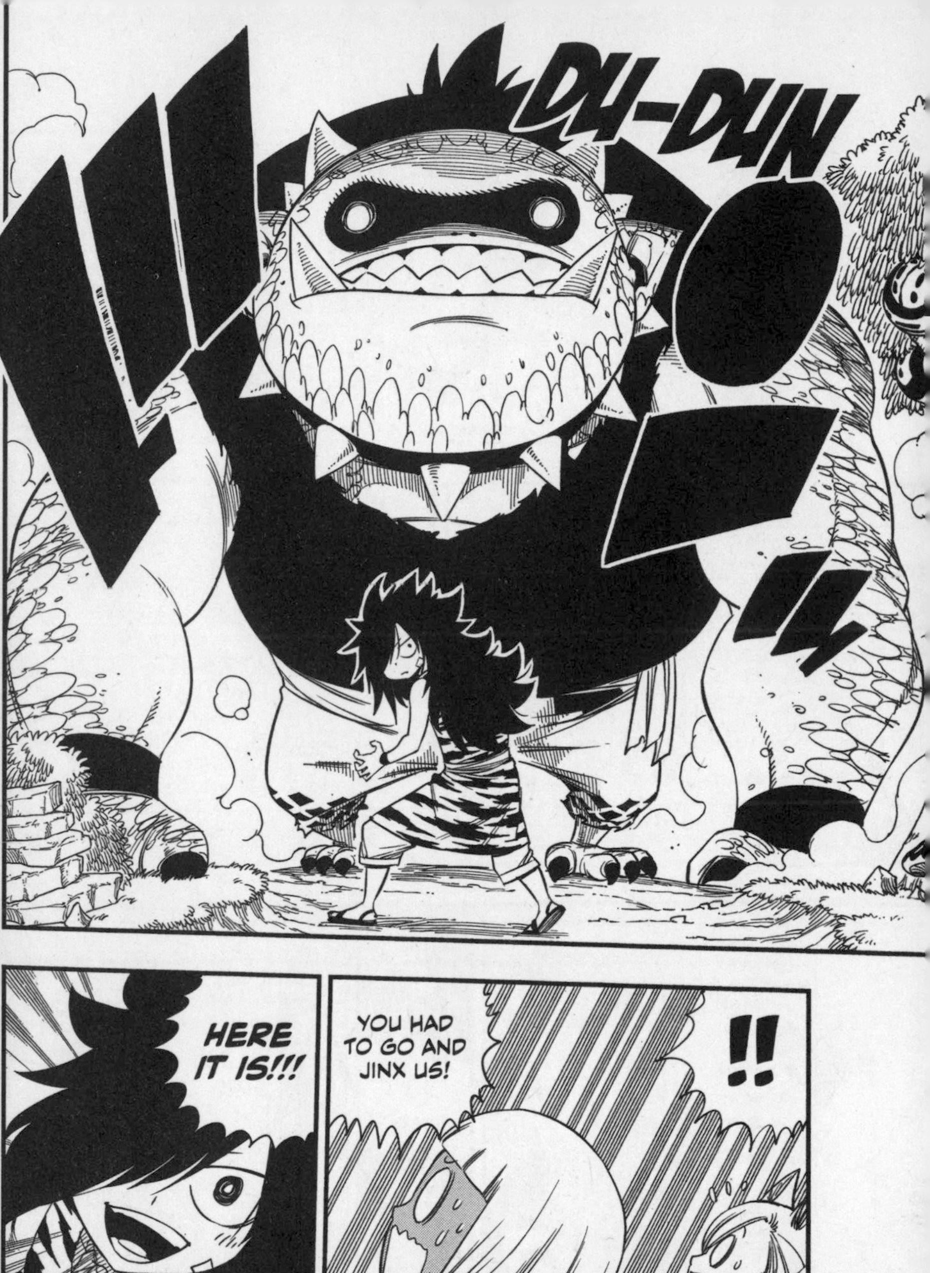
DU-DUN
YOU HAD TO GO AND JINX US!
!!
HERE IT IS!!!

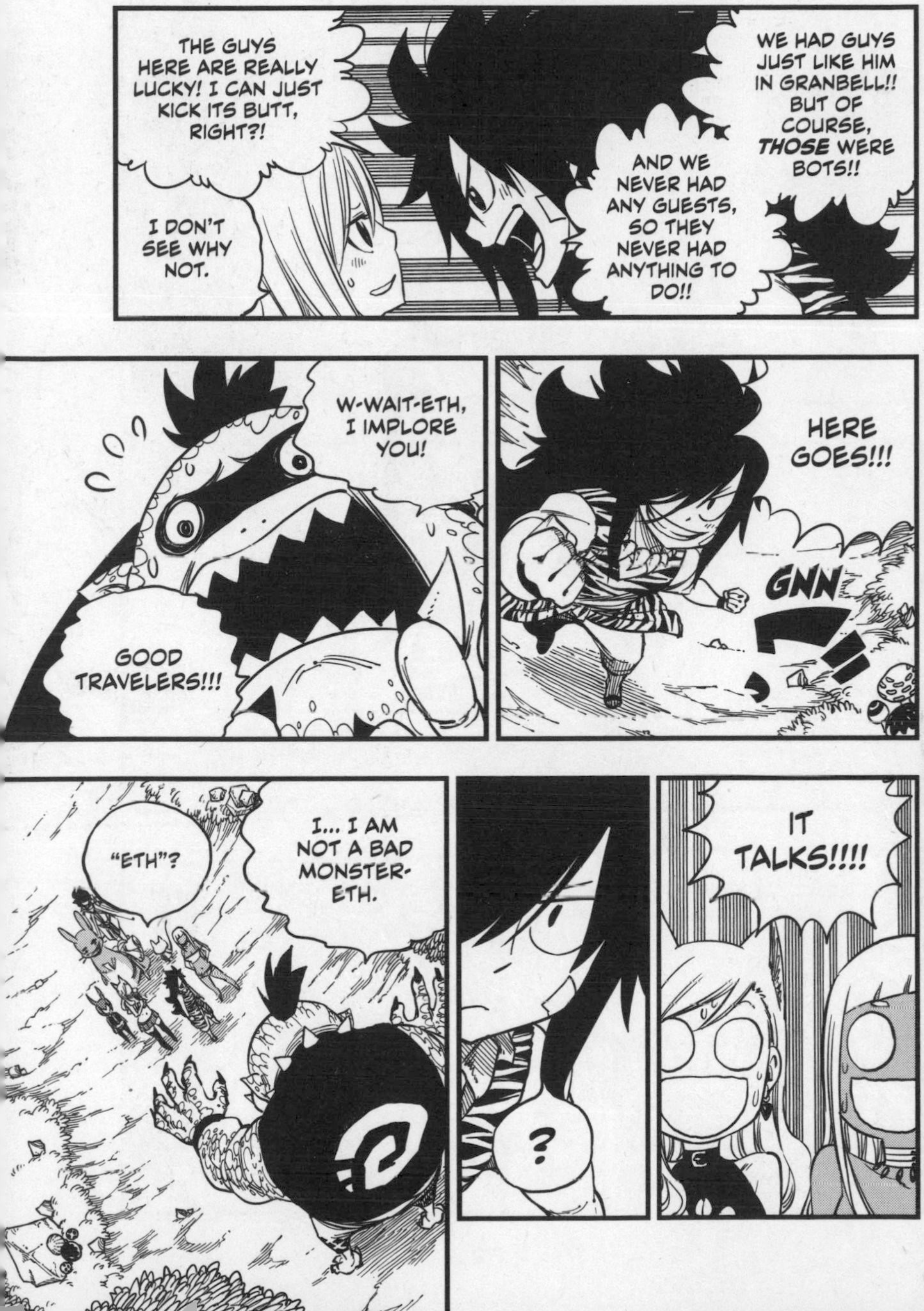
WE HAD GUYS JUST LIKE HIM IN GRANBELL!! BUT OF COURSE, *THOSE* WERE BOTS!!
AND WE NEVER HAD ANY GUESTS, SO THEY NEVER HAD ANYTHING TO DO!!
THE GUYS HERE ARE REALLY LUCKY! I CAN JUST KICK ITS BUTT, RIGHT?!
I DON'T SEE WHY NOT.
HERE GOES!!!
GNN
W-WAIT-ETH, I IMPLORE YOU!
GOOD TRAVELERS!!!
IT TALKS!!!!
?
I... I AM NOT A BAD MONSTER-ETH.
"ETH"?

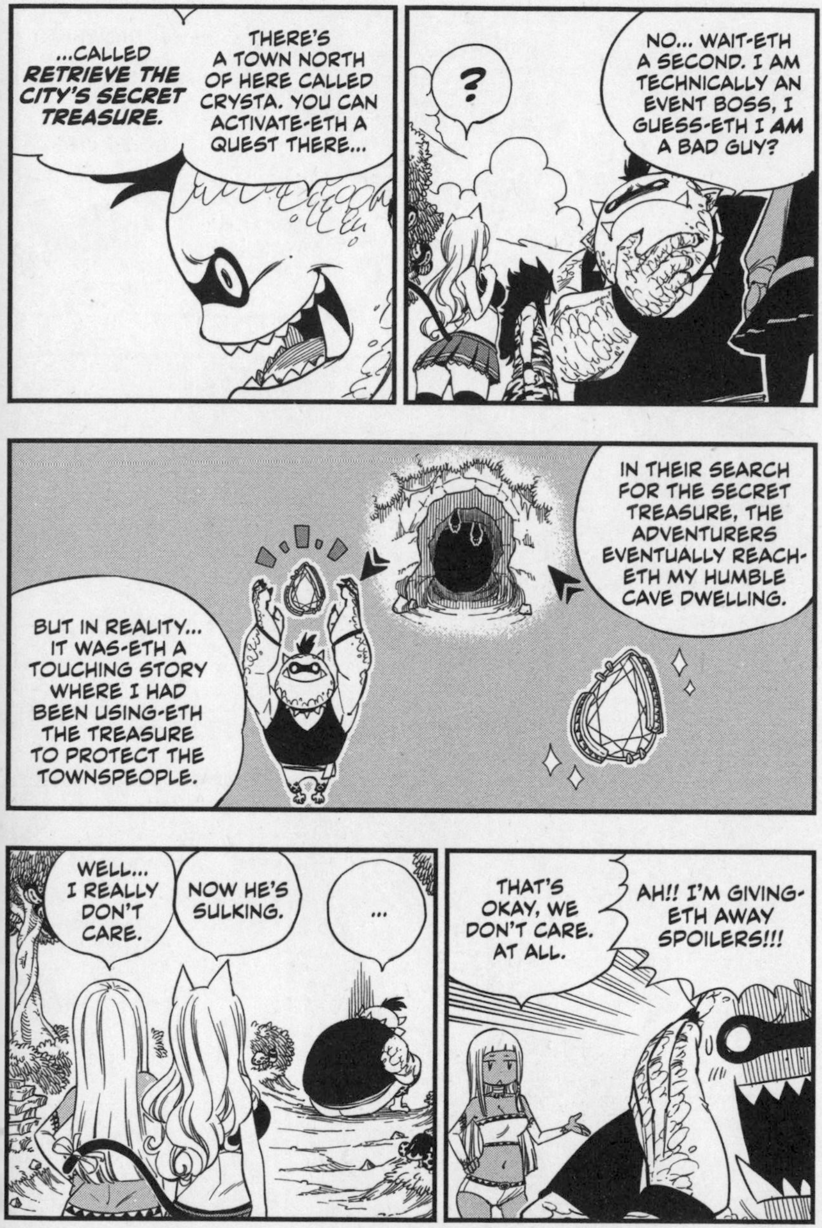
NO... WAIT-ETH A SECOND. I AM TECHNICALLY AN EVENT BOSS, I GUESS-ETH I *AM* A BAD GUY?
?
THERE'S A TOWN NORTH OF HERE CALLED CRYSTA. YOU CAN ACTIVATE-ETH A QUEST THERE...
...CALLED *RETRIEVE THE CITY'S SECRET TREASURE.*
IN THEIR SEARCH FOR THE SECRET TREASURE, THE ADVENTURERS EVENTUALLY REACH-ETH MY HUMBLE CAVE DWELLING.
BUT IN REALITY... IT WAS-ETH A TOUCHING STORY WHERE I HAD BEEN USING-ETH THE TREASURE TO PROTECT THE TOWNSPEOPLE.
AH!! I'M GIVING-ETH AWAY SPOILERS!!!
THAT'S OKAY, WE DON'T CARE. AT ALL.
...
NOW HE'S SULKING.
WELL... I REALLY DON'T CARE.

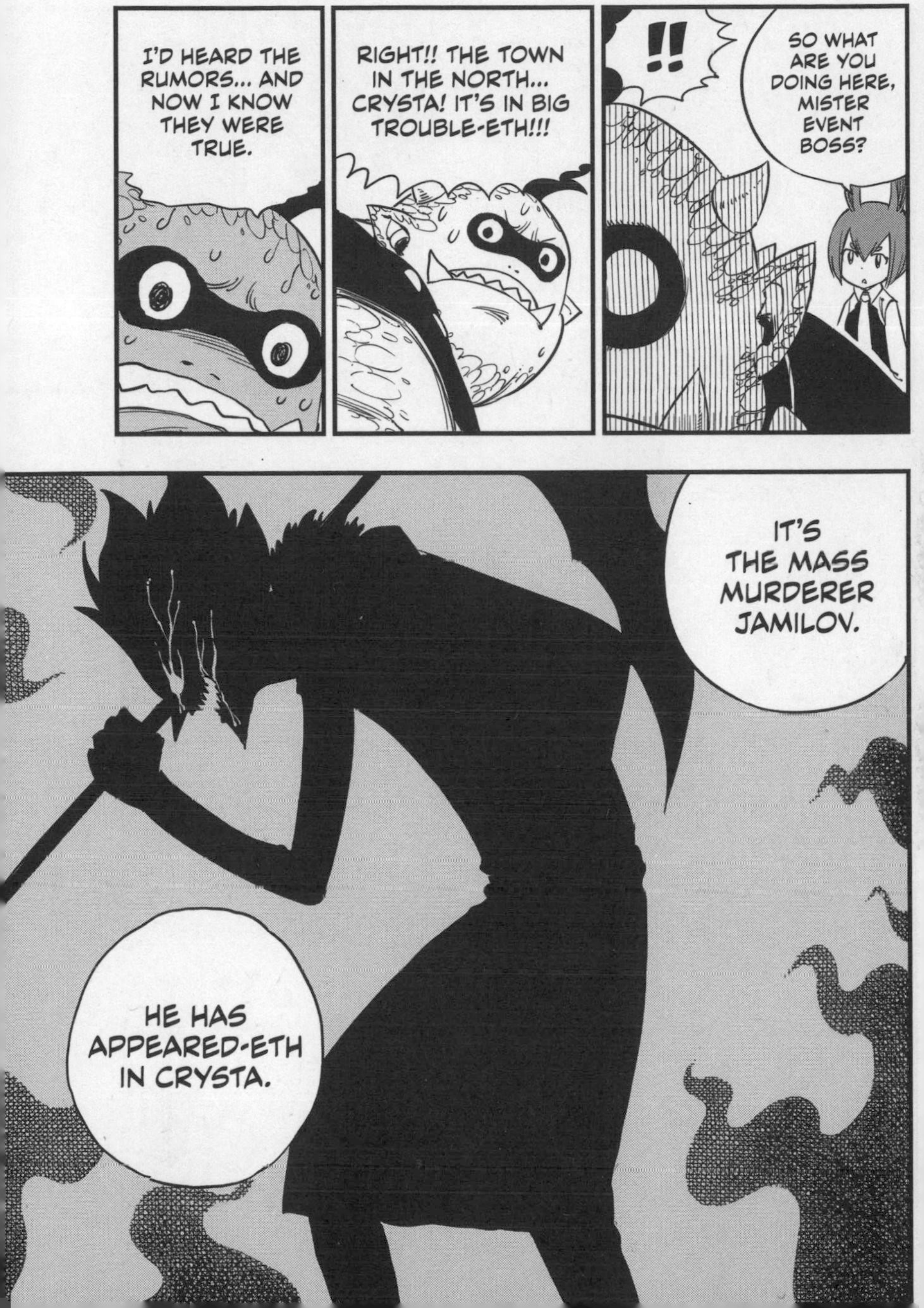
SO WHAT ARE YOU DOING HERE, MISTER EVENT BOSS?
!!
RIGHT!! THE TOWN IN THE NORTH... CRYSTA! IT'S IN BIG TROUBLE-ETH!!!
I'D HEARD THE RUMORS... AND NOW I KNOW THEY WERE TRUE.
IT'S THE MASS MURDERER JAMILOV.
HE HAS APPEARED-ETH IN CRYSTA.

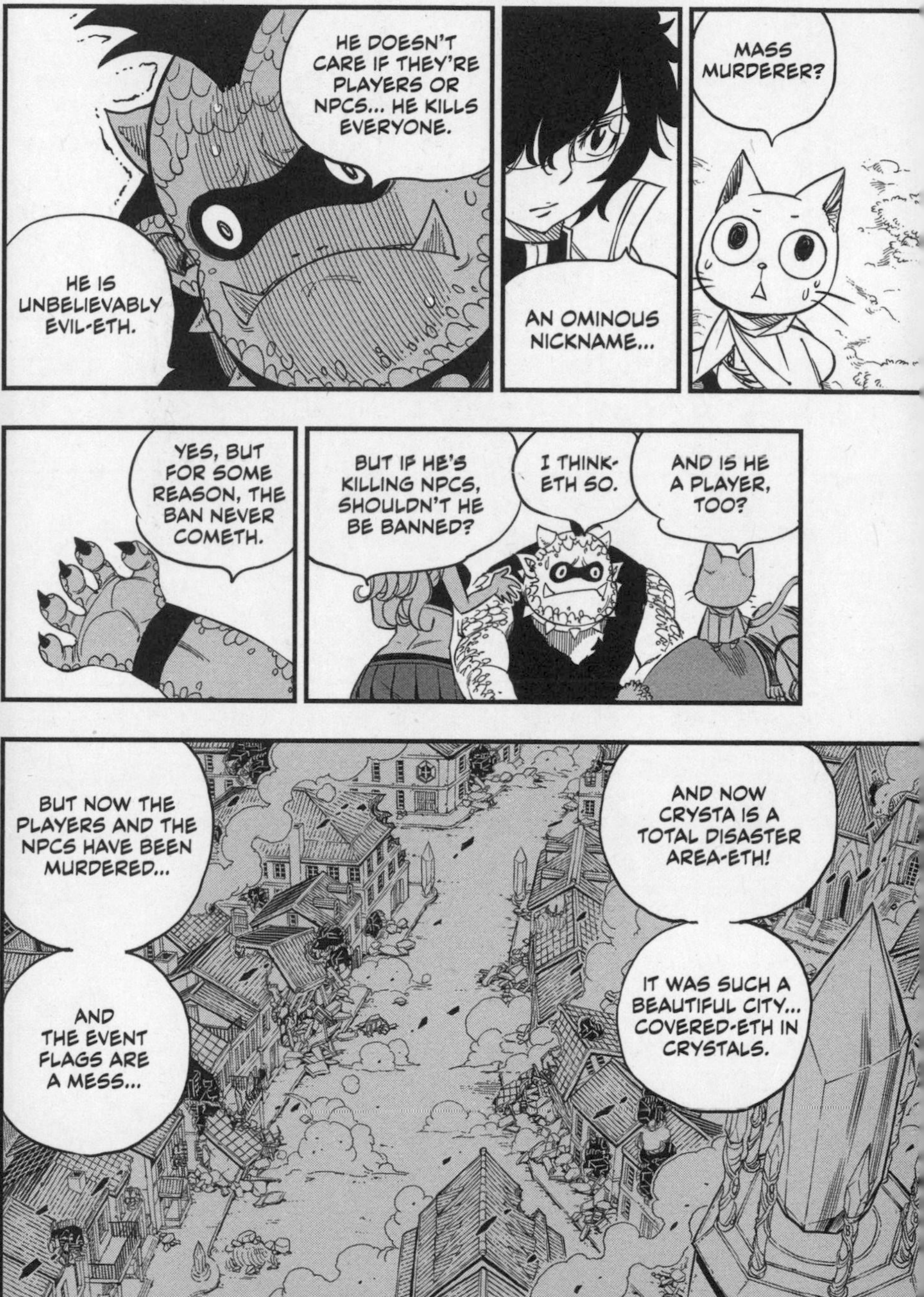
MASS MURDERER?
AN OMINOUS NICKNAME...
HE DOESN'T CARE IF THEY'RE PLAYERS OR NPCS... HE KILLS EVERYONE.
HE IS UNBELIEVABLY EVIL-ETH.
AND IS HE A PLAYER, TOO?
I THINK-ETH SO.
BUT IF HE'S KILLING NPCS, SHOULDN'T HE BE BANNED?
YES, BUT FOR SOME REASON, THE BAN NEVER COMETH.
AND NOW CRYSTA IS A TOTAL DISASTER AREA-ETH!
IT WAS SUCH A BEAUTIFUL CITY... COVERED-ETH IN CRYSTALS.
BUT NOW THE PLAYERS AND THE NPCS HAVE BEEN MURDERED...
AND THE EVENT FLAGS ARE A MESS...

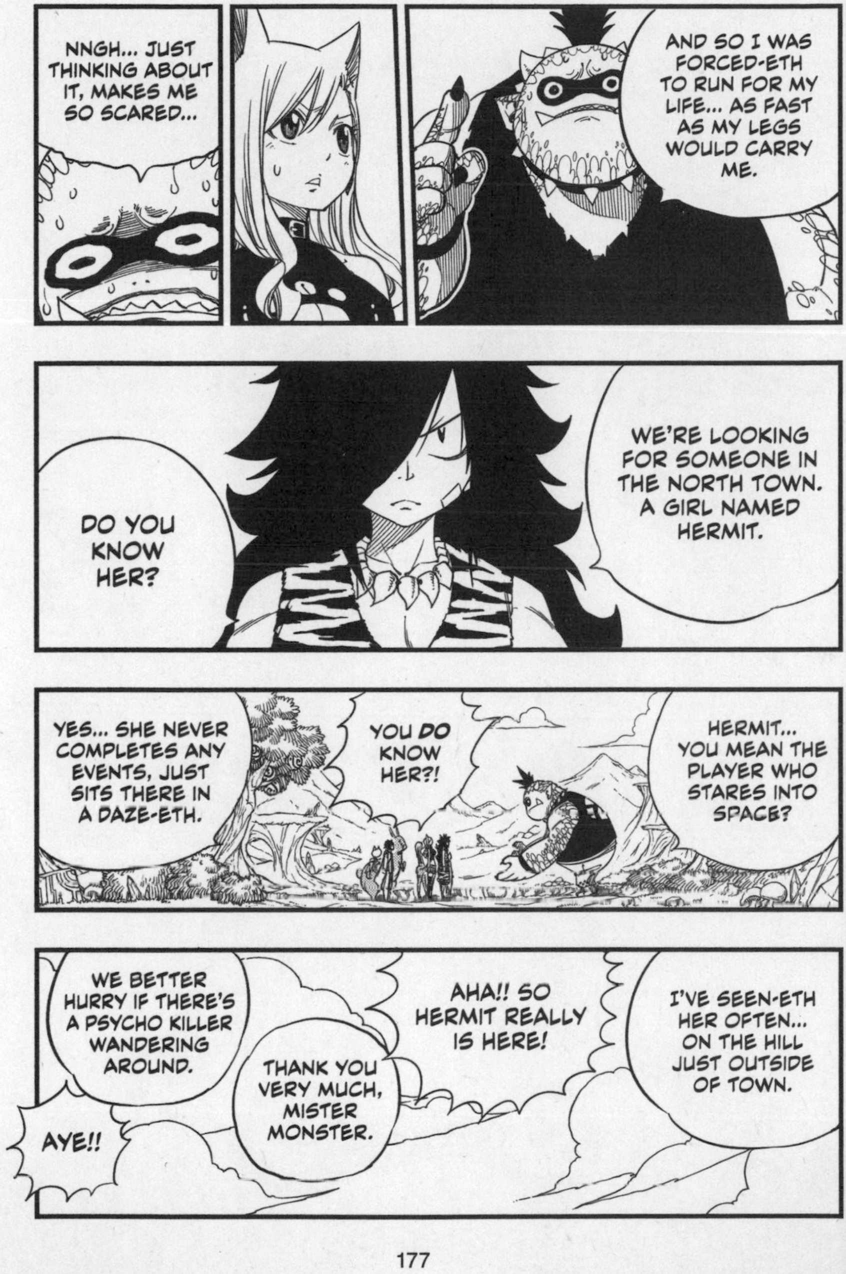
AND SO I WAS FORCED-ETH TO RUN FOR MY LIFE... AS FAST AS MY LEGS WOULD CARRY ME.
NNGH... JUST THINKING ABOUT IT, MAKES ME SO SCARED...
WE'RE LOOKING FOR SOMEONE IN THE NORTH TOWN. A GIRL NAMED HERMIT.
DO YOU KNOW HER?
HERMIT... YOU MEAN THE PLAYER WHO STARES INTO SPACE?
YOU *DO* KNOW HER?!
YES... SHE NEVER COMPLETES ANY EVENTS, JUST SITS THERE IN A DAZE-ETH.
I'VE SEEN-ETH HER OFTEN... ON THE HILL JUST OUTSIDE OF TOWN.
AHA!! SO HERMIT REALLY IS HERE!
THANK YOU VERY MUCH, MISTER MONSTER.
WE BETTER HURRY IF THERE'S A PSYCHO KILLER WANDERING AROUND.
AYE!!

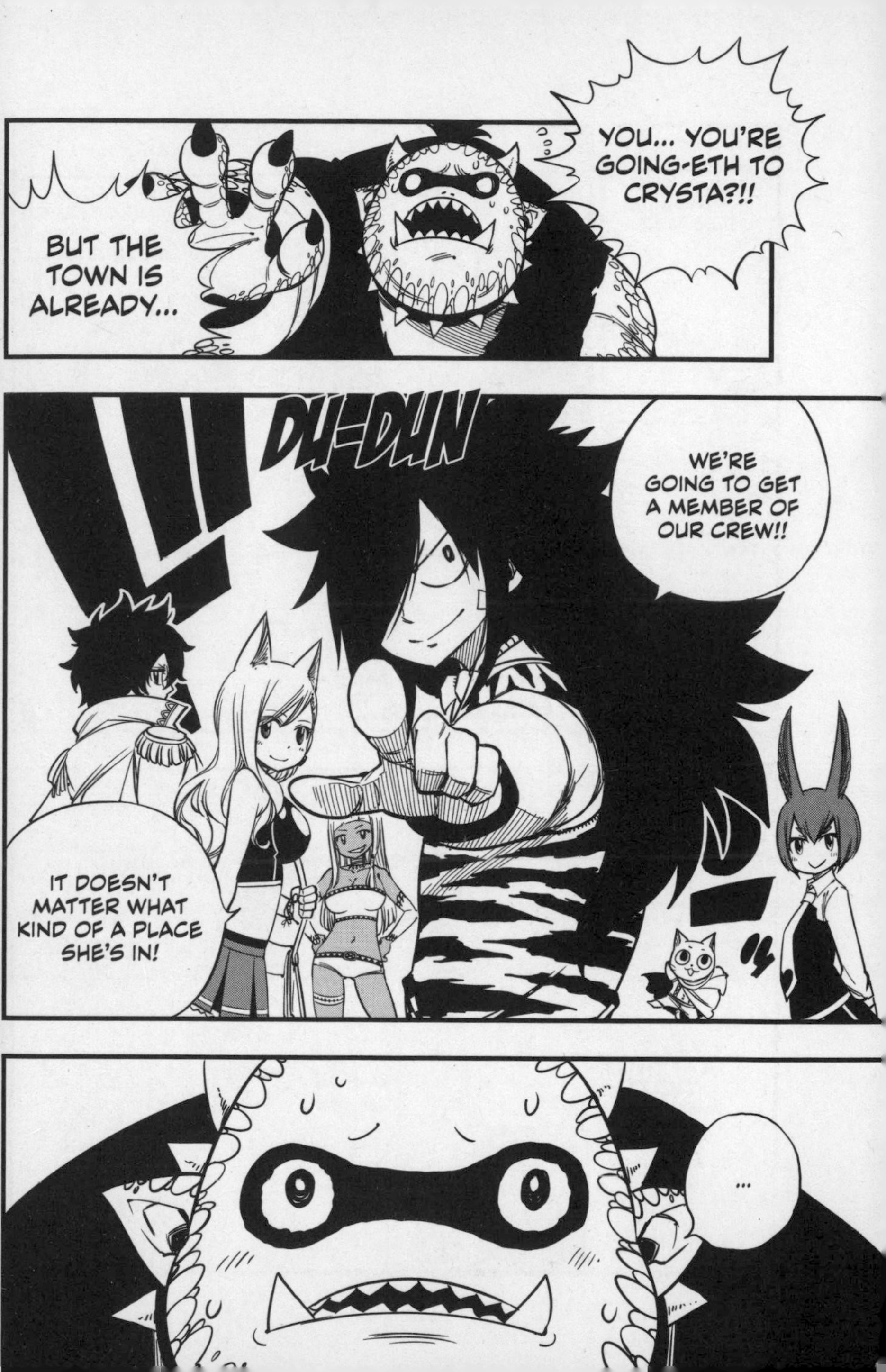
YOU... YOU'RE GOING-ETH TO CRYSTA?!!
BUT THE TOWN IS ALREADY...
WE'RE GOING TO GET A MEMBER OF OUR CREW!!
DU-DUN
IT DOESN'T MATTER WHAT KIND OF A PLACE SHE'S IN!
...

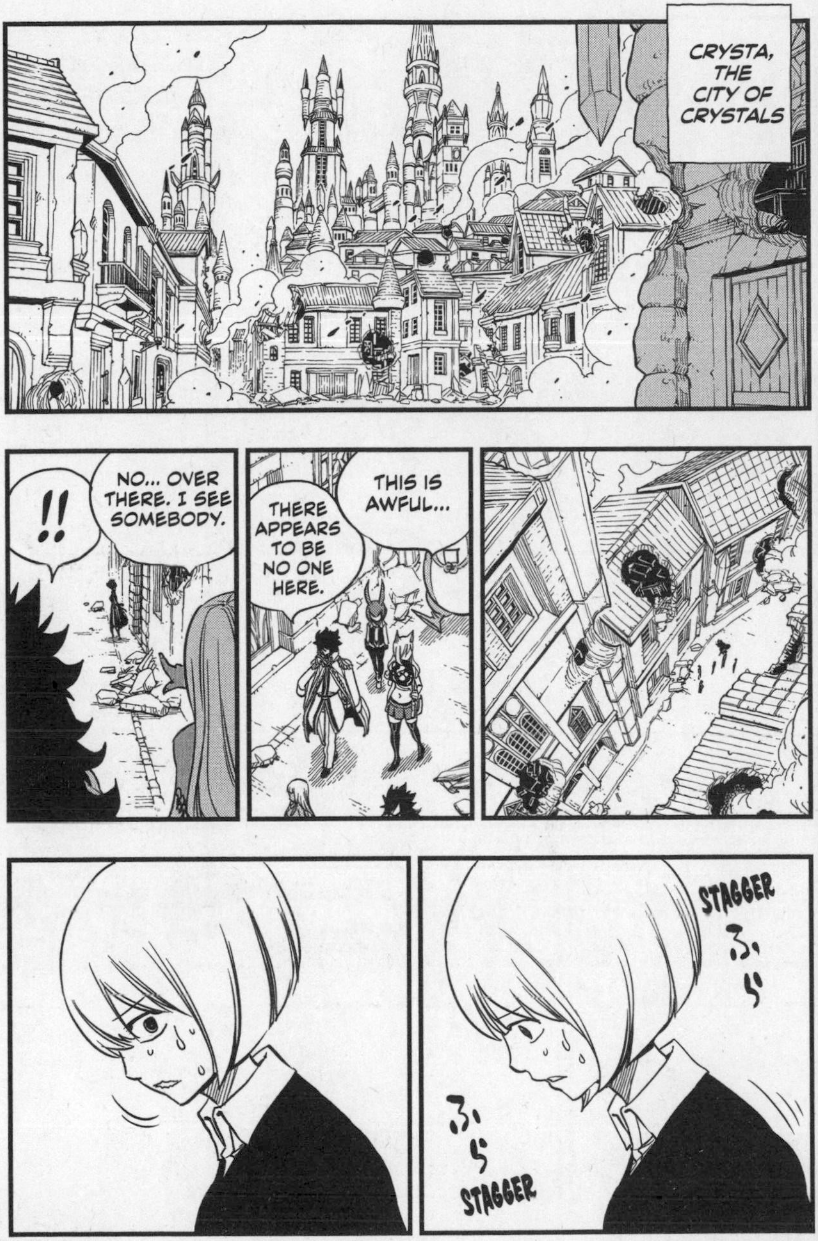
CRYSTA, THE CITY OF CRYSTALS
THIS IS AWFUL...
THERE APPEARS TO BE NO ONE HERE.
NO... OVER THERE. I SEE SOMEBODY.
!!
STAGGER
ふら
ふら
STAGGER

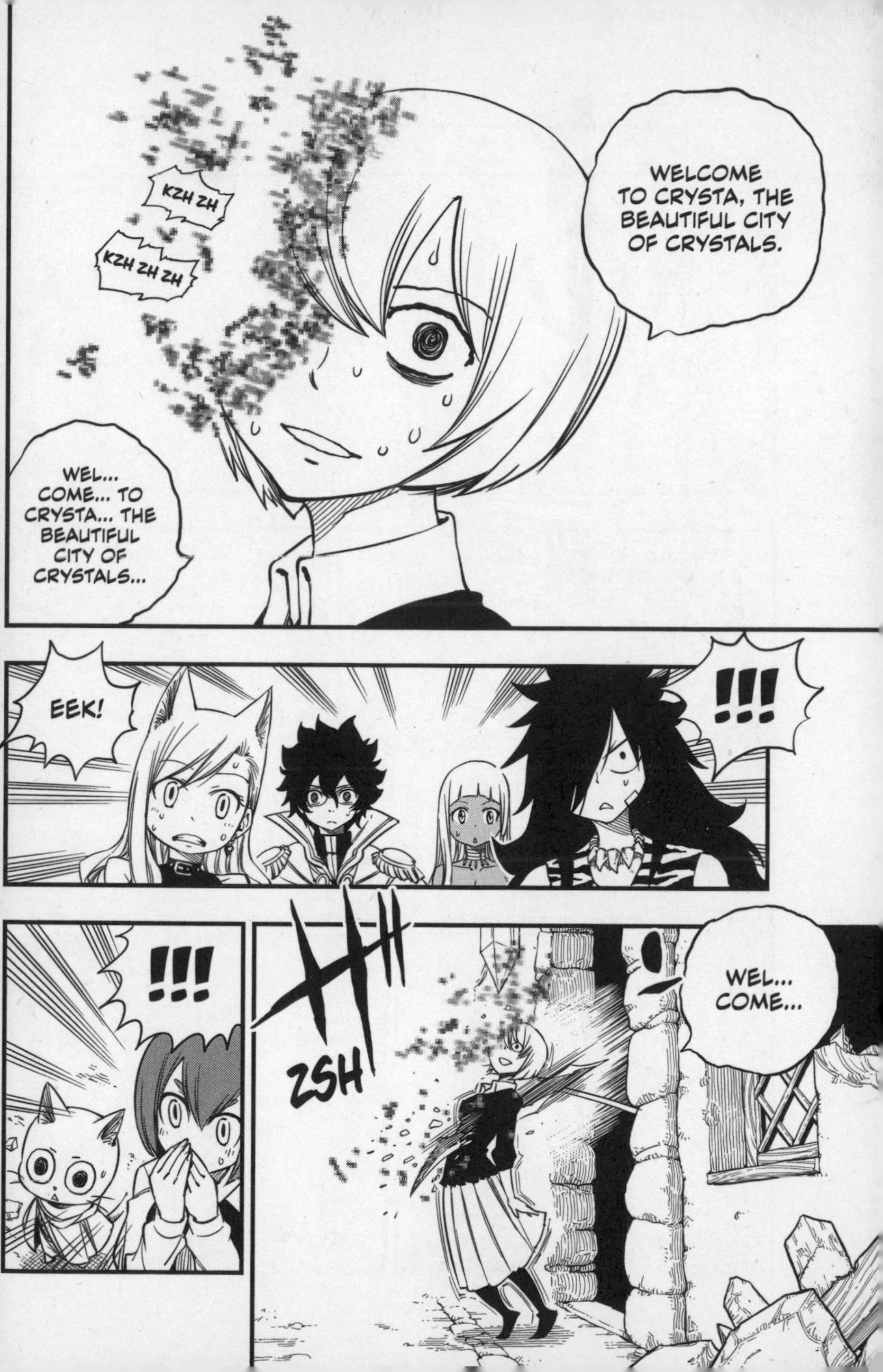

WELCOME TO CRYSTA, THE BEAUTIFUL CITY OF CRYSTALS.
KZH ZH
KZH ZH ZH
WEL... COME... TO CRYSTA... THE BEAUTIFUL CITY OF CRYSTALS...
!!!
EEK!
WEL... COME...
ZSH
!!!

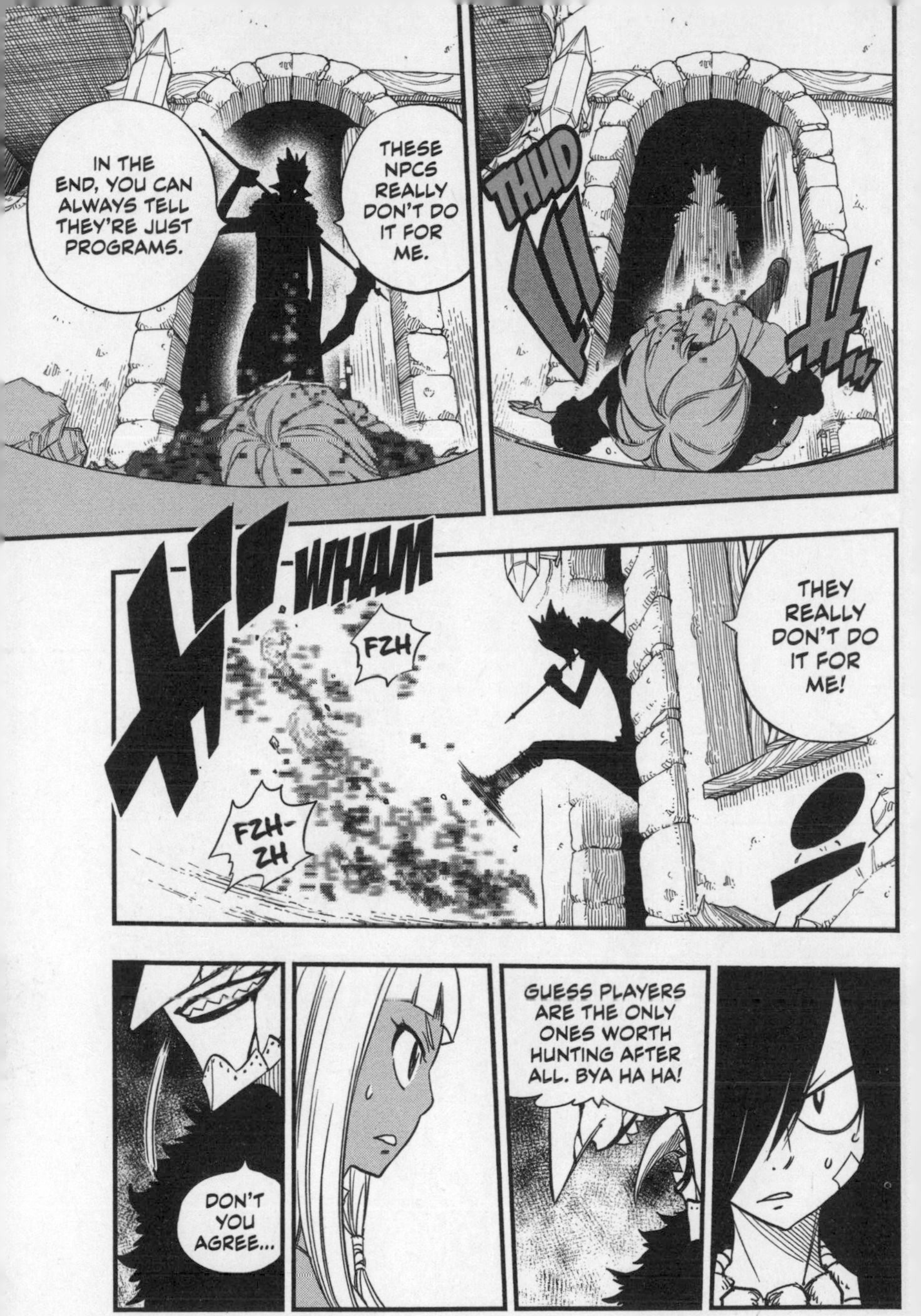
THUD
THESE NPCS REALLY DON'T DO IT FOR ME.
IN THE END, YOU CAN ALWAYS TELL THEY'RE JUST PROGRAMS.
THEY REALLY DON'T DO IT FOR ME!
FZH
WHAM
FZH-ZH
GUESS PLAYERS ARE THE ONLY ONES WORTH HUNTING AFTER ALL. BYA HA HA!
DON'T YOU AGREE...

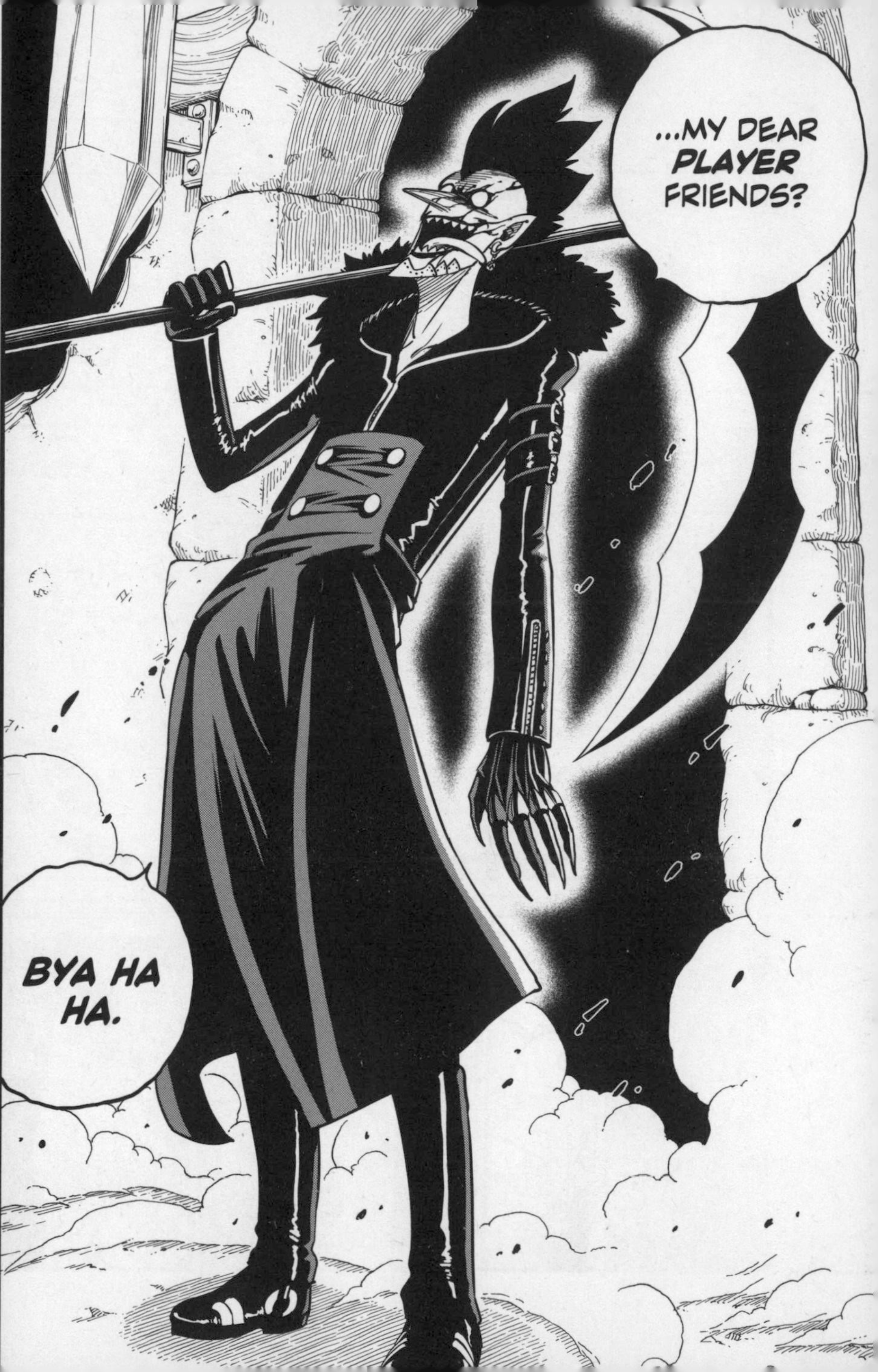
...MY DEAR PLAYER FRIENDS?
BYA HA HA.

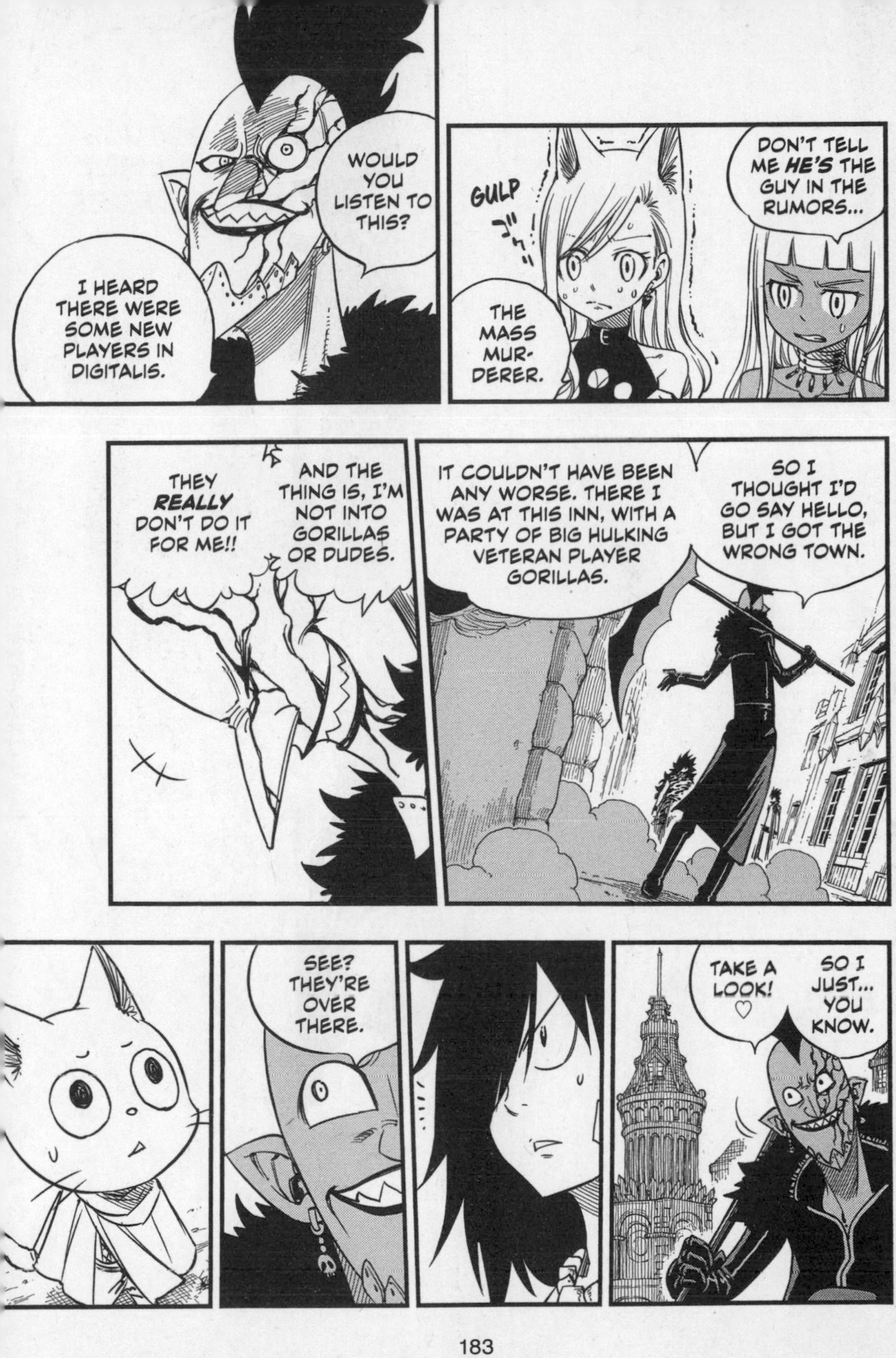
DON'T TELL ME ***HE'S*** THE GUY IN THE RUMORS...
GULP
THE MASS MUR-DERER.
WOULD YOU LISTEN TO THIS?
I HEARD THERE WERE SOME NEW PLAYERS IN DIGITALIS.
SO I THOUGHT I'D GO SAY HELLO, BUT I GOT THE WRONG TOWN.
IT COULDN'T HAVE BEEN ANY WORSE. THERE I WAS AT THIS INN, WITH A PARTY OF BIG HULKING VETERAN PLAYER GORILLAS.
AND THE THING IS, I'M NOT INTO GORILLAS OR DUDES.
THEY ***REALLY*** DON'T DO IT FOR ME!!
SO I JUST... YOU KNOW.
TAKE A LOOK! ♡
SEE? THEY'RE OVER THERE.

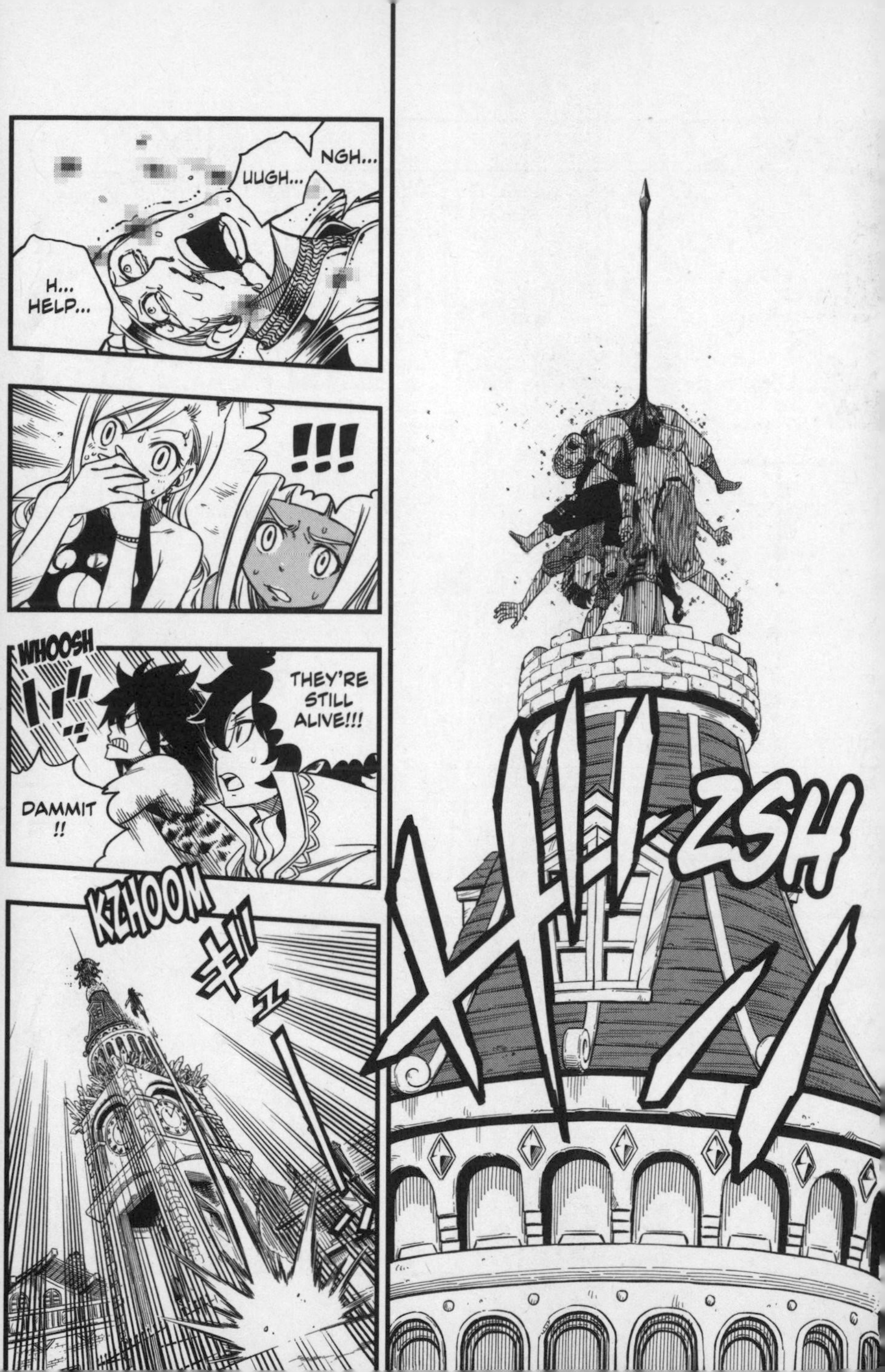
ZSH
NGH...
UUGH...
H... HELP...
!!!
THEY'RE STILL ALIVE!!!
WHOOSH
DAMMIT !!
KZHOOM

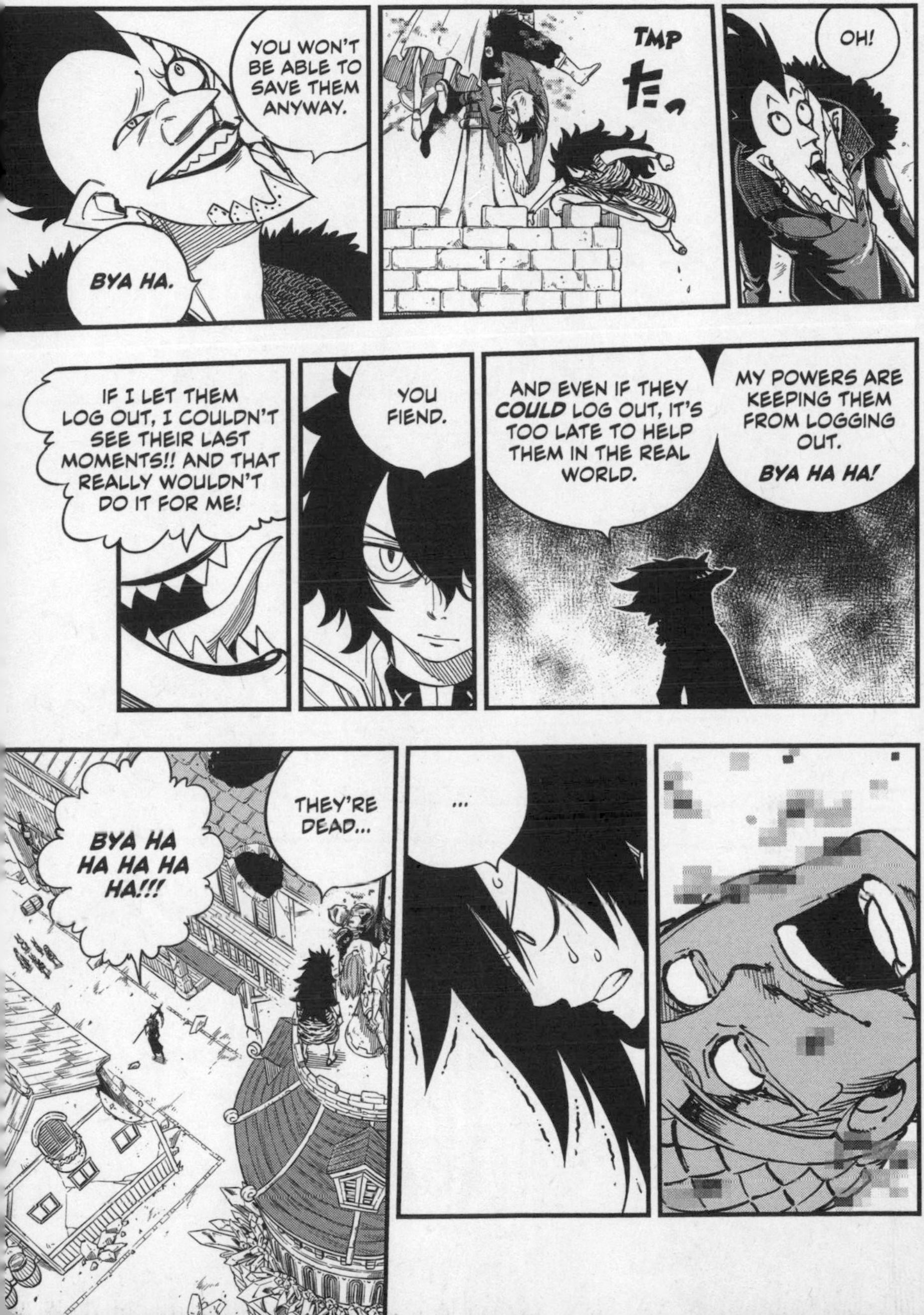
OH!
TMP
YOU WON'T BE ABLE TO SAVE THEM ANYWAY.
BYA HA.
MY POWERS ARE KEEPING THEM FROM LOGGING OUT.
BYA HA HA!
AND EVEN IF THEY COULD LOG OUT, IT'S TOO LATE TO HELP THEM IN THE REAL WORLD.
YOU FIEND.
IF I LET THEM LOG OUT, I COULDN'T SEE THEIR LAST MOMENTS!! AND THAT REALLY WOULDN'T DO IT FOR ME!
...
THEY'RE DEAD...
BYA HA HA HA HA HA!!!

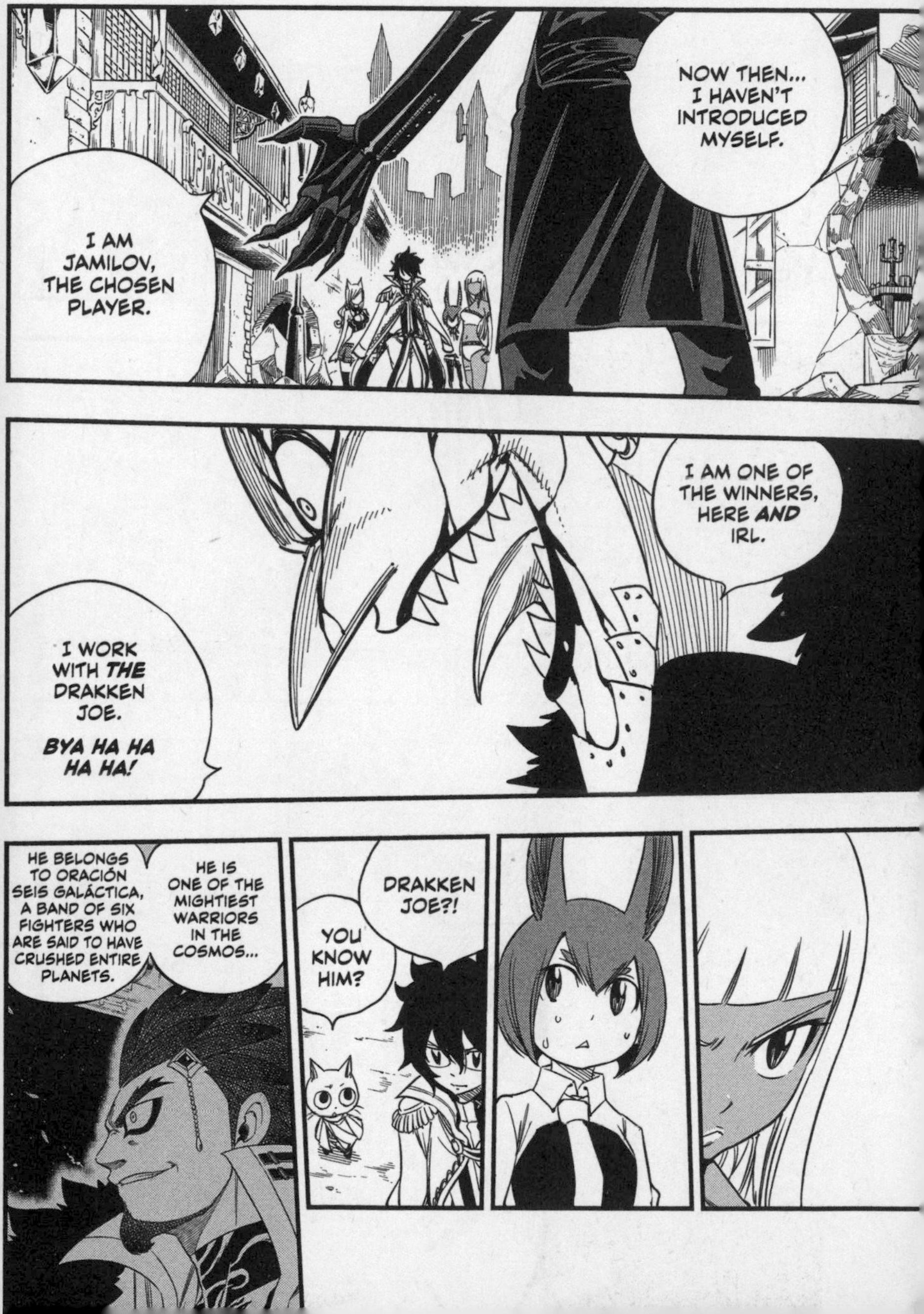
NOW THEN... I HAVEN'T INTRODUCED MYSELF.
I AM JAMILOV, THE CHOSEN PLAYER.
I AM ONE OF THE WINNERS, HERE *AND* IRL.
I WORK WITH *THE* DRAKKEN JOE.
BYA HA HA HA HA!
DRAKKEN JOE?!
YOU KNOW HIM?
HE IS ONE OF THE MIGHTIEST WARRIORS IN THE COSMOS...
HE BELONGS TO ORACIÓN SEIS GALÁCTICA, A BAND OF SIX FIGHTERS WHO ARE SAID TO HAVE CRUSHED ENTIRE PLANETS.

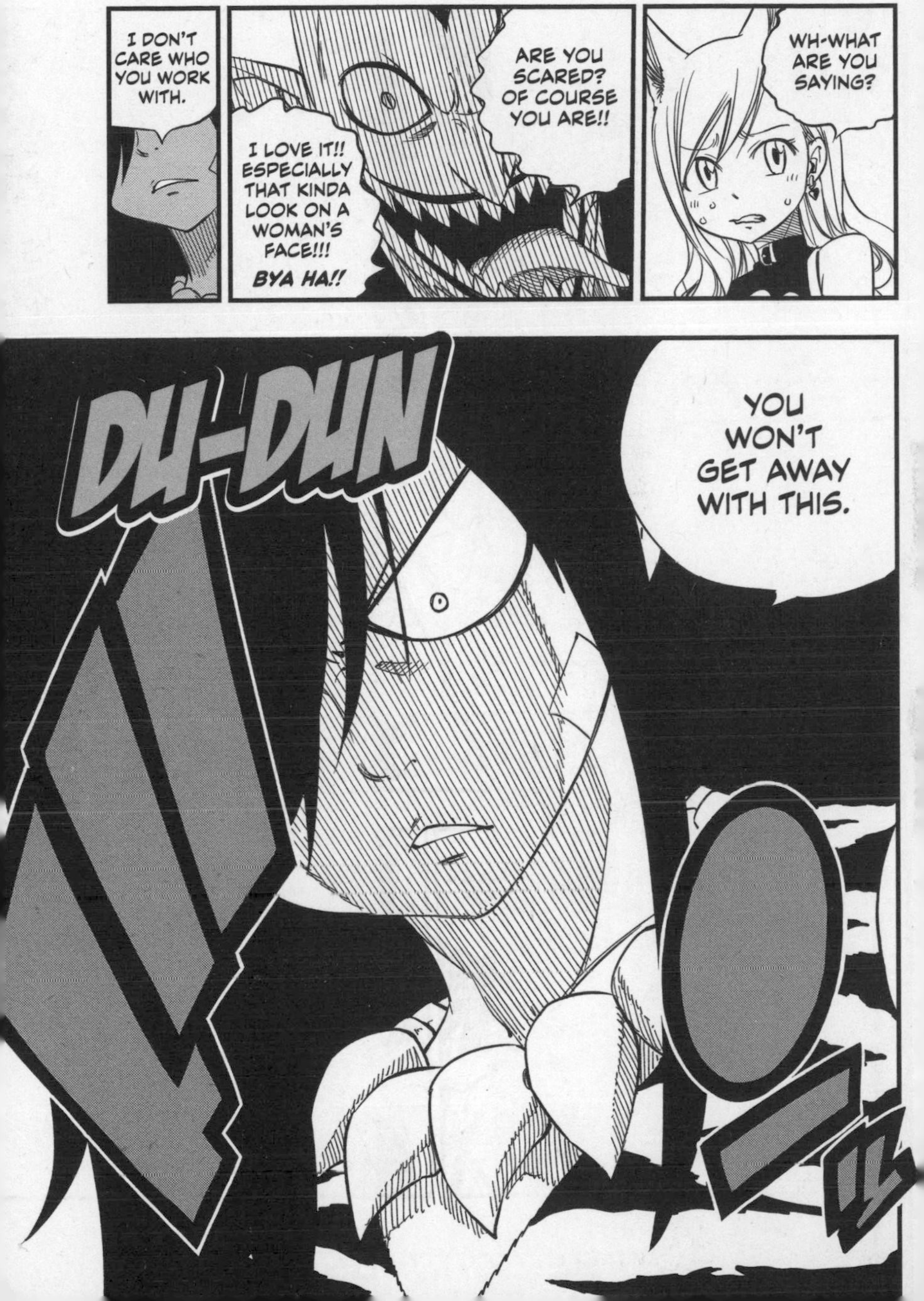
WH-WHAT ARE YOU SAYING?
ARE YOU SCARED? OF COURSE YOU ARE!!
I LOVE IT!! ESPECIALLY THAT KINDA LOOK ON A WOMAN'S FACE!!!
BYA HA!!
I DON'T CARE WHO YOU WORK WITH.
YOU WON'T GET AWAY WITH THIS.
DU-DUN

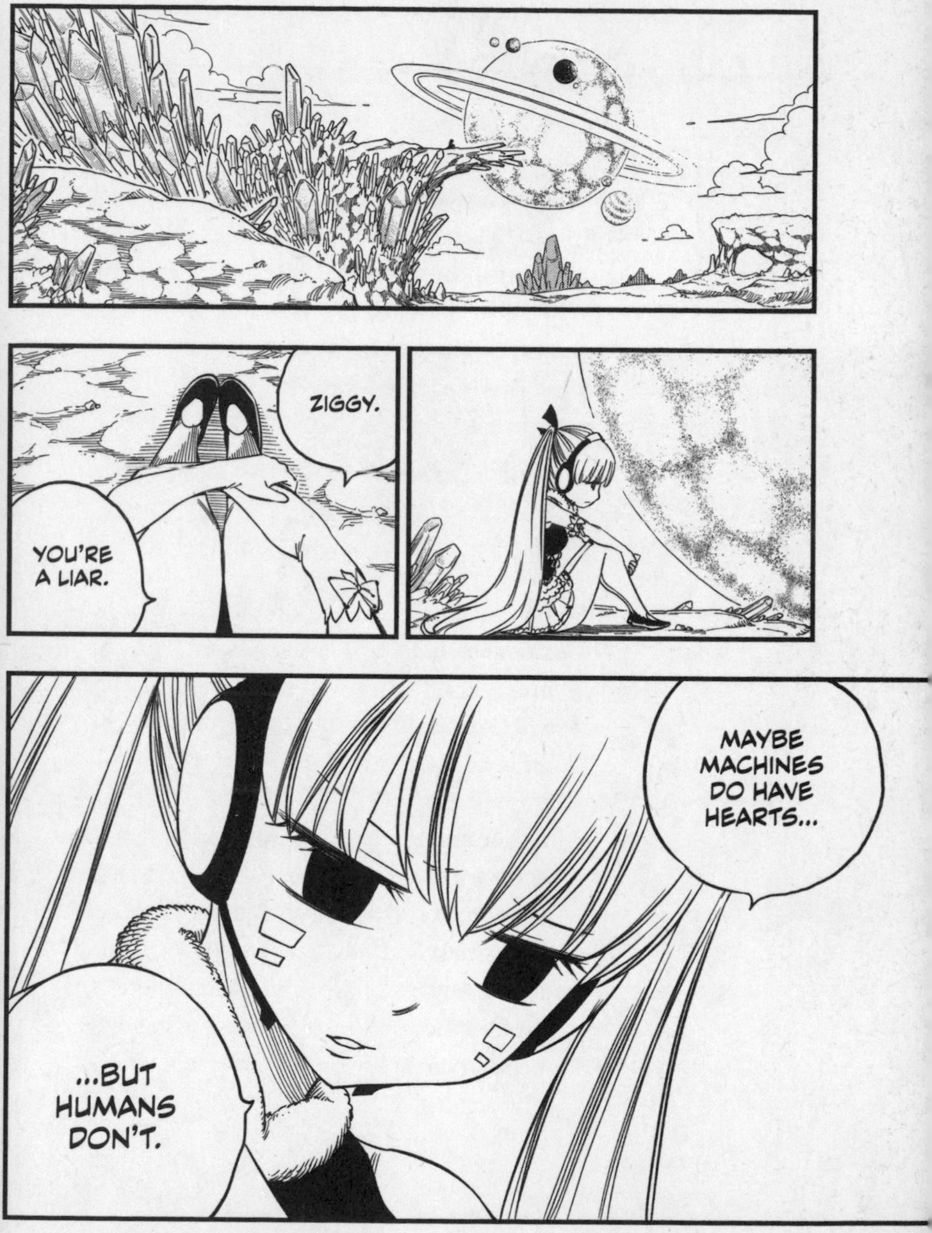
ZIGGY.
YOU'RE A LIAR.
MAYBE MACHINES DO HAVE HEARTS...
...BUT HUMANS DON'T.

TO BE CONTINUED...

AFTERWORD

Moscoy! In this volume, Sister becomes the newest member of the crew. And so does Mosco. I took a liking to Mosco while I was drawing him, and even though I didn't have any plans whatsoever of putting him on the crew, he ended up on the EDENS ZERO anyway. So what am I going to do with him now?

That aside, currently there are a lot of women on the EDENS ZERO crew. This is a little different than what I planned in the beginning—actually there were going to be two more male characters. But a lot happened, and the Shining Stars and Homura made their appearances first. As a result, we have a majority of female characters. There will be more male characters, so any female fans who are reading for the hot guys have nothing to worry about... And after I said all that, I remember that in my last series, *FAIRY TAIL*, of the five main characters, only two were men and three were women. So how **will** the main crew ultimately end up?

I just wrote that I like Mosco, but personally, my most favorite character is Pino. I mean, as an author, I go through phases of favorite characters, so by the time the next volume comes out, I might have a different favorite, but at this point in time, I really like Pino. Of course I like Shiki and Rebecca, too, but as the leading man and lady, I guess they're in kind of a different category. Anyway, I have a lot of story details already worked out for Pino, and the little bot is going to be a very important character in the future. Probably.

‹ KAMOME ›
SHIRAHAMA

Witch Hat Atelier

A magical manga
adventure for
fans of Disney
and Studio
Ghibli!

The magical adventure that took Japan by storm is finally here, from acclaimed DC and Marvel cover artist Kamome Shirahama!

In a world where everyone takes wonders like magic spells
and dragons for granted, Coco is a girl with a simple dream:
She wants to be a witch. But everybody knows magicians
are born, not made, and Coco was not born with a gift for
magic. Resigned to her un-magical life, Coco is about to
give up on her dream to become a witch...until the day
she meets Qifrey, a mysterious, traveling magician. After
secretly seeing Qifrey perform magic in a way she's never
seen before, Coco soon learns what everybody "knows"
might not be the truth, and discovers that her magical
dream may not be as far away as it may seem...

KC
KODANSHA
COMICS

Magus of the Library

Mitsu Izumi

MITSU IZUMI'S STUNNING ARTWORK BRINGS A FANTASTICAL LITERARY ADVENTURE TO LUSH, THRILLING LIFE!

Young Theo adores books, but the prejudice and hatred of his village keeps them ever out of his reach. Then one day, he chances to meet Sedona, a traveling librarian who works for the great library of Aftzaak, City of Books, and his life changes forever...

EDENS ZERO volume 4 is a work of fiction.
Names, characters, places, and incidents are the products of the author's imagination or are used fictitiously. Any resemblance to actual events, locales, or persons, living or dead, is entirely coincidental.

A Kodansha Comics Trade Paperback Original.

Published in the United States by Kodansha Comics,
an imprint of Kodansha USA Publishing, LLC, New York.

Publication rights for this English edition arranged through
Kodansha Ltd., Tokyo.

First published in Japan in 2019 by Kodansha Ltd., Tokyo.

ISBN 978-1-63236-824-9

Original cover design by
Atsushi Kudo, Erisa Maruyama (Gxcomplex).

Printed in the United States of America.

www.kodanshacomics.com

9 8 7 6 5 4 3 2 1

Translation: Alethea and Athena Nibley
Lettering: AndWorld Design
Editing: Haruko Hashimoto
Kodansha Comics edition cover design by Phil Balsman